RALPH BARKER started work as ⬚⬚⬚⬚⬚⬚⬚⬚⬚⬚⬚⬚⬚⬚⬚⬚ but joined the RAF in 1940 as airc⬚⬚⬚⬚⬚⬚⬚⬚⬚⬚⬚⬚⬚⬚ granted a permanent commission. After having three books published in the 1950s he retired voluntarily in 1961 to write full time. He had already become a regular contributor of feature articles to the *Sunday Express*, an association which lasted for more than thirty years.

Many of his books have had an RAF or aviation background, but he has written on a wide range of subjects, including a prize-winning book on a mountaineering expedition, terrorism, biography and the sea.

Praise for *The Royal Flying Corps in France*

'A dashing picture of the ebb and flow of aerial battle, shot through with personal histories and conversations, drawn from the diaries of legendary aces on the one hand and, on the other, the anonymous but dedicated mechanics, pilots and observers who risked their lives in the face of a predatory enemy, fragile machines, unreliable guns and temperamental engines.'
Patrick Garland's *Daily Telegraph Book of the Year*

'Much of his story is about people ... What makes his book ... is its wide use of letters and diaries from the Imperial War Museum, the Liddle Collection and elsewhere. Barker also describes well the ghastly edge of air combat at a time when aircrew without parachutes might have to face the decision to "jump or burn" at any moment.'
Times Literary Supplement

'They are all here – Mannock, Ball, McCudden, the von Richthofens and many less famous but equally worthy witnesses. They tell us, often in grimly laconic style, what Jack Salmond, Trenchard's successor, meant when he called for "Very low flying is essential".'
Herald Express

'The author's style is lucid and accessible ... The research which has gone into this book is considerable.' *Cross & Cockade International*

A BRIEF HISTORY OF
THE
ROYAL FLYING CORPS
in WORLD WAR I

Ralph Barker

ROBINSON
London

Constable & Robinson Ltd
3 The Lanchesters
162 Fulham Palace Road
London W6 9ER
www.constablerobinson.com

First published in the UK as *The Royal Flying Corps in France* (2 vols)
by Constable and Company Ltd, 1995

This edition published by Robinson,
an imprint of Constable & Robinson Ltd, 2002

A copy of the British Library Cataloguing in
Publication data is available from the British Library

ISBN 1-84119-470-0

Printed and bound in the EU

10 9 8 7 6 5 4 3 2

CONTENTS

CONTENTS

1916

1917

1918

ILLUSTRATIONS

George Downing *(Carol Sherwood)*
Albert Ball *(Chaz Bowyer)*
Maurice Kay *(Alex Revell)*
P. B. 'Bruce' Prothero *(RAF Museum)*
J. B. McCudden *(via Norman Franks)*
P. G. Taylor
Eric Routh *(RAF Museum)*
Oscar Greig *(Norman Franks)*
R. F. Glazebrook *(Ben Glazebrook)*
W. Leefe Robinson *(Imperial War Museum)*
Edward Mannock *(Chaz Bowyer)*
W. A. 'Billy' Bishop *(Chaz Bowyer)*
J. T. P. Jeyes *(Anthony Jeyes)*
Arthur 'Bomber' Harris *(Norman Franks)*
Gwilym H. Lewis *(G. H. Lewis)*
Keith Muspratt, Arthur Rhys Davids, and Maxwell
    Coote *(Alex Revell)*
Leonard Barlow *(Alex Revell)*
R. A. 'Dick' Maybery *(Alex Revell)*

Werner Voss with his Triplane *(Alex Revell)*
V. P. 'Versh' Cronyn *(RAF Museum)*
A Group of German 'Aces' *(via Chaz Bowyer)*
A Sopwith 1½-Strutter *(Jack Bruce and Stuart Leslie)*
Sopwith Pups of 46 Squadron *(Jack Bruce and Stuart
    Leslie)*
An Armstrong-Whitworth FK8 'Big Ack' *(Jack Bruce
    and Stuart Leslie)*
P. N. M. 'Puggy' Shone *(Imperial War Museum)*
S. J. 'Squibs' Sibley *(Barry Gray)*
DH4 Bombers *(Jack Bruce and Stuart Leslie)*
A Sopwith Camel *(Jack Bruce and Stuart Leslie)*
The F2B Bristol Fighter *(Jack Bruce and Stuart Leslie)*
J. A. 'Jimmy' Slater *(Bruce and Leslie via Franks)*
C. M. 'Billy' Crowe *(via Franks)*
Arthur Gould Lee *(Alex Revell)*

ILLUSTRATIONS

Clive Collett *(via Franks)*
Alan McLeod in hospital *(Public Archives of Canada)*
Arthur Hammond *(Chaz Bowyer)*
John A. Todd *(Norman Franks)*
Oscar Heron *(Norman Franks)*
Todd's perforated Camel *(Marvyn Paice)*
Alexander Paice *(Marvyn Paice)*
Ewart Stock *(E. J. Stock)*
Ewart Garland *(Patrick Garland)*

ACKNOWLEDGEMENTS

In researching material for this book, I have had generous and enthusiastic help from a great many people. These have included veteran survivors; next of kin and copyright holders of diaries, letters and memoirs; various museums, libraries and institutions; together with a number of distinguished air historians who have made their own work and researches available to me. In expressing my gratitude I must absolve them all from any responsibility for the resultant narrative.

Contact and correspondence with RFC veterans sadly diminished with time, but they included, especially, Maxwell Coote, Gerald Dixon, Cecil Lewis, T. G. Mapplebeck and Harold Tambling; all but Gerald Dixon since deceased.

Material extracted from the Public Record Office files includes: personal memoirs and recollection of individual RFC personnel from files in the Class Air 1 series, including 721, 2126, 2356, 2387, 2388, 2389, 2393, 2395 and 2413. Among those quoted from this series are D. L. Allen, J. O. Andrews, R. M. Bailey, H. M. Le Brock, L. E. O. Charlton, C. C. Darley, W. S. Douglas, P. F. Fullard, R. M. Hill, A. C. Maund, T. Mulcahy-Morgan, G. W. Murless-Green, C. F. A. Portal, C. A. Ridley, J. C. Slessor, R. Smith-Barry and D. F. Stevenson.

Other files from Class Air 1, from which material has been extracted include Nos: 5, RFC War Diary, August 1914; 675, The Air Dropping of Agents, 1915; 687, No. 3 Squadron; 710, An Investigation into the Phenomenon of Spin; 719, No. 3 Squadron Roll of Officers; 724, A History of Aerial Photography; 868, Parachutes for Kite Balloons; 1004, Casualties, Kite Balloons. Also various other Situation statements, Squadron Record Books, Combat Reports, Notes on Air Fighting, Notes on Running a Squadron,

General Methods of Teaching Scout Pilots, and the sequence of meetings of the Parachute Committee.

The Air Board Meetings and Memoranda covering May-June, July-September and October-December 1916 are in Class Air 6, Nos 1-3.

Extracts and condensations from material viewed at the Department of Documents, Imperial War Museum – memoirs, diaries, letters, etc. – are gratefully acknowledged, with thanks for staff help, to next-of-kin and copyright holders as follows: D. L. Allen, G. W. Armstrong, S. Attwater, O. L. Beater, H. A. Blundell, N. A. Birks, L. S. Bowman, W. Sefton Brancker, A. W. Brown, C. Callender, F. Carr, J. G. H. Chrispin, W. Cobb (R. W. Cobb), W. S. Douglas, H. G. Downing (Carol Sherwood), L. F. Field, E. J. Garland (Patrick Garland), M. S. Goodban, S. V. Gorringe (R. S. Gorringe), D. R. Goudie, O. Greig, P. R. C. Groves, T. E. Guttery (D. R. Guttery), P. Haarer, W. F. J. Harvey, J. L. Horridge, R. S. S Ingram (Professor G. I. C. Ingram), Ronald Ivelaw-Chapman (John Ivelaw-Chapman), J. P. T. Jeyes (Anthony Jeyes), J. A. Liddell, A. D. Light, N. Macmillan, J. H. Morris, E. R. Pennell (Renee Duperly), F. C. Penny (James and Joan Seakins), H. R. Puncher, J. C. Quinnell (John Craig), F. C. Ransley (Joanna Wrathall), W. R. Read (G. R. E. Brooke), E. J. D. Routh, H. B. R. Rowell (Elizabeth Rowell), J. G. Selby, H. Seymour, R. J. A. Sheraton (Barbara D. Sheraton), J. C. Slessor, E. E. Stock (E. J. Stock), H. G. Taylor, H. S. Ward (T. C. Le Grice), R. L. Wightman, J. W. Woodhouse, H. Wyllie (John Wyllie). Also A Short History of No. 6 Squadron (Anon); and an Anonymous Diary of a Pilot.

Similarly at the Department of Sound Records, Imperial War Museum: E. Bolt, C. J. Chabot, J. V. Gascoyne, A. T. Harris, J. C. F. Hopkins, A. W. H. James, A. A. N. D. 'Jerry' Pentland, F. J. Powell, H. J. Sanders, J. C. Slessor, A. B. Yuille.

At the Royal Air Force museum, again with grateful thanks to next of kin, copyright holders and staff: F. P. Adams, E. Brewerton, G. I. Carmichael, A. S. W. Dore (Bingham Dore), T. Farquhar, The Henderson Papers, G. P. Jamieson, M. A. Kay, M. M. Kaye, W. R. Read (G. R. E. Brooke), H. J. Sanders, J. G. Selby, C. D. Smart (see also Museum of Army Flying), R. Smith, J. Worstenholme. Also tape and video recordings: J. O. Andrews, E. D. G. Galley, M. M. Kaye, C. B. Lefroy, Mrs Morley (Remembering Albert Ball), J. Oliver, P. N. M. Shone.

At the Museum of Army Flying: Major J. R. Cross, and H. W. Foot, Archivist. Also Wing Commander F. Prince and Anthony Rosen, for help with the tracing and preserving of the Diary of C. D. Smart.

The Royal Aeronautical Society, especially Arnold Nayler, Librarian, and Assistant Librarian Brian Riddell.

At the Liddle Collection, The Library, Leeds University, with grateful acknowledgements to Peter Liddle, for sight of documents in his Archive: V. Brown, P. F. Fullard, A. T. Harris, A. Perry-Keane, H. W. L. Saunders, Bryan Sharwood-Smith, J. C. Slessor, R. Smith-Barry, Thomas Traill, S. F. Vincent, H. P. Walmsley.

The London Library and staff for invaluable assistance

Friends of the Canadian War Museum, Ottawa, and particularly Philip Markham, for advice and for resolving many queries. The Canadian War Museum itself, the Stonewall Branch of the Royal Canadian Legion, and the Winnipeg Free Press, for background on Alan Arnett McLeod, VC.

For help with researches: Eton College Collections, through Mrs P. Hatfield, Archivist; Oundle School, through D. H. Ford, Archivist, for J. P. T. Jeyes and M. L. Hatch; Hertford College, Oxford, through Dr T. C. Barnard, Keeper of the Archives; and Roger Deayton, author of a History of the Old Caterhamians Association (for E. E. Stock); and Roger Lubbock, for extracts from letters written by his uncle Tom Tillard, killed in December 1916. Also the Ministry of Defence RAF Personnel Management Centre, Innsworth, Gloucester.

I have also drawn on my previous work on the operational careers of some of the best known pilots of this era, British and German, on which several series of articles for the *Sunday Express* were based.

For help with finding and producing photographs I am especially grateful to: Chaz Bowyer, R. E. Brooke, Jack Bruce, Bingham Dore, Norman Franks, Patrick Garland, Barry Gray, G., William and

Justin Harvey-Kelly, Peter Hearn, Anthony Jeyes, Stuart Leslie, Wing Commander Freddie Prince, Alex Revell, Carol Sherwood, E. J. Stock and Jean Tambling; also Imperial War Museum, RAF Museum and Royal Aeronautical Society Photographic Libraries.

Among air historians and researchers who have helped me I must especially thank David J. Barnes, who produced a wealth of biographical material for me on a wide range of RFC personnel. I am also indebted to Jack Bruce, Chaz Bowyer, Alan Cooper, Norman Franks, Kevin Kelly, Paul S. Leaman (of Cross and Cockade, GB), Alex Revell, and many others from whose historical work I have benefited.

The published sources I have used in my researches are listed on pages 483–85. In all instances, whether of unpublished memoirs, diaries, letters, tapes, cassettes and videos, or of published works, every effort has been made to trace copyright holders where any substantial extract is quoted. The author craves the indulgence of literary executors or copyright holders where these efforts have so far failed.

PART I

From Mons to the Somme

The Western Front 1914–1916

- – – Frontiers of 1914
- ▬▬ Limit of German Advance 1914
- ▓▓ Direction of B E F's 'Race to the sea'
- ▬▬ Approximate Front Line from late 1914 to beginning of the Battle of the Somme, 1 July, 1916
- ||||||| Allied gains in 1916, including ground conceded by the Germans from winter 1916 to form Hindenburg Line

0 10 20 30 miles 50

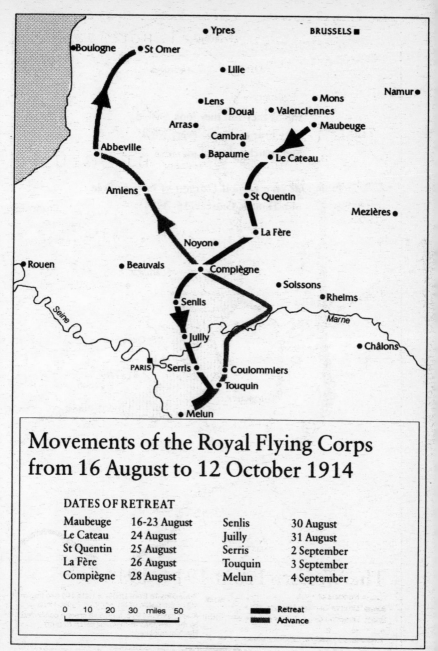

Movements of the Royal Flying Corps from 16 August to 12 October 1914

DATES OF RETREAT

Maubeuge	16–23 August	Senlis	30 August
Le Cateau	24 August	Juilly	31 August
St Quentin	25 August	Serris	2 September
La Fère	26 August	Touquin	3 September
Compiègne	28 August	Melun	4 September

0 10 20 30 miles 50

■ Retreat
▨ Advance

Still as they run they look behind,
They hear a voice in every wind,
And snatch a fearful joy.

From *Ode on a Distant Prospect of Eton College*
by Thomas Gray (1716–1771)

1914

'A USELESS AND EXPENSIVE FAD'

FROM Montrose on Tayside, from Netheravon on Salisbury Plain, from Farnborough near Aldershot (home of the British army), from Gosport on the Solent, and from Eastchurch on the Isle of Sheppey, pilots and observers of the infant Royal Flying Corps converged in their open-cockpit biplane two-seaters on their final take-off point for France. This was on Swingate Downs, high on the grassy cliffs above Dover, near the spot where Blériot had landed from his cross-Channel flight five years earlier. From here they would launch themselves on the greatest of all adventures in the short-lived annals of flight, a massed Channel crossing of some sixty machines to France and to war.

These men were the vanguard of a gallant and adventurous company, most of them in their early and mid-twenties, but destined to give way, as time passed, to extreme youth. They would be among the first to fight to the death for their country in the vast amphitheatre of the sky. Preparing to lead these trail-blazers across the unforgiving water was the commander of the senior unit of the new Corps (No. 2 Squadron), Charles James Burke, a major from the Royal Irish Regiment. Burke was a massive, broad-shouldered, barrel-chested giant, known behind his equally broad back as 'Pregnant Percy'. A decorated Boer War veteran, and a hard taskmaster, he was notorious for his rough landings. Respected for his courage, he had been one of the first to learn to fly at Larkhill on Salisbury Plain and join the Air Battalion; his visionary zeal for service aviation was legendary. He had assigned to himself the role of 'first across'; yet his mechanics, keen students of the form book, were betting on a younger man from the same regiment, the brawny, free-spirited, fearless, irreverent, fair-skinned, baby-faced but highly competitive Lieutenant Hubert Harvey-Kelly. 'Mad as a hawk', according to J.C. 'Jack' Slessor, a future chief of the air staff, he was the popular favourite to win what the mechanics were pleased to see as a race. In their worm's-eye view, 'HK', as they knew him (behind his back again), was the man most likely to win.

Other names to conjure with, many of them acting as squadron or flight leaders of this precarious aerial armada, were: Wilfred Freeman, whom Slessor thought 'the greatest air force man there ever was'; Philip Bennet Joubert de la Ferté, whose memory was said to be as long as his name; Gilbert Mapplebeck, the tallest at 6'3" and the youngest at twenty-one; Gordon Shephard, author of 'Lessons Learnt on Divisional and Army Manoeuvres, 1913', derived from his experiences as both pilot and observer; and the Salmond brothers, Jack and Geoffrey, both future chiefs of the air staff. All but two of these were to survive the war. Equally distinguished in their way were the innovative Louis Strange, of 5 Squadron, and two contrasting Old Etonians whose careers were to be poignantly linked, the lean, aquiline Robert Smith-Barry (also of 5 Squadron) and the solid, soldierly, well-groomed Francis Waldron. 'Ferdy' Waldron, by far the senior of the three, was a flight commander on 2 Squadron.

Among the airmen mechanics, some of whom were filling the observers' front seats because of an order that no two pilots were to be risked together, there were also young men who would one day make their mark. One of them, crestfallen at having to travel by sea because his pilot, the dashing Lieutenant Eric Conran, had been switched from a lovingly tended two-seater to one of the few single-seaters, was destined to outshine peers and seniors alike and to achieve immortality. This was the nineteen-year-old former boy bugler James McCudden.

Following mobilisation on 4 August 1914, the four squadrons

earmarked to accompany the British Expeditionary Force (BEF), representing the entire operational strength of the RFC at that time, moved into prepared positions in the South of England, ready for the penultimate hop to the point of departure. The BE (Blériot Experimental) 2a two-seaters of Burke's squadron, formed two years earlier at Farnborough and subsequently based at Montrose, on the Scottish east coast, actually started their flight southwards on 3 August. Staging at Farnborough, they survived sundry minor accidents and incidents before reaching Dover comparatively unscathed. Before leaving Montrose their pilots secured everything 'not wanted on voyage' in lockers and dared anyone to touch them before their (expected) return. Meanwhile at Gosport, Lieutenant A.E. 'Biffy' Borton, of No. 5 Squadron, dapper, dashing and dare-devil, chuckling his way through life, sporting a monocle more for affectation than astigmatism, was pinning a warning notice to his door: 'No one is to enter this room until the end of the war.' Channel Islander Lieutenant Henry Le Marchant Brock was looking forward to the expedition as 'a great rag' that might last three months. All were confident of being home for Christmas.

The justification for Britain's declaration of war on 4 August was the German invasion of Belgium, whose frontiers Britain had guaranteed. After refusing permission for the Germans to enter their country, the Belgians were putting up a heroic resistance. But the pilots of No. 2 Squadron, in a mood of exuberant optimism, and impatient to get to the war zone, found themselves retained to fly coastal reconnaissances from Dover. Their immediate tasks were to search for hostile submarines that might interfere with the sea crossing of the BEF, and to patrol vulnerable target areas to deter attack by the much-feared German Zeppelins. At Farnborough, where wild rumours of spies and sabotage circulated, the pilots slept under their machines in anticipation of Zeppelin attacks on the airship sheds and on the aircraft factory. Against these bulbous dirigibles, credited with powers of destruction far in excess of their true capability, there was as yet no defence.

At Dover, 'Pregnant Percy' left his pilots in no doubt what was required of them. Unarmed apart from the revolvers, rifles and rifle grenades they were ordered to carry, they were not expected to shun any chance of mortal combat, whatever the odds. There was no special briefing: methods of attack were left to individual enterprise and resource. But lest imagination should fail, 'a certain gallant C.O.' as one of Burke's pilots put it, ruled that in the event of failure to achieve a positive result with their ludicrously inappropriate weapons, the inescapable alternative was to ram any marauding airship head-on.

Pilots seemed little daunted by this dire prospect, consoling themselves with the thought that even without the weight of an observer, who was to be left behind on the ground (for which the observers, feigning disappointment, secretly congratulated themselves), the ceiling of the BE2a was blessedly inadequate to reach the heights at which Zeppelins were known to fly.

The other squadrons bound for France experienced quite as many incidents in transit to Dover but were less fortunate in the outcome. No. 3 Squadron, flying tractor Blériots and Henri Farman pushers (engine behind the pilot, skeletal and transparent, more like kites than aeroplanes), lost one of its best pilots, Lieutenant Robert R. Skene, on 12 August soon after the squadron's dawn take-off from Netheravon for Dover. In a period when aerobatics were regarded as dangerous and unnecessary, Bob Skene, formerly company pilot for the firm of Martin-Handasyde, was both renowned and notorious as the first Englishman to loop the loop. He was not the only RFC pilot to practise this manoeuvre, Mapplebeck stunting spectacularly over Salisbury Cathedral and stimulating an order that no more attempts at looping were to be made: but Skene was certainly not looping that morning. Engine failure, combined with inexperience, was normally the bugbear, but not here. With two men on board whose combined weight varied from plane to plane, together with their kit, which included the mechanic's tools, plus a full load of fuel, it seems probable that Skene's plane was overloaded. McCudden was one of those who witnessed with alarm its bouncing, uncertain take-off run and faltering, taildown struggle to rise. Its disappearance behind the hangars was followed by a reverberating crash. McCudden's friend and colleague, Air Mechanic Ray Barlow, sitting in the vulnerable front seat, was killed instantly and Skene did not long survive him. They were the first RFC casualties of the war.

Lieutenant W.R. 'Willie' Read, of the 1st Dragoon Guards, dubbed a 'live wire' by his colleagues, hid a streak of self-willed obstinacy behind a façade of pipe-smoking maturity. A man of twenty-nine, he mixed easily with seniors and juniors alike, and knew how to look after himself and his men. Flying a Henri Farman of No. 3 Squadron and choosing to stage half-way at Shoreham for refuelling (inner man included), he reached Dover at 10 o'clock. Others of 3 Squadron who got away safely followed his example. One pilot wrecked his machine and injured his mechanic when he side-slipped on landing at Dover.

No. 4 Squadron had made the preliminary move from Netheravon to Eastchurch on 30 July, with no less a task than to protect Woolwich Arsenal – and London incidentally – from air attack. Their record was two machines smashed up on the way, one through engine failure, the other ostensibly through 'pilot error'. Already this phrase, apportioning the blame correctly enough in most instances, had its sceptics, especially amongst the colleagues of dead pilots. An inquest verdict on a pilot and observer of No. 4 Squadron particularly incensed the man who was flying alongside them at the time, Gibb Mapplebeck. He witnessed the structural failure as it happened and landed near the wreck to find both men dead. Of the inquest he wrote: 'I have never been present at such disgraceful proceedings in my life . . . the whole thing was a put-up job to screen the factory . . . the factory official who attended the inquest committed perjury, of which we have proof . . . we hope to carry the matter further but have no great hope of satisfaction.' Still less could exoneration of dead pilots through detailed scientific investigation be looked for in time of war.

'War preparations going on hard,' wrote Mapplebeck on 30 July. 'The worst is now expected.' The squadron's two flights of BE2a's (there was a third, of Henri Farmans) would be going abroad, he thought, at any moment. But at Eastchurch they learned they would be on defensive coastal patrols for at least a week. 'This is rotten,' complained Mapplebeck, who like his colleagues could not get to France quickly enough. Nearly all these men were professional soldiers turned airmen, and however undesirable war might be, it was what they were trained for, and the prospect of putting their skills to the test was an exciting as well as a daunting one. Peacetime soldiering had its rewards but its predictability could be stultifying. Their worst fear was that the war might be over before they got there.

Mapplebeck argued that hostile submarines and airships would still be around in a week's or a month's time: meanwhile the BEF, which began to embark on 9 August under Field Marshal Sir John French, would arrive in France without air support. Yet the squadrons could not leave before their motor transport and administrative tail were in place on the far side, and these were about to sail from various ports. In any case the squadrons were having enough difficulty assembling at Dover; so puny a force could not be in two places at once.

Theoretically the numbering of RFC Squadrons at this stage was consecutive; but No. 1 had been formed originally as an airship squadron under veteran airship and balloon pioneer Captain Edward Maitland (he was also a pioneer of the parachute, had made many jumps from balloons, and in 1913 made the first jump from an airship). Although airships had since been transferred to naval control, No. 1 had not yet been fully re-equipped with aeroplanes. Thus the fourth squadron converging on Dover was No. 5. Owing to a dearth of shipping to embark its administrative back-up, and to a nightmare of mechanical mishaps, 5 Squadron was still at Gosport when, at midnight on 12 August, Brigadier-General Sir David Henderson, the man appointed to command the Royal Flying Corps in the field, arrived at Dover with his second in command, Lt.-Col. Frederick H. Sykes, together with the man he was leaving behind to mind the shop at the War Office, Major W. Sefton Brancker; he promptly issued orders for all machines to be ready to start for France at 6 a.m.

*   *   *

In the years immediately preceding August 1914, Britain had lagged alarmingly behind the other European powers – and particularly France – in military aviation. Although the Wright Brothers had led the world with their flights at Kittyhawk in 1903, the real beginnings of practical aviation had to await the invention of a suitable power unit, and this came in 1909 with the introduction by French engineers of the rotary engine. Up to that time, the chief cause of engine failure had been overheating; but by fixing the crankshaft and rotating the radially-arranged cylinders about its axis, more efficient cooling was obtained. The revolving engine produced more even torque (tangential force) and ran more smoothly, and the power-weight ratio was reduced. French rotary engines were soon being produced elsewhere under licence, and British manufacturers became totally dependent on them, every single machine of the four squadrons bound for France being powered by French rotary engines.

The so-called Blériot Experimental range – the current example being the BE2a – was in other respects a genuinely British-built machine, designed for the government by Geoffrey de Havilland at Farnborough. So too was the Avro 504, less numerous (only four joined the armada), built by the pioneer A.V. Roe. But the Farman brothers, Henri and Maurice, although born in England, had resided in France all their lives, had established their factory near Paris, and were among the foremost French pioneers. A further inadequacy was a reliance on German magnetos.

In 1910 the Chief of the Imperial General Staff had decried the whole notion of military aviation as 'a useless and expensive fad', while the First Sea Lord had estimated that 'the naval requirement for aircraft was two'. Even the French general Ferdinand Foch, later to be appointed Allied Commander-in-Chief, pronounced aviation as 'worthless as an instrument of war'. Cavalrymen, jealous of their forward role as the eyes of the Army in battle, were contemptuous of the early box-kite contraptions, and they warned that their only positive contribution would be to frighten the horses. Connoisseurs of orthodox military and naval warfare saw the air as an element of startling inconvenience. Fortunately there were brass hats on both sides of the Channel who recognised the vital part air observation might play in a future war and foresaw that mastery of the enemy's air forces might be necessary to secure it.

At a lower level there were many enthusiasts. These were not merely the young, the dashing and the venturesome, although they would soon predominate. Among the first to have his imagination fired by Blériot's Channel flight of 1909, and to do something about it, was a 32-year-old mechanical engineer in the Royal Field Artillery named Captain J.D.B. Fulton. Finding his initial resolve to build himself a monoplane of the Blériot type a frustratingly slow process, John Fulton bought himself a Blériot machine and began experimenting with it on Salisbury Plain. But he was beaten to it as the first British officer to qualify as a pilot by a colleague from the same regiment, Captain Bertram Dickson, whose obsession with the dawn of aviation and all it portended for his country had taken him as a spectator to the Rheims Air Show of August 1909, one of the first great landmarks in aviation history. Dickson subsequently acquired a Henri Farman biplane and learned to fly it in France, gaining his certificate on 12 May 1910. Fulton followed in November of the same year.

Dickson flew reconnaissance sorties during the army manoeuvres that autumn with another pioneer, Lieutenant Lancelot Gibbs, but gusting winds impaired their effectiveness and with it their repute. Nevertheless Fulton's work at Larkhill, where he was joined under War Office agreement by the Bristol Company and their School of Aviation, bred a lively airmindedness in the surrounding army camps. Meanwhile the initiative of the Bristol Company in sending three of their boxkite biplanes to India to demonstrate their military value found an able if idiosyncratic disciple in a monocled, deceptively foppish Indian Army officer whose approachability, drive and enthusiasm belied his image. This was W. Sefton Brancker, and for the next 20 years, until his death in the R101 airship disaster in 1930, he was to prove one of the principal motive forces in British aviation. But first, in India, he flew as an observer in one of the boxkites during army manoeuvres and provided such accurate and unprecedented reports of troop movements that the Chief of the General Staff in India was favourably impressed. He was to prove, in the not far distant future, a staunch and appreciative ally of the embryonic air corps: his name was Douglas Haig. Haig was to have another sharp reminder when, in pre-war army manoeuvres at home, the side he commanded lost the 'battle' through inferior aerial reconnaissance.

On 28 February 1911, under public pressure, an army order prepared the way for the establishment of an Air Battalion of the Royal Engineers, to take effect from 1 April. The 14 officers and 150 other ranks of the original establishment formed a nucleus entrusted with the task of creating a body of expert airmen. The training and instruction of men in handling kites, balloons, aeroplanes, and other forms of aircraft would devolve upon this battalion. Officer recruits could be selected from any regular arm or branch of the Service; other ranks would be selected from the Corps of Royal Engineers. The selection of pilots, however, was dependent upon their taking their Royal Aero Club certificate independently at one of the many private flying schools that were emerging. The standard charge at these schools of £75 was reimbursed if and when the candidate passed. High-handed and off-putting as this might seem, it ensured that every aspirant was a genuine enthusiast, suited to the job in hand and not easily deterred.

Belatedly, and some might think stingily, the War Office were officially sponsoring British military aviation. What had previously been known as the Balloon Factory at Farnborough was expanded to become the Army Aircraft Factory, with a brief to build aeroplanes and airships for the Air Battalion in addition to balloons. Airships were originally assigned to No. 1 Company under Maitland, aeroplanes to No. 2 Company under Fulton. Yet in comparison with other European nations the effort was puny. France already had over 200 aircraft in service compared to Britain's meagre dozen or so, and British officers who visited the French army manoeuvres of 1911 noted that French aircraft were being employed not only for visual reconnaissance but also for the control of artillery and for aerial photography. Scepticism about the value of aeroplanes in war,

[11]

however, still lingered, the Germans tending to specialise in airships, attracted by their longer range and greater lifting capacity. But despite this apparent preference they set up corps of military and naval aviation and sought to train pilots and observers in reconnaissance work.

Further evidence of the potential of military aviation was provided in October 1911 when aerial reconnaissance and aerial bombardment were employed for the first time in war in the quarrel in Tripoli (Libya) between Italy and Turkey. But whereas the shelling of Turkish ground targets by artillery and warship attracted no comment, the use of aeroplanes for a similar purpose drew what some saw as illogical protest on moral grounds, initiating the first of countless controversies on the ethics of aerial bombardment.

Arising from this skirmish in Tripoli, governments were forced to review their attitudes, force being the operative word. Asked whether the British ought to seek command of the air as well as the sea in any future war, a naval spokesman replied: 'I do not say we *wish* to do so but I think we will be *forced* to do so.' Under Prime Minister Herbert Asquith, a reluctant Cabinet took the point and requested that a technical sub-committee be formed of the Committee of Imperial Defence to consider future policy and make recommendations. The key members of this committee were David Henderson, then Director of Military Training, and staff officer Frederick Sykes.

The most visionary comment came from one of those early army pioneers who had learnt to fly at their own expense and laid the first foundations – Bertram Dickson. 'In the case of a European war,' ventured Dickson, 'both sides would be equipped with large corps of aeroplanes, each trying to obtain information from the other, and to hide its own movements. The efforts which each would exert would lead to the inevitable result of a war in the air, for the supremacy of the air, by armed aeroplanes against each other. This fight for the supremacy of the air in future wars will be of the first and greatest importance . . .' Not even the great leaders who were to follow could have improved on this.

Thus pressurised from above and below, the appointed sub-committee recommended the formation of a new flying corps, divided into two wings, one naval, one military. A Central Flying School was to be established at Upavon on Salisbury Plain, and the army aircraft factory at Farnborough would become the Royal Aircraft Factory under the flamboyant Mervyn O'Gorman. An Air Committee of the CID, with representatives from both Services, would act as an advisory body. All this was duly approved by the Cabinet, and the Royal Flying Corps, intended to embrace all naval and military flying, was established under Royal Warrant on 13 April 1912. The motto chosen was 'Per Ardua ad Astra'.

The apparent subservience of all forms of naval aviation to an army corps was much resented by the senior service, and the Admiralty, independently and without authority, having developed its own training centre at Eastchurch, established an autonomous existence for its flying branch by proclaiming the birth of the Royal Naval Air Service. Such was the political clout of the Admiralty at that time that this brazen act of unilateralism went unchallenged. It was not officially recognised as the Royal Naval Air Service until 1 July 1914.

One effect of this dichotomy was that two separate agencies were now competing for such meagre resources of aircraft design and construction as existed. War Office policy for both military and naval wings of the RFC, for reasons of economy, had been to build its own aeroplanes at the Aircraft Factory at Farnborough, where Geoffrey de Havilland was both chief designer and test pilot (a fortuitous insurance no doubt). But the policy of the Admiralty, consistent with cutting the RNAS off from War Office control, became to turn to private enterprise. By stimulating firms like A.V. Roe, Shorts, Sopwiths, Vickers and Handley Page to design new machines they overtook the RFC, though doing them a lasting service in the long run by encouraging the emergence of a civilian aeroplane and aeroplane engine industry.

[2]

'FLYING WILL CONTINUE AS USUAL'

AMONG the first of the pioneer flyers later to become famous
in the annals of the RFC (and later still of the RAF), one name
was conspicuously absent, that of Hugh Trenchard. At the
time of the formation of the Air Battalion in 1911, and of the RFC
in 1912, Trenchard was serving as a major with the second battalion
of his regiment in Londonderry. Having previously rebuilt and run
the regiment as a temporary lieutenant-colonel during a long period
of service in Nigeria, he understandably fretted now. All his efforts
to secure a more promising outlet met with rebuttal, often without
so much as acknowledgement, and he was now in his fortieth year.
It would be many years before the War Office pensioned him off,
and his despondency deepened. Several of his contemporaries understood the frustration of this brusque, tall (he was 6′3″), large-framed,
physically arresting soldier with piercing eyes, distinctive visage and
booming voice, but only one came up with any suggestion for alleviating it. This was a comrade who had served under him in Nigeria,
Captain Eustace B. Loraine, scion of a distinguished naval family.
Trenchard recalled the younger man's excitement two years earlier
at Blériot's successful Channel crossing. 'I must find out more about
this flying business,' Loraine had said. Since then he had learned to
fly and joined the Air Battalion, and from there the RFC. Now he
wrote from Larkhill urging Trenchard to transfer. 'You've no idea

[14]

what you're missing. Come and see men like ants crawling!' It was this sense of God-like majesty and power, high above the pygmy affairs of earth, which most of the early flyers found so uplifting.

Nothing was more likely to infect Trenchard with his friend's enthusiasm than opposition, and this was available in plenty. He was too old. Forty was the limit for qualified pilots to join the RFC, and Trenchard was 39 and unqualified. It was a young man's game. He would probably kill himself. Anyway he was far too big and heavy. Had he seen the cramped cockpits of the flimsy flying machines of the day, where leg-room was at a premium? It would be a foolish venture, with no likely military bonus even if he avoided disaster. But no man was more stubborn than Trenchard; it was at once his strength and his weakness. He finally persuaded his commanding officer to endorse his application for three months leave of absence, which, if he succeeded in going solo and passing the requisite tests meanwhile, would just give him time to enrol as a pupil at the new Central Flying School – where he was pleased to learn that one of his instructors would be Eustace Loraine – and book his place on Course No. 1 before his fortieth birthday disqualified him.

As though some final acid test of resolve were called for, the news that confronted him from his newspaper on his return to London on leave provided it. It told of the RFC's first fatal crash, on Salisbury Plain, near Stonehenge, the previous day, 5 July 1912. A Nieuport monoplane of No. 3 Squadron which had set several records in other hands had apparently lost flying speed in the turn, side-slipped and nose-dived, and the pilot had been too low to recover. Both pilot and observer were dead. No doubt it was pilot error – but it was not the first black mark in that period against the monoplane form, leading to a War Office ban on monoplanes and a preference for the sturdier biplane. Staff-Sergeant R.H.V. Wilson, the squadron's senior technical NCO, had been in the front seat. The pilot, as Trenchard read with dismay, was Eustace Loraine.

An order promulgated that same day at Larkhill was to create an undying tradition. 'Flying will continue this evening as usual.' Trenchard's reaction was similar: his grief for his friend and exemplar, wrote his biographer, only steeled his determination. He took care to study the technique of tuition, rented a room within walking distance of the flying school he had selected – Tommy Sopwith's at Brooklands – and impressed his instructor, a man named E.W. Copeland Perry, with his dedication, if not with his skill. 'He would never have made a good pilot,' said Sopwith. Nevertheless he earned his ticket in one hour four minutes' flying time, spread over thirteen inclement days, and according to Sopwith he tackled the task in hand with wonderful spirit. 'He was out at dawn each morning . . . He helped to push the machine out . . . He was a model pupil . . .'

At the Central Flying School, which Trenchard reached in late August that same year, he was quickly co-opted on to the permanent staff as adjutant, where his personality and drive, coupled with an instinctive grasp of the likely function of air forces, handsomely rewarded the gesture. Although he remained an indifferent flyer, he was confirmed in office in October, his grading, poignantly, being as 'an instructor (Squadron Commander) vice Captain E.B. Loraine, deceased.' It was in this period that he conceived the need for the aggressive stance in operations which was to prove the hallmark of the RFC in war.

As it happened, Trenchard was far from being the senior soldier to qualify as a pilot and gain his wings. That honour belonged to RFC chief David Henderson, who learned to fly in 1911 at the age of 49. A man of unusual composure, tolerance and foresight, he was an acknowledged expert in the art of military reconnaissance, and he was quick to see the potential of aerial observation and the urgent need to develop it as a technique. The role of aviation in wartime, it was thought, would be mainly one of reconnaissance, and Henderson, having played a leading role on the CID technical sub-committee, was a natural choice as head of the newly-formed Directorate of Military Aeronautics. Subordinate command of the Military Wing alone (as opposed to the Naval Wing) went initially to Sykes: staff officer Sykes had attended the French Army manoeuvres of 1911 with Fulton and reported trenchantly on them, and he had qualified for his pilot's brevet in the same year.

When the four operational squadrons began their move to Dover on mobilisation, Trenchard confidently expected to go to France with

[16]

them to join the Expeditionary Force, very possibly in command of the RFC in the field. But he was to be disappointed. The Army Council saw Henderson, the man who had nurtured and guided the force from the start, as the logical choice, and Henderson, equally logically, took the politically astute Sykes as his chief staff officer and deputy, leaving command of the RFC at home to Trenchard. Based at Farnborough, Trenchard's prime task, as delegated informally by Henderson, would be to build new squadrons for the rapid expansion that was now envisaged.

Sykes, who was no less of a thruster than Trenchard, now seemed to have been preferred as Henderson's likely successor. He saw Trenchard's role as the subordinate one of direct support of the squadrons leaving for France, and before handing over to him at Farnborough he took it upon himself to tell him so, leading to one of the acrimonious personal clashes which had already characterised their relationship. Sykes, lean and hungry-looking, was hampered by a personality which, it was said, 'strongly engendered mistrust', and the straightforward Trenchard, secure in Henderson's confidence, told him not to talk rubbish. He would get his reinforcements, but the top priority was to produce new squadrons. Trenchard, indeed, had an even more influential supporter in the newly-appointed Secretary of State for War, Lord Kitchener, who took the precaution, on 7 August, of promoting him to brevet lieutenant-colonel, a stratagem which preserved his seniority over Sykes. Nevertheless, with practically the entire reservoir of serviceable machines and experienced mechanics earmarked for France, and with the scheming Sykes having Henderson's ear on the spot as his right-hand man, Trenchard was in for an uneasy as well as an arduous few months.

There was one consolation. Another man who was being left behind, in sole charge of supply and equipment at the Military Aeronautics Directorate, was Brancker, who for all his idiosyncrasies was a man to be trusted. Brancker, like many others at the War Office, had almost despaired in late July and early August when it had seemed that the Government, anxious to avoid hostilities, were going to sit on the fence, an impression which rendered the French attitude towards its ally distinctly ugly. Then came the violation of Belgian neutrality, and with it the declaration of War. Next day, crucially, came the recall to the War office of the 64-year-old Lord Kitchener, 'much to the joy and relief', as Brancker noted, 'of every soldier in the Army'. Yet, as Brancker sought to piece together the scattered remnants of the Military Wing of the RFC, with hardly any pilots or aeroplanes in prospect, Kitchener aggravated his problems by telling him, as a beginning, to raise five more aeroplane squadrons immediately.

At a second interview, Kitchener, one of the few who believed from the first that it would be a long war, ordered Brancker to prepare for a vast expansion, and when Brancker estimated in writing, with much trepidation, that the new armies Kitchener was planning would require as many as fifty squadrons in air support, Kitchener, with prophetic insight, penned a note in his own handwriting at the foot of the minute sheet which deserves to be as familiar to history as the famous 'Your Country Needs You' poster: 'Double this. K.'

Brancker laid down three main requirements, all of them urgent. First, the design and production of aeroplanes and aero engines. Secondly, the recruitment and training of pilots, of air mechanics, and of an administrative branch. Thirdly, the establishment of aerodromes and training facilities. For the supply of aeroplanes, the RFC were obliged by what proved to be a misguided pre-war policy to rely on the Royal Aircraft Factory. The urgent need was to standardise as far as possible on a single general purpose type, for ease of manufacture, training and servicing; and the operational requirement, as envisaged at that time, was for a stable reconnaissance two-seater, one that would virtually fly itself and allow pilot and observer to concentrate on their allotted tasks of observation and artillery support. The obvious choice – indeed there was no ready alternative – was Geoffrey de Havilland's latest development of his BE range, the BE2c. Modifications which gave increased stability, regarded as a bull point for reconnaissance work, and the installation of a 90hp engine of Factory design, the RAF1, improved its performance, but it remained slow and cumbrous and not by any stretch of the imagination a fighting machine. It carried no defensive armament and would almost certainly be difficult to arm and fight effectively. Brancker himself objected to the choice on the grounds that until a satisfactory fighting plane could be evolved the Henri Farman pusher, even more primitive and sedate but with pilot and observer sitting forward of the engine, allowing an arc of fire forward, was preferable. Both the Henri and the Maurice Farman were being produced in Britain under licence from France. But with the need to fight for air space not generally accepted as yet, Brancker lost the argument – and later got the blame for the decision. When it was realised that the Factory was not and could not be geared to mass production, large orders for the BE2c were placed with civilian firms.

The folly of concentrating all aircraft design on a subsidised government factory, instead of encouraging civilian firms to compete, became retrospectively clear. Meanwhile, such firms as had shown interest in aircraft manufacture were now busy with orders for the Admiralty, where there was no keener advocate of private enterprise than the newly appointed First Lord, Winston Churchill. The only other machines the RFC had in more or less immediate prospect, for which limited orders were placed, were: two 'pusher' two-seaters (in which, as with the Farman, pilot and observer sat forward of the engine, allowing an arc of fire forward); the Bristol Scout; and a Factory machine similar to the BE but intended for bombing.

Of the two pusher types, one, the FE2 – Farman Experimental 2 – was a De Havilland design, the other, the Vickers FB5 fighter or Gunbus, owed its embryonic existence more to the enterprise of the Vickers firm, and to an order from the RNAS, than to the RFC.

One other Factory design worthy of mention was the SE2 – Scouting Experimental 2. The prototype was flown occasionally in France by selected pilots in the early months of the war, but it did not appear in its successful SE5 version until 1917.

The Government had shown more foresight early that year in offering a prize for a British aero engine, but the winning design proved far too heavy for practical use and this stimulated the Factory to produce the RAF1, designed for the modified BE2. Meanwhile the gap was filled by substantial new orders for French engines, placed just prior to the outbreak of war.

The recruitment of pilots and mechanics, fitters and riggers presented less difficulty. The favourable rates offered by Brancker enabled him to attract 1,100 of the best mechanics in Britain, and these formed the backbone of the new squadrons he was charged to establish. The only immediate sources of pilots were the civilian training schools, where the intention was to enlist the instructors as sergeant pilots, a breed already existing in the flying corps (one such was an older brother of Jimmy McCudden); but with the RNAS commissioning all pilots, the RFC, in enlisting experienced civilian pilots, had to commission them in order to compete.

The proclivity of established professional pilots for stunting – still strictly forbidden officially – was stifled by making them sign a declaration to the effect that they would not loop or perform any similar manoeuvre while serving in the RFC. But their expertise as instructors was invaluable. Facilities for training raw pilots, rather than recruitment, was the major problem, and the pre-war policy of making pilots pay for their initial training was abandoned, *ab initio* courses being started at CFS and at several requisitioned civilian schools.

When, five years earlier, youthful imaginations were fired by the exploits of Blériot and others, the attendance at aviation meetings had multiplied. Flying, although beyond the reach of the majority except for the occasional joy-ride, became a craze. Now one could learn to fly for nothing – and even get paid for it. The prospect appealed to emotions less immediate than patriotism, although that might have been part of it. Flying gave its practitioners a new conceit of themselves, an individuality, the opportunity to achieve tasks that the earthbound millions could only gaze at in awe. If, as many volunteers felt, they were in a rut, flying would lift them out of it. Self-doubt would be succeeded by self-belief. Subsequently, when the first solo flight was accomplished, a natural apprehension, and the sense of solitude, were submerged in an intense feeling of exhilaration. For the young men who now applied to join the new corps, or to transfer to it, the fact that one could kill oneself in the process of learning only magnified the fascination.

None of these emotions was likely to be stirred by the first question asked of many applicants: 'Why do you want to join the Flying Corps?' And this was only the beginning. Having got past that one, they were faced with what we would now call the 64,000-dollar question. To make a judgement, in a brief interview, on whether or not an applicant had what it took to fly the rickety wood, wire and fabric contraptions of the day was difficult enough, and the class system in which the interviewer operated must inevitably have loaded the dice in favour of the public schoolboy. Anyway, legend – and some reported experience – has it that the second question, intended as a measure of a likely aptitude for flying (it was a question that has been joyously ridiculed ever since), was: 'Do you ride?'

Was it, in fact, so ridiculous a question? A good 'seat', a natural equilibrium, and a sensitive pair of hands, would have been among the qualities the interviewer was looking for. Even more important, perhaps, would be the self-confidence necessary to control an animate object, and the ready acceptance of physical challenge. Many of these young aspirants would fly before they ever drove a fast car or rode a motor-bike as a means of channelling their aggression. And the question was not so élitist as it might appear: far more people were accustomed to horses as a means of transport than would be the case today. And a man who baulked at handling and controlling a horse might baulk at flying and fighting an aeroplane. No doubt the methods of selection were ill-conceived and arbitrary; but they seem to have worked. And the unsuitable pupil was soon weeded out – if he didn't kill himself first.

3

CHANNEL CROSSING:
THE FIRST RECONNAISSANCE

THE airmen alerted in their temporary encampment on Swingate Downs at midnight on 12 August, with a warning that
they would be taking off at six o'clock next morning, had all
won their places the hard way – through personal initiative, financial
sacrifice, the civilian training schools, and the CFS. Now the testing
time had come.

There was not much sleep that night for anyone, least of all for
the pilots, bedded down beside their machines in the hangars, their
rest interrupted by the prodigious snores of Pregnant Percy. They
envied him his capacity to sleep soundly at such a time.

Drawn from over forty different regiments (only a handful, mostly
from No. 5 Squadron, which had not yet reached Dover, were direct
entrants into the RFC Special Reserve), and hailing from all parts of
the United Kingdom (which then included the whole of Ireland, the
Anglo-Irish being strongly represented), they had already developed
fierce squadron loyalties and inter-squadron rivalries; but for the
moment these emotions were subjugated by the infinitely stronger
human ties of shared experience and danger. Already they had suffered losses. Now they faced a flight across a stretch of water which
had already claimed the lives of distinguished pioneer flyers, in flimsy,
ramshackle machines whose power units were continually faltering
and failing. Yet many who encountered them that morning remarked

on their optimism and exhilaration at the prospect before them. Without exception they had joined or been transferred to the RFC for adventure, and now more than ever before they stood on the threshold of it. 'Such exuberance of spirit I have never seen,' was the comment of a non-flying colleague.

Youthful naivety could not wholly account for this atmosphere of zestful panache. Most had attained the rank of lieutenant, all the flight commanders were captains, and the squadron commanders were majors. Nervous tension doubtless contributed, but the excitement was palpable. For many months they had endured the scepticism, even the ridicule, of their fellow soldiers – they were still professional soldiers first and professional airmen second – and now was their chance to prove themselves in battle. This romanticised their resolve to do or die.

Assembled at Dover were not only the aeroplanes of Nos 2, 3 and 4 Squadrons but also another 16 machines that had been allotted to form an Aircraft Park. These machines, together with 4 Sopwith Tabloids in packing cases which were to travel by sea, were the planned nucleus of what would be built up in the ensuing months into a vast system of supply and repair feeding the squadrons in France. They comprised 9 BE2a's, 1 BE2c, 3 BE8s, and 3 Henri Farmans. Half of these, however, had to be supplied to the squadrons at Dover to replace casualties and bring them up to strength before departure. The rump, crewed by spare pilots and mechanics, joined the expedition.

Briefing that morning was properly abbreviated; pilots and mechanics already knew what was expected of them. Maps of France and Belgium had been issued, sealed orders, giving their destination, were opened. Purchasing parties had scoured local suppliers in previous days for tyre inner-tubes, providing a lifebelt of sorts for each man, to be inflated by mouth on immersion. Other equipment to be taken included: for pilots, a revolver, field glasses, and a spare pair of goggles; and for mechanics, a roll of tools. Pilots were also ordered to carry, for sustenance in emergency, a water-bottle containing boiled water, a miniature stove, and a haversack containing biscuits, cold meat, a bar of chocolate, and a packet of soup concentrate. There was no sea rescue organisation, but pilots were not to set course before attaining 3,000 feet, sufficient, it was hoped, to glide across in the event of engine failure. After making landfall at Boulogne they were to coast-crawl south to the Somme estuary before following the Somme river south-east to the aerodrome at Amiens. Shipping bound for Boulogne had been alerted to look out for possible ditchings on the actual crossing.

Squadron ground personnel were sailing for Boulogne that day, mostly from Southampton, while personnel and equipment of the Aircraft Park were leaving from Avonmouth. First to sail, though, were the officers and men of the newly-established RFC Headquarters in France. Under Henderson and Sykes, they would have Major H.R.M. Brooke-Popham as DAQMG and Captain Geoffrey Salmond as GSO2. Others on the headquarters staff included medical and wireless specialists (there was a wireless flight attached rather speculatively to No. 4 Squadron), and the unmilitary and incongruous but urbane and highly literate Hon. Maurice Baring, personal staff officer to Henderson.

Also travelling by sea was a motley collection of motor transport that would have looked more at home amongst the roundabouts and roller-coasters of a fairground. From a pool of requisitioned commercial vehicles assembled in Regents Park in the first days of the war, the RFC, accorded the low priority to which they were becoming accustomed, had had to make do and mend with the remnants, which they proceeded to form into a tumbledown motorcade that towered above their own sombre, functional service conveyances in an orgy of colour. A high-sided roof rack for empty cubical biscuit tins disclosed a past life of delivery work for Peek Frean; and a giant blue-black splash on the side of another van boasted the superiority of Stephens Ink. More appropriate for removals, perhaps, were a white-on-green Maples pantechnicon and a black-on-green Carter Paterson juggernaut. There was a cosmopolitan neutrality in the presence of Sunbeam, Renault and Mercedes tourers and a Rolls-Royce donated by Smith-Barry, and a native touch of amateurism in the recruitment of a private two-seater coupé complete with its volunteer owner/driver, a Mr Weeding from Guildford. Bringing up the rear of this Lord Mayor's Show of vehicles, aptly enough, was a dust-cart.

Even this gaudy cavalcade paled in comparison with its principal exhibit, commandeered to serve as ammunition and bomb lorry for No. 5 Squadron. If other floats in the procession were loud in their praises of their peacetime wares, this one was deafening. Against a backcloth of brilliant scarlet it proclaimed in gold lettering the incomparable merits of HP (Houses of Parliament) Sauce, using the mouth-watering phrase 'The World's Appetiser'. To exchange, as a cargo, such a prompter of digestive juices for the stomach-turning horror of ammunition and bombs might seem Machiavellian; but this was no latter-day Trojan Horse. Neither deception nor camouflage was intended, and no one seems to have considered the vulnerability of these vehicles to observation and attack from the air. But virtue, however unwitting, was to have its reward in the landmark provided by the scarlet van for disorientated RFC pilots and observers during the chaotic retreat that was shortly to come.

First to take off, at 06.25 on what promised to be a perfect August morning, were the pilots of No. 2 Squadron. And first among these, as even the commanders of two of the other squadrons, Jack Salmond of No. 3 and J.F.A. 'Josh' Higgins of No. 5, had forecast, was Harvey-Kelly. He was followed soon afterwards by Burke. For the townsfolk of Dover, the choice of a rallying point so close to their homes created a sensation; and as, one by one, the fragile machines took off and battled giddily for height, the scene on Swingate Downs, overlooked by the Castle and watched by the populace, assumed an atmosphere of jamboree. Pilots and mechanics had too much to think about to be more than subconsciously aware of it, but the spectators were savouring the thrill of history being made.

All the machines of No. 2 Squadron were BE2a's, and all got safely across the Channel. But as Burke led them down the coast to the mouth of the Somme, one of his brood was seen to be missing. On reaching Boulogne, Harvey-Kelly, scorning to use the Somme as a guide, had elected to cut straight across country to Amiens. Just as Burke was gliding down to land at Amiens, he caught sight of another machine: it was Harvey-Kelly's. Landing at 08.20, the favourite beat Burke by two minutes. But with the other machines landing safely one by one, Burke's vexation rapidly gave way to euphoria. H-K, as usual, had got away with it.

No. 3 Squadron, led by its three flight commanders, Captains Philip Herbert, Lionel Charlton, and Philip Joubert (Jack Salmond, the squadron commander, travelled with the ground party), and with a briefed take-off time of 08.15, flew a mixture of BE2s; BE8s (a variant of the BE known somewhat derisively as 'Bloaters' because of their fish-like tail); and Henri Farmans. Lieutenant Willie Read, already mentioned, a man whose contentious individuality was apt to clash with obstacles on the ground as well as in the air, was aware from the start that his engine was not running well, but he managed to coax his BE2 up to 1,200 feet. Determined not to be left behind, he elected to risk it and carry on. One pilot had to abort with engine trouble (he followed five days later), but all the others got through, reaching Amiens at 11.05. Here they again found themselves the centre of attraction. The good people of Amiens, sickened by rumours that perfidious Albion was bent on betrayal, now had welcome evidence to the contrary, and they turned out in force to celebrate. With some thirty strange aeroplanes lined up on the aerodrome as though at a pageant, and the expectation of more to come, they gave the astonished airmen a truly Gallic greeting, showering them with all manner of flowers and goodies. For a brief honeymoon period, the *entente cordiale* flourished as never before.

Last to leave that day was No. 4 Squadron, which included the wireless flight attached to it. Here too it was the flight commanders – two of them in this case, Captains Gordon Shephard and F.J.L. Cogan – who led the way. Two flights of BEs made the crossing, the third flight, of Henri Farmans, being left behind for local patrol duties. Soon after the sea crossing was completed, Cogan's engine cut out, and although he cursed his luck he accepted it philosophically as an occupational hazard and looked for a likely field to force-land in. Unfortunately he had no means of communication with his flight except by hand signal, and his attempts to wave them on their way were misinterpreted; he could not stop them following him down. The field Cogan chose, uncorrugated in appearance, proved to have been recently ploughed, and most of his flight sustained minor damage. If this was not Fred Karno's Air Force it looked very much like it; but skill and resource in repair and improvisation, practised in innumerable forced and unauthorised landings away from base in peacetime, brought a measure of recovery, and after begging facilities for refuelling they got away again the same day and eventually joined the party at Amiens, though one pilot, Patrick Playfair (destined, as an air marshal, to lead another Advanced Air Striking Force to France 25 years later), was obliged to force-land a second time to ask an astonished pedestrian the way. Recording this many years later, he admitted to suppressing it at the time.

Forty-nine machines lay parked on Amiens aerodrome that night, with only two small sheds to accommodate them. Serviceability, in the days to come, would be proportionate to the state of the weather and would be much affected by high winds and rain, but for the moment they basked in perfect August sunshine. So far the expedition had been accomplished without casualty: but Amiens was only a staging post on the way to the selected forward base at Maubeuge, 70 miles to the west-north-west and 12 miles south of Mons. And No. 5 Squadron was still to come.

It was natural that 5 Squadron, the most recently formed of the expeditionary force, should have most of the direct entry special reserve pilots in its ranks, men who were not and never had been regular soldiers and who owed no regimental allegiance. They numbered no more than six, against a dozen regulars, but two of them, already mentioned, were to prove outstanding. The best-known, perhaps, and certainly the most eccentric, was the Etonian Bob Smith-Barry, known from an early stage as simply Smith-B. Sensitive, aesthetic features and a penchant for the unorthodox were rightly indicative of aristocratic descent, but the spare, angular physique scarcely hinted at the single-mindedness of the pedagogue. Nor did one of his early reports at Eton, which described him as '. . . *an awful little boy. He has no aptitude whatever*'.

Smith-B had been flying since 1911 and instructing at the Bristol School since 1912; and at CFS, where they found there was little they could teach him, they had employed him as an instructor. He had approached aviation with the same ardour he had once devoted to a career as a concert pianist, when for two years he had practised for eight hours a day. He believed that the emphasis in training on cautious, unadventurous flying was a danger in itself, leaving the pupil totally unprepared for emergencies, and in his own flying he practised what he preached. Reproached for handling a machine contrary to the rule book, and therefore dangerously, he met the criticism head-on. 'You know, Captain, I felt much safer flying that machine dangerously.' After that they left him alone.

Almost more colourful at first sight was the fearless, inventive, irrepressible Louis Strange. The son of a Dorsetshire farmer, his interests were mechanical rather than agricultural, and he was one of the first to apply his mind to the problems of air firing and air fighting. After taking his Royal Aero Club certificate at Hendon in August 1913 he applied for a commission in the RFC and was eventually posted to the sixth course of instruction at CFS. While he was waiting he offered his services to the Hendon School as an instructor, and he was soon teaching beginners to fly Bristol Boxkites. He flew passengers on joy-rides at week-ends, and he entered for the cross-country races that were gaining in popularity at the time with notable success. Here was a young man who was virtually a professional flyer when he arrived at CFS, perfectly at home in the air.

When war was clearly imminent, all pupils at CFS who were considered sufficiently advanced were posted to active service squadrons, and Strange joined No. 5 at Gosport. Of the three flights of four machines each, A was equipped with Avro 504s, B and C with Henri Farmans. Each flight was a self-contained unit capable of being detached with its own MT workshop and stores. The day after the departure of the other three squadrons for France, the pilots of No. 5 set out via Shoreham for Dover; but their passage was anything but smooth. One of the flight commanders, Captain George Carmichael, found himself without a mount when the interplane struts of his Farman collapsed as he was taxying out, so he set off for Dover by road, having been advised that he might pick up a spare machine from the Aircraft Park when he got there. Another pilot suffered concussion when he crashed near Shoreham, and a third force-landed on the South Downs between Brighton and Lewes with engine trouble, spelling a delay of several days in both cases.

None of these setbacks approached for incident the experience of Louis Strange. The squadron had been held back originally, it will be remembered, by a dearth of shipping. When the squadron transport eventually embarked at Southampton it proved to be short of a driver. Chosen to deputise, despite vigorous protest, was Strange's mechanic. When the missing driver eventually turned up, somewhat the worse for the celebrations that had delayed him, his reward was to be allotted to Strange as substitute mechanic. Since he had never flown before, it was an assignment that was well calculated to sober him up.

He was a big fellow, weighing, in Strange's estimate, about thirteen stone. His kit, too, looked bulky, having been packed to seaborne rather than airborne limits. From past experience Strange knew how to manage an overloaded Blériot, but a Farman, with a top speed of 59 miles an hour, against the Blériot's 72, was even more difficult to handle. To add to his weight problems, the inventive Strange had mounted a forward-firing Lewis gun in the front cockpit of his Farman. (The gun belonged to another 5 Squadron pilot, Lieutenant L. da C. Penn-Gaskell, a ballistics enthusiast who often flew with Strange.) Struggling against headwinds and at times nearly flattened on to the Downs, the Farman took 2½ hours to cover the 70 miles (a ground speed of 28 miles per hour) to Shoreham, where Strange had planned to refuel. He had another reason for alighting at Shoreham – a lady friend had promised to meet him there to say goodbye. The combination of delay at the start and slow-motion flight meant that she had gone when he got there.

At Dover, where the nucleus of a new squadron not yet operational, No. 6, had been given the task of setting up the facilities, red flags warned of obstructions, but an unmarked declivity, aggravated by the Farman's unusual load, caused a broken longeron (longitudinal strut). Into that same declivity, as Strange could not help but notice, his passenger discarded an empty whisky bottle; poor chap, it was Dutch courage he had been seeking this time, but the effect was similar. Strange put him under close arrest, as a kindness as much as anything, and he was marched off to the guard tent.

The next task was to repair the Farman. Finding he could get no spares at Dover, and after having tea at the Castle, Strange set off in Smith-Barry's Rolls-Royce to collect a replacement longeron at Farnborough. It was two o'clock in the morning before he got back to Dover, but he worked through the night fitting the longeron — and was thankful to CFS for the training that had taught him the knack. Then it was breakfast at the Castle and a return to the aerodrome to release his passenger, only to find that he had somehow escaped from the guard tent during the night.

When apprehended, the driver would face a serious charge, perhaps of desertion. But Strange, feeling that the guard must be equally at fault, acted with compassion. Police assistance was sought and the escaped prisoner, still the worse for wear, was run to earth in the town. At last Strange was ready to go.

Meanwhile Carmichael, having picked up the only spare aeroplane available at Dover, a BE8 two-seat tractor biplane from the Aircraft Park, had got away with the rump of the squadron the previous day, 15 August. Carmichael later described the BE8 as 'a nasty contraption with insufficient fin surface, one of the least successful products of the Royal Aircraft Factory', and he was not keen to fly it. But he wasn't going to be left behind, and he coaxed it to Amiens in 2 hours 10 minutes. Others who crossed that day included Smith-Barry. The atmosphere at Amiens remained one of frenzied acclaim, and first General Henderson and then Field Marshal Sir John French visited the camp and congratulated pilots and crews. Henderson told them he hadn't heard so far of any air fighting by the French and added that he 'didn't think there would be any', thinking perhaps to reassure men who, apart from Louis Strange, carried only revolvers and rifles. He was soon to revise this opinion.

Next day, 16 August, a Sunday, the weather broke, but Strange finally got away from Dover at midday. At once he was faced by a strong north-east wind, and it took him an agonising forty-five minutes to cross the water by the shortest route to Cap Gris Nez, with a rough, inhospitable sea swirling beneath him to remind him of the caprices of aero engines and the frailty of tyre inner-tubes.

His grudging sympathy with the predicament of his abducted, half-inebriated front-seat passenger was enhanced. But despite deteriorating visibility he identified his pinpoint, and he was amazed, when he circled the aerodrome at Amiens, to see crowds of people milling around the perimeter, undaunted by the drizzle, and a phalanx of more than fifty aeroplanes lined up in rows as though on display. Landing and taxying up to align his Farman with the other machines, he had scarcely come to a halt when his passenger sprang to life, stood up in the front cockpit, and waved another empty bottle to acknowledge the cheers of the throng.

For Strange there was the satisfaction of catching up with his squadron colleagues after the lone flight across. For his passenger, somewhat unkindly perhaps, there was a reckoning with his commanding officer, the monocled Josh Higgins, who had crossed by sea with the ground party. Fidgeting as was his habit with eye-glass and swagger stick when obliged to deliver a reprimand (his jutting backside had earned him the sobriquet of 'all bum and eye-glass', sometimes shortened to 'arsy-glassy'), and a man generally popular because he flew whenever he could and also looked after his men, he nevertheless awarded the unfortunate MT driver 56 days' field punishment. It could, of course, have been much worse for the man but for Strange.

All four squadrons had been ordered that morning to fly to their forward base at Maubeuge, ten miles behind the section of the line to be guarded by the BEF. But low cloud had delayed them, only No. 2 Squadron getting off before Strange's arrival. No. 4 Squadron followed, and then No. 3. All went well until the last aircraft but one took to the air. The pilot, Second Lieutenant Evelyn Copeland Perry, was one of the most experienced flyers in the Corps (he was the man who had taught Trenchard to fly). But he was piloting one of the dreaded BE8s. He was climbing over the aerodrome when the plane stalled and appeared to catch fire. Last to take off was Copeland Perry's flight commander, Lionel Charlton, and as he circled before heading east he saw below him on the ground the machine which had preceded him, crumpled and burning. Both Perry and his air mechanic, a lad named Herbert Parfitt, were killed.

Carmichael, having himself flown a BE8 to Amiens for 3 Squadron, was given the task of collecting one of three new Henri Farmans from the French base at Buc. Another pilot, Lieutenant R.M. Vaughan, forced down with engine trouble in a machine which bore no national markings, was arrested as a spy by the gendarmes and dumped in the local jail, where he languished for three days until he was released into the hands of the local mayor and his two lovely daughters.

Carmichael's good fortune was compounded when Smith-Barry, the pilot selected to fly his BE8 on to Maubeuge, suffered a control failure near Peronne and sustained multiple injuries in the subsequent crash. His mechanic, Corporal Frederick Geard, in the front seat, was killed.

Languishing in hospital at St Quentin with two broken legs and a smashed knee-cap, Smith-B was heartened by a letter he received from his squadron commander, Josh Higgins. 'Don't worry about the smash. I am quite sure it was not your fault.' This uncritical verdict, written before the causes of the crash were known, was a tremendous compliment to the known skill and natural ability of Smith-Barry. In Higgins's experience – and few knew better, since he flew all machines delivered to the squadron himself and learned their tricks before allowing others to fly them – no one in the Corps handled and manoeuvred aeroplanes with the confidence and indeed the mastery of Smith-B, and he guessed that somehow he would get back to flying.

The third of the replacement BE8s provided by the Aircraft Park was written off soon afterwards, happily without serious injury to the crew.

On the approach to Maubeuge – in stark contrast to their reception at Amiens – several machines were fired on by the French. Fortunately their marksmanship was poor, only Waldron's plane being much damaged.

They were now near the Belgian frontier, billeted in a fortified town no more than forty miles from the invading German Army. But they were reassured, on 18 August, by their first glimpse of the BEF, marching boldly through the town on their way north to Mons to the stirring accompaniment of regimental bands. However, as Joubert noted, the arrival of the British only meant, for the RFC, an impartial peppering from the ground by ally and compatriot alike, both armies having sensibly resolved to shoot first and face questions afterwards. As soon as anyone took off and crossed the Maubeuge –Mons road he was welcomed by a roar of musketry. To counter this the crews worked all night painting Union Jacks on the underside of lower wings and on fuselages, only for these emblems, in the days that followed, to be mistaken for the German cross and riddled accordingly. It wasn't only the British who suffered. In the middle of a Zeppelin scare, the French shot down one of their own airships.

Read was told to hold himself in readiness to take off as soon as any Zeppelin was sighted. He and his observer were armed with three bombs to drop on the Zeppelin from above, supposing they could outclimb it, and a revolver each to deter interference from hostile aeroplanes. 'There was no sign of the gasbag,' wrote Read sardonically.

For the ground party, steering a triumphant, flower-bedecked course by road and rail from Boulogne through Amiens to Maubeuge, fêted at every stopping place and showered with gifts, the euphoria lasted a little longer. Even at Maubeuge, where they bedded down on the aerodrome, the French did their best to make them comfortable. But for the flying men, the sequence of accidents and crashes, the loss of comrades, and the novel experience of being fired at, especially by their own side, led to some unspoken but gloomy forecasts. What would happen when the fighting started, Read asked himself – as it was surely about to do? 'Estimates are that not more than 5% of those who have come out with the Corps will go back,' he noted. Proud of being in the vanguard, and as high-spirited as ever, pilots began to accept that they might not be home for Christmas after all.

The German invasion plan, prepared some years earlier by Count von Schlieffen when he was Chief of the German General Staff, was a daring scheme aimed at knocking France out of the war at the outset. Inherent in the plan was the blatant infringement of Belgian neutrality, the German armies sweeping round through Belgium and Northern France to encircle Paris and cut off the major portion of the French army from reinforcement, compelling the French Government to surrender. The plan had since been modified by von Schlieffen's successor, von Moltke, to take account of an expected French counter-offensive in Alsace and Lorraine, Moltke strengthening the left wing at the expense of the strong right wing which von Schlieffen had seen as the decisive element. Despite the delay imposed on the advance by the heroic resistance of the Belgians, the anticipated French counter-offensive was stillborn by setbacks and losses, and General Joseph Joffre, the French Commander in Chief, ordered a retreat on the whole front. The British contingent had barely taken up its positions to make a stand at Mons on a 25-mile sector when the French on their right were forced to pull back, leaving the British right flank exposed. This was on 22 August. News of the French retreat was not immediately passed to the British, though the Germans soon found the gap and started pushing through.

The distinction of flying the first RFC reconnaissance of the war – they took off at 09.30 on 19 August – had meanwhile fallen to Philip Joubert of No. 3 Squadron and Gibb Mapplebeck of No. 4. Each had a designated task. For the first part of their reconnaissance they were to keep together, so that if one were forced down through mechanical trouble – a perpetual anxiety – the other could report where he was. To save weight and improve performance they flew without observers, but this proved a false economy, both pilots losing their way – and each other – in poor visibility and low cloud. Mapplebeck somehow completed his task, reporting only a small cavalry force at Gembloux instead of the concentration suspected; but Joubert, despite landing several times to fix his position, lost his way repeatedly and spent an abortive eight hours before returning to Maubeuge. It was not a very convincing performance.

Reconnaissances flown on 20 and 21 August disclosed no enemy troops immediately in front of the BEF; but on Saturday the 22nd the twelve reconnaissances that were flown built up a picture of a substantial enemy force moving towards the British front. GHQ had previously been wary of Intelligence based purely on air observation, but it was afterwards admitted that the RFC's efforts that day, led by Gordon Shephard, 'did much to dissipate the fog of war'. Trust in and reliance on the RFC, although still far from complete, was at least embryonic. But there was a price to be paid. Several machines came under accurate rifle and machine-gun fire and Sergeant-Major D.S. Jillings, an observer with No. 2 Squadron, was hit in the leg by a rifle bullet, the first British soldier to be wounded in an aeroplane. Worse was to follow when one of 5 Squadron's Avros failed to return; it had been shot down by ground fire while the crew were noting the progress, from 2,000 feet, of a German infantry column. After the chastening experience of Joubert and Mapplebeck the rule that two pilots must not fly in the same plane had inevitably been relaxed in order that qualified observers could be carried, and Lieutenants V. Waterfall and C.G.G. Bayly were missing.

Gordon Bayly's half-completed reconnaissance report, picked up near the crash site, survived in the hands of Belgian peasants, who secreted it, and it eventually found its way to the War Office – too late for practical use. Stranger still, the arrival of the Avro in enemy-held territory seems to have given the Germans their first sure knowledge of the presence in France of British forces.

On the same day the first German airborne intruder, alerted perhaps by Waterfall's crash, appeared over Maubeuge airfield at 5,000 feet, and two BE2 crews went after it with hand grenades and bombs. Meanwhile Strange took off in his Farman, with Penn-Gaskell to work the gun. Struggling for altitude, he had got no higher than 3,500 feet when the German, having had plenty of time to complete his reconnaissance, bade them a disdainful farewell. Frustrating as this was for Strange and Penn-Gaskell, it was nothing to their disappointment when Higgins, blaming the weight of the gun for their ponderous ascent, ordered them to dispense with it. In vain did they argue that the Blériots had done no better. 'You'll have to manage with a rifle in future,' ruled Higgins.

4

THE RETREAT FROM MONS:
THE MIRACLE OF THE MARNE

THE BEF under Sir John French consisted of two army corps, a cavalry division, and a cavalry brigade, comprising a total, at most, of 80,000 men and 250 guns, a contemptible enough little army in all conscience by comparison with France's 72 divisions, and even on this 25-mile front it was heavily outnumbered and out-gunned by the First German Army under von Kluck. Horace Smith-Dorrien's Second Corps were to hold the line westwards from Mons, Douglas Haig's First Corps eastwards to Binche. For these men, the cream of the British Army, war was their job, and they expected to stem the tide of the German advance before mounting an offensive that would drive the invaders back on their tracks. But with the battle of the frontiers impending, and liaison with the Fifth French Army on the British right not yet established, GHQ gave the RFC — even more contemptible in its way — a new task. In addition to locating enemy forces and reporting on their strength and progress, they were asked to find out what they could about the movements of their Allies.

Philip Joubert and Dermott Allen of 3 Squadron, as pilot and observer, were among those detailed, their machine — a rarity — being a Blériot two-seater monoplane. The Anglo-Irish Allen, a slim, upright figure with piercing blue eyes, had already proved himself an above-average interpreter of what he saw from the air, his verbal amplifications, despite a marked stammer, always being worth waiting for. From heights varying between 1,500 and 2,000 feet, in good weather, they found they could detect practically all ground movement; and as they flew over the battle area in and around Charleroi they saw quite clearly that the French were being driven back. Yet despite the reputation they had earned, their report, when they landed back at Maubeuge, was coolly received, no reference to a withdrawal having yet been made by the French. It was not long, however, before the report was confirmed and Joubert and Allen were vindicated. The BEF had barely reached their decreed positions when they were seen to be untenable. From the start it was a case of retreat or be annihilated.

That evening, 22 August, Sir John French held a conference at Le Cateau with Haig and Smith-Dorrien at which the request of the commander of the Fifth French Army that the British, to relieve pressure on the French, undertake a local offensive action at Mons before joining them in a strategic retreat had already been pre-empted by events. Yet they could not disengage without making a stand and fighting their way out, thus providing the requested cover for the French left wing. Next day, 23 August, the British infantry, supported by artillery, fought the Battle of Mons. By inflicting losses on the enemy almost comparable with their own they delayed the German advance, and despite almost intolerable pressure they somehow covered their own retreat from daybreak on the 24th. Men snatched what sleep they could where they fought, and the withdrawal did not develop into a rout; but to the RFC the sight of their comrades returning to Maubeuge in war-torn disarray, so soon after their triumphant passage north, was agonising.

Some of the RFC contingent had already abandoned Maubeuge for Le Cateau, to the south-west, while the Aircraft Park had begun withdrawing from Amiens to St Omer, 30 miles inland from Boulogne. Among those who witnessed distressing scenes of chaos near Maubeuge was Read. 'Roads everywhere were crowded with troops retiring,' he noted, 'not a good sight.' The atmosphere was one of dejection and even despair. 'Poor fellows, they've had no sleep and little food for three nights and days, being driven back and pressed always by the advancing enemy. The Germans have us on the run, fighting a rearguard action against big odds.' It was easy to see they were in a tight corner, with men, guns and transport blocking the roads, and he was reminded of campaign histories he had studied describing disorderly retreats. Some of the casualties were riding on the limbers of guns, and walking-wounded were throwing away their haversacks, even their rifles. He made one of these men pick his rifle up, but others were carrying their wounded pals, and he turned away in embarrassment.

The notion of making a stand before the fortress of Maubeuge was collapsing as fears of envelopment grew. When shells began falling close to the aerodrome, Brooke-Popham sent Read to take up a position on a low hill which gave a commanding view of the surrounding countryside. He took two orderlies with him to act as couriers for the warning messages he expected to initiate. Suspecting and then confirming that German cavalry were using a wood in the middle distance as cover, he sent first one orderly then the other back to report. He was already aware of increasing activity behind him on the aerodrome, but no message came for him to abandon his post, and when he finally returned, without orders, practically everyone had gone. One defective Henri Farman had been set on fire lest the Germans capture it, but his own Farman was still there, his mechanic, bless him, was standing by to swing the prop, and they took off for Le Cateau as German cavalry approached.

Le Cateau was a pleasant enough town, but accommodation was lacking. 'We slept', wrote Maurice Baring, 'and when I say we I mean dozens of pilots, fully dressed in a barn, on the top of, and underneath, an enormous load of straw ... Everybody was quite cheerful, especially the pilots.' Baring's phrase, of course, included observers, who were spending their days directing pilots over and behind the battlefield, looking for enemy movements and locating enemy batteries, and learning fast. German uniforms were appearing with increasing frequency where once there had been British, and the threat was evidently aimed at Le Cateau. On the afternoon of the 25th, while the BEF prepared to make a stand at Le Cateau, the RFC retreated south-west to St Quentin.

That afternoon Lieutenants C.W. Wilson and C.E.C. Rabagliati of No. 5 Squadron, having just filed a reconnaissance report, were refuelling their Avro, No. 398, when an intruder was seen approaching the aerodrome from the south. 'There you are,' shouted Josh Higgins, adjusting his monocle, 'go and take his number!' Already the swept-back wing-tips of the intruder had identified it as an Etrich Taube. Heading north and climbing steeply, Wilson and Rabagliati were tacitly agreed on putting into practice the tactics they had often discussed, namely, getting ahead of and below the 'hostile' (enemy aircraft) so that Rabagliati, in the forward seat (but aft of the tractor engine), could fire upwards and rearwards over Wilson's head. Wilson was forced to duck below his cockpit coaming when the firing started, to avoid the ejected 'empties', but when it ceased he followed Rabagliati's pointing finger earthwards. The Taube pilot appeared to have surrendered: he continued to descend, and he finally force-landed in a field. They would have liked to land beside him and claim their prize, but they could see troops nearby and could not identify them, so they decided to return to Le Cateau. In fact the action had taken place so close to Le Cateau that they were applauded on landing, a dubious pleasure as it exposed their poor navigation, and they now wished they had landed beside their victim.

They were to wish this even more fervently when they caught up some time later with Harvey-Kelly, who had also tangled with the Taube and was posing as the victor. He had landed beside it and he and his observer had chased the pilot into a wood. They had removed a small plaque from the wreckage, which they were now displaying as booty. 'Stopped him in full career,' wrote Wilson in his diary, 'and claimed first Hun for 398. H-K handed the plaque gracefully to me. "Your bird I think."' Wilson and Rabagliati passed the trophy on to Higgins laconically. '"Number you asked for, Sir."'

The contrasts between luxury and discomfort experienced by the crews from day to day as the retreat accelerated were extreme. Sometimes they slept on billowing feather beds surrounded by lace curtains, with all the comforts of a provincial hotel, sometimes they were billeted in private houses; but more often they dossed down in the open, under hedges or the wings of their machines, sheltering in their greatcoats from thunderstorms that muddied and water-logged the fields and drenched the flimsy contraptions they must fly again next day. Yet several pilots managed to nurse their original steeds throughout the retreat.

Their routine, as recorded by Carmichael, although mainly reconnaissance, included patrolling the rear of von Kluck's army, searching for targets for their makeshift bombs, and attacking enemy machines with rifle fire whenever opportunity offered. They were even called upon, when units of Haig's Corps lost contact with Smith-Dorrien's, to help in locating them. Towards the end of each day they would be looking for their next landing ground, often at dusk and sometimes after dark, homing as often as not on their motley column of transport. Yet rations and fuel, even letters and parcels, continued to reach them, striking proof of the efficiency of Brooke-Popham and his supply services, while the mechanics often laboured all night to repair damage and wear and tear to the machines. No wonder they found that whenever and wherever they could get their heads down they slept. Yet, as Carmichael wrote, 'it was a picnic' compared with the nightmare horrors and privations from which, for the infantry, there was no escape and no respite. This bred in them an anxiety and determination never to let their earthbound comrades down, accounting, in the days ahead, for sacrifices that in retrospect sometimes seemed obstinately wasteful. RFC leaders were imbued – even perhaps obsessed – with this same anxiety.

Meanwhile the retreat continued. Stragglers who had lost touch with their comrades were often visible from the air, some with their rifles and equipment but 'too many without either', noted Charlton, while the Corps staff, whenever he reported to them, looked increasingly haggard. As a former fighting soldier and Staff College graduate his sympathies were engaged, and he developed a guilt complex about his own comparative immunity. Meanwhile the military retreat was hampered by multitudes of civilian refugees and their animals and impedimenta, jamming the roads in a panic attempt to escape the consequences of enemy occupation. Their own vulnerability, too, increased as they harassed advancing enemy troops and transport columns with grenades, *flechettes* (steel arrows), and improvised petrol bombs. Yet they often felt safer in the air than on the ground.

'Our Second Corps was unable to disengage without fighting,' noted Dermott Allen, 'and was being heavily attacked by four German Corps on the line Cambrai–Le Cateau.' Anxious to know how the battle was going, GHQ called that afternoon for further air reconnaissance, and 2nd Lieutenant Vivian Wadham, with Allen as observer, was sent to search and report. For more than an hour they flew over the battle, the pattern of which Allen found clearly discernible. He watched the withdrawal of some British guns, the crews of which had all apparently been killed or wounded, and saw salvoes of enemy shrapnel bursting continually amongst the relief teams of cavalry as they galloped up. It was a sickening sight, when the smoke cleared, to see groups of wounded horses struggling panic-stricken on the ground. 'The general retirement along our whole line could be seen,' continued Allen, 'with officers rallying and reforming the infantrymen as they streamed back over the fields.' His urgent message pinpointing the German concentrations did not immediately reach GHQ, which was in the process of evacuating St Quentin, but on landing he was taken to report personally to Sir John French and his Head of Intelligence, a welcome sign of the enhancement of RFC prestige. He returned to the aerodrome to see aircraft hurriedly preparing to fly off to the south-west, directly into an approaching thunderstorm.

Such was the speed and pressure of the German advance that they were driven out of St Quentin after a single night, falling back on La Fère, fifteen miles to the south. Short of fuel and sustenance, forced down to 300 feet by the rain, and with all pinpoints blotted out by the mist, they had their digestive juices activated by a glimpse, through the murk, of the old sauce lorry, in the middle of the circus-like convoy heading for La Fère.

Left behind in hospital in St Quentin was the unfortunate Smith-Barry. 'What's going to happen to me?' he demanded of the hospital staff. The evacuation of the town, he was told, meant that immobile patients would be left behind. The idea of being exposed to the mercies of the advancing German Army did not appeal to Smith-B, and he shouted to one of the hospital orderlies, 'Get me a cab.' Despite his broken legs he got himself out of bed, down the stairs, and into the horse-drawn four-wheeler that was somehow procured for him, placed his splinted legs on the front seat and, still in hospital pyjamas, was driven out of the west side of the town as the Germans entered the east. For the rest of his life he would limp and walk with a stick, but his escape was to prove infinitely more significant than anyone could have foreseen at the time.

The move south to a makeshift aerodrome at La Fère was accomplished without casualties despite the thunderstorm, pilots landing almost anywhere on the outskirts of the town. Two days later, on the 28th, with the noise of battle creeping ever nearer, those about to head north on reconnaissance or bombing were told to fly approximately 30 miles south-west from La Fère after completing their tasks and to look out for machines on the ground near Compiègne. Again the sauce lorry proved the best pinpoint. Here they were billeted in a school. The move was undertaken under continual threat of encirclement and capture, with no semblance of aerodrome defence, yet, according to Baring, spirits were high.

An appeal for high calibre replacement observers to improve interpretation of what was seen from the air brought two temporary attachments, Captains H.C. Jackson and E.W. Furse, both former students of the Staff College at Camberley. Jackson soon established a reputation as the best observer with the RFC, and his reports were given special credence at Smith-Dorrien's headquarters, exerting a notable influence on orders for each day's retreat. Jackson sometimes flew with Read, who found him an aggressive partner. 'Jackson spotted a German Taube machine,' wrote Read. 'I'd also seen him, but we'd done our job and I didn't want a fight.' According to Read, this was the conversation that ensued:

Jackson, excitedly: 'Look, old boy!'
Read, dismissively: 'Yes, I know.'
'I think we ought to go for him, old boy.'
'Better get home with your report.'

    Jackson, more urgently: 'I think we ought to go for him, old boy.'

    Resignedly: 'All right.'

Read altered course, and, as they passed the Taube, Jackson got in two shots with his rifle, which the German returned. This happened several times as the pilots manoeuvred, until ammunition on both sides was exhausted.

    'Have you got a revolver, old boy?'

    'Yes, but no ammo.'

    'Give it to me then, old boy. And this time, fly past him as close as you can.'

Humouring Jackson, and assuming he carried some ammunition of his own, Read did as he was asked. To his amazement, as they got opposite the Taube, Jackson flung the revolver at the German's propeller. 'Of course it missed,' said Read. Honour being satisfied, they flew home. How Read explained the loss of his revolver, a court martial offence, is not recorded. Soon afterwards Jackson returned to his regiment, though this must surely have been coincidental: he went with one of the RFC's first individual mentions in despatches.

After two days at Compiègne under the protection of a military guard, with the enemy in the vicinity of the aerodrome, they moved again, eventually escaping across the Marne. The French retreat, too, continued, while understanding and confidence between the Allied commanders, so far from improving, deteriorated. Bombed at each new aerodrome, the squadrons only just got away as the enemy closed in. The Germans, having crossed the Marne a day after the BEF on 4 September, were now approaching to within 30 miles of the capital city, and pilots strove hourly to keep Headquarters informed.

'In spite of the great efforts of the First Army,' wrote von Kluck later, 'the British had escaped the repeated attempts to envelop them. They continued their retreat southwards.' He made one final attempt to settle with the British, but again they eluded him, finishing up south of Paris at Melun. Eventually he abandoned the encirclement of Paris from the west and changed tack, turning to cut inside Paris to exploit the successes of the German Second Army on his left against the French: by executing a wheeling movement to the south-east he would develop a threat to the French flank. The switch was soon suspected by the RFC, Captain Furse, with 'Biffy' Borton as pilot, being among the first to interpret the signs and warn GHQ.

It seemed to the British, regrouping south of Paris, that the apparently endless retreat had been halted. Yet the High Command remained uneasy. Although pressure from their pursuers seemed to have relaxed, the enemy cavalry corps was unaccounted for; it had not been seen for two days. Misgivings multiplied as widespread air reconnaissance failed to locate it.

Joubert, with Allen as observer, was sent out in the late evening in an attempt to solve the mystery. They located groups of German infantry of about company strength on the BEF's right, presumably acting as advanced guard, but they seemed unusually thin for the numerous divisions supposed to be lurking behind them. Where, Allen asked himself, studying his map, were the serried ranks of marching men, the long columns of horse-drawn artillery, the endless supply trains they were accustomed to seeing? It was not until darkness was falling, when hundreds of bivouac fires suddenly twinkled, that the picture became clear. As Allen finished marking the main concentration of fires on his map, he and Joubert simultaneously made the same discovery. Around a haphazard formation of streams and backwaters which had been selected as watering-places, groups of horses were so crowded together that only one interpretation was possible: the missing German cavalry corps had been found.

Flying low in the gathering dusk, almost unseen from the ground, Joubert and Allen could easily discern the horses drinking at their waterholes, with horse lines concentrated round every farmhouse. They flew back at once to report.

It was clear beyond a doubt that von Kluck, ignoring the BEF to the south, had turned east of Paris to assist the German armies on his left, aiming at a final showdown with the French. Moving, undiscovered until now, across the British front, the cavalry corps had taken up their orthodox position in the van of von Kluck's wheeling movement.

The Germans believed that the Allies were virtually beaten and that victory was within their grasp. What they failed to appreciate was that the French retreat had been genuinely strategic, and that the French Army, although suffering severe casualties and forced to give ground, remained a cohesive force. Trusting to the strength of their eastern fortifications, the French High Command had even withdrawn troops from that area and formed a new army of 150,000 men to operate north of Paris.

When further air reconnaissance revealed that von Kluck's change of plan had left his right flank exposed, an opportunity presented itself for counter-attack, and General Joffre, exhorted and cajoled by General Galliéni, the military governor of beleaguered Paris, seized his chance. On 5 September he told Sir John French that he intended to take offensive action forthwith: next day he did so. For three days, from 6 to 8 September, on a 100-mile front from Compiègne east to Verdun, the course of the battle fluctuated. At one point the newly-formed French Sixth Army was under such pressure that 600 taxis were requisitioned to ferry vital reinforcements from Paris. But the line was held, and with the British now moving forward purposefully and recrossing the Marne, the Germans feared a breakthrough. On 9 September the German attack was called off and the entire invading forces, monitored hourly by the RFC, began a 40-mile fighting retreat to the River Aisne.

The 'Miracle of the Marne', recognised as one of the decisive military engagements of history, had been wrought, frustrating the German plan for a lightning victory. With the 'contemptible' British Army, according to the plan, cut off and rendered impotent, a brief but victorious campaign against Russia had been scheduled to follow. Instead, despite heavy casualties on both sides, the Allies had won a strategic victory.

Withdrawing northwards until they had crossed the River Aisne, the Germans halted on 13 September on high ground above the river. On the same day the Allies began to cross in pursuit, in torrential rain and under heavy fire. The RFC had moved forward in support the previous day, but that night the wind rose to gale force. The spotting and ranging of hostile batteries now became the primary task – but the RFC could not discharge it. Blinded by mist and rain, pilots returned to their bases empty-handed only to see their machines wiped out on the ground as the storm raged. One Farman of 3 Squadron, hurled 30 feet into the air, crashed on top of another in a lethal coupling. BEs of 2 Squadron, caught by a sudden shift in the wind before they could be pegged down, were blown across the aerodrome in fragments, presenting an appalling spectacle next morning. Screw pickets were used from this point on, undercarriage wheels were sunk so that wing skids rested on the ground, and vehicles were parked to windward as a screen. But it was a chilling reminder of the dependence of pilots and observers and their flimsy machines on the weather.

Even the hasty first-aid administered by the ground crews could not put more than ten or a dozen soggy machines in the air next day, and the reports rendered by pilots and observers, braving appalling weather in patched up machines, were inevitably sketchy. Unhappily, the best use was not made of such information as was gathered, at great personal risk, and heavy casualties were sustained in the Battle of the Aisne.

Frontal assault by infantry alone had been shown to be unavailing, and outflanking movements, attempted by both sides, were successfully countered. As Joffre moved his forces north-west, the BEF were switched to coastal defence, and the RFC, following them northwards, established themselves at St Omer. The enemy now concentrated on seizing the Channel ports, and the subsequent race to the sea developed into the First Battle of Ypres. Although often grounded by bad weather, the squadrons gave warning of German build-ups and reported accurately on troop movements. When the Germans did finally break through, a counter-attack by an improvised force achieved such success that Ypres, which thereafter stood as a symbol of Allied resistance, was saved.

A defended front line had meanwhile been established on a roughly north–south axis from Dunkirk to Compiègne before swinging east for Verdun and south again for the Swiss border. Within a few weeks the war of movement had thus given way to the beginnings of the static and attritional trench warfare which, punctuated by costly and abortive offensives, was to characterise ground operations for three and a half slaughterous years. In such a war, it was confidently expected, the Allies, with their greater resources of manpower, must prevail.

How the RFC would adapt to this change to static warfare remained to be shown. The story so far was not one of unqualified success, far from it, but the tiny nucleus of what was to grow into a massive force of nearly 300,000 officers and men and over 22,000 aeroplanes had justified its existence under enormous pressures. Their earlier reconnaissances had detected the enemy's attempt to encircle the BEF at Mons. As the BEF sought to escape they had hedgehopped to pinpoint their pursuers and even to harass them with makeshift bombs. Above all, with their French allies, they had spotted the wheeling movement executed by von Kluck's army and the dispositions of his forces which opened the way to victorious counter-attack.

'I wish particularly to bring to your Lordship's notice', wrote Field Marshal Sir John French in his despatch on the retreat, 'the admirable work done by the Royal Flying Corps under Sir David Henderson. Their skill, energy and perseverance have been beyond all praise. They have furnished me with the most complete and accurate information which has been of incalculable value in the conduct of operations. Fired at constantly both by friend and foe, and not hesitating to fly in every kind of weather, they have remained undaunted throughout.'

5

THE BEGINNINGS OF BATTLE FATIGUE: 'BOMB THE KAISER!'

AFTER the nomadic, precarious but eventful life of their first weeks in France, pilots and observers of the four RFC squadrons began to complain of boredom as the front line stabilised and they found themselves scouring much the same ground every day. Yet they accumulated a variety of fresh experience that winter.

It was not long, either, before the enemy co-operated in relieving their boredom. This co-operation, far from fraternal, lay in the proliferation and improved accuracy of their anti-aircraft weapons in and behind the front line. In the early days the German system of ranging was so rudimentary it was derided, and by skidding sideways on an even keel after each salvo it was generally possible to avoid the next one. 'Biffy' Borton was one of the first to demonstrate this. Each time the ploy succeeded he gave one of his typical chuckles and sang out, in triumph, a phrase from a George Robey music-hall monologue charged with that comedian's infamous innuendo: 'Archibald, certainly not!' Abbreviated to 'Archie', it became the standard RFC vernacular for all anti-aircraft fire.

As the shell-fire intensified, pilots sought to fly at safer heights. But it was difficult to get most machines above 5,000 feet, and below that they were vulnerable. Rifle fire frequently caused minor damage and casualties, but only a lucky hit was likely to be serious; indeed, to come back without boasting a few bullet-holes suggested over-caution. Flesh wounds, so long as they were minor, could be a source of envy, resulting in a few days' leave, perhaps in Paris. But sympathy sometimes gave way to hilarity, as when Mapplebeck, although seriously hurt in the groin, sustained a real 'flesh' wound by losing the tip of his penis.

Mapplebeck had set off with the idea of destroying a German observation balloon by dropping petrol bombs on it, taking no observer or firearms to save weight. At the mercy of an intercepting enemy aeroplane, he had been wounded while manoeuvring to bomb that instead. Losing consciousness, he had recovered in time to land without damaging his machine. This exploit, coming on top of another in which he blew up an ammunition train, brought him a DSO to soothe his wounded feelings.

There was less laughter over the prospect of a direct hit from Archie, though even here familiarity bred fatalism, though hardly contempt. 'Very glad to get out of the heaviest fire I have been under so far,' noted Strange on 4 October. 'At one time shells were simply bursting all round; in addition to the deafening roar of their guns we could easily hear the whistle and shriek of bullets.' Yet he added: 'I am getting used to being shelled now, almost indifferent to it in fact; it is marvellous that we don't get hit more often.'

Read, too, out spotting for the artillery, was heavily Archied. 'The air was thick with shell-bursts from anti-aircraft guns,' he noted. He kept turning, diving, and climbing, but in doing so he lost height. Finally at 3,000 feet a shell exploded near enough to put a splinter through his propeller, but he managed to limp home. The fair-minded Read could not help but admire the zeal of the German gunners: they had brought nothing down by shell-fire as yet but it was not for want of trying, and it was only a question of time. 'Archibald can reach you at 10,000 feet, it belches forth dirty yellow and black smoke and chain shot, and the noise of the shell bursting is almost enough to make one stall the machine with fright.' This battering, in an ever more concentrated form, was what the crews were to face for the next four years.

'It was normal for each crew to do two operational flights a day,' wrote Carmichael. 'Owing to low cloud, close reconnaissance and artillery observation were frequently carried out below 1,000 feet, and one Henri Farman was hit twelve times in three days.' Read wondered how his nerves would stand this daily bombardment. 'I notice several people's nerves are not as strong as they used to be. I'm sure Archie is responsible for a good deal. I would not mind quite so much if I was in a machine that was fast, and would climb a little more willingly.' Pilots were already conscious of the inadequacy of their machines.

Read was up four times on 23 October, totalling four and a half hours, mainly observing for the artillery. 'A good dressing-down from Archibald,' he wrote, 'and the Germans shelled the airfield after we got down and we were very lucky to escape. Some of the shells burst much too near and I could hear the pieces of shell whistling past. Well, I suppose the end will be pretty quick if one of Archie's physic-balls catches one. I think I would rather it caught *me* than crumple up Henri, because one would have too long to think when falling from 4,000 feet.' The helpless, falling-leaf plunge to destruction, more and more protracted as greater heights became commonplace, was to be a recurring nightmare. At least there was no resentment at the absence of parachutes, which had barely been tested yet in practical form for heavier than air machines.

After two months in France, pilots were beginning to feel, if not to show, the symptoms of battle fatigue. '27th October: arrived back at camp at 5pm,' wrote Read, 'nearly dark, feeling dog tired and absolutely fed up, having done 14½ hours' flying in the last five days, 4½ again today, and tonight I do not feel as if I shall be able to go on for long at this rate without an easy. It isn't that my nerve is going but I feel stale.' Archie was not the only threat. Every flight was a gamble, either through engine fallibility or structural decay caused by weeks of exposure to storm winds and torrential rain. One Henri Farman climbed so ponderously that it was opened up, disclosing a rear spar so saturated that it was sprouting fungus.

One of the most abiding handicaps was the meteorological phenomenon of the prevailing westerly wind, which drove them deeper into enemy territory than they sometimes intended and then treacherously delayed their return. For Farman pilots it was especially burdensome; an optimum speed of under 60 m.p.h. could sometimes leave them hovering motionless over the lines, the target of every gun within range. Lieutenants Abercromby and Small, of 5 Squadron, elected to abort a reconnaissance when, turning into wind on the outward flight to test its strength, they found they were actually going backwards.

The greatest toll still came from crashes on take-off and landing, not always from pilot error. Read himself, given a new Henri Farman, smashed it when the engine failed at a critical moment near the ground. It was his third crash in a week. He tried to pancake, the wheels touched prematurely, and the machine did a somersault. Everyone thought he and his observer must have been killed, but miraculous escapes from apparently fatal crashes through structures breaking up at slow speed were among life's compensations. Read was knocked out, but he got away with a broken nose. His sympathies were all for the man in the front seat, Major L.B. Boyd-Moss, the squadron's senior observer, incapacitated with back injuries.

As if the inherent dangers in handling these obsolescent machines, coupled with the broadsides of the enemy, were not enough, the shoot-first-and-face-questions-afterwards mentality of the troops, however understandable, was bound to cause tragedy sooner or later. When disaster came, the victims had descended to 1,000 feet in order to locate the batteries whose fire they were briefed to observe, only to be mistaken by the infantry for an enemy reconnaissance machine. German small arms fire had been generally wayward, but the British gunners, mistaking the Union Jack painted under the fuselage for the Maltese Cross, were right on target. Lieutenant Cyril Hoskins and his observer Captain Theodore Crean were the unfortunate crew, the plane caught fire and came down in flames. It was the first of the many 'flamers' that were to become the obsessive dread of some of the most famous 'aces' of later years.

The French, whose infantry never seemed able to distinguish British aircraft from German, and who fired impartially at either, were taken to task on one occasion with impeccable courtesy by the stuttering Dermott Allen. 'Do you m-mind t-telling your m-men not to f-f-fire on us,' he asked a French infantry commander. 'It p-p-puts us off.' To this masterpiece of understatement the commander pleaded, in justification, that the red cross on the Union Jack was all that was clearly visible from below and that it was sometimes mistaken for the German marking. Typically, it took the loss of Hoskins – one of the pilots who had helped to identify von Kluck's wheeling movement – and his observer to induce a change. Wouldn't it avoid confusion, suggested the French commander, to adopt the same circular marking as the French? National pride could not quite stomach this, but a compromise was reached in which the French roundel replaced the Union Jack but with the blue and red circles in reverse order (red centre and blue on the circumference, with white between).

Although a sharp reminder to British troops ordered them not to fire on any machine unless they were absolutely certain of its identity, pilots and observers, with their military background, understood without bitterness that ground troops were bound to be trigger-happy when there were aeroplanes about. It was just another hazard to be faced. Here too it was a wonder so few aircraft were hit. However, special detachments of flights and squadrons briefed to work direct with chosen formations in forward areas were already operating, and as this closer association between soldier and airman developed, errors became less frequent.

Valour, fear, aggression, apprehension were often a matter of mood. A good night's sleep could work wonders. Forty-eight hours after committing his self-doubt to his diary, and twenty-four hours after his flight commander Philip Herbert, noticing his nervous tension, had offered him a week's leave in England to recharge his batteries, Read noted: '. . . feel awfully fit today, after my long lie-in this morning.' He appreciated Herbert's thoughtfulness, but 'I do not want a rest. Feel as fit as when I came out.' Nevertheless it was a welcome treat next day when he and fellow pilot Alexander Shekleton had a day off to go into St Omer. He noted that the methodical Shekleton, whom he greatly admired, had not broken a single machine since coming out with the squadron in August. Yet on a recent 'show' (every trip was a 'show', not a sortie, or a mission, or an operation), he had had to turn back through feeling unwell.

'A few days rest at St Omer would do him good,' diagnosed Read.

The strain got to everyone sooner or later. 'After a long day's flying you feel you have had enough and don't ever want to go up again,' wrote Strange, 'but after a day's rest you are as keen as ever.' His reactions varied. 'One day you come down absolutely sick and tired of it all, while on another you just feel you have enjoyed a fine flight.' Rifle fire still caused more casualties than Archie, but 'it is the continual shelling that puts such a strain on you.' It would have been horribly monotonous, thought Strange, but for the opportunity to drop a few bombs on their tormentors. These home-made bombs, released haphazardly over the side, with no bomb sight devised as yet, could be little more than an irritant, but 'you feel you can get a bit of your own back.'

Squadron commanders, many of whom did little or no flying themselves, had already concluded that every man's stamina was exhaustible. Flight commanders, too, seeing their charges' reactions in the air, soon knew, when men turned back, whose excuses were genuine and whose were not. For all Read's independence of mind, there was never any question of his reliability, but he soon had further evidence of an intention to rest him. 'It was my turn for recce today and he [Herbert] went instead. Never felt less like wanting a rest in my life.' This may well have been a false bravado, the onset of a compensating aggression that could lead to recklessness. Anyway, when a major strike of a dozen machines was mounted next day, 1 November, Read was again omitted.

The target, openly and unashamedly, was none other than Kaiser Wilhelm himself. 'Hang the Kaiser' was to come later; it was 'Bomb the Kaiser' now, perhaps the first modern attempt to assassinate a war leader. The order came at the crisis of the first battle of Ypres: the Kaiser was reported by Intelligence to be inspecting forward troops at Gheluvelt, six miles east of Ypres. His approximate programme was known, and each pilot was given a place and time to bomb. 'Everyone went off bristling with bombs,' recorded Read. Observers had been left behind to increase the bomb-load. Critical of the exaggerated expectations of the effects of aerial bombing, Read added, with conscious irony: 'No official information so far

[53]

that the Kaiser is dead.' Carmichael provided an excuse: 'He had left before we arrived.'

Nerve and luck were apt to run out simultaneously; it happened too often to be purely coincidental. 'The next day,' wrote Read, 'I stopped one with my leg at 5,000 feet over Courtrai and was invalided to England.' The day he got his 'Blighty' wound, as he put it, his observer was the famous actor and pre-war flyer Robert Loraine.

Matinée idol Bobbie Loraine had earned his pilot's certificate on 21 June 1910 at the age of 35. A complex and contradictory character, he could be charming and infuriating in turn, and as an actor his undoubted talent was rarely taken seriously because of his physical beauty. As a pilot, as in life, he was erratic and accident-prone, but his courage was undoubted, and he enjoyed great success as a pioneer aviator before the theatre reclaimed him. His French air mechanic, asked whether his boss was lunatic or hero, answered that he was both in turn – and often both at once. Volunteering his services on the outbreak of war, Loraine was accepted by the RFC – but rejected as a pilot when he crashed several machines. He still pleaded to go to France, and Brancker sent him there as an observer on probation. He was attached to No. 3 Squadron and was soon flying his first reconnaissance.

A fortnight after Read's departure, Loraine himself was wounded, so seriously that 'for a week it was touch and go'. But he recovered, and his acceptance of the supporting role of observer, despite a reputation for megalomania, compensated for his record at Farnborough. In September 1915 he was back in France as a flight commander with 5 Squadron, where his popularity with the mechanics contrasted sharply with the resentment of his pilots at being ordered about by 'this old man', who was not a brilliant pilot, was an erratic disciplinarian, and worst of all, was an *actor*. An attempt to force him out failed, and he was awarded the MC for shooting down an Albatros (after which he dropped a sympathetic message over the lines). 'We had to admit,' said his 19-year-old senior lieutenant, 'that there was something in Loraine.'

Read, too, got back into action in France that year, but it was not intended that he should stay long. The experience of some of those first across was needed to form new squadrons at home and help with training. Gordon Shephard, Biffy Borton, George Carmichael, Lionel Charlton and many others had either gone or were earmarked, and Read was booked for a spell of instructing. 'A great loss' was the squadron's verdict on Read's departure: but he would be back.

Gibb Mapplebeck, after hospitalisation in Paris, refused home leave. He had been befriended by an attractive nurse who made him an equally attractive offer: she would drive him to a villa in Nice to recuperate – in the bosom of the Mumm family, to which she was related. There he was introduced, among other luxuries, to vintage champagne. The medicine worked, and early in 1915 he was back on the squadron, fully operational in all respects, according to his brother Tom (the nurse was not consulted).

6

HUGH DOWDING: LANOE HAWKER: LEWIS AND JAMES AND THE 'CLOCK CODE': AERIAL PHOTOGRAPHY: TRENCHARD LANDS IN FRANCE

EARLY attempts at air fighting were often more farcical than frightening, though the first sight of an unidentified aeroplane never failed to somersault the stomach. Willie Read's experience, apart from the Jackson incident, had not been untypical. 'Had an awful fright today. Saw a strange-looking machine coming along at the same height, 5,000 feet. We got rifles and revolvers ready – and then we saw, to my great relief, that it was a French Voisin.' They passed each other peaceably at 20 yards' range. Not so the Taube which, unarmed but carrying bombs, Read had tried to chase off while observing for the artillery. 'He was about 300 feet higher than we were,' which Read reckoned was quite a handy position in a Henri, giving his observer a good field of fire. While Read closed the range, his observer opened up with the rifle. 'The German turned twice, trying to get us immediately below him so as to drop a bomb on us, but I kept clear.' Bombing a stationary ground target without a bombsight was speculative enough: hitting a moving target with a bomb in mid-air reduced air combat to the level of Mack Sennett comedy. Yet Read took it seriously. Two machines flying one above the other on the same course at the same speed might conceivably narrow deflection to something like point-blank level.

Armament in RFC machines remained crude and ineffectual: the Bristol Scout, for instance, a single-seater tractor of pre-war racing design, was fast and manoeuvrable by contemporary standards, but its potential was cramped for this reason. It was also delicate and unforgiving, which meant that any examples available tended to be appropriated by squadron commanders, not always the best shots. The armament improvised initially was a rifle with a sawn-off stock clamped to shoot diagonally forward, missing the propeller but leaving the pilot aiming round corners. Josh Higgins loved it, but unlike Borton he did not wear a monocle merely for show, and Carmichael wrote that 'unfortunately his sight was not equal to his enthusiasm'. He could never get close enough to his quarry to shoot.

After being ordered to abandon the mounting he had improvised for Penn-Gaskell's machine-gun, Strange introduced an alternative modification in his Farman which moved the pilot forward to the front cockpit. This allowed the observer to stand up in the rear cockpit, secured by a safety strap, and fire in almost any direction. It was the best arrangement so far devised, though Strange recorded a rueful comment. 'The noise the observer made when shooting over my head was something terrific.'

Strange's Farman was the last survivor of the original machines of No. 5 Squadron that had left Gosport two months earlier; every other Avro or Farman had been crashed or otherwise lost. Finally, on 15 October, Strange was allotted a brand new Avro 504, all-British apart from the 80 h.p. Gnome engine. It was a development of this type, the 504K, that was later to become the standard trainer in the RFC. Any sentimental attachment to the old Farman was minimised for Strange by the much improved performance of the Avro. This improvement, however, did not extend to the armament, which was much the same as that generally adopted as standard in the Blériot with the observer in the front seat firing a rifle upwards and rearwards over the pilot's head. When a German reconnaissance machine overflew the aerodrome at St Omer, Strange and his observer, eager to test the Avro in combat, ran to their machine and climbed in without helmets, coats, or maps. It took them an hour to get within range of their quarry, and then the observer fired 70 rounds at about 100 yards' range before the German pilot escaped unscathed into cloud.

Angered at their impotence, they unwisely chased after the German – and with their primitive instruments, and without maps, they got lost. Running out of fuel over the North Sea, they managed to glide in and land on the beach near Le Touquet. It was a chastening experience, teaching Strange that it was folly to put themselves at risk in combat with such feeble armament. Against orders, he fitted a cross-bar between the centre section struts over which a rope was slung, so that a Lewis machine-gun, mounted on top of the fuselage decking, could be hauled up on a pulley in mid-air, free to fire in all directions. A chance to use it came on the morning of 22 November when, on reconnaissance with observer Lieutenant Freddy Small, they spotted a German reconnaissance machine heading for St Omer at about 7,000 feet. Recognising it as an Aviatik, Strange climbed and turned in front of it, manoeuvring for position. When he gave the signal, Small fired two long bursts, after which Strange closed the range to 50 feet only to see the German observer taking pot shots at them with a Mauser pistol. Small was in the act of changing a drum, standing up immediately in front of Strange, when his face suddenly contorted and Strange saw blood oozing from his gloved hand. Nevertheless Small completed the drum-change, and after another long burst the Aviatik pulled up, stalled, and side-slipped before flattening out and coming down near some reserve trenches on what appeared to be the British side of the line.

Landing at an aerodrome nearby, Strange delivered Small for first aid before cadging a motor-cycle to see what had happened to the Aviatik, convinced that Freddy Small had shot it down. He found it just where he expected, with twenty bullet holes in it but apparently capable at the very least of having continued into friendly territory. Presumably the pilot thought he had already crossed the lines. His observer and superior officer, of the Prussian Guard, was furious at being captured, and when he discovered his NCO pilot was uninjured he broke away from his captors, knocked him down, and began kicking him viciously before he was overpowered and dragged away.

There were differences of opinion between pilot and observer in the RFC – as with Read and the impulsive Captain Jackson – but there is no record that they ever came to blows. The status of observers fluctuated with the tasks they were expected to perform, and a practice that crept in of taking almost any volunteer was disapproved of and corrected; but it was soon established in the RFC that the man at the controls was in charge.

The rage of the German observer, although perhaps understandable, was a poor advertisement for discipline and comradeship in the German Air Force. But it seems – unfortunately for the RFC – to have been untypical. A shortage of trained observers probably accounted, in this instance, for the selection of an unsuitable man. The choice in the RFC, too, was limited, and a call went out for men with artillery experience to volunteer for transfer. One who answered the call was a young man named W.S. Douglas, Sholto Douglas. Training for these volunteers was 'extraordinarily little', wrote Douglas, 'nearly all at the front'. He told the story of a flight with Harvey-Kelly when, because they were both big men, they had discarded rifles to save weight. The confrontation that followed with an unarmed 'hostile' produced frustration on both sides but ended with a smile and a comradely wave. A bond quickly developed between opposing airmen, a bond of shared experience in an exciting new element, which sometimes brought reactions approaching chivalry.

Recruits from the artillery brought with them an experience of battle conditions which was invaluable; but they did not all prove eagle-eyed. 'We have a lot of new observers,' Mapplebeck learned from his CO on his return to duty. 'The pilots have to do all the observing nowadays.' Many pilots felt that they were better placed anyway for accurate observation, while observers found themselves concentrating increasingly on gunnery, and this eventually became the pattern.

The first squadron to reinforce Nos 2 to 5 in France was No. 6, the squadron which, when in embryo, had prepared the ground at Dover for the August departure. Under Major John H.W. Becke, with a mixture of BE2a's, BE8s, and Farmans, they flew to Bruges on 7 October, to support a ground force that was to attempt the relief of Antwerp. This plan was soon overtaken by events, and they joined their fellow squadrons at St Omer. One of the flight commanders was Cyril Newall, who, 25 years later, when World War II began, was to hold the highest post in the Royal Air Force. And a man of even greater subsequent achievement actually flew with the squadron as an observer; this was Captain H.C.T. Dowding.

Hugh Dowding had shown his peculiar brand of stubborn independence by negotiating a unique no fly no pay contract with the Sopwith school. He had refused to put down a penny of his own money: they were to teach him to fly on credit, and he would pay up when he got his ticket and could claim a refund from the army. Sopwith must have been impressed by the man's implicit assumption of superiority, because he agreed.

On mobilisation, Dowding had been retained by Trenchard to run the despatch camp at Dover, and he chafed at being kept in England, just as Trenchard did, pestering Trenchard for a posting to France. The more extrovert, self-assertive Trenchard was up against a man of quiet reticence who proved as stubborn as himself: it was a case of the irresistible force and the immovable object. When the exasperated Trenchard finally relented, however, it was with characteristic abruptness, and with a sting in the tail. 'You want to go to France, do you? Very well, you shall go tomorrow – with No. 6 Squadron, as an observer.' Dowding was undismayed. Once in France, the right opening would come.

Dowding's facility for seeing things as they were and not as others, especially his seniors, wanted to see them, was soon demonstrated. The day before Antwerp fell he was sent to observe the roads west of the city. He spotted Belgian troops but no Germans, and after filing his report he was called, with his squadron commander, to the headquarters of Sir Henry Rawlinson, the general responsible for that section of the front. 'You say you saw no Germans?' queried Rawlinson. 'But they're there, we know that they're there.' Dowding stood his ground. 'Well, sir, you wouldn't wish me to say I'd seen them if I hadn't. It was a very clear day, and if there had been any Germans I must have seen them.' This direct contradiction of a general marked Dowding as a man not easily shaken from his convictions.

Of more immediate significance, perhaps, was the arrival with 6 Squadron of a 23-year-old former sapper of varied experience named Lanoe Hawker. Hawker had given up a naval cadetship through ill-health before studying at the RMA at Woolwich, meanwhile learning to fly at Hendon, and in March 1913 he transferred to the RFC. A man of moods, sensitive and introspective, with an exceptional capacity for friendship, he was deeply upset by the loss of a contemporary in Gordon Bayly, who, with Waterfall, had been the first RFC crew to be reported missing. Hawker, who had become a friend of the family and was in love with Bayly's sister Beatrice, still hoped to hear that his friend had survived as a prisoner, as indeed Waterfall had.

Whether the loss contributed to Hawker's belligerence is uncertain: he seems from the first to have set an exceptional standard of tenacity and aggression, foraging deep into enemy territory to seek antagonists. His pugnacity, especially when facing superior numbers in inferior machines, did much to inspire that eagerness for combat which was to characterise the operations of the RFC. No one was more skilful at handling and fighting the BE2c than Hawker, and he became the first of the RFC's great fighter pilots, many months before the emergence of Albert Ball. This, though, was in a period when Trenchard, deploring the publicity given to French and German 'aces', as against the anonymity of the tenacious and vulnerable men on artillery co-operation, succeeded for a time in keeping the Press at bay.

Opportunities for aerial combat that winter, though, were rare, and the RFC, like its adversary, was frequently grounded by the weather. There was no thought as yet of forming specialist homogeneous scout squadrons; each squadron held one or perhaps two scout-type machines on strength. When conditions allowed, pilots demonstrated the aggressive spirit that was to become a byword by bombing approved targets and ground-strafing enemy troops. But with the front now static, the dominant factor was the artillery, and far and away the main priority lay in co-operating with the gunners to seek out and pinpoint enemy batteries and correct the fire of our own batteries on these and other targets.

As with air fighting, so with artillery co-operation, early attempts had been crude, cumbersome and chancy, such vague phrases as 'south of the final e in Compiègne', or 'above the d in Gueudecourt', to give an enemy battery's position on the map, being both wordy and imprecise. A simple and accurate method was urgently needed. Even more pressing was the need to pass the required information rapidly and efficiently from air to ground. Klaxon horns blasting messages in morse code from the heavens were at the mercy of wind and weather. Signalling lamps and flags were too easily misread, and coloured flares, fired by Very pistol, were limited in scope. The ideal method of communicating information to battery commanders was by wireless telegraphy, and attached to No. 4 Squadron, it will be remembered, was a wireless flight. It was during the opposed crossing of the Aisne that the spotting of hostile batteries became of prime importance, and when the war of movement was succeeded by static trench warfare, the artillery settled into prepared positions and the pilots of the wireless flight came into their own. Co-operation extended to taking up gunnery officers to help with aerial survey work, while the sites of enemy batteries were confirmed and noted on maps. Positions were continually revised and copies of amended maps circulated. Soon the wireless flight was expanded into No. 9 Squadron, with Hugh Dowding to command. He had found a niche.

Much of the flying was done by two pioneers whose enthusiasm and perseverance had overcome the usual peacetime inertia and eventually convinced their masters of the potential of wireless telegraphy in aerial reconnaissance. Both men were lieutenants in the Royal Engineers, both had learned to fly in the summer of 1912, and both were signals specialists in their middle to late twenties who knew precisely what they were about. Their names were Donald Lewis and Baron (usually contracted to Bron) James. Lewis proved a natural organiser and leader, James had been head of his house at Harrow. Recognition of their expertise brought demands for their services exceeding all possibility of supply. Because of their bulky wireless equipment — it weighed 75 lbs and filled the front cockpit of their BE machines — they were obliged to fly solo, controlling their machines with one hand, frequently under fire, and operating the wireless 'buzzer' with the other. How much the Harrow-educated James enjoyed these lone forays is not recorded, but Lewis was said to revel in them. 'Lewis came in from spotting with his machine full of holes,' was one comment. 'I believe he likes it!' These two machines, easily recognisable from the way they were flown, seemed ubiquitous to the troops on both sides that winter.

Both men were professionals who worked tirelessly to improve their effectiveness and for whom soldiering was a career. Like most of their kind, they had no personal quarrel with the enemy and respected his professionalism in turn. 'Why,' demanded Lewis of a visiting 'personality' (it was Hilaire Belloc), 'do the newspapers abuse the Germans in so foolish a manner?'

Running commentaries on the fall of fire, which would be acknowledged by the laying out of ground strips by the battery (there was no reverse communication by wireless, just a transmitter in the aeroplane and a receiver on the ground), followed a familiar pattern. After contact was established and the firing started it might continue: 'A very little short . . . Fire . . . Fire . . . Fire again.' Each time a correction was transmitted, two or three minutes might elapse as the gun-crew adjusted their aim and resumed firing. Then might come: 'Over . . . Over and a little to the left . . .' Another short wait, and then, of the next salvo: 'You were just between two batteries . . . Search two hundred yards either side of your last shot . . .' The same terse, staccato, dispassionate morse later announced that success was imminent. 'You have them!' (The exclamation mark was understood.) Four minutes later would come: 'Hit . . . hit . . . hit!'

Another twenty minutes might be spent over the target, refining directions and reporting results. Finally, after an hour or more of intense concentration, half-smothered at times by Archie, it was time to leave after a job well done. Unemotional as it appeared, the pilot's understandable relief was implicit in his final message: 'I am going home now.'

The use of such approximations as 'left', 'right', 'short', or 'over', to indicate the correction required, still lacked precision, and eventually Lewis and James devised between them what they called the 'clock code'. Having already learned to 'square' his maps and those of the battery commander with whom he was working, Lewis fashioned a transparent celluloid disc, with a centre spot which he placed at the chosen point on the map. Eight concentric circles on the disc signified varying distances from the target, from 10 yards to 500, each circle being identified by a letter. A set of radial lines on the disc numbered by the hours on the clock face, one to twelve, indicated direction. Thus by means of a brief coded message containing a single letter and a single number the target was located with some accuracy, time was saved, and the chances of error reduced if not eliminated. As each shell landed the pilot or observer signalled to the gun battery the ring within which it had fallen and the hour on the clock face. The squared map and the 'clock code' became standard on the western front throughout the war.

The greater sophistication of air-to-ground wireless communication conferred no immunity on its practitioners, and it is surprising, in view of their persistence, that the two pioneers lasted as long as they did. James, who had been promoted to flight commander on 6 Squadron, was ranging a battery alone as usual in July 1915 when his BE was hit by a shell and plunged to destruction. There is no doubt that the Germans recognised the specially adapted plane and knew of the pilot, and fears that James's last moments must have been anguished were dispelled when they dropped a note to say he was dead when he fell.

Gordon Shephard, by this time commanding 6 Squadron, had believed that in Strange, Hawker and James he had the three best flight commanders in France. Of James's death he wrote: 'He is a great loss to me: much the best artillery officer out here. He also started wireless in the RFC and has never been properly recognised by the authorities.' He and Lewis had shown, from the earliest days, the momentous contribution to artillery shoots that wireless communication could make, and as more compact equipment became available it was widely introduced.

At about the time of James's death, Lewis was appointed to succeed Jack Salmond in command of No. 3 Squadron, by then equipped with the French-built Morane Parasol (a monoplane two-seater); but this did not stop him flying, nor did a subsequent promotion to command what had become the RFC Second Wing, with the rank of lieutenant-colonel. But on 10 April 1916, with an artillery officer to whom he had been showing the results of his own battery's trench mortar fire, he was shot down and killed by a direct hit from the guns he was pinpointing.

The loss of such men could be ill-afforded, stimulating Trenchard to order that squadron commanders must no longer be risked over the lines. Many were to chafe under this ruling, though there were some who ignored it.

Although there were pre-war pioneers of aerial photography in the RFC as well as of wireless telegraphy, mainly in No. 3 Squadron under Salmond, most of them were little more than dabblers, pilots who modified their own personal cameras and took photographs mostly for the fun of it. But on one pre-war exercise they undertook a genuinely useful experiment by producing a photographic mosaic of Britain's south-coast defences, to show what might be done. Outstanding was Lieutenant Charles Darley who, with Lieutenant George Pretyman and others as pilot, began taking photographs experimentally once the front stabilised.

'I don't think anyone else in the squadron did any photography at this time,' wrote Darley later. 'I had to buy my own chemicals in Bethune, develop the slides in an emergency dark room in the stables of the château in which we were billeted, and send them out. I personally took the results each evening to Corps HQ (Fourth Corps) and explained them, often to Henderson himself.' But Darley found non-flying topographers slow in comprehending aerial pictures, each of which, from medium altitudes, covered only a small area. Often in a Blériot he could get no higher than 4,000 feet, but he began to do better when the squadron got a few Morane Parasols in the New Year.

The potential value of Darley's work went unrecognised at first, still less was much thought given to the science of photographic interpretation. As an instance, Sholto Douglas, when he became an observer on 2 Squadron, was appointed air photographer to the unit 'because I had had a box camera as a boy'. But towards the end of January 1915, a map of the trenches that Darley had produced largely for his own use so impressed Jack Salmond that he took it to Headquarters. Sykes, who had seen something of French efforts in this field, sent Salmond's brother Geoffrey to study their methods, and it was immediately apparent to the younger Salmond that he was among experts. A four-man Wing Photographic Section was formed under Lieutenant J.T.C. Moore-Brabazon, holder of the Royal Aero Club's Aviator Certificate No. 1, with Sergeant Victor Laws, who had been taking photographs from airships and man-carrying kites since 1912, as his technical chief. (In time Sergeant Laws was to become Wing Commander Laws, chief photographic officer with the Air Component of a later British Expeditionary Force.) These men set about designing a camera specifically for air use.

After the departure of the four operational squadrons to France in August 1914, only two RFC stations remained in action at home: the Central Flying School at Upavon and the Royal Aircraft Factory at Farnborough. Thus the task given to Trenchard by Henderson, under Brancker's patronage, to recruit and train men to form new squadrons for France, demanded pertinacity and drive. None of the machines being built by a variety of firms under Government contract – the BE2c, the Avro, the Henri Farman, even the Vickers Gunbus – possessed the armament or fighting qualities that were going to be needed when the Fokker *Eindecker*, with a synchronised machine-gun firing through the propeller arc, was introduced in the second half of 1915. Meanwhile the bulk production of the BE2c that was in progress at selected factories would ensure that the majority of pilots and observers would be condemned to battling for their lives in this sedate and comparatively toothless biplane ('Stability Jane' was one of its nicknames), against infinitely superior opposition for many months to come. Yet it is hard to see how it could have been otherwise. Most of the new designs ordered were little beyond the development stage, and if there was a lack of urgency in conceiving and building more advanced types, and in improving their fire-power, the requirement was barely apparent as yet. Certainly Brancker and Trenchard, left with a seemingly impossible task, rose to the challenge, acting expeditiously and often precipitately to speed the progress demanded by Kitchener. New RFC stations were opened, pilots, riggers, mechanics and fitters were recruited and trained, and the nucleus of new squadrons was formed. Expansion was the watchword, and if it was largely expansion for its own sake, that was inevitable. To expect Brancker and Trenchard to have hastened slowly in the circumstances would surely be unrealistic. But for the airmen they were taking such trouble to recruit and to train, quantity without quality was to prove lethal.

For three months Trenchard channelled his frustration at being denied what he deemed his rightful place at the front into sowing the seeds of abundant growth. But in November, at last, came the call to France. Ironically it emanated from a decentralisation of the RFC in France masterminded by Sykes. As the line stabilised, and the work of the crews became more and more localised, squadrons worked increasingly in direct contact with corps commanders, and in November these attachments were regularised by the creation of Wings. The First Wing, consisting of Nos 2 and 3 Squadrons, was to operate with the Indian Corps and the Fourth Army Corps, the Second Wing – Nos 5 and 6 Squadrons – with the Third Army Corps. Command of the Second Wing fell, on promotion, to Lieutenant-Colonel C.J. Burke (Pregnant Percy). Command of the First Wing went, again on promotion, and at Henderson's insistence, to Trenchard. No. 4 Squadron and the wireless unit (soon to become No. 9 Squadron) were retained under the direct control of RFC Headquarters. A Third Wing was formed in March 1915 under Brooke-Popham.

At home, the Military Wing at Farnborough, formerly under Trenchard, was split into two central commands, an Administrative Wing, with headquarters at Farnborough, commanded by Lieutenant-Colonel E.B. Ashmore, and a Fourth Wing, a training wing, with

headquarters at Netheravon, commanded by Josh Higgins, repatriated after picking up a thigh wound in his Bristol Scout. This wing
embraced squadrons preparing for France.

1915

7

THE BATTLE OF NEUVE CHAPELLE

'If you can't fly because of the weather,
I shall probably put off the attack.'

DOUGLAS HAIG

T AKING aerial photographs with the new box camera, the 'A'
Type, manufactured by a civilian firm to the photographic
wing's specifications, required the observer to hold the
camera by its straps or handles, while he leant over the side of the
cockpit and performed eleven distinct operations for the first
exposure and ten for each subsequent one. During this laborious
process, he was usually being well quartered by Archie. Yet by early
February the whole German trench system facing the British First
Army had been photographed, building up a detailed mosaic of the
area.

It was with the help of this mosaic, and the registering by the RFC
of enemy batteries, strong points, and possible transport bottlenecks,
that Sir John French based his plans for a spring offensive. Weakened
though he was by his losses so far, and unable to deliver a heavy or
prolonged assault, he had nevertheless been able to expand the two
corps of the original BEF into armies, and he was anxious to keep
them active and to exploit any enemy tactical weakness that air
reconnaissance might reveal. It soon became clear that the Germans
in the village of Neuve Chapelle were holding a salient in no great
strength, open to assault on two sides.

The immediate objective of the British plan, devised in detail by
Sir Douglas Haig and agreed by French on 19 February, was to

capture the village. If this went well, the Aubers Ridge, further to the north-east, might come within their grasp, threatening Lille. This was a capture that might prove of lasting significance. 'For the first time,' records the official RFC history, 'the British army went into action with a picture of the hidden intricacies of the enemy defences.'

Against this, Intelligence reports suggested that the Germans would be capable of rushing in substantial reinforcements within a day or so. Here, too, in addition to their primary tasks of reconnaissance, photography, and artillery co-operation, the RFC was asked to play a vital role. They were to bomb railway facilities in the enemy's lines of communication so as to harass and hamper the drafting in of reinforcements.

The bombing of enemy targets had hitherto been of a whimsical, free-lance nature, carried out with makeshift bombs that were man-handled over the side, aimed at targets of opportunity. Pilots and observers engaged on other duties got a wry satisfaction from hitting back at their tormentors, but the influence of their bombs on the campaign was nil. Now they were to be detailed for the first serious attempt at disrupting enemy communications by bombing. Indeed, a bombing mission aimed at a specific target was to spearhead the assault.

Early in March Haig sent for Trenchard and revealed something of his plans. What could the RFC contribute? It was the first time the two men had met. Strangely incoherent at the best of times, Trenchard was the worst possible advocate when arguing a case verbally, and he began badly, his explanations sounding faltering and inadequate even to him. But Haig didn't want to be bothered with detail: he was judging the man. Trenchard scored through avoiding exaggeration and not promising more than he was confident he could deliver. He indicated the positioning of the reconnaissance and artillery co-operation squadrons of his wing in relation to the First Army and described the tasks of which he believed them capable, subject always to the weather. This, he warned, could quite conceivably ground the whole force, Second and Third Wings – the wings that were to bomb the lines of communication – as well as the First.

Haig's reaction gave tremendous encouragement to Trenchard. 'I shall expect you to tell me before the attack whether you can fly, because on your being able to observe for the artillery, and carry out reconnaissance, the battle will partly depend. If you can't fly because of the weather, I shall probably put off the attack.'

Trenchard could hardly believe his ears: here was a brass-hat who properly appreciated the contribution the RFC could make. Even if Haig's reaction was no more than a psychological ploy, aimed at inspiring the RFC to redouble its efforts by emphasising, even exaggerating, its importance to him, it was a welcome change from the cynicism of the past. Indeed, it was the start of a rapport between soldier and airman that had its foundations in the pre-war Brancker reconnaissances in India.

Soon after six o'clock on the morning of 10 March, three machines of No. 3 Squadron set out to bomb what was believed to be an enemy defence headquarters at Fournes, six miles east of Neuve Chapelle. The raid was led by Eric Conran (now promoted to captain and flight commander), with whom McCudden still flew occasionally; but on this day the man in the front cockpit was squadron commander Jack Salmond. The other two pilots flew solo in order to increase their bomb-load. Attacking at three-minute intervals, they reported direct hits which set fire to the target; Conran and Salmond made doubly sure by dropping their bombs from a hundred feet in three separate runs. Whether the enemy's battle control was seriously hampered by this raid was not known.

The main tactical bombing programme for the first day of the battle was timed for mid-afternoon, to coincide with a lull in the infantry attack. Considering the hopes of violent disorder that were vested in it, it is instructive that it consisted of no more than a single aircraft on each of two targets. Such were the illusions, in 1915, of the effects of aerial bombardment, curiously naive from men who would have given a much more realistic estimate of the weight of shell-fire required to eliminate a similar target.

Confidence in the men who were to discharge the duty was similarly blithe, though perhaps with better reason. Both the men selected had served with the BEF from the beginning. Strange was the natural selection on 6 Squadron: following reports that German reinforcements were already passing through Courtrai station by the train-load, that was to be his target. He would be flying a BE2c. Stripped of all armament and with an empty front cockpit to compensate for the weight of the bombs, it had crude bomb-racks fitted under wings and fuselage for carrying and jettisoning three French-made bombs. With these weapons, each weighing less than 25 lb, Strange was expected to devastate a target whose destruction, he was led to believe, was a matter of life or death to the soldiers of Haig's First Army. Imagining the reception he was likely to get, he did not rate his chances highly.

The second target chosen was a railway junction north of Menin station, some ten miles short of Courtrai. Here the choice of pilot, although limited, was less clear-cut. The task was allocated to Strange's old squadron, No. 5, where the squadron commander decided that the most suitable bomb-carrier was the new single-seater Martin-and-Handasyde S1, a small sporting tractor biplane which had been adapted for military purposes and fitted with a Lewis gun above the centre section, firing outside the radius of the propeller blades. It had a maximum speed of 87 m.p.h. and was capable of carrying a 100 lb bomb. Competition for the privilege of ferrying this monster was limited to the only three men on the squadron who had mastered the Martinsyde – Carmichael, Rabagliati, and Wilson. All three were among the original contemptibles, 'Daddy' Wilson, at 37, being much the eldest. But it was bulk rather than age that disqualified him, and Carmichael and Rabagliati tossed up for the honour. Carmichael won.

The two attacks were roughly synchronised. First to take off, at 15.23, was Strange in the BE2c, with Carmichael following seven minutes later. The weather, which had promised well enough for Haig to open his attack, was beginning to break; the cloud-base had lowered to 3,000 feet, and visibility was poor. To keep track of his position Strange stayed below cloud, but as he neared the lines the flashes of the German guns, piercing the afternoon gloom, and the dark puffs that hung with menacing proximity around him, forced him to seek the cloud's sanctuary. He aimed to the north of Courtrai, easing gently down to the level of the cloud base before sighting the clustered roofs of the town. A diving left-hand turn and there below him, through straggly low cloud, he saw the railway, running in a straight line towards his target.

Flattening out below two hundred feet, he followed the track and almost immediately sighted the station. It was time to descend even lower. A train was standing at the platform, several coaches long, probably a troop train. Perhaps after all he could do something positive for his comrades in the infantry. A solitary German sentry was aiming a rifle at him from the platform, and he remembered the hand grenade he had thrust into his flying jacket before take-off. Gripping the control stick with one hand, he withdrew the grenade with the other and extracted the pin with his teeth. Then he pitched it overboard. It fell at the sentry's feet as the plane careered on.

Small-arms fire was now converging on him from all angles, and suddenly the platform roof was rushing towards him. He yanked back on the stick and pulled the bomb-release lever before skimming the roof. After twisting his neck round to see where his bombs had fallen, he straightened up to find his escape route blocked by a stockade of telegraph poles. Another yank on the stick and a climbing turn and he was shooting a final, kaleidoscopic glimpse at the mayhem he had evidently caused.

Three dozen bullet holes in the BE2c testified that once again Strange's luck had held. He was lucky, too, in getting first-hand evidence, through an Allied agent in Courtrai, of the results of his attack. It had indeed been a troop train standing at the platform, about to unload. Seventy-five men had been killed or wounded and rail traffic had been delayed for three days.

Carmichael's brief was no less compelling: his task, too, was directly related to the ground battle. And whereas Strange had carried a stick of bombs any one of which might score, success for Carmichael depended on a single shot. Aware how chancy this must be, he had a hole cut in the cockpit floor between his feet so that he could look vertically down at the railway line, the better to judge his approach.

With its unaccustomed load the Martinsyde climbed ponderously, and even before he crossed the lines at 4,000 feet a shell fragment pierced the fuselage inches behind his back. Picking out the railway line leading to Menin, he switched off his engine with the idea of making a stealthy approach, but as he descended to 800 feet a solitary machine-gunner dissuaded him and he restarted the engine, dived for the track and clung to it, descending from 300 feet to 100. The sleepers raced by under his feet, but he still had to judge the right moment of release. This he had worked out beforehand, and five seconds after Menin station passed beneath him he pulled the toggle. Nothing happened. He had expected the aeroplane, freed of its load, to soar involuntarily; the release mechanism must have failed. But then the blast seized the Martinsyde and thrust it forwards and upwards on a billowing cushion of air. Half-concussed himself, but collecting his senses, he looked back to see a column of black smoke rising 200 feet or more above him, the point of impact, so far as he could judge, being just about right, a few yards short of the junction.

Turning east to confuse the German gunners, he found himself over a parade ground, with troops rushing to and fro, taking pot shots at him. He threw a rifle grenade at them to put them off their aim, but his machine was badly hit, one engine cylinder was put out of action, and his only remaining lateral control was his rudder. Nevertheless by low flying and jinking he crossed the lines without further damage and landed safely after what he afterwards called 'two hours 10 minutes of a somewhat exhilarating afternoon'.

On that first day the German positions were overrun and the village was captured, but next day, 11 March, the weather clamped. Little could be seen from the air, and artillery co-operation ceased. The Germans were rushing in reinforcements and preparing to counter-attack, and the British were unable to exploit their advantage. However, early that morning three pilots of No. 4 Squadron took off in darkness from Bailleul, using electric torches to monitor their instruments, their objective another rail junction, this time at Lille. They had moved up to Bailleul to be near their target, their course was indicated by lamps on the ground, and they were to arrive over

Hugh Trenchard. 'He gave the RFC determined leadership and a clear sense of direction.'

W. Sefton Brancker. 'Deceptively foppish' – but a man to be trusted.

J.F.A. 'Josh' Higgins. 'All bum and eyeglass.' Seen here with the squadron mascot.

Frederick H. Sykes. 'Hampered by a personality which strongly engendered mistrust.'

Charles James Burke (centre) with pilots of No. 2 Squadron, the first across the Channel. On Burke's left is 'Ferdy' Waldron. Top left (standing) is Hubert Harvey-Kelly.

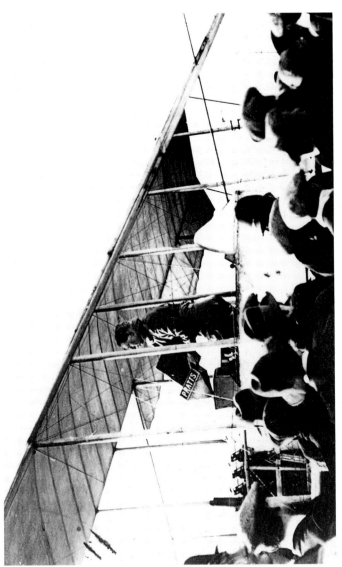

Hubert Harvey-Kelly refuelling his Maurice Farman Longhorn on a pre-war flight. 'He kept one in roars of laughter the whole time.'

Philip Bennet Joubert de la Ferté, said to have a memory as long as his name.

John D.B. Fulton. Bought himself a Bleriot monoplane and began experimenting with it on Salisbury Plain.

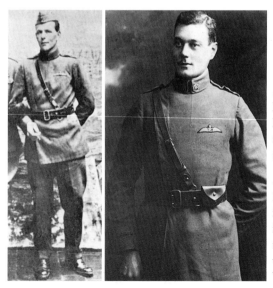

Far left: Bob Smith-Barry. 'An awful little boy' – but he revolutionised air training world wide.

Left: Louis Strange. Handsome, fearless, innovative, irrepressible, he flew right through the war and again in World War II.

Dermott Allen. His verbal
dilations, despite a stammer,
were worth waiting for.

'Bron' James. 'Much the best
artillery officer out here.'

W. Sholto Douglas fought
Boelcke and Immelmann.
'I was thoroughly frightened.'

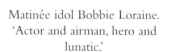

Matinée idol Bobbie Loraine.
'Actor and airman, hero and
lunatic.'

Will Rhodes-Moorhouse VC.
'If I must die, give me a drink.'

Aidan Liddell, VC, MC, in the
uniform of the Argyll and
Sutherland Highlanders. He gave
'an astounding display of fortitude.'

Fokker fodder. BE2c's of No. 13 Squadron about to take off
for France, October 1915.

The Fokker *Eindecker*. This is an EIII.

A Vickers FB5 Gunbus in enemy hands after being forced down intact.

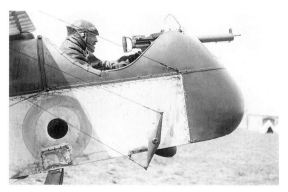

The cockpit of a DH2, the RFC's first single-seat fighter. 'Spinning incinerator?' Not so, said Lanoe Hawker.

Oswald Boelcke.
'Our brave and chivalrous foe.'

Max Immelmann.
Animal magnetism –
and the inventor of the
Immelmann turn.

Manfred von
Richthofen. He called
Lanoe Hawker 'The
English Immelmann.'

A captured Albatros DI. With the DII and
the Halberstadt it turned the tables on the
RFC in the autumn of 1916.

the target at daybreak. Apart from a short practice flight at St Omer on the previous evening, none of them had flown at night before.

Sending three aircraft against a single target might seem more realistic, but the weather was such that Major Charles Longcroft, the squadron commander, sought a cancellation. Someone at GHQ, surely with his tongue in his cheek, said that if the raid was successful it might end the war: therefore the pilots must go. The order, described as ridiculous by the forthright Longcroft, brought disaster. One pilot crashed soon after take-off and the other two failed to return. One of these was shot down and died from his injuries, the other, also shot down, but enjoying better luck, was Mapplebeck. He had just set fire to his BE2a when he glimpsed three figures approaching out of the mist. Hiding in a convenient ditch, and sub-sisting on chocolate, he somehow avoided discovery from a massive search before being kitted out by the Belgian he eventually approached. But the garb only accentuated his height, and he was grateful to another Belgian for hiding him for a week in a garret in Lille. He did not know that he was being personally protected by the Mayor. When the hunt got too hot he moved on, tramping across Belgium, always at night and always in fear of compromising the good people who helped him. After another night in a ditch near the Dutch frontier he crossed while the sentry was lighting his pipe, and the shots that were fired at him missed. Next he crossed Holland, took passage on a fishing smack, and presented himself at the War Office, where they feigned surprise: they had known of his escape but dare not reveal it for security reasons. Among the mementoes he brought with him was a poster offering a reward for information leading to his capture and threatening death to anyone who helped him, signed by the German military governor of Lille. Sadly the Mayor of Lille, M. Emile Jaquet, and three other Belgians, were later apprehended and shot by the Germans. Mapplebeck was back with his squadron five weeks later.

The third day of the battle was marked by storms and enemy counter-attacks, and the British took no more ground. RFC tasks included locating the line of battle and reporting its fluctuations. The bombing of tactical targets, too, was resumed. This time the raiders included No. 1 Squadron, recently arrived from England under Geoffrey Salmond and comprising eight Avros and four of the hitherto unlucky BE8s.

Further bombing raids were made, notably by Pretyman of 3 Squadron on the railway station at Don, where he blew up the centre carriages of a train; but an accident to a Morane of the same squadron while it was being loaded with French bombs resulted in an explosion in which twelve men, including the pilot, were killed and four more seriously wounded.

Later that day it was discovered that some of the bombs had not gone off, and Jack Salmond, commanding 3 Squadron, put the wreckage out of bounds until further notice. 'Next morning,' wrote Pretyman afterwards, 'we found some of the wreckage had been cleared and the remaining bombs removed and buried. Major Salmond had done this himself at daybreak.' Fifteen years later Jack Salmond was to succeed Trenchard as chief of the air staff, to be succeeded in turn by his brother Geoffrey.

The influence of the RFC on events at Neuve Chapelle lessened as the weather worsened, and the very limited success of the First Army – a dent in the German line little more than a mile wide and 1,000 yards deep – scarcely justified the gamble or the casualties. For many it was their first experience of battle, and one young infantryman who later transferred to the RFC described it in detail, from the initial bombardment, when his rifle 'steamed like a boiling kettle and became so hot I could scarcely hold it', to the taking of about 300 prisoners, many of them wounded, and the occupation of their forward trenches. The reporter was Private Goodban, Monty Goodban, of Clapham High Street, where his father ran a domestic store. 'We have to wade through trenches waist deep in water, which is like soup and as cold as ice, not much worried by our personal discomfort, the excitement is too great. This is our first glimpse of real warfare. What a sight. I cannot describe it.'

Hungry, wet, and smothered in mud, they were ordered to make a bayonet charge, across fields which were believed to contain the original German trenches. 'What a gruesome sight. Dead and wounded strewn everywhere, the latter groaning and moaning in the most heartrending manner. There are British and Germans all mixed up lying side by side.' An attempt to take the new German positions after dark failed disastrously. 'As soon as the Huns discovered us they opened a terrific fire of machine-guns, rifles and artillery, cries of chaps getting hit go up on all sides.'

Goodban and three of his pals lost touch with their battalion and tramped back to their base. 'Arrive there at 5.30 a.m. absolutely done up. All day chaps kept turning up who had got lost in a similar manner to ourselves.'

That summer Goodban 'stopped about 20 pieces of a rifle grenade with his leg' and was evacuated home. Commissioned in January 1916, he volunteered for the RFC later that year, one of a great many who felt, with some justification, that they had had enough of the trenches and would like to try something else. On 7 May 1917, after 22 hours 50 minutes' solo flying, he was posted back to France to fly two-seaters on 22 Squadron. It was a period of catastrophic inferiority in the air, especially for newcomers, and twelve days later he was shot down and killed.

Insulated as they were from the horrors of the trenches, it was through transfusions like this that the men of the RFC were continually reminded, even in the midst of appalling losses, how lucky they were.

8

THE RFC's *RAISON D'ETRE*:
ITS FIRST VC:
THE BALLOONATICS

'No call from the army must ever find the RFC wanting'

HUGH TRENCHARD

PREPARATIONS for a combined Allied offensive, intended to dwarf the limited objectives of Neuve Chapelle, were begun in mid-April with an assault on an eminence dominating the Ypres area – Hill 60 – to test the enemy's strength. But the plan was pre-empted by a surprise German assault. A recently captured German prisoner had been boasting of a lethal gas which he claimed was about to be used against the Allies to eliminate the Ypres salient and force a major breakthrough. Special reconnaissances were flown to see what could be detected, but it was not until 22 April that Louis Strange, cruising to and fro over the salient at dusk, noting the flashes from the German 17-inch howitzers which had begun the bombardment that morning, watched aghast as the evil secret unfolded: borne on a breeze that for once was blowing off the German trenches, a stream of bilious, yellow-green smoke was being wafted westwards towards the Allied lines. The captured German infantryman had been right: this could only be poison gas. Strange landed and reported at once to Headquarters.

The eruption was indeed a cloud of toxic chlorine gas, and its effect was immediate, the bewildered Allied troops, after a moment's asphyxiation, fleeing in terror. The gap was eventually closed, and minor counter-attacks restored the position, but ground was conceded. Subsequent air reconnaissance prepared the Allies for a German attack north of the salient, and this was beaten off, but a second gas attack forced further withdrawals.

When agents reported strong reinforcements moving towards the salient, the two newly-formed RFC squadrons attached to Brooke-Popham's Third Wing at St Omer, Nos 7 and 8, were ordered to attack trains and rail centres in the feeder line, armed with 20 lb bombs. When these attacks proved futile (some of the crews lost their way, some of the bombs failed to release), First Wing were called in to attack vital targets. Four machines were despatched, each carrying a 112 lb bomb, but even of these, only two reached their objectives.

One pilot, from 2 Squadron, was briefed to bomb the railway junction and marshalling yards outside Courtrai station, 35 miles behind the lines: Intelligence reports indicated that as many as 40,000 troops were being rushed through Courtrai to the salient, making this a priority target. The pilot chosen was a man whose background was unique. Because his grandparents, cattle-farming in New Zealand, were childless, a liberal Maori chief had sent one of his daughters to co-operate in bearing them a child. She duly obliged, and father and stepmother adopted the girl that resulted as their own. When the girl grew up she married her step-mother's brother; soon afterwards they moved to England. Their second child, Will Rhodes-Moorhouse, now twenty-five, was the pilot briefed to bomb the vital rail junction at Courtrai.

Small and slight, he exuded vitality, and he was well known pre-war on both sides of the Atlantic as a fearless and even recklessly competitive car racer and aviator. Marriage did not change him, and as soon as the war started he joined the RFC.

The vortex of fire that was known to surround Courtrai seemed likely to be almost impenetrable, and Rhodes-Moorhouse was warned not to come down too low. But he knew well enough that the only chance of creating havoc with a 112 lb bomb, with no proper bomb-sight, was to attack from low level.

Air interception was extremely unlikely, and there were no

navigation problems, so observers were left behind. The man spared in Rhodes-Moorhouse's machine was Sholto Douglas.

The expectation that a single aircraft with a single bomb could eliminate a sprawling and complex target emphasized the misconceptions of the Allied commanders. Pilots knew better, but they wouldn't admit it; for them, optimism was everything. Rhodes-Moorhouse took off in his BE from the aerodrome at Merville at five minutes past three that afternoon, 24 April 1915, and set course in good heart. Crossing the lines at 1,000 feet, he got through safely to Courtrai and easily located the junction. He dived on the target, dropped his bomb from 300 feet, and felt the blast as it exploded.

At once he was the focus of a nest of guns ringing the junction, backed up by hundreds of rifles and machine-guns fired by the assembling troops he had come to delay. A direct hit from a gun being fired at him point blank from the belfry of a church rocked the biplane to its roots and a bullet pierced his thigh, but somehow he pulled away. Bleeding profusely, with his plane crippled, his best chance of survival was an immediate forced landing; but half the value of the destruction he had caused lay in making it known, and he headed back to the lines. Wounded again, this time in the abdomen, he could still have crash-landed with honour and sought medical help, but surrender was not in his lexicon. He must file his report.

Among those who helped him from his machine back at Merville was Sholto Douglas. 'We were amazed,' he wrote afterwards, 'that he ever managed to get back.' A cluster of bullet holes in the observer's seat told him what his own fate would have been.

Rhodes-Moorhouse still shunned medical help until he had made his report; he made it verbally, in Trenchard's hearing. Mortally wounded, he disclaimed any tag of heroism. 'If I must die,' he told the padre, 'give me a drink.'

A last request that his body be sent back to England, to be buried on the family estate in Dorset where he had planned to build a cottage for his wife and infant son, was granted by Sir John French. Three weeks later he was posthumously awarded the Victoria Cross, the first RFC man to be so decorated. He had set an example that many would follow.

This was not quite the end of the Rhodes-Moorhouse story. In 1937 his son joined 601 (Auxiliary) Squadron, fought as his father had done in France, from the same airfield at Merville, won the DFC in the Battle of Britain, and was killed in his Hurricane at the height of the Battle, on 6 September 1940.

We know what the son achieved. What of the father? Confirmation came that he had indeed blasted the junction, delaying enemy reinforcements, and an official despatch rated his 112-pounder 'the most important bomb dropped in this war so far'. Yet his contribution stood out more for its rarity than for its influence on the battle – the Second Battle of Ypres, as it came to be known. Of 141 bombing raids launched between 1 March and 20 June 1915 only three could be regarded as successful, and the cost in men and machines was prohibitive.

What was needed was a complete reappraisal of the effectiveness of aerial bombardment, together with a more sophisticated bombsight than the crude contrivance, consisting of little more than a few nails and some lengths of wire, improvised by Louis Strange with the help of an Intelligence Corps officer, Second Lieutenant Robert Bourdillon, whose fascination with the subject led to his transfer, late in 1914, to the experimental flight at the Central Flying School. A graduate of Balliol and St Mary's Hospital, London, Bourdillon had returned to Balliol as a Lecturer in Chemistry. He had enlisted in August 1914 and was now 25.

At CFS, by mid-1915, Bourdillon had combined with others to evolve a less primitive instrument. Speed over the ground was measured, with the aid of a stop-watch, by two sights taken on one object, the same principle being employed to give the correct angle for release of the bomb. The new CFS bombsight was adopted by both the RFC and the RNAS, gave much improved results in the offensive that autumn, and remained in use on the western front until the end of 1916.

A review of bombing policy was also attempted, one conclusion being that bombs were most effective when dropped on railways, especially in cuttings, where the blast was contained, diversion difficult, and the line might be blocked for days. A more realistic estimate of the weight of bombs required to destroy a given target was also attempted, with the resolve that British and French air units should co-ordinate their attacks in future in strict conjunction with ground operations.

The British had clung to Ypres as a symbol of their obligation to Belgium, and the salient, although diminished in size, was held. The RFC kept GHQ in touch with enemy movements as they occurred and even in one instance gave a résumé of the battle as it unfolded, penetrating the veil for army commanders otherwise 'blinded by the fog of action'. Meanwhile many hundreds of hours were flown spotting for and directing the artillery, achieving a fair degree of mutual understanding. Much could be seen from the air, photographed, and even sketched by war artists, that was otherwise hidden – but against this, mist and low cloud could frustrate even the persistence of a Bron James or a Don Lewis, blanketing the battleground just when enlightenment was most wanted. Some commanders were still sceptical of the reliability of air reconnaissance, leaving crews to risk their lives to get information that was mistrusted and even ignored. 'Where,' asked one corps pilot bitterly, 'would the artillery be without us?'

Another VC, in circumstances similar to those of Rhodes-Moorhouse – severely wounded twenty miles beyond the lines but concerned only to get back with his report, together with machine and observer – was recommended in June by Pregnant Percy, then commanding the Second Wing: the presumptive pilot was none other than Biffy Borton, a man who in other respects so looked after his comforts that he sent home for all manner of luxuries. But there was one circumstance that told against him: he had survived. His chuckle when he realised he'd missed a posthumous VC may be imagined. Curiously enough his brother 'Bosky' (they were family nicknames) *did* win a VC – in the army.

For the armies of the BEF, support that summer for continued Allied aggression in the Neuve Chapelle region was attenuated and then suspended through heavy losses and a shortage of ammunition, so that reorganisation and the replenishing of supplies in preparation for the major offensive planned for the autumn became the rule. It was a time of consolidation, too, for the RFC. But there was no diminution in the work of reconnaissance and artillery co-operation during the build-up. Sorties began with a telephone call from the observer to the battery with which he would be working to learn or confirm the objectives, check map co-ordinates on the large-scale squared map, and agree the time the shoot was to start. Over the target the observer, having let out his trailing aerial, called up the battery in morse code. The ground operator put out his coded strips, and when all was ready the observer called upon the battery to fire. After he had reported on the fall of shot, the battery corrected its sights and fired again. Eventually, when the range was found, the observer signalled the OK. Throughout this sequence, as always, he would be under fire.

A weakness became apparent in the lack of standardisation of procedures for air/ground communication. Squadrons and flights were allocated to work with particular batteries, they exchanged visits, mixed socially and developed a mutual respect and understanding; but there was a loss of efficiency when they were called upon to work with unfamiliar units. There was also a conspicuous void, frustratingly revealed during the fighting for Hill 60 in April, when splendid opportunity targets, which a number of guns were in a position to have engaged, escaped unscathed because no appropriate signals procedure existed. Only in No. 1 Squadron (one flight of Avro 504s, two of Morane Parasols), was a method evolved, the observer sending an agreed signal and a map reference, the code letters meaning 'I see a good target. All guns please engage it.' Pressed by Geoffrey Salmond, Henderson called a conference in June, and a pamphlet was issued laying down a basis for future army/air co-operation.

Following his posting to No. 6 Squadron as an observer, Hugh Dowding, having drawn attention to himself by his confrontation with Rawlinson, had soon found an appointment more to his liking by being placed in charge first of the wireless flight attached to 4 Squadron and then of the two wireless flights that formed 9

Squadron. When it was decided, in February 1915, that wireless should play a part in the routine work of every squadron, 9 Squadron was disbanded, to become the first home wireless school, and Dowding was appointed to take over No. 16 Squadron, with the warning that its pilots had been driven too hard by his predecessor, and that it was not a happy squadron.

To seventeen-year-old Second Lieutenant Herbert Ward, who had learned to fly as an Eton schoolboy and was now reporting to 16 Squadron at an aerodrome near Merville, the rather squalid farmhouse that served as Dowding's office accentuated Dowding's dry, scholarly appearance and general air of detachment: he seemed decidedly off-putting. 'Pernickety, interfering, querulous, and impossible to work with', was the summary of Dowding by a contemporary, Archibald James, who later gained distinction in Parliamentary and diplomatic circles.[1] But when Dowding quoted to Ward something from Hilaire Belloc's *Cautionary Tales* and Ward was able to volunteer the next couplet, a working relationship seemed possible. Dowding then announced his intention of accompanying Ward on a test flight to see if he was ready to go over the lines, which Ward interpreted as a brave and avuncular gesture. He evidently passed the test, because afterwards he was presented with a BE2c for his personal use. Yet it was soon apparent to him that Dowding lacked that outward show of geniality that makes for popularity, and he must have seemed a perverse choice for the task of revitalising a tired and disaffected squadron. Ward could not help but notice that two of the flight commanders cordially disliked each other, and he felt that Dowding could have been more forthcoming in knocking their heads together – a curious parallel with his failure to intervene nearly a quarter of a century later in the Keith Park/Leigh-Mallory Big Wing controversy. 'He seldom allowed his dry style of humour to emerge from behind a barrier of terseness,' wrote Ward later. 'Thus he acquired a reputation for unfriendliness. We were an oddly assorted group.'

1. Wing Commander Sir Archibald James, MC, educated at Eton and Trinity College, Cambridge, retired from the RAF in 1926 and was MP for the Wellingborough Division of Northants, 1931–1945.

Ward's great friend on the squadron was Duncan Grinnell-Milne, who described the atmosphere under Dowding as one of 'chilliness and gloom'. But whereas Ward, a more gentle creature, bore the Germans no personal ill-will, Grinnell-Milne detested them. Ward liked the BE2c for its ability to extricate itself from the most provocative handling, and he enjoyed photographic missions because of the concentration demanded. Having manoeuvred his machine over precisely the right map square, he then had to insert each fresh photographic plate into the externally mounted camera, at an angle which would prevent it from being snatched out of his hand by the force of the airstream. Most of his reconnaissances were relatively uneventful until October, when he had cause to appreciate the superiority of the Fokker *Eindecker*. He was eventually shot down on 30 November, a few days before his eighteenth birthday; but he survived as a prisoner, and later made a successful escape.

At home, the need for an officer of more senior rank than Brancker to argue the RFC's corner in the battles for men and material led to Henderson's return to the War Office. Replacing him, on 19 August, in command of the RFC in France, was Hugh Trenchard. He had arrived where he had always expected to be.

Trenchard's guiding principles were simple and clear-cut. First and foremost, the RFC was part of the British Army, and no call from that army must ever find the RFC wanting. This was the RFC's *raison d'être*, never to be forgotten. Second, air superiority must be fought for, gained, and retained at any cost, necessitating an aggressive posture even in adversity. Third, war could not be conducted effectively without casualties. It was in this spirit that he sent countless men to face the enemy against fearful odds – in plain words, to their deaths. There were times when he was forced by events to temper all-out aggression with defensive measures, but he relied throughout on the morale of his crews, visiting them frequently and encouraging them personally. Many spoke of the inspiration his presence provided. Yet they were well aware of his ruthlessness. He accepted, as Haig did, that it was a war of attrition, in the air as on the ground: of keeping it up longer than the Hun.

Archibald James, the man who had been so dismissive of Dowding, thought Trenchard the greatest man he had ever met, calling him 'a totally inarticulate genius'. His opinion was later supported by historian Arthur Bryant.

The man in France who proved of the greatest value to Trenchard was Maurice Baring, who had been Henderson's ADC. Yet, as opposites, the brusque, dominating military personality and the urbane, highly literate civilian, they viewed each other with mutual suspicion. 'I'm prepared to let you stay on a month's trial,' said Trenchard in his abrupt manner. 'If you're no good to me you'll have to go.' Then, softening, he added: 'I'd also like you to give me a trial. Whatever you've heard to the contrary, I think you'll find I'm not such a bad person to work for.' It is revealing that even the orderlies employed by Trenchard supported this. After returning to England to consult Henderson (an act of loyalty to his old boss and friend of which Trenchard did not disapprove), and finding nothing there to excite or distract him, Baring agreed to the trial month with Trenchard. Shortly came the famous incident with the Oxford marmalade, a jar appearing on the breakfast table soon after Trenchard had expressed a wistful longing for it. 'I see you've got a memory, Baring. I shall use it.'

Baring was to accompany Trenchard wherever he went, and the command 'Take a note, Baring,' was to become a catchphrase. It proved the happiest of partnerships, linking Trenchard's single-mindedness, mastery of detail, and flair for getting things done with the interpretive powers of Baring, who translated Trenchard's apparent incoherences into lucid and convincing prose. Trenchard's reputation for following things through, never letting them rest until they were accomplished, owed much to Baring and his note-taking.

Henderson's return released Brancker to take over the Third Wing. Ashmore, formerly commanding the Administrative Wing in the UK, took over the First Wing from Trenchard, and Jack Salmond replaced Burke (sent to Canada to discuss an air training scheme) in the Second. Of the twelve squadrons then in France, Ashmore and

Salmond controlled four each and Brancker three: the twelfth was attached to GHQ. A squadron still consisted of three flights of four aircraft with one or two spare machines. Not all squadrons were homogeneous, but the ubiquitous BE remained the most numerous. Other types were Morane Parasols, Maurice Farmans, and the Vickers FB Gunbus. All squadrons carried one or two so-called scout machines in addition, on the principle, later reversed, that each should have a leavening of offensive aircraft, rather than grouping such aircraft together in special squadrons. The Germans, initially, made the same mistake.

Useful aids to artillery co-operation, hitherto neglected by the RFC, were kite balloons. Prompting came from Douglas Haig, who had learned of the successful spotting and direction of artillery fire by the French using hydrogen-filled balloons. Before the summer ended, four kite balloon sections, lent by the RNAS and comprising fourteen balloons in all, were in position opposite their German counterparts, responsibility for them being gradually taken over by the RFC. The advantage of the balloon was that, unlike the aeroplane, it could stay up all day, only needing to be hauled down for a change of observer, or to escape air attack. A deterrent to such attack could be provided by anti-aircraft batteries located nearby; but there was no defence against long-distance shelling. Although captive, the balloon came complete with its own transport and engine-operated winch and could be moved to a different site as required, giving a degree of mobility.

Working generally in pairs, the observers climbed into the basket suspended from the balloon and were released to a height of anything from 1,000 to 5,000 feet. They carried with them the call-sign of the relevant battery and the co-ordinates of the target which the battery was to engage. A telephone line gave them direct communication with the battery. Having located the target, the method of correcting the fall of shot was exactly similar to the code established by Lewis and James for the corps squadrons.

So useful was the information gleaned by the 'balloonatics', as they were known, that within a few months there were more than 40 kite balloons dotted along the British front, roughly parallel but a mile or more behind it. Their enemy opposite numbers were equally numerous. 'In good, cloudless weather,' wrote balloonatic G.D. Machin, 'visibility was superb.' But being so near the front they had 'no cosy safe billets as the aeroplane flyers had', recalled another balloonatic, Sergeant Bernard Oliver. Instead they found themselves 'camping in dug-outs in the mud . . . often blasted out by shell fire.'

Whereas batteries could remain silent when aircraft were spotting, and thus remain virtually invisible, opening up again for business when the air was clear, they could hardly hold their fire all day, while balloon observers, relieved at intervals, could remain aloft indefinitely. 'In theory,' wrote 18-year-old balloonatic Leonard Field (who later, appropriately enough, rose to the heights of brigadier), 'nothing could be simpler.' But he cited one factor which made life 'less than idyllic', and a second 'which tended to shorten it'. As with heavier-than-air machines of the period, the wind was a natural enemy. It acted on the balloon capriciously, spinning it round on itself 'like a polo pony', always choosing the most inconvenient moment. Worse still was the bending of the cable in a gusting wind, which might yank the balloon down by a hundred feet or so. Then, when it eased, the balloon shot up again. All these disturbances could happen suddenly and speedily, with disastrous effects on the balloonatic's stomach.

One who was not so fortunate as Field was West-End actor and entertainer Basil Hallam, whose balloon broke free in a high wind – an occurrence not totally unknown – and, in the prevailing westerly, headed for the trenches. Hallam and his companion, after jettisoning their maps and instruments, took to the parachutes provided, but Hallam's failed to open.

The third particular unpleasantness was enemy action. Just as the British disliked being overlooked by prying eyes, so did the Germans, and like the British they took active steps to prevent it. 'One of the more interesting sights on a fine clear day,' reminisced Field, 'was that of an enemy fighter suddenly appearing out of nowhere and shooting up a row of balloons like a child popping toy ones at a

Fair.' Field was grimly aware that his compatriots in the front line found this as diverting as did the Germans. 'Life in the trenches was monotonous,' he said, 'and this gave them something to look at.' There were also the German heavy guns, some of which could be elevated sufficiently for target practice on kite balloons.

'It was a matter for nice judgement when to get to hell out of there,' said Field. Sometimes, if the winch crew thought things were getting too hot, they pre-empted the decision, hauling the balloon down. But if a balloon was set on fire, the occupants jumped.

The extreme vulnerability of balloon observers was recognised from the start by the provision of parachutes. 'You'll have to jump out of one of these things sooner or later,' Field was told on arrival, 'so you may as well learn how to do it now.' The learning process was minimal. 'When you go up, just jump out. Oh – and try to keep your feet together when you land.'

Parachutes, of the C.G. Spencer Static-Line (Automatic) type, were attached to the outside of the basket, packed into an elongated wicker container shaped like a candle-snuffer. When the observer jumped, his weight pulled the canopy open. 'You hoped, first,' said Field, 'that the parachute would come out of the container without tearing itself, and second, that it would open.' For Field it always did, but only after he had fallen several hundred feet, when 'it opened with a bang which shook you in the tenderer parts.' Bernard Oliver recalled that, because of the discomforts of the Spencer-type harness, 'we made our own harness with webbing and string.'

'These flyers were the pioneers of the parachute,' wrote Oliver, and the claim is well-founded. The types of parachute and packing, however, would have been too bulky for the confined cockpits of the time, and for use in heavier-than-air machines a miniaturisation was needed, also a means of clearing obstacles, interior and exterior. The problem should not have been insurmountable, but there were other obstacles to be cleared. For instance, it was argued that air crews, unlike balloon observers, were in a position to defend themselves, removing, it was suggested, the moral imperative.

Because of the intense protective fire that was assembled on the ground by both sides, balloon-busting became a specialised and highly dangerous sport. Jimmy McCudden, after a particularly fraught attempt, wrote: 'I was very glad to get down, and since then I have never liked balloons.' Albert Ball, at a second attempt, got his balloon and set it on fire, but his engine was hit. 'Oh, it was rotten, for I only just got back.'

At first, pilots were content to shoot down the balloon: they recoiled from shooting the balloonatics when they were down – or half-way down. But they came to realise that the balloon was more easily replaced than the trained balloonatic, and the man in the basket was at the mercy of the man in the cockpit.

An incident that occurred on a September evening was not untypical. An ascent to 3,000 feet was made at 6 p.m. by a balloon with a crew of two, a Lieutenant Walls and a Flight Sergeant Moncreiff. Reports that hostile aircraft were approaching caused the winchmen to start hauling down at 6.27. At 6.31 the hostile was sighted – it was an Albatros single-seater – and the ground gunners opened fire. The balloon was still on the way down. At about 200 yards range the pilot opened fire, aiming at the men in the basket. The tracer was clearly seen.

Next the pilot went for the balloon, attacking from the stern. Finally he banked round and attacked from the bow before making off over the lines, pursued by artillery and machine-gun fire.

The basket crew were unhurt, but the balloon itself was aflame and descending, and at 6.32 Moncreiff jumped, followed almost immediately by Walls. Prior to jumping they had thrown out all their maps and papers, but these were sucked in by the furnace of the burning balloon. Somehow the two observers managed to avoid the flames and land safely.

Thirty-three balloons had to be replaced that month, which was about average for the period. Destruction by shelling (eight, with two unserviceable) was double the destruction by enemy aircraft (four, with one unserviceable), which was an emerging trend. Half the replacements were simply due to wear and tear, mostly through porosity.

The balloonatic, then, like the men of the corps squadrons, faced protracted and sometimes concentrated exposure to enemy fire.

Many wartime hazards were reduced as experience was accumulated, but the law of averages decreed that, with some hazards, the longer the exposure the greater the risk. Enemy guns were no respecters of persons, and the Spencer parachute, as we have seen, sometimes snagged or suffered damage from enemy fire and failed to open.

In most other respects, experience remained the key to survival. G.D. Machin, shot down in flames on his second ascent but surviving, saved his balloon on two other occasions by electing to stay aloft rather than be winched down once an attack had started. 'The German machines took the "easy ones" at low level.' On yet another occasion a chapter of accidents, including a broken winch and a collapsed balloon when it was too late to jump, ended with Machin, this time with Oliver, falling in the basket into a clump of trees, which cushioned the impact.

Whereas a great many aeroplane observers applied for pilot training and re-emerged at the front as pilots, graduation from balloons to heavier-than-air craft was rare. This was partly because many had become balloonatics after failing the tests for aircrew. They were specially trained for balloon work and had to master varying skills, including the theory and practice of balloon flight. They were no more transferable than trained air mechanics. Also, having got used to the idea of escape by parachute, it may be that they didn't much fancy going without. But there were certainly balloon observers who transferred to aeroplanes. One who succeeded was the ambitious Leonard Field, who later enjoyed a distinguished career in Military Intelligence.

9

HAWKER AND STRANGE
AND THE FOKKER *EINDECKERS*

L IFE in the RFC squadrons in that summer of 1915 was tolerable enough, with the newer squadrons gradually knuckling down alongside the old. Setting off for France remained an adventure, as one young second lieutenant on No. 7 Squadron, Francis P. Adams, flying an RE5 (the first of a series of Reconnaissance Experimental types to go into production at Farnborough), recorded in his diary. Delayed at Folkestone by bad weather, they finally took off on 8 April, by which time they were so exhausted by their celebrations over the Easter weekend that they were glad to get away. Their early reconnaissances, flown at excessive heights, betrayed their inexperience, and they were directed not to exceed 7,000 feet. They then became vulnerable to ground fire, of which Adams wrote: 'Some of the Archies are quite white bursts, apparently shrapnel, and some are black, evil-looking things. The bursts sometimes shake the machine and the shell fragments can be plainly heard.' But by the end of the month he felt blooded. 'More holes in the machine – this is now becoming a matter of course.'

So far as enemy aircraft were concerned, although there was a noticeable increase in activity, there was little more than skirmishing as yet. But it was inevitable that the Germans, too, would seek to spy on the activities of their foes and, as the Army pioneer Bertram Dickson had foreseen, sooner or later this kind of Intelligence-gathering would attract armed confrontation. Yet both sides were sluggish in providing their pilots and observers with suitable weapons; rifles and pistols were still the norm in the early months of 1915. The obvious answer was the machine-gun, and on the British side the choice fell on the Lewis, which was lighter than the alternative, the Vickers: a bonus was that the chilling effect of the airstream provided an inbuilt cooling system and allowed radiator casing and cooling fins to be discarded. A drawback was that, until an efficient non-freezing lubricant became available, oil in the gun's mechanism was prone to congeal, causing stoppages. A further inhibition was that these guns were in demand elsewhere, Britain having contracted to provide a number to the French, who had been generous in turn in supplying aircraft and engines to Britain.

The problem of mounting and firing such a gun in a tractor machine to penetrate the propeller arc without damaging the propeller was shortly to be solved, though not, in the first instance – and to their cost – by the British. Meanwhile several improvisations were attempted. Louis Strange was a pioneer in offsetting the Lewis to one side, though heading in one direction and aiming in another required a freakish marksmanship. More effective was fixing the gun high enough above the top plane for the bullets to clear the propeller-tips. It was with a BE2c so fitted that Lanoe Hawker first went jousting into enemy airspace.

Although the new Fokker monoplanes fitted with interrupter gear, which synchronised the gun with the engine, allowing the bullets to pass between the propeller blades, made their first appearance that summer, they were too scarce and too cautiously flown as yet to cause alarm. 'Hun machines always over their own lines and generally much lower,' noted Adams on 29 May. 'They immediately run for it and dive to earth if one pursues them.' This was just as well as at this stage Adams and his observer still boasted nothing more lethal than a rifle and revolver between them. Their main concern was engine trouble, for which they frequently had to turn back.

Nevertheless newcomer Adams found many compensations, not least lunching with the artillery on his days off, discussing methods of co-operation, and getting to know the men on the ground and their problems. Like many others before him and after, Adams was conscious of the extremes of his own life, and especially of his home comforts, compared with the men at the front. 'It's exceedingly pleasant to return to an ideal billet, a hot bath and a shave and a leisurely breakfast, with a London newspaper only 24 hours old. Life is certainly quite pleasing.' If he reflected that it was likely to be short, he confided no such qualms to his diary.

By early June Adams's RE5 had been armed with a Lewis gun, operated by an observer named Meakin, and they soon had a chance to use it. 'Had an exciting time on June 5th', related Adams. They seem, on this occasion, to have been mixing business if not with pleasure then at least with some kind of prank: their reconnaissance was aimed at the railway junction at Valenciennes, but they were to drop a message bag addressed to the Hun Flying Corps on Lille aerodrome on their way home: in the bag was a copy of the squadron magazine, with some friendly taunts for German pilots. After being spotted by German observation balloons they were crossing Lens at their briefed height of 7,000 feet when Adams espied a Hun machine some way astern and shouted to Meakin: 'Get the Lewis gun ready!' Two abrupt left-hand turns brought them roughly parallel with what they took to be an Aviatik. 'At 300 yards she let off a belt from her machine-gun,' Adams wrote later. 'All the bullets were heard, but nothing seemed to hit. We held our fire, then let her have a couple of bursts.' The Aviatik was still circling threateningly when a second machine, of the pusher type, startled them by firing at them and scoring hits, Meakin being fully occupied at the time in changing a drum. Then an Albatros swung in underneath them, and bullets began to come up through the fabric from below.

These encounters, before the Fokkers got to work, were not as desperate as they sounded. Adams and Meakin completed their reconnaissance, by which time they were again being chased. Yet they were still doggedly determined to deliver their message. Over Lille aerodrome they were tagged by another hostile, but they dropped the message bag, a feat which would be wildly applauded over a couple of drinks in the Mess. 'Furious shelling greeted us near the lines,' noted Adams, which no doubt they deserved. 'Soon after that my engine stopped and I managed to land.'

Such combats, if they can be so called, were not untypical of the inconclusive nature of air fighting that summer. Nevertheless Adams felt a glow of pride at completing his mission. He felt warmer still after a few sets of mixed doubles at a nearby château. 'Extraordinary interlude, so near the war,' he noted. 'Started off with fizz!' Emotional warmth, though, seems to have been absent, due to the plainness of the mesdemoiselles. 'None very striking,' was his verdict, 'but some could play tennis rather well . . .' Like so many other front-line diaries, it was to end abruptly, the last entry being penned on 2 July. But the two men were safe, interned in Holland, and were repatriated after the war.

As the summer progressed, attacks on our reconnaissance machines, although still spasmodic, became more determined, and squadron commanders generally entrusted the more distant reconnaissances to the better-armed aircraft. This did not always afford them safety. A note dropped over the British lines from a German machine recorded the death of a British pilot and the capture of his observer on a lone long-range reconnaissance in a French machine. 'The German pilots have the highest praise for their opponent,' concluded the note, 'who died in an honourable fight.'

Better able to take care of themselves were the crews of the FE (Farman Experimental) 2b's, a pusher-type of pre-war de Havilland/Farnborough design, four examples of which were delivered to No. 6 Squadron in June. It was easy to fly, had a reliable (120 h.p. Beardmore) engine, and gave pilot and observer a wide view from a spacious cockpit. Two machine-guns, linked together and fitted to a pivotal mounting, could be fitted in the front cockpit, and the observer could stand up and fire to the rear over the top planes and over the pilot's head, giving some protection astern. This left the pilot free to fly the plane. But Lanoe Hawker still packed his rifle, getting his own back on his observer by firing it forward over *his* head. Here was a fighting machine well able to hold its own with the new and faster German machines then coming into service. Unfortunately, deliveries that summer were restricted to the four to

No. 6 Squadron, and the type failed to appear in any numbers before the end of the year.

Hawker's main interest at this time was the new Bristol Scout he had been allocated. Even in the virtually unarmed BE2c, as already mentioned, he had shown a flair for air combat almost before it was thought of, and he was soon evaluating, testing and stunting his new Bristol and designing, with the practical help of air mechanic E.J. Elton, with whom he shared the credit, his own front mounting for a machine-gun. After study and trials he arranged to fire the gun obliquely forward, crabwise, as Strange had done, to port of the propeller arc. A speed of 89 m.p.h., and a climb to 6,500 feet in ten minutes, against twenty in his previous machines, with a ceiling of 15,500, placed Hawker in his element. He knocked nothing down at first due to the inherent aiming difficulties, and he made no claims, but he forced several aircraft to spin down in confusion, trailing smoke. 'It's quite exciting, diving at 120 miles an hour and firing a machine-gun.' And of the Bristol Scout: 'She is a little beauty . . .'

Hawker had a habit of waiting on the ground, ready to start, until he got warning from ground observers or from pilots already airborne of 'hostiles'. Then he would take off and go hunting. But his exploits were not confined to air combat: he fitted his forays in the BE2c and later the Bristol Scout into his routine squadron work. When the Zeppelin raids began on England, 6 Squadron were given the task of destroying the lair of one of the raiders near Ghent, and Hawker was chosen as the most likely man to succeed. Floating menacingly over the target lay a captive balloon, manned by a machine-gunner, and Hawker decided to neutralise that first. He 'proceeded to execute some split-arse spirals round the balloon and heaved grenades at it', according to his report. Of the three bombs he subsequently dropped on the shed, two scored hits; but ironically the offending Zeppelin had been destroyed in the air shortly beforehand. Account was taken of his earlier work, however, and he was awarded the DSO.

Shot in the foot on one of his forays, Hawker had to be lifted in and out of the cockpit, but he continued flying although hobbling about with the aid of a stick. One day, enjoying the peace at high altitude, he had a revelation, soon to be confirmed, that his friend Bayly was indeed lost and would never return.

Palpably exhausted, with the carefree impetuosity of earlier days blunted, he was sent home on leave, where he renewed his friendship with the bereaved Baylys. Returning refreshed, he earned further plaudits from his squadron commander. 'He's now back,' wrote Gordon Shephard, 'flying as daringly as ever, and has inflicted damage on German aircraft by combat in the air.' Although Trenchard's policy kept Hawker's name unknown outside the RFC, his reputation within it as the outstanding scout pilot of his time was firm. His appearances over the lines in his Bristol Scout also won the respect of the enemy.

Early in July Hawker's fellow flight commander Louis Strange was posted to home establishment to form a new squadron after eleven months at the front, a record for any pilot at that time. Before he left he survived one of the most bizarre escapades of the war. No. 6 Squadron had also acquired a single-seater Martinsyde S1, which attracted Strange because of its machine-gun mounted above the centre section, and Shephard allotted it to him as his personal aeroplane. But it was slower than Hawker's Bristol Scout, and when they got news of an intruder, usually by wireless from Bron James, Strange sometimes used it as a decoy, enabling Hawker to attack unseen. The main problem with the Martinsyde was that to change the ammunition drum the pilot had to loosen his safety belt and stand up in the cockpit to reach it, a perilous procedure, especially during combat. Add to this the weight of the drum, the force of the airstream, and a machine that was sluggish, climbed ponderously, and was inherently unstable, and Strange's preference for it emphasises the faults of the alternatives. Its armament, and its top speed of 87 m.p.h., just about justified its label of 'scout'.

Strange was chasing an Aviatik from Lille, on his own this time, at 8,500 feet, both machines being near their respective ceilings. The German observer had been taking pot shots at the Martinsyde with a parabellum pistol, and Strange, having hitherto held his fire, replied with a drum from his Lewis. But when he tried to change the drum, it jammed.

Unable to remove it with one hand, he wedged the stick between his knees and tugged at the drum with both hands. When this failed he loosened his safety-belt and raised himself out of his seat to get a better grip. As he struggled, the safety-belt slipped down, he lost his knee-grip on the stick, and the Martinsyde, still climbing, stalled and flicked over into a spiral. As he was already more than half-way out of the cockpit, he was thrown clear of the machine, legs kicking, hanging on desperately to the drum.

A moment earlier he had been trying to free the drum with all his strength. Now its stubborn resistance was preserving his life. How long would it hold?

The edge of the drum was cutting into his fingers and he had to catch hold of something more permanent. The Martinsyde was now flying upside down, and he had the sense to realise that the top of the centre section strut must be behind and above him. Dare he let go of the drum with one hand to make a grab for it? There was no alternative. He groped for the strut and gripped it fiercely, transferred the other hand to it, and began kicking upwards until he got first one foot and then the other hooked inside the cockpit, thrusting around until he coiled his legs round the stick. He jammed on full aileron and rudder – and the machine obligingly rolled out right way up. Dropping into his seat with a bump, he grabbed the stick in shell-shocked triumph.

The crew of the Aviatik went home and claimed a victory: they had seen the British pilot thrown out of his cockpit. On the strength of this the Germans spent half a day searching in vain for the wreckage of man and machine.

Strange's departure two months later left the squadron short of a flight commander, and for a time Hawker took command of both A and B Flights. This was the prelude to perhaps his finest period. He continued to alternate scouting sorties on the Bristol with brilliant reconnaissance work in the FE2b, but it was on a designated offensive patrol that he set out in a new Bristol Scout (he had run out of fuel in the old one and crashed it), on the evening of 25 July. Soon after crossing the lines he spotted two enemy two-seater biplanes over the Ypres salient. Any chance of surprising them was defeated by Archie, whose pattern of bursts warned them of his approach. One of the hostiles stayed long enough to return his machine-gun fire, and the Bristol was hit, but Hawker discharged a whole drum at him with such accuracy that the German spun down. Twenty minutes later, still over enemy territory, Hawker intercepted another two-seater. This one, too, was armed with a machine-gun, but again Hawker's fire was the more accurate and he crippled its engine and forced the pilot to land.

The sun was setting and Hawker was conning the evening sky from 11,000 feet, nearing the end of his patrol, when he spotted an Albatros two-seater that had ventured over the British lines, confident in the power of its bristling machine-gun, palpably intent on some specific artillery spotting. Hawker had been obliged to seek his prey almost exclusively on the German side, where proof of his marksmanship was rarely available: here was a chance to provide the doubters – and there were always doubters – with the evidence.

Manoeuvring so as to put the apparently unsuspecting German a thousand feet below him down sun, scarcely daring to breathe, he dived on his target, holding his fire. When the Albatros filled his sights, a single burst sent it diving out of control. Seconds later it turned on its back, ejected the observer, and burst into flames. Exultation at this spectacular outcome would have been complete but for the pity aroused by the sight of a fellow aviator plunging puppet-like to his death.

Strangely enough, the body of the observer, thus preserved from the flames, yielded invaluable Intelligence. Not only was he carrying a map on which he had marked the exact location of a British battery that was firing at the time, the same map also showed the position of four German batteries, one of which, persistently troublesome for weeks beforehand, had long been searched for in vain.

This trio of victories in a single evening, climaxing in the swift and spectacular destruction, in a clear sky, of a high-flying and apparently invulnerable Albatros, witnessed by thousands of troops, together with its Intelligence bonus, coming on top of many months of unparalleled aggression against the enemy, surely called for some special recognition, and Hawker was immediately recommended for a VC.

Hawker had heard about the new Fokker *Eindeckers* with the synchronised forward-firing machine-gun, but so far he hadn't encountered one. He would hardly have chosen to do so near the end of a patrol in an FE2b, with fuel and ammunition – not to mention his own stamina – running low, nor would he have relished the thought of being dived on unawares on first acquaintance by what was fast becoming a dreaded antagonist. But it was as he and his observer, Lieutenant Noel Clinton, returned from a reconnaissance via Lille that a Fokker fired on them in what was becoming a typical swooping shock attack. Only Hawker's exceptional skill saved them from the *coup de grâce*, and eventually he so outmanoeuvred the German pilot that a point-blank burst from Clinton sent the *Eindecker* crashing down on the outskirts of Lille. This was almost certainly the first of the *Eindeckers* to be shot down in combat, justifying the phlegmatic Clinton in rating the patrol 'a nice little outing'. Hawker's reaction, as always, was ambivalent. Enthusiasm at his victory was tempered by fellow feeling for his victim.

Hawker's mood swings could be of some amplitude, and there can be little doubt that he was overworked that summer, with two flights to lead and run and two types of fighting aeroplane in which to take the war to the enemy. It was strenuous and nerve-racking work, and it was perhaps inevitable that the most capable and aggressive pilots should get the bulk of it, especially for anything non-routine. Gordon Shephard noted the dark rings appearing round Hawker's eyes, the unaccustomed gauntness, and the overall signs of strain, and he sent him on leave. Happily Hawker was home when his VC was gazetted. The award was a landmark, the first VC to be won for valour in air combat.

Shephard did not feel he could spare Hawker for long, and when he returned to France he was still tired. 'I'm not quite as well as I should like,' he admitted, 'and if I don't get better soon I shall apply for a home job.' But he didn't want to go just yet. 'I'm very keen on completing a full year out here, something no one else has done.' After the lay-off, work proved the best cure, and he was soon feeling 'much more chirpy', recording further successes and giving his mind to reorganising the technique of artillery co-operation in the FE2b.

But he was denied his immediate ambition. There were still only twelve squadrons at the front at the end of that summer, but the expansion that was in progress at home meant that Hawker was earmarked to command a new squadron, and on 20 September, five days before the start of the Battle of Loos, he was posted home, having completed all but seventeen days of the year he had set his heart on. He was the last remaining of the original pilots of No. 6 Squadron who had crossed the Channel on 6 October 1914; and he knew he had just about worn himself out.

Had he known what awaited him in England he might have preferred to stay where he was. He was ready enough for the challenge of forming and commanding a new squadron, No. 24, with the prospect of flying a brand-new single-seat pusher aeroplane, the DH2, designed by Geoffrey de Havilland (who had meanwhile left Farnborough and formed his own company, Airco). It would be the first single-seat scout squadron to be formed in the RFC. But he was unprepared for the situation that confronted him at the squadron training base on Hounslow Heath. Just as the demand for rapid expansion had bred hurried decisions on aircraft selection, so the training of pilots had had to be rushed. Most of the men joining 24 Squadron were raw and inexperienced; many were still in their teens. Hawker checked them out individually on the various hacks available at Hounslow and in most instances was obliged to instruct them afresh. He also assumed responsibility for their physical and mental fitness during the winter months, when they were awaiting delivery of the DH2s and when flying opportunities were few and boredom threatened. Leading the pack himself, he had them running round the Heath before breakfast. A saving grace was the personal interest he took in all their problems.

There was no chance of boredom for Hawker: the shortage of experienced leaders was such that he was placed in charge of two of the night-flying stations ringed around north-east London whose task it was to attempt to intercept raiding Zeppelins, a tiresome and, it was considered, almost hopeless assignment. Here again he found himself filling the role of instructor, and there was always competition to fly with him because of his reputation. He didn't even get a break at week-ends. 'They will have to give me leave soon,' he wrote on 27 November, 'or I shall collapse.'

Rejuvenation did not come until the arrival at Hounslow, on 10 January 1916, of the first de Havilland DH2 scout. Powered by a 100 h.p. Gnome Monosoupape of French design and manufacture, it was to earn a reputation, when first introduced, of a liability to spin. Hawker was kept busy convincing his pilots that this reputation, if not altogether without substance, was exaggerated, and that correct piloting could counter any such tendency. One of the problems was that those of his pilots who had trained on Stability Jane had to be retaught when they came to fly an unstable machine like the DH2. Farmans and Avros had to be nursed through every manoeuvre, whereas, with a BE, a touch on the controls and the machine did the rest. Trainees could be passed out more quickly on the Blériot, but their skills were strictly limited. Nevertheless a month later, on 7 February 1916, the squadron moved to France.

News of the further depredations of the Fokker *Eindeckers* had already percolated through. But FE2b's were also beginning to arrive in strength, and the crews of these, with Hawker's DH2s, and a third pusher type, the Vickers Gunbus, braced themselves for the task of neutralising what, in Hawker's absence, had become known as the Fokker Scourge.

Anthony Fokker, a Dutch aviation engineer, had had a monoplane built to his own design as far back as 1912. Of clean outline and fair performance for its time, it was very similar to the French-built Morane Saulnier monoplane, the main difference being that part of the structure was of welded steel tubing instead of wood. The Germans saw its potential, improved the design, and put it into quantity production. Powered by an 80 h.p. Oberursel rotary engine, its clean lines gave it the ability to make long almost vertical dives on a target. But this feature was not utilised immediately; it was employed at first as an unarmed reconnaissance machine.

The change came with the chance capture of a modified Morane Saulnier Type L parasol monoplane flown by the French pioneer aerobatic pilot Roland Garros, who in 1913 had been the first man to cross the Mediterranean by air. To solve the problem of aiming a machine-gun straight ahead, Garros and designer Raymond Saulnier had fitted wedge-shaped metal plates to the blades of Garros's propeller, believing that the proportion of bullets that would strike the blades would be small and would anyway be safely deflected. On 1 April 1915 Garros took off to try out this theory, and it worked. With no more than superficial damage to his propeller, Garros shot down a German two-seater in flames. After he had repeated the feat twice in the next seventeen days, the French began fitting the device to all similar aircraft, and very soon another pre-war stunt pilot, Adolphe Pégoud, was chalking up victories.

Failing to appreciate the immense advantage they had gained, the French seem to have made no attempt to safeguard their secret. Eventually the Germans must surely have tumbled to what was afoot and reacted accordingly, but engine failure in Garros's plane while on a bombing run over Courtrai, and the prevailing wind which carried him deeper than he intended into enemy territory, ensured that cognizance came sooner rather than later. Realising the implications too late, Garros tried to set fire to his machine, but was unsuccessful; he brooded on this so guiltily as a prisoner that he plotted to retrieve his reputation by escaping and rejoining the fight. He eventually did so, only to be killed in action. But he could not undo the damage he – or those who had countenanced his bombing mission – had done.

Gun, engine and propeller of Garros's machine were passed to Anthony Fokker, with orders to copy it for installation in his very similar monoplane. But Fokker and his staff went further; aware of a pre-war patent for a synchronised gun, they introduced a timing mechanism which allowed bullets fired from a machine-gun to pass between the blades of a revolving propeller, rendering deflector plates superfluous. In addition, bullets fed from ammunition belts removed the necessity for changing drums. Crude as the device was, and primitive as was its carrier, together they constituted the first efficient gun platform for scout pilots.

Yet the Germans, too, failed at first to appreciate how decisive the development was. The first Fokker E1s, as the armed machine was designated, were produced in small numbers and allotted in pairs in

July 1915 to various flying units, to operate as escorts for two-seaters. Although the Germans were already smarting under the unopposed bombing raids of the French, appreciation of the potential attacking role of the Fokkers came slowly, and then from the pilots themselves, principally from two men who were to become national heroes in Germany, Oswald Boelcke and Max Immelmann.

Boelcke, who was involved with Fokker in testing the E1 from its inception, was at least Immelmann's equal in flair and aggression, and he surpassed him in strategic and tactical vision. He laid down four basic principles of air fighting: height advantage; attacking out of the sun; the use of cloud for concealment; and close range. He also showed tactical awareness in choosing attacking positions where the target aircraft's guns could not be brought to bear on the attacker. Yet the 'Eagle of Lille', as Immelmann was dubbed, gained the greater immediate fame through his romantic appearance and his invention of the turn which bears his name.

The Fokker's hawk-like ability to dive vertically in surprise attack took the aggressor too far beyond his target for a quick follow-up strike; Immelmann's answer was to use his diving speed for a swift zoom to gain height, pulling up into a loop before a half-roll off the top so that he was upright and above his target, flying in the opposite direction. By falling away into a stall turn he was then ideally placed for surprise attack, or to escape if need be. And it was Immelmann who launched what was later to develop into the Fokker Scourge when he shot down a British two-seater bomber on the German side of the lines on 1 August 1915, the first officially confirmed Fokker victory.

The head-on form of attack, in which the aircraft itself was aimed at the target, revolutionised air marksmanship and with it air combat. Fortunately for the Allies, however, the initial impact was attenuated by a mistaken distribution of the new *Eindeckers* in penny packets, and it was not until that autumn and winter, rising to a crescendo in the New Year, that the successors of the E1s, the E11s and the E111s, with more powerful engines and concentrated into special units (though never totalling more than 50 at any one time and 300 in all), shot down several hundred Allied machines and reduced their principal victims, the unfortunate crews of the BEs, to 'Fokker Fodder'.

The day before Immelmann's first victory, and six days after Hawker's triple success, a third VC was won, by a man who was not an experienced flyer like Hawker, nor the callow youth that many newly-arrived pilots were beginning to be. At twenty-seven Aidan Liddell was two years older than Hawker, and his VC was remarkable not so much for the action itself, which was similar to many other brave attempts by mortally wounded pilots to coax a crippled aircraft home with their report (and often, as in this case, preserve the life and freedom of an observer), as for the man and his background. No conventional hero, he was an academic of delicate health and physique, with a first in zoology at Balliol, one whose exceptional gifts, it was said, would have brought him distinction in any pursuit. An Argyll and Sutherland Highlander, born in Newcastle, he had learned to fly in 1914 for his own interest, without thought of transfer to the RFC. He went to France in August 1914 with overall responsibility for the machine-gun sections of his battalion, and at Christmas 1914 he took part in the famous (or infamous) fraternisation, of which he wrote: 'On that day everyone spontaneously left their trenches and had a meeting half-way ... The Germans gave us cigars, and we gave them chocolates and tobacco. They seemed very pleased to see us! Some had lived in England for years, and were very bucked at airing their English again!'

Then it was back to the killing. 'You don't know how nerveracking this trench business is, and how far off the end of the war seems. It would appear that it must go on until the Germans are quite exhausted, which might take a little time.' The flash of wry humour was typical, the reference to his nerves prophetic. A mention in despatches and a Military Cross (a DSO was recommended) confirmed his fortitude, but in February 1915 he was sent home on sick leave, and having already taken his ticket, a transfer to the RFC after six debilitating months in the trenches seemed natural. On 23 July he returned to France to join No. 7 Squadron, flew his first reconnaissance patrol on the 29th in an RE5 and his second and last two days later. It was for another astonishing display of fortitude, when he brought his crippled machine under control and made a forced landing on the Allied side despite hideous wounds, that his VC was awarded. He died a month later. Sadly the life that he saved, that of his observer, Second Lieutenant R.H. Peck, was to be sacrificed later.

Having been posted home from 6 Squadron in July, and finding the promise of a squadron frustratingly delayed, Louis Strange wangled himself a posting as a flight commander on 12 Squadron under Cyril Newall, and he was back in France by mid-September. Trenchard visited the squadron with Baring and expressed approval of the new gun mountings Strange had devised for the BE2c, but when he saw Strange he bristled. 'What are you doing here? I thought I sent you home to form a squadron.' Strange wisely kept his peace. 'You must go home. Make a note, Baring.' Strange thought his presence would be forgotten, but a few days later, after a Bristol Scout had been allotted to the squadron, a delighted Strange was fitting a Lewis gun to it when Trenchard appeared again with Baring. 'I thought I told you, Baring, to remind me to send Strange home?' Then he turned to Strange and boomed, 'Strange, go home at once.'

Surely he couldn't mean right this minute? But he said again, 'Go home at once.' Then, pointing to an old Maurice Farman, he added, 'in that machine, now!' There was nothing for it but to salute and order the machine to be started up. But with a 35-knot headwind Strange had no intention of crossing the Channel that day. Instead, he dropped down into Abeele and 6 Squadron, where his old boss Gordon Shephard accepted his excuses. But he had to promise to leave early next morning, after what he called 'a most hectic and hilarious night with my old friends'.

Strange proceeded to form a new squadron, No. 23, but the night before they were due to leave for France (16 March 1916) he went down with appendicitis, an overworked surgeon left a swab inside him, and he was fourteen weeks in hospital and unfit for flying for many months. When he recovered he went to CFS as a flight commander and instructor. But his operational career was not quite finished yet.

10

THE BATTLE OF LOOS: DERMOTT ALLEN AND A BOMBING CAMPAIGN: LIVES THROWN AWAY

G REAT hopes were pinned by the French General Joffre in a 1915 autumn offensive, starting in September, deploying the growing strength the Allied ground forces had accumulated that summer, and taking advantage of the known transfer of German divisions to the Russian front. Joffre's offensive was to be mounted on an ambitious scale: he planned to advance across the bare, undulating Champagne country and achieve a decisive breakthrough, developing an attack along the entire front which, if successful, would drive the enemy from French soil. Despite objections from Haig that ammunition was still short and the terrain unsuitable, the British, aware that failure to back up the much stronger French contribution could leave them isolated, agreed to develop a subsidiary attack in the region of Loos, directly north of Vimy Ridge and the important town of Arras. Haig's First Army was to push up between Lens and La Basée while the Second Army made diversionary attacks east of Ypres.

The RFC in France now comprised three wings controlling twelve squadrons, numbering some 160 miscellaneous aircraft, mostly BE2c's and Morane Parasols; there was still only a leavening of Gunbuses and FE2b's. And the RFC had its problems. 'We'll be in a chaotic state if we do advance,' wrote Dermott Allen, now a flight commander on 8 Squadron in Third Wing, after a spell of photographic work. 'It is pitiable how short we are of spares.' For weeks the bombing squadrons slaved day and night in preparation for the offensive, keeping their machines active on reconnaissance and artillery-spotting by day, devising and fitting bomb-racks by night. 'Life is very strenuous,' said Allen. His day began at 06.30, he had his flight to run, and to keep in touch he did a reconnaissance or artillery 'show' every second day. 'Yet one hears of railway unrest in England.' The jingoism of the early days, it seemed, had cooled, with strikes proliferating, arousing great bitterness in France. 'The British working man is really a swine of the first water,' wrote Allen intemperately, 'till he gets really properly hunted and straffed.' Social inequalities, exacerbated by wartime restraints and controls which bore most heavily on the working population, were largely to blame.

The First Wing was to be solely occupied in artillery co-operation with Haig's First Army; indeed the entire programme of artillery bombardment that was to precede and accompany the British attack would depend on their persistence and skill, first in locating enemy batteries and then in directing the fire that would aim to silence them. The Second and Third Wings were to delay and harass the expected flow of enemy reinforcements by bombing the important Lille–Douai –Valenciennes rail communications triangle. French bombers would be similarly active on the Champagne front.

'The first signs of the big push showed themselves on 20 September,' noted Allen. The preliminary bombardment began next day in a tense atmosphere but in good weather, and the bombing programme opened two days later. Then on the 24th it began to rain, and it was still raining on the 25th when the infantry went over the top. The corps squadrons, all visited and motivated before the attack by Trenchard, did well enough until the visibility deteriorated, but they failed altogether to provide information on the progress of the attacking troops, mainly through a breakdown in the primitive air/ground signalling methods that had been planned but insufficiently practised. There was also a failure to appreciate the value of low flying to observe changes and gaps in the dispositions of the enemy force, so that, as it afterwards became clear, golden opportunities were missed.

In the opening attack the British used gas for the first time, and

Lieutenant J.G. Selby, seconded to the RFC from the gunners and observing from a Morane Parasol of 3 Squadron, applauded at first: we were giving the Germans a taste of their own medicine. But he soon changed his mind. 'We were flying at about 8,000 feet. The wind had changed and we could see the gas visibly drifting back over our own trenches. My pilot throttled down and turned round and said: "Thank God we're in the Flying Corps, old boy!"' It was a moment of ambivalence for Selby, his relief at his good fortune being balanced by guilt.

The aerial bombardment enjoyed some spectacular successes, among them an attack, on the 25th, by a BE2c of Allen's squadron from a height of 150 feet, on a bridge which carried a light railway over the main line in the Valenciennes triangle. The pilot succeeded in cutting the one and blocking the other; this was Sholto Douglas. Next day, despite appalling weather, an attack on the locomotive sheds at Valenciennes blew up two ammunition trains and exploded twenty trucks of shells, halting all traffic at this vital junction at a critical time. Reconnaissance flights, too, bore fruit, pioneer air photographer Darley reporting rail activity further south near Cambrai which stimulated raids in which the permanent way was cratered by direct hits. (Soon afterwards Darley was shot down by Immelmann, but he survived as a prisoner.)

'My special job', wrote Allen, 'was to interrupt communications on the Valenciennes–Douai line. Any train but Red Cross was to be bombed from low altitude, which meant going down to 7–800 feet, although the bombsight, except when used in the vertical plane, was not much good at this height.' Flying without an observer, he carried one 112-pounder and six 20-lb anti-personnel bombs. Going in second of three, he dropped his 112-pounder 'on or near' a busy junction north-west of Valenciennes, obliterating the area round the points with dust and smoke. But much to his disgust, four of his 20-pounders failed to explode.

Allen believed that the bombing campaign was proving effective: the Valenciennes–Douai line had been continually blocked and traffic held up. At the very least the enemy must have been caused great inconvenience, forcing him to employ batteries of rockets and reinforcements of troops in an effort to protect the route. The Germans were also going in for camouflage, daubing their trains and suppressing tell-tale emissions of smoke. The result, for the RFC, was prohibitive losses, largely from ground fire but also from the increasing aggression of units of the German Air Force, particularly the Fokkers, which emerged for the first time as more than a threat. 'It's hard to believe that I've lost every single officer that I had a month ago,' lamented Allen. 'They simply disappeared one after the other.' Yet the daily routine continued. 'I'm afraid one gets very callous to this sort of thing. It all happens so quietly and unobtrusively. A machine goes out and does not return. It is shown on the daily state as missing for a couple of days and is then struck off charge. I tell someone to take an inventory of the missing officer's kit. A new pilot or observer arrives and has to be trained. Then one gets a letter from the relatives of the missing. These have to be answered. War is a beastly business. I can't conceive any normal person liking it, and yet one could not dream of remaining at home.' (After a short break at home through illness, he had agitated to return to a squadron.)

Yet the losses in the air paled before the slaughter on the ground. Rumours, all too accurate, were reaching the squadrons of a total of 50,000 casualties. Most of the flyers had been regimental officers, and they rated their own sacrifices as nothing compared to those of the fighting troops.

Assessing the impact of the bombing was difficult. Brancker, talking to Allen at the height of the campaign, thought that although German communications had been disrupted, the lines had never been completely cut. German records later revealed that substantial damage was wrought but that debris was quickly cleared: all reinforcements were said to have reached their destinations on time.

The Germans demonstrated the truth of this by launching fierce counter-attacks, and when the reserves requested by Haig were delayed, due reputedly to French's desire to keep them under his own control through jealousy of his subordinate, the British were forced to pull back. Meanwhile in Champagne the Germans, having had advance warning of the French attack through their Intelligence agents, and enjoying the advantage of higher ground, held on.

The Allies also used agents, or 'spies', but information from behind enemy lines was scarce, and assaults tended to be continued even when failure seemed inevitable. 'Tomorrow I am for a bombing show,' noted Allen. The target was the same, but losses had bred caution: there was to be no low flying unless trains were actually seen.

'The First Army is going to attack,' noted Allen on 12 October. 'I hardly think they seriously think they're going to get through. It's awful to think of the lives that are going to be lost tomorrow to gain a few hundred yards . . . If only we had the ammunition to absolutely annihilate the Bosch batteries and trenches.'

Allen realised that the material damage his squadron could inflict was small, but he had been indoctrinated with the Trenchard dogma. 'It is a means of forcing the Hun to come up and fight us at our own time and choosing.' The Fokker pilots, led by Boelcke and Immelmann, were all too ready to oblige, even sometimes crossing the Allied lines – unusual for the Germans – and the vulnerability of the BE2c was ruthlessly exposed. Allen still believed in the doctrine of attack, but he was begging for faster machines and stronger escorts. 'Once you have the Hun in the air he must not be allowed to get away.'

From 30 September the bombers were given an escort, generally one for one, Third Wing being fortunate in having the only Vickers Gunbus squadron so far formed (No. 11) to protect them. Alternatively, two or three bombing machines might be sent together while Gunbus patrols endeavoured to keep the air clear. The corps squadrons, too, found themselves obliged to fight for the information they sought, necessitating escorts.

'Bombing seems to be off for the present,' noted Allen later that month. He saw this as a bad sign: bombing and the ground offensive went hand in hand, so there must be a lull in the fighting. Rumours, mostly of a discouraging nature, were rife. 'Two more fellows missing from the squadron,' Allen recorded on 12 October. 'They went on a long recce in one of my "spot" machines and unfortunately didn't come back. One is affected by one's own show a great deal.'

Immelmann recorded his fourth victory (a BE2c) on the 10th, yet the Germans, by continuing to split the Fokkers up into penny packets, still failed to maximise their advantage. And to give the crews of the outclassed British machines their due, it was amazing how well most of them held their own.

The wintry weather that set in as October advanced came as a blessed relief. Haig's casualties, as was usual for the attacking force, were more than double those of the enemy, the French lost 190,000, and by early November Joffre had finally abandoned his plan, anyway for the time being. He was still convinced that, although his losses were half as many again as the German, the Allies could stand it and the Germans could not: he believed he was wearing them down. On the British side, Sir John French got the blame for the débâcle, especially for the delay in providing reserves, and he was replaced as commander-in-chief by Douglas Haig.

'Life,' wrote Maurice Baring, presumably thinking of those who survived, 'resumed its normal course.' Allen wrote with equal fatalism. 'One has now quite fallen into a groove. This war has quite become part and parcel of one's existence.' Peace was a thing of the dim and distant past, and no one cared to guess when it would return. Leave, which was the one thing everyone longed for, was something it was better not to contemplate: one only started counting the days. Yet the idealism with which Britain had begun hostilities remained strong. 'If it is left to the folk out here, I don't think there would be any thought of chucking it until the Bosch has taken it properly in the neck.'

Allen was one of the few who tried to keep the many facets of the war in perspective. 'It always strikes me as peculiar how really little interest nearly everyone takes in the war in general. We each have our own little job, such as servicing engines or procuring spare parts. We are dominated by our own little corner.' Absorbed in the task in hand, people just didn't concern themselves further. As for the flyers, survival was a consideration but not an obsession. 'Personally I admit I never worry. As for the big issues, one knows practically nothing.' The gap between the brass-hats and the men at the sharp end, despite Trenchard's frequent visits to the squadrons, remained wide.

Nevertheless Allen retained his critical faculties. Several more of the originals were booked for a return to France in charge of squadrons or flights: Brock was to lead 15 Squadron (BE2c's), Carmichael 18 Squadron (Gunbuses), and Borton 27 (Martinsyde Scouts). The policy was that no one could command a squadron in France until he had first commanded a reserve squadron at home, which meant that Allen could not be promoted direct in France. Mapplebeck, too, was wanted as a squadron commander, and he went home to take over a reserve squadron at Joyce Green, near Dartford, where, with few Zeppelins to intercept, he spent much of his time making night flights over defended points around London to give practice to the searchlight and gun crews. Perhaps he got bored with this, as there are accounts of low level stunting over the houses of some particular friends in Shooters Hill. 'We lay flat on the grass and were quite sick with fright,' was one comment. This exuberance came to a tragic end when, having called at Shooters Hill unexpectedly on 24 August to persuade them to come and watch him try out a recently acquired Type N Morane monoplane known by the British as the Bullet, difficult to fly because of its high wing loading, he descended in a succession of spirals which steepened until the machine hit a hangar roof, the whole ghastly sequence being watched by his horrified friends. It looked like a typical show-off misjudgment, in a machine in which the pilot was inexperienced; but a doubt was later expressed about this particular model's basic airworthiness. It was ironic that Mapplebeck, whose scepticism about the glib assumption of pilot error had been so well founded, should have a similar question mark surrounding his own death.

Even amongst his larger-than-life contemporaries Gibb Mapplebeck had stood out, and he had had so many narrow escapes he had seemed indestructible. 'There are few of the early pilots,' wrote Strange, 'whose loss was felt as deeply as his.'

Operational experience was also a requisite for appointment to command a squadron, but Allen saw this rule being manipulated to give preference to favourites at home. 'People who've done very little operational time are being promoted immediately to flight commander, and after a couple of trips over the lines are being sent home to form new squadrons.' This was galling for a man like Allen, who had pressed for a return to the front line but could not be appointed to a squadron while in France. Even if these men were outstanding, he reasoned, surely it would be better to put them in charge of an existing squadron rather than expect them to form and train a new one from scratch.

Allen was also critical of the amount of flying the squadrons were required to do that winter, with several reconnaissances daily, often when the weather was not really fit, two or three machines on artillery ranging, and two or three bomb raids a week. It was right to maintain the offensive spirit, as Trenchard demanded, and it looked good in the summary of work; but it seemed to Allen that flying time was often being amassed with an eye to the summary alone. Reconnaissances often took off as soon as possible after dawn, and, with myopic regularity, followed a well-worn route, inviting interception. Bombs were dropped for the sake of bombing something. 'Wouldn't we have done better to husband our resources?' asked Allen.

It was not until January 1916 that the Fokkers 'really took the game up seriously and made our lives unbearable', according to Lieutenant H.B.R. Rowell (later knighted after a career in shipbuilding): he arrived on 8 Squadron in October. Nevertheless Allen recorded that by Christmas 1915 his original group of pilots, four to a flight, had been replaced three times over. Forty-nine RFC pilots and observers were lost in action in the last two months of the year, partly owing to the standard of the replacements, who usually arrived with no more than twenty hours' solo flying, often less, and who displayed a woeful lack of flying expertise. They had no idea how to avoid trouble, or how to extricate themselves when they got into it, only underlining the case for a period of consolidation.

Experienced crews, too, were needlessly over-exposed, often in atrocious weather, leading to gaps not easily filled. Lieutenant H.W. 'John' Medlicott, of 2 Squadron, one of the few genuine 'aces' so far, had five victories, three in a Bristol Scout and two in a BE2c;

with him on 10 November 1915 as observer was Lieutenant Arthur Whitten Brown, almost equally experienced. They were on a reconnaissance to Valenciennes when their escort lost them in a snowstorm: typically, they continued with their mission. By all accounts it was absurd weather for such a long reconnaissance to be attempted, but after ten blank days urgent orders had come through from wing headquarters to get the job done. Under fire, they were eventually forced to crash-land, and Brown, having already sustained a bullet wound, was badly hurt as they crashed. Both men survived as prisoners, but Brown spent many months in hospital. They had prepared themselves well for escape in case of capture, but Brown had to give up the idea. Medlicott made several attempts, only to be shot dead with another escaper in the last of them, in May 1918. Brown lived to navigate John Alcock, in 1919, on the first direct air crossing of the Atlantic.

11

SCRAPS WITH BOELCKE AND
IMMELMANN: McCUDDEN AND
PORTAL AS OBSERVERS:
HARVEY-KELLY AGAIN

INSULATED though they were from the carnage in the trenches, news of the death of erstwhile comrades at the front upset them almost as much as the daily recital of fellow pilots and observers missing or killed, and this stimulated their resolve. When an aeroplane did not return there was always hope, postponing or alleviating shock. Pilot and/or crew might well have survived to be taken prisoner. Most such incidents occurred out of sight over enemy territory. Crashes on the aerodrome were not infrequent and could be nasty, but more often than not they were survived. Even when German infantrymen fell wounded or killed during bombing and strafing there was something impersonal about it. This protective cocoon, though, could be rudely sundered, as Allen found on a long reconnaissance in the middle of the battle. He had crossed the lines just south of Albert on his way home and was looking at the statue of the Virgin on the church when a German two-seater dived to the ground in front of him. He noted the spot where it crashed and was sent out afterwards with a mechanic to land nearby and guard the wreck until a ground party arrived. Artillery and a Gunbus were sharing the credit. A crowd had gathered round the wreck and there had already been some souvenir hunting, but Allen recovered most of it. 'I just glanced at the bodies,' he wrote. 'The two poor Huns were riddled with bullets and one was horribly mutilated. I felt most awfully sorry for the poor devils . . . I don't think I will forget the sudden glimpse of that machine crashing through the air . . . When I tried to shave on my return my hand shook so much that I nearly had to give it up.'

Allen was pained to see that whereas the national papers summed up the work of the bombing squadrons in the Loos battle in a couple of lines, they gave colourful accounts of the depredations of the Fokkers. It was bad for morale, as were many of the rumours and counter-rumours from home. He heard of one raw pilot in No. 4 Squadron who sighted three hostiles on his first trip over the lines and at once headed for home. 'They say he is now in bed with nervous prostration and has acquired a bad stutter. I'm not surprised. Officers come out here with an exaggerated idea of Hun frightfulness and not having much experience sometimes get a bit panicky.'

Propaganda excesses at home left the front-line flyers sceptical: they had a healthy respect for the Hun, with whom a chivalrous enmity was still being maintained. When Allen heard, as he later did, that some of his crews had survived to be taken prisoner, the first tidings, in at least one instance, came in a message dropped on the aerodrome by the enemy.

Allen had learned to fly at Hendon in 1912, graduated on the first course at CFS, joined 3 Squadron under Brooke-Popham in January 1913, flown to France with the armada on 13 August 1914, and remained until January 1915, when he was injured in a crash. He managed to get himself posted back to reconnaissance work in France three months later and thence to 8 Squadron as a flight commander under Lionel Charlton; but his health broke down again in March 1916 (he was then twenty-five). After running a training squadron in Scotland he was appointed to develop major training schemes overseas as senior staff officer, first in Canada and later in Texas. The Canadian scheme had first been examined by 'Pregnant Percy' – Lieutenant-Colonel C.J. Burke – in 1915, but it was not until 1917, under the pressures of expansion, that a school was established in Canada. More than 4,000 pilots were trained under these schemes, and Allen, on his return to England, was awarded the Air Force Cross.

When Willie Read returned to France in June 1915 to join No. 5 Squadron (Avros and BE2c's) as a flight commander, he had virtually commandeered the squadron's only Bristol Scout, which he christened 'Priscilla'. And when, in mid-December, he was posted home a second time, he announced that he 'must have one more go with Priscilla'. The two enemy machines that he intercepted returned his fire, penetrating his fuel tank, and he only just got back. It was nearly the end of Priscilla, if not of Read, who left for home next day with a Military Cross for 'conspicuous gallantry on several occasions'. 'It was an easily won MC,' he said, 'as I could not recall any conspicuous gallantry.' This was typical of Read. Next time he returned to France he would be commanding a squadron.

The fraternisation of the first Christmas of the war was frowned on as liable to weaken resolve and was discouraged in 1915, but there was tacit agreement to do no more that day than go through the motions. 'Only three machines from 8 Squadron [BE2c's] left the ground,' recorded Robin Rowell, who led them. 'I wandered over the lines just to see that all was quiet, when Brother Bosche started firing at us with anti-aircraft guns.' But the firing, like the flying, was more festive than furious. 'These three machines were then seen to turn round towards the lines and fly homewards in a series of loops and other stunts,' recorded a witness. 'Archie stopped firing at once, and loud cheers were heard from both sides of Nomansland.'

It was the BE2c crews, partly because they were still the most numerous, who suffered worst at the hands of the Fokkers, and indeed the German pilots seemed intent on picking them off. Thus they became known as Fokker fodder. The best way of countering the Fokker's advantage of having synchronised guns firing forward through the propeller arc became a subject of lively debate among the Blériot crews.

Four days after Christmas, as they walked out to their machines to look for enemy reinforcement activity between Cambrai and St Quentin, two of the best pilots on 8 Squadron found themselves in disagreement. 'If a Fokker dives on you,' said Scotsman David

Glen, 'the best thing to do is to fly straight on. That's the only way to give your observer a chance.' Glen's observer had already shot down a Fokker using these tactics, which gave weight to what Glen said. But his companion, Sholto Douglas, another Scot, while admiring Glen's nerve, was far from convinced. 'I prefer to turn in underneath them. Your method may work against the rank and file, but you wouldn't stand a chance against men like Boelcke and Immelmann.' The adulation heaped on these two men in Germany had become well known.

The air was clear, but from 6,500 feet they could spot no special activity, they had seen no enemy planes, and they were not far short of the limit of their reconnaissance when they saw six tiny, thin black lines suspended in the sky in the direction of Douai. The *Eindecker* was notoriously difficult to spot, especially head on, but Glen and Douglas saw them simultaneously. 'I was thoroughly frightened', said Douglas afterwards, 'and I longed to turn and run for it. We were outnumbered by six to two, and it might have seemed prudent to turn back, but then we would have failed to complete our task and the German scout machines would have achieved their object. Someone else would only have had to try again later.'

As he kicked the rudder and thrust the stick hard over to port, turning towards and under the attack, Douglas saw Glen bravely holding his course. When he straightened out, four of the Fokkers were pulling out of the dive, but two others were hurtling downwards, whether in pursuit of Glen or having been hit he could not tell. Then, far below him, he saw Glen's BE2c spiralling down in flames.

The four remaining Huns were now turning to him. 'In the heat of the fight I was too busy to feel frightened. Mostly I felt angry, furious with these Huns who were undoubtedly trying to kill me. There was only one thing to do, and that was to kill them first.'

As Douglas turned and dived underneath his attackers he heard the racket of the Lewis gun immediately above his head and smelt the choking stench of cordite. Then his observer, James Child, waved excitedly and pointed to one of the Fokkers. 'I've got him!' Douglas looked up just in time to see another Fokker pull up in front of him in a steep climb prior to beginning a loop. 'At the top of the loop he seemed to twist on to one side, reverse his direction, and come straight for me. Immelmann!'

The man who had executed that spectacular manoeuvre was indeed Max Immelmann. And one of the pilots who now sought to finish Douglas off, as he afterwards learned, was Oswald Boelcke.

Douglas's mad, writhing helter-skelter to get back to safety prostrated his gunner with sickness, leaving them easy meat for the Fokkers. Douglas – and his pursuers – thought Child was dead. But Douglas's fear of his plane breaking up was less than his fear of being shot down, and he went on rough-handling his machine in desperation. As the Fokkers attacked in succession, one of the German pilots – in fact it was Boelcke – came in so close Douglas could almost feel the bullets spraying into his back. Boelcke had indeed fired at point-blank range, only for his guns to fail. He had run out of ammunition.

As the Fokkers forced him nearer the ground, Douglas feared his loss of height and therefore manoeuvrability would prove fatal. But making a virtue of necessity, he sacrificed his last 300 feet or so, letting the plane fall out of the sky for the sake of the protection he hoped he might get from the ground itself. Now they could not execute their favourite diving attack without flying straight in.

For a moment, thinking their adversary was about to land, Boelcke and Immelmann chivalrously held off. Or that was how it seemed. Then Child, recovering now they were flying more or less straight and level, surprised Immelmann with a burst that seemed to come from a corpse, forcing him to retire to 1,000 feet.

Douglas was still about ten miles from safety when one of the Fokkers overtook him in a shallow dive, banked steeply, and turned back towards him on a collision course. Again it was Boelcke. His aim was to flush the BE2c up like a pheasant, where Immelmann and the remaining Fokker pilots would be waiting for it. But Douglas's hunch was that the instinct of self-preservation that demanded he hold his course would force Boelcke to break off.

With the slower flying speeds of the time, a collision course was not a sudden moment of involuntary terror but a deliberate span of hypnotic tension. Both men were under a spell which might lock them into immobility until it was too late. The ultimate moment seemed almost to have passed when Boelcke broke off.

The Germans kept up the chase until Douglas was within a mile of the front line. Then they gave up. Soon afterwards Douglas's engine seized and he landed in the middle of a gun battery south of Arras.

Douglas described his escape as his most hair-raising experience of the war, and the story made the headlines at home, embarrassingly so as it was written up by an Army Intelligence officer who knew very little about flying. Trenchard was to blame for this, for not appointing an RFC Press liaison officer to ensure accurate reporting.

The German Air Force were said to be out of sympathy with the 'playing fields' attitude attributed to RFC men, the outlook of their own pilots being presented as fearless but clinical. They did not see air combat as some superior form of school sports. Boelcke's comments on the Douglas incident, however, seem at variance with this view. He saw it as a fine fight and a 'joyous scrap'.

Of the two pusher types, the Vickers Gunbus and the FE2b, the Gunbus was effective at first, but its origins dated back to 1912, and it was too limited in speed and ceiling to stand up to the Fokker, while there was still only one flight of FE2b's at the front for the Battle of Loos. In time the FE2b's were to work out a method of frustrating their attackers by forming a defensive circle, but the Gunbus was soon to be withdrawn from the front. It was powered by the 100 h.p. Gnome Monosoupape, which behaved erratically in the Gunbus, as the experience of an eighteen-year-old named Oscar Greig confirms. Commissioned in May 1915, he arrived in France in July with fifteen hours solo on the Gunbus and, like many other eighteen- and nineteen-year-olds of his era, under twenty hours in all. Whereas most of the pilots who fought and flew in 1914 and early 1915, young though they were, had attained maturity, most of those now arriving at the front had come straight from school via the training stations and were little more than schoolboys. Yet with their physical and mental vitality they were ideal recruits to the air war. Theirs was the age group notorious for risking life and limb on motor-bikes, and their contempt for death made them formidable fighters. Unfortunately, because of the demand for expansion at all costs, they were inadequately trained and poorly served by their machines, and often by their seniors.

Again and again young Oscar Greig had to return to base with a dud engine, but his persistence soon earned the respect of his fellows, and his extreme youth was more apparent when he put pen to paper. 'The major has sent in my name for a decoration,' he recorded. 'I do hope I get it. It would please Mummy so. Anyhow it would be topping!' But he had been in action barely a month when he had a cylinder blow, and this was the beginning of a loss of confidence. In October he got into a horrific spin from high level, and although the Gunbus eventually came out after falling for many thousands of feet, both Greig and his observer were left with shattered nerves. Soon afterwards a sensitive commanding officer, recognising good material when he saw it, posted them home for a rest. Greig's observer went on to pilot training, and Greig became an instructor, to return to France in 1917 for a short and unpleasant spell on FE2b's.

Another newcomer in the same month was an army despatch rider who had applied successfully for transfer to observer, RFC. This was Charles 'Peter' Portal, who was to become the most distinguished of all chiefs of air staff after Trenchard, holding that appointment from 1940 to 1945. Although 22, he qualified under the motor-bike test: despatch riders were notorious for speeding. When he reported to No. 3 Squadron (Morane Parasols) at Auchel he had never been in an aeroplane nor seen a Lewis gun, but he had learnt the morse code, and as a despatch rider he could read a map. No doubt this was why, posted to A Flight, he was at once selected to observe for the new flight commander, Captain T. O'B. Hubbard. Or perhaps, since 'Mother' Hubbard, as he was inevitably dubbed, seemed too gentle a character for the role, had only just arrived, had only once flown a Morane, and had crashed it at that, Portal was ripe to be sacrificed. He soon learned that the Morane was treated by pilots with great respect: the old hands assured him, just to cheer him up, that he had much more chance of being killed by a Morane than by the enemy.

Portal was disappointed that no one attempted to instruct him in his squadron duties. He would have much to say on the subject of training. But Hubbard did tell him to find out how to work a Lewis gun. 'We'll do the early tactical reconnaissance', he said, 'the day after tomorrow.' Portal spent several hours dismantling and reassembling the Lewis and learning how to clear stoppages, only to be told when the time came that the Morane couldn't carry both him and the gun. He did the tactical recce with a stripped rifle and a hundred rounds of ammunition.

On this first flight with Hubbard, the 80 h.p. Le Rhone engine kept missing, the Archie was alarmingly accurate, and Portal confessed to being 'very afraid'. Yet he soon became inured to the Archie. Unlike the BE2c, the Morane had to be 'flown' every minute, but Portal soon realised that Hubbard, for all his gentle nature, was an excellent pilot, while the observer's position behind the pilot made the Morane superior to the BE2c as a fighting machine, with some pretensions to defending itself from stern attack. The main drawback, as Portal saw, was that few of the observers really understood the Lewis gun – another black mark against training.

When a Morane was shot down by Immelmann over Valenciennes, three more were sent off together for mutual protection. Portal was allotted to Harvey-Kelly, by this time with 3 Squadron as a flight commander, and he persuaded H-K to let him mount a Lewis. The second Morane, whose observer also carried a Lewis, managed to reach the briefed height of 10,000 feet, but H-K and Portal could get no higher than 8,000. The third Morane, which held Jimmy McCudden, now a sergeant observer on C flight, staggered along behind them at 6,000. McCudden, with fantasies of flaming Fokkers, had packed not only a Lewis but also enough ammunition for a brace of dog-fights. Tight lateral formations were in any case considered unsafe because of the risk of collision, several hundred feet often separating one machine from another; here the height separation made mutual protection impossible. But H-K was not a man to turn back. Immelmann duly appeared and was recognised by his antics, and he attacked the top Morane, leaving McCudden and

Portal, for all their obvious potential, impotent. But the unknown observer drove Immelmann off.

In November 1915 Captain Edgar Ludlow-Hewitt, whose work with the artillery as a flight commander on No. 1 Squadron had been outstanding, assumed command of No. 3 Squadron on promotion to major, and for his observer he chose McCudden. An application for pilot training had been made by McCudden in July, but he had been told he was too valuable as an observer. Yet he knew a safe pilot when he saw one, and he developed a great admiration for Ludlow-Hewitt 'for his coolness under fire – not batting an eyelid when shells burst around him continually.' McCudden, although he had done a lot of flying as corporal and sergeant observer, had not, it seems, yet acquired this degree of serenity. 'As for myself, I was in a terrible state of funk.' If this was true, it clearly did not affect his performance. More revealing of his character was his admission that he 'didn't much care for the dashing, extrovert type of pilot; all right for him but not much good for the passenger.' (He had been flying earlier with Harvey-Kelly.) But the more he flew with Ludlow-Hewitt, the more intensely he disliked flying with anyone else.

Many of Harvey-Kelly's contemporaries were now commanding squadrons, and H-K appears to have been passed over because of his unpredictability: his exploits, and his manner of relating them, had become legendary. 'The funniest man I've ever met,' was the opinion of Archibald James. 'He kept one in roars of laughter the whole time.'

Many of H-K's stories were told against himself. On leave from France, he failed to report back at the due time. Orders sent to various leave addresses in England and Ireland went unacknowledged, and hotels and bars in London where RFC men congregated were combed unsuccessfully. When he eventually turned up at the War Office he followed his combat philosophy: get your blow in first. He flung a sheaf of telegrams and letters on the table and demanded to know how the hell he could go to all these places at once. He added that he was already fed up with England and wanted nothing more than to be sent back to the war. As usual he got away with it; but it may have delayed his promotion to squadron commander. This came, with No. 3 Squadron, in the New Year.

The enforced delay to the development of McCudden's career was ended in January 1916, when Ludlow-Hewitt unselfishly granted his wish to be sent home on a pilot's course. Now twenty, he had already been awarded the MC and the Croix de Guerre. His elder brother, Flight Sergeant William, had been killed instructing in March 1915, but a younger brother, John Anthony, had applied for a transfer from despatch riding to the RFC. Jimmy was back as a pilot in time for the Somme battle that summer.

12

AGENTS AND PIGEON FANCIERS:
A SPY IN THE MOTOR TRADE

BEFORE the two warring armies became entrenched, secret agents had little difficulty in passing from one side to the other, to gather information, and to report back. But as the front line consolidated, and parallel trenches were dug in close proximity, crossing the strip of neutral earth known as no man's land became perilous. At a conference attended by the three RFC wing commanders at Trenchard's headquarters shortly before the Battle of Loos, Trenchard told them he had a job for them, specially requested by GHQ. They wanted him to send an aeroplane to land behind the German lines, dropping an agent at a secret rendezvous near Courtrai. The agent's mission, it was stressed, had an important bearing on the forthcoming battle. 'The French have already done this sort of thing 28 times,' Trenchard told them, '27 times successfully.' The wing commanders would love to have known what had happened the twenty-eighth time, but they knew that Trenchard would never say no to an earnest request from the Army, and they were not disposed to argue, especially when they learned they would not have to despatch a second aeroplane to pick the agent up afterwards – an altogether trickier assignment. He would be armed with carrier pigeons who would home back to GHQ with his reports. When his task was finished – if he survived it – he would work his way back, normally through Holland or Belgium.

The task was allotted to No. 6 Squadron, the pilot chosen being one of the contemptibles who had crossed the Channel with 4 Squadron and, by nursing his aircraft right through the retreat, rightly gained a reputation for reliability and resource. He had force-landed his machine many times in ticklish situations but never broken it, though it had sometimes needed running repairs, which he had performed single-handed before taking off again, just the sort of coolness under pressure that might be required. This was the 25-year-old Captain T.W. Mulcahy-Morgan, formerly of the Royal Irish Fusiliers, and few could match his record. His brief was to land the agent, name of Van de Leene, at dawn on the edge of a village known to the agent, a suitable field being indicated adjacent to a wood, into which the agent would beat a hasty retreat.

The chosen field turned out to be small and enclosed by trees. Even in the slow and stable BE2c the glide before landing had to be judged to a nicety, and at 04.45 on 13 September, twelve days before the battle opened, in the poor visibility of first light, Mulcahy-Morgan had the misfortune to leave his port wing behind in a tree. Both pilot and passenger were badly hurt, Van de Leene, in the front cockpit, being saved from mortal injury by the bulky pigeon basket he carried in front of him. He broke both legs and suffered internal injuries, while Mulcahy-Morgan broke his jaw. The pigeons survived unhurt. First on the scene were some friendly civilians, who seized and secreted papers and pigeons, but the two men were too badly injured to be hidden, and eventually the Germans arrived and took them prisoner.

A pilot captured at the moment of setting down his spy was liable to the death penalty. The spy would be shot for sure. And when they were interrogated, in hospital in Courtrai, their chances looked bleak. But threats were accompanied by the usual blandishments – the more help they gave, the better would be the prospects of leniency. Mulcahy-Morgan got the impression that things weren't going too badly for Van de Leene, who he guessed was probably being 'turned' – if he wasn't a double agent already. His own position looked the more precarious, and he took refuge in his broken jaw, feigning dumbness, and got away with it. Five days later another agent sent back news of the crash, and of the safe custody of papers and pigeons.

After two years in captivity Tom Mulcahy-Morgan escaped, returning to England in April 1917. He was awarded the MC and Bar.

The first successful spy-dropping attempt by the RFC was made a fortnight later, on 28 September, the pilot being Captain G.L. Cruikshank of 3 Squadron, the machine a Morane Parasol. Guy Cruikshank, aged twenty-five, and a Cambridge graduate, was also one of the contemptibles, highly regarded by Trenchard and already holding the MC. Thanks to Cruikshank the drop was a model of its kind and he was awarded the DSO. But the third of these adventures, five days later, was anything but trouble-free. The pilot this time was Lieutenant J.W. 'Jack' Woodhouse, of 4 Squadron; even at twenty-seven he passed the motor-bike test, having before the war won over a hundred British and Continental motor-cycle events including the International Race at Le Mans.

Woodhouse seems to have had by far the most meticulous preparation of the three. At a conference in the office of his CO, Charles Longcroft, at which a number of staff officers were present, large-scale maps were produced and various landing fields considered. This time the drop was to be made at dusk, so that the agent could escape in darkness, although for Woodhouse this meant a night landing back at base.

Over a period of several days Woodhouse made a number of flights to memorise landmarks, while light bombing took place simultaneously so that his familiarisation flights should not be conspicuous. The agent, a middle-aged French ex-army NCO named Le Marrier, tough, gregarious and immensely popular, arrived in time to get to know Woodhouse, not to mention the whole of the Sergeants' Mess, where he was accommodated before the drop, a security risk that accorded ill with the otherwise secretive preparations. Then at last, with tanks half full and the BE2c stripped of all impedimenta to improve its climbing rate and reduce landing and take-off runs, Le Marrier squeezed his swollen bulk (plain clothes underneath French uniform, one pigeon basket on his lap and a second strapped to the wing, pockets bulging with personal gear and a large bottle of Sergeants' Mess wine), into the front cockpit and Woodhouse climbed to 7,000 feet and waited for dusk.

Descending to 1,000 feet, they were approaching their recommended field when they saw lights and heard the crack of a rifle, and Woodhouse instinctively opened up and started to climb. He decided to give Le Marrier the chance to abort, but Le Marrier shook his head and pointed north, where an alternative field was located, alongside a wood like the first, about eight miles south of Cambrai. As dusk fell, and with a ground mist aiding concealment, Woodhouse made an even more silent approach than he had planned, his switched-off engine failing to pick up as intended just before landing, but the touch-down was smooth and the run short. He helped Le Marrier out of his cockpit with his many accoutrements and waved him off towards the wood. So heavily laden was Le Marrier that he dropped one of his baskets of pigeons and didn't notice it at first, then had to turn back to retrieve it. Meanwhile Woodhouse had set the throttle, switched on, and swung the propeller. He had prepared the tail skid to hold the ground as firmly as possible when the plane started to move; but now the engine, over-rich from the windmilling descent, backfired.

Woodhouse switched off, opened the throttle fully, and started to turn the propeller backwards to clear the surplus petrol that had accumulated during the descent. Suddenly he was shocked to see a figure emerging from the wood, coatless and empty-handed: he was considerably relieved to recognise Le Marrier, who had seen his pilot's predicament and come back to help. He tried to grab the propeller, but Woodhouse, anxious not to be found in the company of a spy, chased him off. 'He laughed,' said Woodhouse afterwards, 'but I don't think I did.' After pulling the prop backwards a few more times Woodhouse sat down for a rest. At last, after he had stuffed his gloves into the air intake for the 'suck in' sequence, he again swung the prop and this time the engine fired. He scrambled back into the cockpit as the machine moved forward.

It was now pitch dark, the engine was missing badly, and soon he had to land again, fortunately in a level, deserted area. After running the engine in short bursts to burn out the surplus oil he got off again, and the engine behaved rather better, but he was hopelessly lost. When he was sure he had crossed the lines he put the machine into the slowest possible glide, lit a cheroot to steady his nerves, and waited for the bump, hoping to see enough at the last moment to flatten out. The landing was heavy and the machine came to a halt on its nose, but only the propeller was damaged. He had been away nearly two-and-a-half hours.

'I consider,' wrote Brancker, commanding Third Wing, 'that Lieutenant Woodhouse deserves very high commendation.' For this and other stirring exploits, he too was awarded the DSO.

Selection for the task of dropping agents was haphazard at first, though some preparation was given. Sergeant Sidney Attwater, a skilled toolmaker and A.V. Roe apprentice from Preston who had inevitably been enlisted as an air mechanic, had graduated to air observer and finally, after training, to pilot on FE2d's (250 h.p. Rolls-Royce engine). 'I received orders to report one morning at 2 a.m. to my flight commander,' he recorded. It was a perfect moonlit night, and he had to do three night landings without flares, which he accomplished safely. Next day he was sent on a trial run in daylight to a small German aerodrome, and on the next moonlit night he was introduced in the CO's office to a French agent. At 01.15 'Monsieur Victor' boarded the FE2d with a large basket containing pigeons, ammunition, money etc., which was duly affixed to the starboard wing. He also carried an old-fashioned string bag which he revealed was full of dainties and gifts for his wife and family. Spies were generally natives of the district they were being dropped in, with special knowledge of the country, more often than not civilians, but 'Monsieur Victor' wore French uniform, and Attwater noted with some disquiet the number 13 on his cap. 'How are you going to get away after I've landed you?' asked Attwater. This was not answered until after the landing, when the agent asked to be taxied to a wood at one end of the aerodrome. 'Turn round ready for take-off,' said Monsieur Victor, 'and wait for another agent to come back with you.' Attwater agreed to wait for a minute or so. 'I was getting a bit windy', he admitted, 'by the time he arrived.' To Attwater's alarm, the replacement let off a few rounds at a solitary hangar as Attwater prepared to take off. There had evidently been some answering fire, as he later found several bullet-holes in the FE2d. But to Attwater's enquiry about the fate of Monsieur Victor, the reply was: 'It is impossible for him to be caught.' There is some evidence that these two agents were identical twins, working a familiar deception. Attwater rated these agents 'the most courageous men in the war'.

Once the agents had despatched their reports back to GHQ by pigeon post, a re-supply operation was required to furnish them with more pigeons. How were these pigeons to be dropped? A pilot named Edward Pennell was assigned to the task of concentrating on methods of pigeon dropping. Reflecting that it was pigeons themselves which generally did the dropping, he braced himself to become the first of the pigeon droppers.

In conjunction with an unnamed airman from Hartlepool, who was an expert on homing pigeons, and an air mechanic named Callender, Pennell began his experiments. The valuable homing pigeons had to be settled at GHQ so they would return there, and they could not in any case be risked on practice drops, so the barns in nearby farms were scoured for wood pigeons. Two of these pigeons, each wearing a tiny harness, were tied together with a six-foot cord, on the principle that when tethered and released they would fly against each other and gradually descend to the ground. In practice the unfortunate birds became hopelessly entangled and died. A better method was evolved, using the same principle, in which four pigeons were placed in separate compartments in a rectangular metal box fitted in the bomb rack under the fuselage, with doors opening earthwards. When the release cable was pulled by the pilot, the doors opened, the pigeons fell out individually, flew off in different directions, and, being tethered, slowly fluttered to the ground.

The operation was to take place in daylight when there was good cloud cover interspersed with clear patches: on crossing the line, Pennell was to climb above the cloud, fly for a given time on a prearranged compass course allowing for drift, descend through a clear patch on estimated time of arrival, and look for six large hay or straw stacks in a field which would also contain a herd of black and white cows. After releasing the pigeons at the lowest height consistent with safety, Pennell was to seek cloud cover again as quickly as possible.

Cruising around at 5,000 feet on ETA, Pennell searched for a break in the cloud. 'I had now got the wind-up pretty badly,' he said afterwards: he was expecting the whole German Air Force to be waiting to pounce. Diving through a convenient gap, throttling down as he did so, he circled at 1,000 feet, looking for hay stacks and cows, but there was nothing to be seen. It suddenly occurred to him that his chances of finding his target must be hundreds to one, and that a protracted search would give the whole show away as well as attract opposition. It was not long before he turned for home. When the pigeons were offloaded back at base it was found that the cold and perhaps the height had been too much for them; half were dead.

Another attempt a week later, when the pigeons were actually dropped, was no more successful, the agent reporting that they mostly died before reaching the ground. For the next attempt the pigeons were fitted with small parachutes, but it was no more successful.

As the number of agents proliferated, a special flight of four BE2c single-seaters was formed by Guy Cruikshank under Biffy Borton of 27 Squadron to land them at chosen rendezvous, the agent being strapped to the lower wing, close to the fuselage, shielded by a strip of three-ply wood. The front cockpit was simply faired over. After Woodhouse's experience the timing of the drop reverted to early morning, with the pilot taking off shortly before dawn. Successful drops were made, but after an occasion when pilot and machine failed to return, suspicion fell on the agent, and Cruikshank decided to take the next flight himself, fully prepared for skulduggery. Immediately he landed, the agent turned a gun on him and fired, but Cruikshank was quick enough to get in a single shot which proved fatal for the agent. Although wounded in the arm, Cruikshank brought the plane back safely and with it the revelation of the agent's treachery.

By 1916 a Special Duty Flight, now transferred to Headquarters

Wing under Cyril Newall, was formed by Jack Woodhouse, Cruikshank having been appointed a flight commander on 70 Squadron (Sopwith 1½-strutters). Meanwhile Woodhouse had greatly augmented his night-flying experience by attacking raiding Zeppelins while based at Dover. As before, the job was to drop spies behind the German lines, but this time by parachute, 'much more pleasant for the pilot,' wrote Woodhouse, 'but I suspect rather dicey for the spy.' The parachute selected was of the C.G. Spencer type, the one used by observers in kite balloons, and it was carried in a casing under the fuselage. The agent wore a harness which was attached to the parachute by a line: when he jumped his weight pulled the parachute from its casing and it opened immediately and automatically. Or so the agent was assured.

Woodhouse, flying a BE12a (a single-seater with 140 h.p. RAF engine), carried the agent very much as in the BE2c, lying flat on the strengthened wing. But shortly before he was due to jump, the agent would naturally peer down into the darkness to try to recognise the dropping area. On one occasion the agent, transparently doubtful of Woodhouse's navigation, stood up reluctantly when alerted, steadied himself in the airstream by gripping the side of the cockpit, and stamped about uncertainly on the wing, showing a marked reluctance to leave. Woodhouse had already throttled back, they were barely above stalling speed, the fellow's movements were upsetting stability, and soon control would be lost and they would spin in. 'I had to help him to make up his mind,' was Woodhouse's masterpiece of understatement. He had the man on his conscience afterwards and was relieved to hear some time later that his reports were duly arriving.

When there were no agents to drop or to supply, Woodhouse was employed in bombing specially selected targets from a level impossible in daylight. This, with the agent-dropping, meant a lot of night flying, and as landing behind the lines was not involved any more he chose to fly with full tanks and cruise about waiting for dawn to find his base aerodrome. Returning early one morning with a French cheroot stuck in his mouth, he found Colonel Newall sitting on a shooting stick waiting for him and his report. 'Smoking in open cockpits was definitely not done,' recorded Woodhouse later, 'but the future chief of the air staff never turned a hair.'

For the agents themselves, the actual descent was only the beginning, their fate often depending on an accurate drop. The use of parachutes introduced an assumption of pinpoint accuracy which it was not always possible to achieve. And however remote the rendezvous, there was always the danger that the passage overhead of an aeroplane would alert ground observers. The facility with which agents merged into the background on the enemy side of the lines, and passed back their reports, is explained by the fact that they were mostly operating in home territory that had been overrun by the Germans but remained friendly to the Allied cause.

This certainly helped another agent dropper, Claude Ridley, of 60 Squadron, to 'do a Mapplebeck' during the Somme battle, when he force-landed with engine trouble with his passenger still on board. The agent told Ridley to hide in a ditch, disappeared, and returned with civilian clothing and money, after which Ridley had to shift for himself. 'I am a British officer trying to escape,' he told any locals he met. 'Will you help me?' They always did. Challenged aboard a tram, he punched his way clear and jumped, crossed an electrified fence at the Belgian frontier, and arranged his own passage back into France, bringing with him much useful Intelligence. Welcomed back at 60 Squadron, he was awarded the DSO.

Some years after the war, Jack Woodhouse renewed acquaintance, quite by chance, with a man in the motor trade against whom he had raced at Brooklands pre-war. 'It's a long time since we met,' was Woodhouse's greeting.

'Not so long as you think,' was the reply.
'Oh?' queried Woodhouse. 'How's that?'
'Do you remember a night at Auchel when you took off to drop a spy by parachute?'

All Woodhouse could remember of Auchel was of dropping a man with a shockingly untidy beard. This fellow was clean-shaven. But he went on to describe precisely what had occurred prior to take-off, even to the extent of what Woodhouse had said in his halting and indifferent French. 'Not all agents', he added, 'were Frenchmen – but keep what I've said under your hat.'

There the conversation was interrupted, leaving Woodhouse to ponder whether his old racing antagonist had been an Intelligence Officer involved in the drop, or the agent himself, minus a very untidy false beard.

1916

13

FOKKER FODDER – 'MY GOD! IT'S MURDER!': HAWKER AND 24 SQUADRON: THE LESSONS OF VERDUN

THE Allied Strategy for 1916 aimed at something far more ambitious than the costly but disappointing engagements of the previous year. At Neuve Chapelle, and again at Loos, breaches had been made in the enemy lines, but the exploitation of these breaches had been frustrated by the enemy's ability, rapidly and decisively, to draft in powerful and seemingly inexhaustible reserves. It was clear that before any deeper penetration could be achieved, those reserves must themselves be eroded. This was the objective of a joint Allied offensive planned for the summer of 1916 in which the initial breakthrough was to be made by the British, with the French following up to soak up the German reserves and inflict a crushing blow. The assault was to be preceded by a massive bombardment intended to annihilate the German first and second line trenches and open the way for the infantry. The Somme was chosen as the battleground because the Allied armies could fight there side by side: this was at the insistence of the French, whose army was double the size of the British and whose scepticism about British reliability was ingrained.

There were thirty-eight British divisions in France by January 1916, and nineteen more would have arrived by mid-summer: Haig expected to be ready to mount his assault by that time. Would the RFC be ready to play its part? It was now accepted that the role of air forces in visual and photographic reconnaissance, in spotting for and directing the artillery, and in denying these facilities to the enemy (by bombing their airfields and intercepting their intruders), was of paramount importance, and each of the four British armies now in France was supported by an RFC brigade. Each brigade had two wings, one for the corps (army co-operation) squadrons and one for the army (bombing and fighting) squadrons, and each squadron, on paper at least, was brought up to a total of eighteen machines from the previous twelve. By mid-summer, all being well, the RFC would have doubled in size in the space of nine months to twenty-six and a half squadrons, which looked impressive; but many were still equipped with the same basic BE2 machine, and not all the new squadrons were yet up to strength. Against this, the delivery in quantity of the Fokker EII, with its more powerful engine, and the EIII, with a further speed increase, in recent months had added to the disastrous inferiority from which the RFC aircraft had suffered since the introduction of the Fokker EI. The German pilots still operated almost exclusively over their own side of the lines, but Trenchard's insistence on maintaining an aggressive posture – anything else, in his book, spelt disaster – inevitably meant that whenever a penetration of any depth was attempted, either for reconnaissance or bombing, the Fokkers were waiting. No longer distributed in penny packets, they now operated in groups of three or four, and of the machines they ambushed, most were shot down and the occupants killed. As the carnage reached crisis point, Trenchard was obliged, on 14 January 1916, to issue an order whose effect was to weaken his force dramatically just at the moment when the demands made upon it seemed likely to increase.

The order began with a humiliating admission of inferiority. 'Until the RFC are in possession of a machine as good as or better than the German Fokker it seems that a change in the tactics employed becomes necessary.' Trenchard proceeded to lay down as a hard and fast rule that any machine employed on reconnaissance must be escorted by at least three fighting machines. 'These machines must be flown in close formation and a reconnaissance should not continue if any of the machines become detached.' Since it was rare for any group of aeroplanes to escape fragmentation, if only through engine trouble, this was an operational restriction of extreme severity. The ruling was to apply to both short- and long-range penetrations, and the implications of the obvious tactical reversal were acknowledged and even emphasised. 'Flying in a close formation must be practised by all pilots.' Hitherto, as already indicated, formation flying in anything like close proximity had been shunned as dangerous.

As it happened, the RFC already had in prospect the introduction of machines which it was hoped would prove as good as or better than the Fokker. These were the DH2 and the FE2b, and later the FE2d, already mentioned. Both types were designed by Geoffrey de Havilland, the Fee, as it came to be known, originating as early as 1910, and both had the open lattice-work fuselage, beam spars and bracing wires of the period. But being of the pusher type, they were not dependent on interrupter gear for firing straight ahead.

Led by Lanoe Hawker, No. 24 Squadron (DH2s), Britain's first single-seater scout squadron, arrived in France on 8 February 1916 in great excitement but was immediately absorbed in a crisis of its own. The day after their arrival, one of the flight commanders, on the first flight of a DH2 from a French airfield, got into a spin and failed to recover. Five days later, another pilot spun in, and this time the machine caught fire. It had happened before, earning the DH2 the grisly sobriquet of the 'spinning incinerator'. With the morale of his pilots, all inexperienced and nearly all under twenty-one, severely shaken, Hawker responded by taking up a DH2 and, according to his biographer, spinning it from every conceivable angle, engine on and engine off, and demonstrating how, with correct remedial action, and provided there was sufficient height, it always recovered. 'It's all right, you fellows,' he is reported to have said after landing. 'You can get the DH2 out of any spin. I have just tried it out.'[1]

The mysteries of the spin had not yet been solved, and Hawker's discovery – on the face of it – was a momentous one. Apparently his pilots 'gathered eagerly around . . . while he explained the correct manoeuvres until they all understood them clearly . . . Out they all went to follow his example.' But what these manoeuvres were is not

1 Hawker, Tyrrel M., *Hawker VC* (The Mitre Press, 1965).

specified, nor was the discovery publicised, which seems inconceivable. Another pilot on Hawker's squadron is said to have been the first man to stunt a DH2, but neither man was mentioned when an investigation into spinning and those who solved its secrets was later published (see Chapter 18).

Within its limitations the DH2 was to prove an agile little single-seater, wonderfully manoeuvrable, almost capable of turning on the proverbial sixpence. But its time was not yet. The first bulk delivery of the two-seater FE2b's, too, with its spacious front cockpit in which the observer could move about freely and enjoy a wide field of fire, aft over the top planes and in a wide arc ahead and abeam, had reached No. 20 Squadron in January, but like the DH2 it had yet to establish itself. Meanwhile, despite a marked improvement achieved by the introduction of tighter formation flying and the provision of escorts, losses mounted.

Bitter criticism of the War Office for its general failure to design and supply suitable modern machines for its air crews, and in particular of its apparent tolerance of the shortcomings of the BE2c, was shrugged off by the routine appointment of a committee. This did not divert a flamboyant, egocentric but far from uninformed ex-RNAS pilot named Noel Pemberton-Billing from pressing charges in the House of Commons of criminal negligence by RFC commanders. Pemberton-Billing had earlier distinguished himself by his brilliant planning of an RNAS bombing raid on the Zeppelin sheds at Friedrichshaven: he had since resigned his commission to stand (and be elected) as a member of Parliament, posing, with some authority, as an expert in air matters. On 22 March 1916, two years ahead of his time, he demanded the creation of a single force that would consume what he called the inertia of the RNAS and the blunders of the RFC. He particularly stressed the over-ordering of the BE2c (of which over 2,000 were built), which he claimed the pilots themselves were stigmatising as Fokker fodder. Continuing what amounted to a blistering attack on the RFC leaders, he went on to suggest that 'quite a number of our gallant officers in the Royal Flying Corps had been rather murdered than killed'. This latter calumny referred to accidents in training rather than in action, which he attributed to faulty construction. Certainly it was true that the majority of fatalities were occurring at the training stations rather than at the front.

The outcome of Pemberton-Billing's charges was a judicial inquiry, a first step on the road to amalgamation of the two air services. But its immediate impact was small. Trenchard's fury was directed at the alarmist insinuations of Fokker invincibility, which were taken up enthusiastically by sections of the Press (especially by the trenchant C.G. Grey of *The Aeroplane*), and the effect this was bound to have on the morale of his pilots. There might also, it was feared, be a knock-on effect on recruitment.

Judging from the quality and lack of experience of new pilots arriving in France, it was clear that reorganisation of the entire training programme was urgently needed, and on 16 February Trenchard sent Jack Salmond home to undertake this task. One young man, perhaps hardly typical, reporting for duty at St Omer that spring was the seventeen-year-old Cecil Lewis. There was certainly no faulting his enthusiasm. 'In those days,' he wrote later, 'I lived for the air. There was nothing in life to compare with taking a machine off the ground, wheeling away into the sky, trying turns, spirals, dives, stalls, gliding, zooming, doing all the stunts a pilot needs to give him confidence and nerve in a tight corner.'[1] But he recognised that as yet he was hopelessly ill-equipped for action. Even after being given a BE2c, told to regard it as his own, and to do all the flying he wanted, he confessed a day or so later that his total flying time was fourteen hours. 'It's absolutely disgraceful to send pilots overseas with so little flying,' he was told by his flight commander at St Omer. 'You don't stand a chance.' Perhaps his obvious youth had aroused his mentor's pity. 'I'll speak to the major and try and keep you here for a bit . . . another 50 hours and you might be quite decent, but 14! My God, it's murder!' In two quite separate contexts the same crime was being alleged.

At this time, replacement pilots were arriving at St Omer at the rate of about ten a week, an insufficient number inadequately trained. The deficiency was caused partly by the winter weather, which had

1 Lewis, Cecil, *Sagittarius Rising* (Peter Davies, 1936; Greenhill Books, 1993).

delayed and truncated training programmes, partly by an inevitable failure to fulfil over-optimistic estimates, and partly because, in the phenomenal expansion being attempted, new squadrons were being formed and sent out before they were ready. Despite Pemberton-Billings's calumnies there was in fact no shortage of volunteers, rather the reverse. '. . . to belong to the RFC in those days was to be singled out among the rest of the khaki-clad world by reason of the striking double-breasted tunic (the maternity jacket, as it was known), the wings, and the little forage cap set over one ear, but more than this by the glamour surrounding "birdmen"', wrote Cecil Lewis. 'Flying was still something of a miracle. We who practised it were thought very brave, very daring, very gallant: we belonged to a world apart.' The shortage was not of young men willing to chance their arm but of instructors, especially of men of the right calibre. Pilots sent home on rest from France were not always temperamentally suited to so specialist a task.

In those early months of 1916 the crews of the new pusher-type fighters were granted an unexpected hiatus in which to work up: on 21 February 1916, with the Fokker menace at its height, the planned Allied offensive was pre-empted by a massive German assault on a nine-mile front in north-eastern France along the banks of the Meuse, opposite the ancient French town and fortress of Verdun. The German objective was to bleed France white in a war of attrition, forcing the British to take over more and more of the line; they would deal with them later. Meanwhile they relied on the French co-operating in their own destruction by defending the fortress, for reasons of national pride, to the bitter end. Meanwhile the bulk of the German fighter force under Boelcke would be concentrated in the skies above Verdun.

In the longest and bloodiest battle of the war, repeated German assaults were met by sacrificial French resistance in what became known as the 'hell of Verdun'. Joffre, having decided to hold the fortress at all costs, placed Pétain in command on this front, and in establishing a supply route, and by frequent rotation of units, Pétain contributed decisively to the failure, despite recurring crises, of the

German assaults. These culminated in a final abortive bid on 11 July. By that time, Pétain's appeals to the British to relieve the pressure at Verdun by opening the planned campaign on the Somme had borne fruit.

For Trenchard and the RFC – and for Commandant Paul-Fernand du Peuty and the *Aviation Militaire* – the lessons of Verdun were starkly clear. Du Peuty was already sympathetic to Trenchard's doctrine of the offensive, of the absolute necessity of dominating the enemy's air space or he would dominate yours; but if he harboured any doubts, the experience of Verdun would have quelled them. To begin with, the *Aviation Militaire*, keeping on the offensive, attained a marked superiority, so much so that the Germans were forced to deploy their Fokkers to protect their air reconnaissance machines. Nevertheless the German two-seaters were sometimes able to penetrate French air space and harass French troops, leading to complaints that the only aeroplanes ever seen over the battle area were German. Weakening under intense pressure to provide protective patrols for the French infantry and artillery, du Peuty surrendered the initiative, allowing the Germans, under Boelcke, to move in quickly and bomb the ground troops, shoot them up, bomb their installations, inflict increased casualties, and generally gain the ascendancy, even to the extent of shooting down French reconnaissance machines. The more the army demanded direct air support the more the Germans dominated, both on the ground and in the air. Finally, ignoring the blandishments of the generals, du Peuty reverted to his original tactics and proved to his detractors that he had been right in the first place. Aiding him in this demonstration were new types of machine, the latest Morane and particularly the Nieuport 11 or Bébé, a single-seat V-strut sesquiplane (biplane with the upper wing-span – or wing-chord, as in this case – greater than the lower), small in size but speedy and with a good rate of climb, and with a Lewis gun on the top wing firing over the propeller arc. It was in machines of this type, superior in most respects to the Fokker, that reputations were made above the Verdun battlefield by the first clutch of French aces – notably Charles Nungesser, Jean Navarre and René Fonck. And it was in a Nieuport Bébé, one of a number received by the RFC in March 1916, that the first of the publicised British aces, Albert Ball, scored his first successes.

Meanwhile Hawker was cementing his reputation within the service as a tactician and leader, although, inhibited by the restrictions placed on squadron commanders, he rarely led his men into combat. But unlike many in his position he flew regularly, allowing one of his flight commanders to lead. Despite the numerous administrative and personnel problems involved, he found running a squadron in France much easier than he had found the working-up period at home, and he accepted that his job now was to drive and inspire. When called upon to send his pilots on risky assignments in which he had been ordered not to take part, he felt the moral authority granted by the VC and DSO ribbons on his tunic and was glad of them, and he took part when he could in order not to lose touch. He was aware that many of the orders he received from wing headquarters, especially for providing escort for deep reconnaissances designated urgent despite poor weather, resulted from insistent and sometimes unreasonable army demands which Trenchard would not deny. Above all he remained an operational pilot, improvising and inventing, popular with his own squadron and with the squadrons they were escorting, a model for every DH2 pilot, several more of whom were now arriving in France with new squadrons.

Expectations of a protracted tussle with the Fokker *Eindeckers* for supremacy did not at first materialise. With the majority of Boelcke's men engaged elsewhere, Hawker's pilots were given time to accustom themselves to the formation flying ordered by Trenchard, patrolling the lines north of the Somme. Meanwhile a second FE2b squadron, No. 25, arrived from England. Both FE squadrons, when called upon to provide escort beyond the lines, found themselves under surveillance, but when challenged they generally gave as good as they got. Often, by retaining close formation, they deterred attack altogether. They also developed the frustrating defensive tactic of forming themselves into a circle, which meant that no Fokker pilot could get on the tail of one FE2b without coming under direct fire from one or more of the others.

14

THE ARRIVAL OF BALL:
THE DEPARTURE OF IMMELMANN

B Y April, Hawker's DH2s (No. 24 Squadron) had perfected their tactics and had begun escorting reconnaissance and photographic machines beyond the lines. The Fokkers tried to get at the two-seaters, but they were confronted by the DH2s before they could do so. On 24 April, a group attack by Fokkers on five reconnaissance BE2c's was effectively repulsed by four escorting DH2s, and next day another succession of determined Fokker attacks on a reconnaissance machine was beaten off by two of Hawker's pilots. These two engagements finally confirmed that the manoeuvrability of the DH2 was more than a match for any Fokker pilot, Boelcke and Immelmann included. The Fokkers still tried to interfere, and although the DH2 also proved superior in speed, climb, and general fighting efficiency, the Fokker pilots could always escape by diving, so not many were actually shot down.

Because of the penetration attempted daily on behalf of the army, RFC losses were always greater than those of the enemy, but not a single machine was lost when under escort by Hawker's squadron. And the contrast between the massive information gleaned by the RFC, against the trickle obtained by the few enemy planes that ventured over the British lines, was immense.

Of particular value was the work of the photographic crews, who, as always, were obliged to fly straight and level while operating the camera. In the FE2b the work was done by the observer; in the BE2c, still far more numerous in this period, the observer, sitting in front of the pilot under the small centre section, top plane above, lower plane below, could see little. Thus the pilot, sitting slightly aft of the mainplanes with a fair downward view, had to operate the camera, which was clamped outside the fuselage beside him. To sight it he had to lean over the side and direct his gaze through a ball-and-crosswire finder: controlling the machine with his left hand, he then selected the area he wanted to photo, put his right arm out into the 70-knot wind, and pushed the camera handle back and forth to change the plates, pulling a ring on the end of a cord for each exposure. It was a tedious process, and, with escorting machines similarly obliged to fly straight and level to maintain protection, a hazardous one. Losses there certainly were, and at times the Fokker pilots operated with all their old panache; but in the course of four consecutive days in mid-May the whole of the enemy's trenches facing the Fourth Army – the first line, the intermediate line, and the second and third lines – over a front of more than twenty miles, were successfully photographed without any interference from the Fokkers. The Fokker threat had been repulsed, and command of the air, so essential to the forthcoming battle, had been secured.

Similarly reassuring were the dummy combats staged against a Fokker captured intact on 8 April, which revealed it as outmoded except for its interrupter gear and 500-round belt-fed machine gun. All the current machines performed well against it – except, of course, the BE2c, which 'just wasn't in it', according to one of the test pilots.

There were two especially notable personnel occurrences to report in the months before the Somme battle. On the British side it was a unique acquisition; on the German side it was a tragic depletion. First, on 18 February, the nineteen-year-old Albert Ball, described as a 'quiet, shy, simple little chap', but with a chin that suggested a stubborn, rebellious streak, arrived at No. 13 Squadron on BE2c's, where he was engaged on artillery work and occasional bombing missions. Ball not only disliked twin-seat flying, he hated being responsible for another man's life; nevertheless his aggressive potential emerged and was recognised, and on 7 May he was posted to 11 Squadron. Here the basic machine, recently replacing the Vickers Gunbus, was the FE2b, but this heterogeneous squadron also boasted three Bristol Scouts and three of the tiny Nieuport 11 single-seaters, offering Ball a taste of the aerial freedom he craved. It did not take him long to make his mark. Four days later, while flying a Bristol Scout, he scored a probable victory over an Albatros two-seater and was mentioned for the first time in an RFC communiqué, bringing his name to more general notice. It was with 11 Squadron, under the benevolent eye of his new commander, 'Mother' Hubbard, and with the help of his mechanic, F.J. Land, that he built the small wooden hut, surrounded by flowers, on the edge of the aerodrome, near the hangar where he housed the Nieuport Bébé he was now allotted, and where he lived on his own and stood immediately ready for action. It was here, too, that he delighted in lighting a magnesium flare outside his hut at night and walking round it in his pyjamas playing the fiddle. No doubt this was a contributory factor in his desire for solitude – and in the granting of it.

A practising mechanic even as a boy, Ball had volunteered for army service with the Sherwood Foresters, transferring to the RFC after learning to fly privately during the summer of 1915 – necessarily at dawn so as to be back on parade at 6 a.m. Already commissioned as a second lieutenant, he was awarded his wings on 26 January 1916 and posted to France three weeks later.

Ball is reputed never to have flown for amusement: but he neglected no opportunities for practising his stalking talents, putting the wind up many a BE2c pilot he happened to encounter on his own side of the lines. One day Lanoe Hawker, whose habit it was to make flying visits to the corps squadrons to discuss escort problems, was airborne in the only machine that could be spared, a BE2c, when he spotted a Nieuport Bébé. The pilot started stalking him at once, and Hawker, the finest of all handlers of the BE2c, thoroughly enjoyed the battle of wits that followed. Neither man knew who he was up against, but Ball, in the far superior fighting machine, could never quite attain the position he wanted and eventually conceded defeat. But he noted the BE's identification markings, and he rang up the squadron after he landed to find out who it was. He was considerably mollified to learn that it was Hawker.

Despite his quiet simplicity Ball was highly strung, and for all his eccentricities he suffered from acute nervous tension, so much so that in no time at all he asked for a rest. This unseemly request was referred to his brigade commander, none other than Josh Higgins, who noticed, while inspecting the squadron machines, that Ball's gun wasn't mounted as ordered. 'Put it lower,' ordered Higgins. 'Take it off and put it lower.' Ball had his own method of operating the gun, but he was in no mood to explain. 'Who has to fight it?' he demanded. 'You or me?' For this piece of insolence, and the premature request, he was punished by being sent back to BEs, this time on 8 Squadron.

Ball described this as a cad's trick, but he still seems to have been treated with an amused and even respectful tolerance, as someone altogether out of the ordinary, and on 27 June his first decoration, a Military Cross, was gazetted. Meanwhile Patrick Playfair, now commanding 8 Squadron, gave him plenty of interesting work, including night bombing and spy-dropping. After landing his passenger safely on one of these nocturnal spy-dropping trips he couldn't get the man to leave, so he threatened to shoot him if he didn't go at once, before they were discovered. Ball eventually 'helped' the man out of the cockpit.

Among the new FE2b pilots was an eighteen-year-old South African named G.R. McCubbin, survivor of an episode in his training that verged on the farcical. While a pupil at Joyce Green, George McCubbin force-landed his machine in the grounds of an officers' convalescent home, though without doing himself any damage that might have qualified him for admission. His machine too was undamaged, and next morning, after being entertained overnight by the nursing staff, who proved appreciative of the company of an able-bodied visitor, he took off safely but could not resist executing a few stunts in salute. Losing control, he crashed in almost the same spot as before, but this time smashed up his plane and broke a leg, qualifying for admission after all. When he joined 25 Squadron in France some time later, however, he and his observer, Corporal J.H. Waller, were responsible for the tragic depletion of enemy strength already mentioned – or so the British have always claimed. Of seven FE2b's which took off on an offensive patrol over Lens in the late evening of 18 June, two, piloted by Second Lieutenants J.R.B. Savage (leading) and McCubbin, sighted three Fokkers some distance below and immediately dived to the attack. In the mêlée that followed, the precise manoeuvres of each of the combatants remain typically obscure, but certain it is that the pilot of one of the Fokkers was Immelmann, and that he turned the tables on Savage by rolling into a steep climbing curve that brought him above and behind his target, and that Savage was mortally wounded by a burst from Immelmann's guns and dived away out of control.

Seeing that McCubbin was already seeking revenge, and aware that he was vulnerable, Immelmann broke off his attack on Savage, but too late. Corporal Waller opened fire point-blank, and the Fokker failed to recover from its dive, careering on down until it crashed. McCubbin and Waller did not know it until later, but they had removed a major threat to the supremacy Trenchard was demanding. A second FE was shot down by the other Fokkers and its crew taken prisoner, but the Eagle of Lille was dead.

The Germans could not believe that their hero had been outfought, and they attributed his last despairing dive to a defect in his interrupter gear damaging his propeller; it was a fault that had occurred before. He would not be the only 'ace' about whose death an air of mystery was to linger. The evidence appeared to be conflicting, although later it was reported that the Fokker's control wires had been shot through. More immediately, Immelmann was accorded the tribute of having a memorial wreath dropped by another South African pilot over a German aerodrome, with a message of condolence. McCubbin got the DSO and Waller the DCM.

The drawback – perhaps the folly – of according extravagant praise and publicity to a few outstanding pilots was the blow to morale when their invincibility was seen to have been illusory. This could well be why reasons other than enemy action were found for Immelmann's death, although reports of the action left the British in no doubt. The Germans decided not to risk a second similar blow, and Boelcke was withdrawn from the line.

Two of the scout squadrons attached to the Headquarters Wing under Dowding, No. 27, (flying Martinsyde G100s, which featured a much larger wing area than the S1 and a Beardmore 120 h.p. engine), and No. 60 (Moranes under Ferdy Waldron), reported no interference next day during escort work and offensive patrols. The G100, a single-seat tractor biplane designed as a long-range escort fighter, was quickly dubbed 'Elephant', or 'Jumbo', for obvious reasons, and it did not last long as a fighter. Its weight and size made it sluggish in combat, and 27 was the only complete squadron so armed. Yet Oliver Stewart, the aviation commentator, thought its good qualities were underestimated, while air mechanic C. Callender said it did 'yeoman service' as a fighter and bomber on the Somme. 'The majority of machines turned out by factories at this stage of the war', added Callender, 'were not up to standard, but many modifications and improvements were made in the field.' This was often at the behest of disgruntled pilots, and the work of the ground crews in refining and rearming unsatisfactory machines often went unsung – but not by Trenchard. 'These men,' he repeatedly emphasised, 'are the backbone of all our efforts.'

Equally remarkable was the composition of 60 Squadron, both in personnel and equipment. Old Etonian Ferdy Waldron had enlisted three more OEs as flight commanders, the senior being Bob Smith-Barry. Other squadron pilots included Peter Portal and the eighteen-year-old Harold Balfour. Each flight sported, at first, a different type of Morane Saulnier. First was the Type N monoplane, adapted from a pre-war racing machine, with a maximum speed of 90 m.p.h. at sea level and a good rate of climb. Because of its superior streamlining, the British christened it the Bullet. Second was the Type L (later LA), the first of a series of 'Parasol' monoplanes, so named because of their umbrella-like single wing. Third was the BB, a two-seater biplane otherwise resembling the Bullet. Only the Parasol, the type to which Raymond Saulnier fitted deflector plates and in which Roland Garros was captured, was much used by the French.

Trenchard was especially wary of the Bullet because of its high wing loading, high landing speed and extreme sensitivity to elevator control, but in the build-up to the Somme battle he was glad of what he could get. 'They were tricky little brutes to handle,' according to Balfour, and Mapplebeck had killed himself in one. But shortly before the battle the Parasol flight on 60 Squadron was re-equipped with them.

Meanwhile No. 3 Squadron, now commanded by Harvey-Kelly, was still flying the Parasol. 'It was a machine you could never relax in,' wrote Cecil Lewis. It needed the greatest skill and care and a light but accurate touch. 'People killed themselves on Moranes with alarming rapidity.' But it was to carry him right through the Somme battle, during which he won an MC and was mentioned in despatches. *'Good old Parasol!'* Anything he flew after that, he wrote, was child's play.

15

THE SOMME – A COMPLETE WASH-OUT: BOMBER LOSSES: A WELSH VC

ALTHOUGH the original plans for a combined offensive on the Somme had been pre-empted by the German assault on Verdun, the British for their part continued to prepare for a summer campaign, while continually under coercion from the French to act as early as possible to relieve the pressure on them. On 21 May, and again on 21 June, the situation at Verdun impelled Pétain to plead for Haig to start a diversionary action. Haig's plan was for the British Fourth Army under Rawlinson to develop his main assault on an eighteen-mile front stretching from Maricourt, north of the Somme, to Gommecourt. On Rawlinson's left, in support, was the right-hand corps of the Third Army under Allenby: nineteen British divisions in all. South of the Somme, eight French divisions were to hold a ten-mile front opposite Peronne. Opposing these armies, and holding strong positions on high ground, well protected by deep dug-outs, was the German Second Army under von Below.

Haig's plan was to subject these fortified positions to eight days of crippling bombardment beforehand, using a massive concentration of artillery on targets registered in previous weeks by air observation. Stunned and bemused, the enemy would then have to face the advance of the British infantry across no man's land. Meanwhile the RFC, in addition to its routine work, was to mount an assault on enemy kite balloons, which now stretched away 'like a palisade', it was said, on the German side of the lines (and were duplicated on the Allied side), while the bombers would aim at airfields and communications targets. Working back from a D-Day of 1 July, the bombardment was to start on 24 June. But, inconveniently, a thunderstorm on the 23rd wrought havoc to preparations, the damage being specially severe to the British kite balloons, several of which were struck by lightning and destroyed. One unfortunate crew, when their balloon was wrenched from its winch in an electric snowstorm, were blown across the lines and whirled up to 13,000 feet before being blown back and deposited safely but miraculously behind Arras. And on the 24th, although pilots flew low in order to direct the artillery, the planned opening bombardment was hindered and curtailed by rain.

Thus the softening-up barrage that was to shatter the resistance of the German front-line troops got off to a dismal start. On the 25th the RFC did well in destroying five German balloons, four by *Le Prieur* rockets attached to interplane struts and fired electrically by the pilot (the eponymous inventor was a lieutenant in the French navy). Meanwhile the barrage rose at last to an awesome crescendo, exceeding anything in military experience. Things went well again on the 26th, when the bombardment was halted for a time so that its effectiveness could be judged from air photographs, corps commanders finding this visual evidence 'of the greatest value'. Then, for four days, although the barrage continued, nearly all air work was hampered by fog.

So to 1 July, by which time the RFC's total active aeroplane strength in France had reached 421, plus over 200 in reserve at the depots and parks; this was an increase of some 150 since March. And on that first day the corps squadrons embarked for the first time on a systematic attempt to provide regular contact patrols. In previous battles, advancing troops had frequently found themselves cut off from their support, commanders sometimes being unaware of their precise whereabouts. The contact patrol, flown at heights of 500 to 1,000 feet, and lower when necessary, aimed to provide liaison between the front line and the battalion or brigade headquarters, closing the Intelligence gap. 'A pilot patrolling at low level,' wrote Cecil Lewis, 'could see the red flares which the Tommies carried and were instructed to light at different times.' The observer marked the position on the map provided, recorded the co-ordinates, and put a message in a weighted bag; the pilot then swooped low over the relevant headquarters and dropped the bag. By this method, pinpointing of the flares fixed the movements of the forward troops for the commanders hour by hour.

This was the principle of the contact patrol. It had been tried briefly but unsuccessfully during the Loos battle, and now the same understandable inhibitions on the part of the ground troops contributed to another disappointing result. For them it was against nature to reveal themselves so openly. All too often their flares remained unlit, and Cecil Lewis described the intended air co-operation on the first day as 'a complete wash-out'; indeed he saw 1 July as 'an entire failure'. There was, he wrote, 'no co-operation from the very men we were there to help'. As for the air crews, they found themselves weaving through the shells of their own guns to get the information they sought. Operating for five and six hours a day, sometimes more, for days on end, they flew so low they could soon distinguish which side was which from the colour of their uniforms. Co-operation with the ground troops improved within a day or so, the use of klaxons by aircraft proving audible and mostly translatable, but Lewis blamed the sequence of frustrations that followed on the disastrous start.

The Allied troops began to advance across no man's land at 07.30 that morning. But the plan to destroy the enemy's first and second line trenches had been only partly successful, and it was the French, whose heavy artillery was the stronger, who achieved an early success. The Germans, forewarned by the barrage, and with their natural topographical advantages, put up such a fierce resistance that the British were mown down, making minimal progress. Again and again the tidings brought back by the corps squadrons were grim. Any element of surprise had been forfeited, and the result was 57,000 casualties, among them 19,000 killed, the biggest loss ever suffered by a British army in a single day.

In the first few days of the battle the RFC also suffered serious losses, if not in quite the same proportion. It almost seemed as though

Trenchard was determined that they should. If soldiers died, so must airmen. He continued to pursue his two-pronged policy of, one, continual aggression, and two, never failing the ground forces whatever the odds. Still most numerous among the squadrons were the BE2c's (and its refinements d and e), whose crews, scarcely resting, varied long hours spent on artillery control and photography by loading up a few 20-lb bombs and heading for enemy aerodromes, railheads and sidings. Meanwhile FE2b's; Martinsyde and Morane scouts; two flights of Sopwith 1½-strutters lent by the Admiralty after an appeal from Trenchard, the first two-seater to mount a synchronised gun; and two more squadrons of DH2s (No. 29 under Eric Conran and No. 32 under a pugnacious Welshman named Lionel Rees), joined No. 24 in escort work and in long offensive patrols to re-affirm air superiority and make the work of the corps squadrons possible.

Noticeable was the extreme youth of many of the newcomers. Each was given a fitter and a rigger to look after his machine and was made 'absolutely responsible for them', according to the eighteen-year-old Gwilym Lewis, the youngest pilot on 32 Squadron. Lewis's virile, Clark Gable-ish looks would have been identified with that actor in a later era. Now his natural fears were considerably attenuated by the reluctance of the enemy scout pilots to challenge intrusions; he was much more scared of the German two-seaters. He found it astounding how many RFC machines crossed the lines and how promptly the Huns turned tail. It was reassuring to find that the enemy had the wind up just as much as he did. An awful lot of hot air, he thought, was talked and written about pluck. He would love to bring a Hun down – but when the scrapping began he was scared to death. 'You have no idea,' he wrote, in a letter home, 'how scared I am when I go for these brutes.' Yet he found dogfights 'wildly exciting'.

Of Lionel Rees, his squadron commander and a fellow Welshman, he wrote: 'Everyone knows that the major is mad. He is never happier than when attacking Huns. I wouldn't be surprised if he comes home with a VC.' But he reserved his greatest admiration for the crews of the FEs of 25 Squadron, whom it was often his job to escort. 'They recce and bomb all day long.' Of his own morale he admitted: 'A nice cushy wound would suit me all right,' but that otherwise, even if he had the chance, he wouldn't go home. Despite frequent losses, 'it's not such a bad little war if it wasn't so cold.' This, in open cockpit pushers like the DH2 and the FE, was a daily affliction, even in mid-summer.

Of the bombing, much was opportunist, and even when major raids were attempted, although the concentration on a single target was greater than hitherto, machines still tended to be despatched in dribs and drabs. Most of these raids were calculated to delay enemy reinforcements. Of the twenty-eight BE2c's which took off on specific bombing missions on 1 July, beginning soon after midday, only one hit its target. Of six machines that set out to bomb the well defended town of St Quentin, only three got back.

One who didn't, Second Lieutenant Laurie Wingfield, had enjoyed the variety of his corps squadron existence, knowing that by comparison with the infantry he was living in luxury. But he recognised the bombing of the railway station at St Quentin, thirty-five miles beyond the lines, as a special job. 'The "eggs" we were carrying were large ones,' he wrote later, 'weighing 110 lbs each full of TNT and I had to carry two.' This meant sacrificing all superfluous weight – which included an observer. Even a machine-gun was thought an unjustifiable load, but Wingfield decided to take one – and regretted it when it reduced his rate of climb. He was told he would be escorted by a squadron of DH2s, but when he arrived at the line and they failed to appear, he set course alone. When he reached St Quentin he dropped his bombs on the railway station as briefed and was rewarded by a huge column of smoke, rising, as he looked back, to 2,000 feet. 'On the way home,' he wrote later, 'I met a Fokker, and that was the end of the story.' Completely outclassed though the BE2c was, Wingfield put his six months' experience to good use and it took the Fokker pilot fifteen minutes to shoot him down.

It was still not the end of the story. The bombing of St Quentin that day had not only been costly, it had also, like so many of these attacks, been abortive so far as Headquarters knew. And Wingfield, now a prisoner, could not enlighten them. But German prisoners captured later that month revealed the spectacular truth. Having received urgent orders to entrain that afternoon for the Somme front, two enemy battalions had been crammed into the station, arms piled up and transport standing by to be loaded on to a train, when one of Wingfield's bombs hit and exploded in an ammunition shed. There were two hundred ammunition wagons lined up in the station sidings, the fire spread to them, and sixty were destroyed before the rest could be got away. More than that, the fire destroyed the train and the whole of the equipment of the two battalions. Men fled panic-stricken in all directions, leaving 180 dead and wounded, and the regiment which suffered most had to be sent back to be re-equipped.

Even then Wingfield's story was only half told. Fifteen months later, in October 1917, he escaped from prison camp, crossed the Dutch frontier, and returned home, to begin a distinguished career in the aviation industry.

The BE2c's and d's of No. 7 Squadron, under Major F.J.L. Cogan, were directed to railway targets in the Cambrai area, where the station was hit for the loss of one machine. But it was a classic opportunist attack later in the day which brought the best results when Second Lieutenant Arthur Gordon-Kidd spotted a train on the line approaching Cambrai. The train was nearing a cutting situated on a curve, and Gordon-Kidd was well aware that such enclosed areas gave exceptional force to bomb-blast if the weapon could be accurately aimed, with wreckage sometimes blocking a cutting for days. Coming down to 900 feet to give himself every chance, he approached the train head on, timed his run perfectly, and scored a direct hit on the middle carriages, which caught fire and exploded. For this exploit he was awarded the DSO. Later a pilot of 16 Squadron (also BEs), found the train still burning and dropped two more bombs on the rear coaches. Further massive explosions confirmed that the train was carrying ammunition, and it was still blazing fiercely that evening.[1]

---

1. In August 1917, flying Spads of 19 Squadron, Gordon-Kidd was mortally wounded.

All day, standing patrols of DH2s and FE2b's went out in pairs to cover specific areas, waiting over the lines until they were relieved by the next pair. Although their primary job was to fight, they watched for enemy movements, and, in the case of the FE2b's, carried 20 lb bombs for targets of opportunity. These patrols engaged in many scraps, and two FE2b's were shot down, but they helped to keep enemy aircraft occupied while the corps machines, at lower altitudes, carried out their tasks for the army.

When targets were attacked in sufficient numbers, with a strong escort, the German pilots rarely interfered. This was demonstrated on 2 July, when six RE7s (developed from the RE5 and capable of carrying a 336 lb bomb) set out with an escort of four Martinsydes to bomb an enemy infantry headquarters and ammunition dump at Bapaume: six Moranes of 60 Squadron patrolled the area while the attack was in progress. The heavy-cased bombs carried by the RE7s started a fire which, it was said, 'grew in intensity and still coloured the eastern sky when darkness had closed over the day's fighting'.

Euphoria at the occasional bombing success, however, was tempered by dismay at the losses suffered in those first few days of low-level attacks on rail targets. Reconnaissances on 3 July reported many troop movements in the neighbourhood of Cambrai, but the bombing of trains, which resumed early that morning, met with sterner opposition. Some of the bombers were shot down, others were forced to turn back, few reached their primary targets. Bombing raids on St Quentin also suffered losses and rebuffs. Throughout these days Trenchard was continually touring the squadrons, inviting the men to 'gather round', encouraging and, according to the crews, inspiring by his presence, and he turned up with Baring at 60 Squadron that day in time to wish Waldron luck on an offensive patrol. Waldron, evidently not under an embargo, believed in leading his men, and on this day five Bullets were required to act as a decoy for the BE2c's bombing St Quentin. Among the pilots were Smith-Barry and Balfour. Not only were they unable to help the bombers, they were soon hard pressed themselves, running into a dozen enemy machines at 8,000 feet twenty miles beyond the lines, several Fokkers among them.

In armament and manoeuvrability the Fokker was superior to the Morane, but Waldron attacked at once. Balfour spotted a Fokker on Waldron's tail and forced it to break off, but soon afterwards he saw Waldron going down, apparently under control. Smith-Barry drove the other Fokkers east, but his Morane too was badly shot about and he and his colleagues were forced to return. There was no further sign of Waldron: he had been shot down and killed. 'One of the best men we ever had,' was Trenchard's verdict. Although losses were a daily occurrence, somehow it struck home more forcibly when it was one of the original few. Smith-Barry was appointed to take his place.

The tally amongst the bombers, on those first three days, was eight missing, with many others out of action for varying periods, if repairable at all. The inescapable conclusion was that deep penetration by BE2c's, flying without close escort and without observers, and with their performance, such as it was, further restricted by bomb-carrying, was unsustainable. Even the successes were rarely quantifiable, and Trenchard, whose daily tours of the squadrons revealed the bomber crews as being, in his own phrase, 'a bit rattled' (with good reason), acknowledged that the BEs would be more usefully employed in their routine corps duties, to which they were returned. Trenchard considered putting in for a couple of VCs to sustain morale: meanwhile, when switched to bombing, the BEs were ordered to fly in formation under escort.

If Trenchard did in fact recommend any pilots on this front for VCs, they weren't granted, the only VC of the opening days of the battle being won in the Loos area, by a squadron commander subject to the normal embargo that he must not cross the lines. Yet no one was unduly surprised – least of all Gwilym Lewis – at the name of the recipient. On the morning of 1 July a formation of ten enemy bombers crossed the lines near Festubert. DH2s of 32 Squadron under Lionel Rees had been airborne in this area since 03.40, but it was not until Rees himself took off with Lieutenant John Simpson, a 26-year-old Canadian, at 05.55 that contact was made with the German formation, and it was Simpson, who had lost touch with Rees, who made it. As was not unusual in German formations, the leader was an observer, Leutnant Erich Zimmermann. Despite the odds against him, Simpson attacked immediately. Three of the hostiles broke towards him, and after a sharp exchange Simpson's machine was hit. Watchers on the ground saw the DH2 descend some 5,000 feet, apparently under control, but in fact Simpson had sustained eight bullet wounds in the head and was already dead. Rees had seen nothing of this, but he now caught sight of the enemy formation. It was so unusual for hostiles to penetrate to any depth that he took them for a British patrol – until he spotted their markings through binoculars.

When the Germans saw a second DH2 climbing towards them they were confident of scoring a second victory, but Rees, holding his fire, splintered the fuselage of one hostile from short range with his first burst and then attacked another, which wobbled crazily before going down apparently under control. When the leader and two other machines turned away, Rees began chasing them and was soon overhauling them, only to be hit in the leg by a burst fired from long range, losing proper control of the DH2s rudder. Yet he still bore down on the leader. His subsequent account concluded: 'I finished firing about ten yards away, and saw the observer sitting back firing straight up in the air . . . He was firing an immense amount of ammunition. Just before he reached the lines I gave him one more drum. Having finished my ammunition I came home.' Rees had scattered a major German bombing raid single-handed, and German records confirmed in detail his account of the fight. One German crew actually jettisoned their bombs over their own lines. The observer firing so blindly into the air had indeed been the leader, Leutnant Zimmermann: it had been a dead man's hand on the trigger. The pilot, although wounded, got the plane down.

Gwilym Lewis, in a letter home, wrote: 'Archie batteries say they have never seen anything so gallant or comic in their lives . . . I told you he was the bravest man in the world.' But the leg injury proved worse than feared, and it was the end of Rees's operational career.

Here was another man, like Hawker, whose watchword was 'Go in to attack! Whenever you see the Hun, no matter where he is, be he alone or accompanied, go for him, and shoot him down.' It was an attitude that, once inculcated, it was hard not to follow, costly though it often was, as in the case of the Canadian Simpson. No scout pilots of this or any period adopted this attitude more enthusiastically than the Canadians, but none excelled the Welshman Lionel Rees, who had earned his reputation – and an MC – as a flight commander on Gunbuses with 11 Squadron. Together with men like Hawker, Harvey-Kelly, Don Lewis and Bron James he exerted an almost messianic influence on the ethos of the RFC, long before the advent of the aces.

16

FLAMERS AND FROSTBITE:
NO EMPTY CHAIRS

THE first phase of the battle, in which the British, at enormous cost, gained a six-thousand-yard footing on the main or Bazentin ridge, despite stubborn German resistance, lasted a fortnight. During that time, and beyond, Trenchard's declared objective of keeping the German Air Force too preoccupied in defence either to interfere significantly with the work of the corps squadrons, or to intrude effectively over the British lines, was achieved. General von Below later complained of three areas of dominance by the RFC in these early weeks. First: 'The enemy's aerodromes enjoyed complete freedom in carrying out distant reconnaissance.' Secondly: 'With the aid of aeroplane observation the hostile artillery neutralised our guns and was able to range with most extreme accuracy on our trenches.' And thirdly: 'By means of bombing and machine-gunning from a low height against infantry, battery positions and marching columns, the enemy's aircraft inspired our troops with a feeling of defencelessness.'

This dispassionate summary was supported with some vehemence by the German troops themselves. 'The English are always flying over our lines directing artillery shoots,' was the burden of one lament, 'thereby getting all their shells right into our trenches. This moral defeat has a bad effect on us all.' As for their own air force, the letter continued: '. . . one must be too ashamed to write, it is simply scandalous. They fly as far as this village but no further, whereas the English are always flying over our lines.' German records subsequently described July and August 1916 as 'the blackest days in the history of the German Air Force'.

The second phase of the battle, which lasted for two months, until mid-September, settled into a tense and debilitating struggle for possession of the main ridge. Most significant for the RFC was that the German Air Force began to show signs of a recrudescence. To match German expansion and reorganisation on the ground, which included, on 29 August, the appointment of Field Marshal von Hindenburg as Chief of the German General Staff, assisted by General von Ludendorff, General von Hoeppner, until recently chief of staff of the von Below's Second Army, was made responsible for the centralised administration of the German Air Force. Meanwhile Boelcke was brought back to organise the formation of *Jagdstaffeln* or *Jastas* (pursuit or hunting squadrons), each to consist of fourteen newly-developed machines, namely the D-type Albatros and Halberstadt. Both mounted two fixed machine-guns firing through the propeller arc, and all would be flown by carefully selected pilots who had been through advanced air training schools. Command of *Jasta* 2, which was formed on 30 August, was given to Boelcke, who invited a two-seater pilot and former observer whose enthusiasm had impressed him, Manfred von Richthofen, to join him. The first batch of new machines was delivered on 6 September, and Boelcke's first combat mission was flown on the 17th, two days after Haig renewed the assault in what became the third and final phase of the battle.

For most of that summer, however, the RFC enjoyed an air superiority they were never to know again, and life in the better equipped squadrons seemed ideal, so far as soldiering could be ideal in wartime. Visits to artillery units, partly to talk shop, partly to kill time in bad weather, and partly for good will, offered continual reminders of how lucky they were. Gun emplacements and dug-outs under fire, existence on hard rations in the midst of shell-holes and mud – this was indeed a different world. By comparison the RFC lived a civilised life, still to some extent officers and gentlemen, comfortably housed in farms and sometimes châteaux, or in Nissen-hutted camps, with three-course meals in the Mess, and even, in the quieter sectors, the correct wines and the traditional circulation of port, coffee and liqueurs. Many, like Captain P.N. 'Puggy' Shone, a newly-arrived observer, had experienced both worlds, and after ten months in the trenches he felt he had moved from an East End dosshouse to the Savoy. 'Five minutes behind the lines,' he noted, 'you were in complete safety,' while, with the help and ingenuity of ground tradesmen, the functional hut furnishings were transformed. 'In our hut we had running water,' boasted Shone, 'and to sleep in a camp bed – amazing!'

Another man with dual experience was Sergeant-Observer H.G. Taylor, of 25 Squadron (FE2b's): Taylor, after a boyhood in rural Surrey, had served with the Machine-Gun Corps on the Somme and would never forget the appalling conditions. 'In the trenches you faced death every second, not knowing when it might come; in the RFC you could certainly say between flights that you had so many more hours to live. On the other hand, in the air, you could see death coming, especially if you caught fire at height. With no parachutes, whether you stayed in the machine or jumped, the result was the same.'

Some people believed that only those airmen who had once fought on the ground and retained an indelible impression of that experience could ever have a proper sense of responsibility towards the men in the trenches. But the evidence, from Trenchard down, is that this was not so, and that all were fully aware of their luck. Even in Messes close to the front there was almost always a piano, and a gramophone playing the latest London theatre hits, as well as newspapers and the companionship of kindred spirits. Parties and binges, and the horseplay of Mess games, were discreetly encouraged, as a release from the perpetual strain of facing Archie and a highly skilled and courageous adversary, not to mention the missing faces and the perpetual fear of a 'flamer'. 'Once you see a machine fall from the sky in flames, especially when it contains your friends,' wrote H.G. Taylor, 'you always have this fearful picture in your mind.' This was the unmentionable dread, which only surfaced in ghoulish ditties that were rendered with frenetic gusto as comic songs.

Volunteers from overseas often formed a grudging admiration for the atmosphere created in RFC messes: one who commented on it approvingly was Canadian Harold E. Hartley. He noted the studied avoidance of controversial subjects, the understatement, and the absence of selfishness and swank. The habit of sleeping in hutted dormitories he found far preferable to single rooms or bunks, making for closer companionship, and he relished the clubbable blend of leg-pulling and old-fashioned courtesy which was extended to new-comers. He likened the ambience to that in a college fraternity. If at first it was dominated by the public school element, it was beginning, by 1916, to be democratised as casualties increased and men from all walks of life, not to mention 'colonials', as they were still apt to be called, contributed their own distinctive aura to the mixture. Hartley was also pleased – and perhaps surprised – to find his com-manders understanding, helpful, and fair.

If there was one discomfort from which the airman suffered to a greater degree than the soldier it was the cold. One of the first to arm himself with fur-lined thigh-boots was Hawker, and even in the FE2b's, which rarely reached a height above 8,000 feet, the spacious but draughty and exposed open cockpit became a refrigerator. The wearing of silk underwear, silk gloves, leather gauntlets and a leather face-mask, with fur-lined garments from head to foot, was never proof against 70- and 80-knot winds at temperatures far below zero. It was worse still for the pusher crews, where any warmth from the engine went to waste behind them, and where the crude bombsight necessitated the setting of a stop-watch with bare hands. 'I got frost-bite setting that stop-watch,' said Sidney Attwater when still a cor-poral observer, 'and so did many others.' An issue of whale oil to protect exposed facial areas proved unpopular because of its revolt-ing smell, and most men substituted cold cream.

Patrick Playfair and his observer, after landing from three hours at 7,500 feet in a Gunbus, were unable to move from their cockpits for several minutes, and when they did manage to climb out they were unable to straighten their legs. Both collapsed and had to be helped to their feet and supported to the rest hut. The problem was quite fortuitously solved by an Australian RNAS pilot named Sidney Cotton (later a pioneer in aerial survey and air spy photography). In the very cold winter of 1916/17, Cotton was tuning up the engine of his Sopwith 1½-strutter, dressed in dirty, begrimed overalls, when he and others were despatched in a hurry to intercept an intruder. They saw nothing, but when they collected together afterwards, everyone was frozen stiff except Cotton. 'That's funny,' he said, 'I'm quite warm.' He hadn't had time to don flying kit and was still wearing his dirty overalls. On examining them he found they were saturated with oil and grease and must have acted as an airtight bag and kept the body heat in. He asked for leave, went to London, and had a flying suit made up to his own design. It had a lining of thin fur, then a layer of airproof silk, then an outside layer of light Burberry material, the whole being made up in one piece like overalls. The neck and cuffs had fur pieces sewn inside them to prevent the warm air escaping. Deep pockets just below the knee allowed pilots seated in cramped cockpits to reach down into them easily for maps and accessories. After searching tests the Sidcot suit, as it was eponymously known, came into general use, replacing the old-fashioned boots and coats. Frostbite sufferer Sidney Attwater wrote: 'They were splendid.' They were still widely used in World War II.

Many squadron commanders found the restrictions placed on their flying distasteful, and Hawker still flew on patrols, regularly if not frequently. This was how he kept in touch. He shared the problems of most squadron commanders in that his seniors, under pressure from army or corps commanders, often exaggerated the urgency of their requirements, forcing him to order his pilots out when the odds against them could have been improved given more time.

Planning was a feature of Hawker's leadership, and after a show there was always a de-briefing – an innovation then – and a lively discussion. There were many anxious days for Hawker that summer as he waited for his pilots to return from patrols. Men who were overdue were not necessarily missing: Hawker could still hope for a phone call to say they had got down elsewhere. When a man was confirmed as missing there were letters to write, effects to be sorted, replacements to be requested. Trenchard's dictum, for reasons of morale, was 'no empty chairs at the breakfast table', and sure enough another raw newcomer would arrive the same day. None of Hawker's young pilots was married, but there were families and girl friends to be advised and, if possible, soothed. Sometimes he could truthfully say there was a good chance of the man being a prisoner; sometimes he would know with virtual certainty that the man was dead. Sometimes there would be debts, even pregnancies. Next day there was a new man to be trained.

One replacement, who had only recently taken his ticket, was awakened by his batman on his first morning to be told that 'Mr A has been shot down and Mr B has crashed in flames in the village'. That morning Hawker put the newcomer through his paces and ticked him off for 'showing off, and for losing height in the turn'. These unfortunate fledgelings were the inevitable result of expansion outstripping supply, and their shooting, like their flying, was often appalling. One man arrived never having seen a Lewis gun before.

Nevertheless it was the DH2 squadrons, with No. 24 in the vanguard, which largely defeated the Fokkers. The FE2b's contributed, giving the German pilots some nasty surprises at first by their wide field of fire, and so did the Moranes, though the latter suffered a disastrous July. Smith-Barry was not one to mince words, and he complained to Dowding, at wing headquarters, of one batch of replacement pilots: 'They've only seven hours flying, sir, it's bloody murder.' He refused to send anyone out on patrol until he'd brought him up to a standard that he felt gave him a chance; according to one recruit, nineteen-year-old S.F. (Stanley) Vincent, when Trenchard visited the squadron Smith-B 'as good as told him he was a butcher'. Another new pilot, Peter Portal, recognised his commander as a daring and spectacular airman, despite the embargo on his leading the squadron into action, and noted how he encouraged individuals and tolerated no divisions of race or class. Portal also thoroughly approved of the care Smith-Barry took of his pilots: they 'had a good chance to learn the real principles of safe flying from precept and example'.

Yet Smith-Barry was intolerant of anyone he suspected of over-caution. Borrowing the Morane of a new flight commander, he found a neatly rolled package stowed in the cockpit. 'Emergency rations,' he was told by a mechanic. Examination disclosed silk pyjamas, razor, toothbrush, 500 cigarettes, and other insurances against misfortune. Tearing the parcel open and scattering its contents for all to see, S-B shouted: 'One of my pilots is preparing to be a prisoner!' Many would think such preparations prudent, and they were widely popular, but S-B wouldn't have it. His attitude was on a parallel with that of the Air Board over parachutes: that given a possible alternative to fighting to the death against the enemy before coaxing his machine home, a man might choose it.

For all Smith-Barry's professionalism and paternalism, not to mention his eccentricities, one thing he could not change was the basic inferiority of the Morane. By 3 August half the squadron's original pilots had been killed or wounded or posted missing, and he requested that the squadron be taken out of the line to recuperate. He had scarcely made the request when he lost yet another pilot, Claude Ridley, missing from a spy-dropping mission. (In fact, as already recorded, he turned up later.) Dowding supported the request, and Trenchard, belying Smith-Barry's accusation, told Haig: 'I have had to withdraw one of the GHQ fighting squadrons from work temporarily ... This squadron, since the battle began, have lost a squadron commander, two flight commanders and one pilot – all killed or missing, and yesterday it lost two more machines and two pilots and two observers by anti-aircraft fire. Besides this, they have had several officers wounded. They have a very difficult machine to fly, and I think a rest away from work is absolutely necessary.'

Three weeks later, when the squadron resumed operating, there was only one flight of Moranes remaining: the other two had been replaced by the Nieuport 17 or Super-Bébé, far and away the best single-seater scout at that time. Their arrival coincided with the posting in of Albert Ball. Given a free rein by Smith-Barry, Ball made an immediate impact. Roderic Hill, who joined the squadron a month

Above right: Lanoe Hawker, VC, DSO. His motto, posted on the squadron notice board, was 'Attack EVERYTHING'.

Above: 'She is a little beauty'. The Bristol Scout with the obliquely mounted machine-gun in which Hawker won his VC.

Left: Jack Woodhouse with the agent, a French ex-army NCO named Le Marrier, whom he dropped from a BE2c behind the German lines.

C.F.A. 'Peter' Portal. Astounded at the ignorance of his instructors.

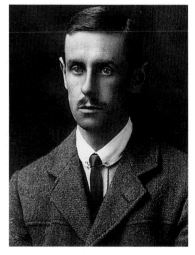

Hugh Dowding. 'Pernickety, interfering, querulous' . . . but not easily shaken from his convictions.

Gwilym H. Lewis. 'You have no idea how scared I am.' Yet he found dogfights 'wildly exciting'.

Lionel Rees, VC. 'Everyone knows that the major is mad . . . I told you he was the bravest man in the world.'

Above left: 'Willie' Read. Looked after his men – but kept himself warm.
Above right: Read with Leslie Porter. 'I lost my best flight commander.'
Read blamed Dowding.

The Sopwith 1 1/2-strutter. Flown by 43, 45 and 70 Squadrons.

S.F. Vincent. Overheard Smith-Barry 'as good as tell Trenchard he was a butcher.'

George McCubbin. Crashed his machine showing off – but later, with observer Corporal J.H. Waller in an FE2b, accounted for Immelmann.

Harold Balfour in the cockpit of a Caudron trainer at the Ruffy-Baumann School of Flying at Hendon.

Roland Garros in the boxlike Type L Morane Parasol monoplane in which he scored his victories and was himself shot down.

The Morane Parasol Type LA, with rounded fuselage. 'It was a machine you could never relax in,' wrote Cecil Lewis – but it took him right through the Somme battle.

The Morane Type N, which the British called the Bullet. 'They were tricky little brutes to fly,' wrote Harold Balfour. Mapplebeck killed himself in one.

Sidney Attwater when a corporal observer on 8 Squadron (BE2c's). Later, with his fellow Lancastrian Tom Mottershead, he was nearly court-martialled.

Tom Mottershead, DCM, VC. Set on fire by an Albatros DII, he got plane and observer back safely.

An FE2d of the type flown by Attwater and Mottershead.

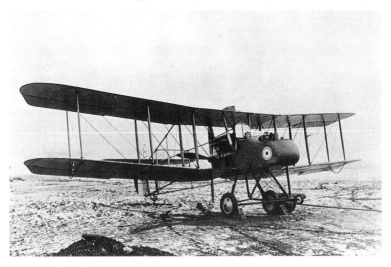

Ball's Nieuport – showing the contrasting wing chords.

Albert Ball, VC, DSO and two bars. 'A quiet, shy, simple little chap,' he protested that he 'did not think anything bad about the Hun.'

Flight Sergeant James McCudden as an observer, 1915. Whereas Ball was the gifted amateur, McCudden was the seasoned professional.

Ewart Garland. An Australian who 'kept on flying to the limit of endurance and beyond.'

Arthur Gordon-Kidd. A classic opportunist bombing on the first day on the Somme.

18-year-old Harold Tambling during training on the Bristol Fighter. 'We have a completely new squadron every few weeks.'

earlier with an exceptional rating, but was still confined to Moranes, clashed with his commander on being thus restricted, but made the best of the Morane and soon earned S-B's respect. He described Ball as 'sitting in his hut on the aerodrome, gramophone going, working out schemes'. Although a boy of a kindly nature, he was 'uncannily swift and sure' according to Hill. 'He had one idea, to kill as many Huns as possible.'

Contemporary sources emphatically deny that the appellation Hun was derogatory or derisory. 'I would go as far as to say,' wrote nineteen-year-old Australian pilot Ewart Garland, 'that flying men on both sides felt less personal antagonism than say footballers in the heat and excitement of play ... There was no hate between enemy airmen, and quasi-affectionate references to German airmen were quite usual.' Cecil Lewis wrote: 'They were our friends the enemy. We treated them well when they were captured, and they us.' Only when the Zeppelins and later the Gothas were bombing London did Lewis experience a brief access of rage. He spoke of a strong magnetic attraction between airmen matched against each other at altitude. 'I have felt this magnetism engaging an enemy scout three miles above the earth.' When Ball's father wrote to him to say 'Let the devils have it,' Ball replied: 'I do not think of them as devils. I only scrap because it is my duty, and I do not think anything bad about the Hun.'

The speed and manoeuvrability of the Nieuport 17 soon attracted basic tasks like photography: by putting a camera in a Nieuport, photographs could be taken more quickly and more safely than in a slower machine. With malice aforethought, Smith-Barry had a camera installed in the machine of the one man on the squadron whom he suspected of being a shirker, sent him on a photographic sortie with an escort of three of his colleagues, and awaited results. Sure enough the pictures revealed the tentative nature of the flying: the pilot had tried, by tilting his machine, to cover the area without penetrating it. Smith-Barry called the four pilots in and told them they had wasted everyone's time and would have to go again. To the escort pilots he then proposed a novel method of ensuring success: two of them were to fly one on each side of the leader and a little behind, with the third astern. 'If Blank leaves what you consider the correct line or height, you have your guns to remind him to get back into position.'

Stanley Vincent was on the leader's right, and he was soon putting a burst of fire, 'with tracer bullets much in evidence', past the leader's wing-tip. Both the other escorts had occasion to fire off similar reminders, the one astern going into action when the leader began climbing above the height for which the cameras were focused. 'The photographs were quite satisfactory this time,' said Vincent. However he added: 'The very next day this chap, then well over the German side of the lines, had engine failure and went down and landed behind the enemy lines and failed to destroy his machine. The Germans thus found out that the Nieuports were carrying cameras, and their guns paid that much more attention to us.'

As for the faint-hearted leader, although he could expect to survive the war, he would, when repatriated, have to face searching interrogation by a specially appointed committee, in common with all former prisoners.

On another occasion Vincent was one of three on an offensive patrol when they clashed with five of Richthofen's *Jasta* and had to fight for their lives. When it ended, as suddenly as it had begun, and the sky was clear, the leader, exhausted and slightly airsick as they all were, turned for home. In effect they were cutting short their patrol, and when they landed S-B was furious. 'We'd deserted our post, we'd left a gap in the sky where the enemy could pour through and attack our corps machines, we'd let ourselves down.' Smarting under this tongue-lashing, the nineteen-year-old Vincent retired to his tent in suicidal mood. Some time later, in came S-B with a bottle. 'Hello Vincent,' he said. 'Have a brandy.'

17

BALL AND McCUDDEN: THE CONTACT PATROL: THE MEN OF THE FE2b's

OFFENSIVE patrols, photography, escort work – all these were the daily diet of the Nieuports, and Albert Ball, for all his individualism, could be an asset on bomber protection. Accompanying the FE2b's of 11 Squadron, he was confronted by about twenty assorted hostiles in three groups. He crashed one, sent another down in flames, and, with the last of his ammunition, downed a third. Returning to the nearest aerodrome, pursued by the enemy for much of the way, he rearmed and returned to the scene, only to find it deserted. Short now of fuel, he was attacked by two hostiles on the way back and his Nieuport was riddled. Compelled to land away from home, he slept by his machine, organised repairs, and flew back next morning. Six days later, when the bombers he was escorting came under attack, he drove two hostiles down, forcing them to land, and crashed a third on its nose. No wonder he loved his Nieuport.

Intolerant of help and advice himself, Ball never sought to advise or correct others, disliked anyone flying with him, and, with Smith-Barry's connivance, enjoyed a roving commission. In a description of Ball's method, Hill wrote: 'There was a curved rail down which the gun had to be run to change drums. By exerting pressure on one side of the stock, Ball held it rigid when nearly down, pointing up at about 80 degrees. [Curiously Hawker had done something similar in the DH2.] By skilful manoeuvre he was able to zoom up underneath his victim, then by a slight oscillation of the control stick cause his guns to rake the target fore and aft at a range of about 30 feet.' This approach, often unseen, was just as often fatal for the victim.

Ball fought with his head, according to Hill, who called him 'the offspring of a vixen and a lion'. He was not all blind aggression. As an instance of his animal cunning – Hill dignified it as astuteness – he related an incident when Ball flew most of the way to Cambrai just under one of the Moranes, totally unsuspected by the pilot. 'His security', said Hill, 'lay in the fact that he fought at such close range that the rest of the hostile formation dare not fire at him for fear of hitting each other.' In a hectic six weeks with 60 Squadron, from 23 August to 4 October, Ball increased his tally of victories to thirty, higher than anyone on the Allied side except the Frenchman Guynemer with thirty-seven. The sight of the red spinner on Ball's propeller boss so terrorised the enemy that there were times when even the pilots of the new *Jastas* shrank from attacking him. 'Figuratively speaking,' wrote Hill, 'he did the work of a whole squadron, setting the model of courage and determination, though not of leadership; we were instructed in formation flying by others.' A short leave, the award of a DSO, and promotion to captain, which placed him technically in charge of a flight, didn't change him. When he saw a flock of Huns he opened his throttle and flew straight at them, using his guns in hosepipe fashion, and leaving his flight to fend for themselves.

Meanwhile Jimmy McCudden, having completed his pilot training, had returned to France on 8 July as a flight-sergeant pilot on FE2d's on 20 Squadron. Of four NCO pilots who arrived that day, none was to survive the war, although two were to win the highest award. McCudden himself was one, the other was a Lancastrian named Tom Mottershead, also bound for an FE squadron, No. 25.

McCudden's ambition to join a single-seater scout squadron was satisfied four weeks later when he was posted to 29 Squadron on

DH2s under his old pilot Eric Conran. But he was confined mostly to escort work, and it was another month before he scored his first victory. Even then his diffidence prevented him from making a claim, and he was credited with the two-seater Albatros he attacked on 6 September on the evidence of ground witnesses who saw it crash.

Jimmy McCudden's long apprenticeship – two years as air mechanic, gaining the rank and responsibilities of sergeant at twenty, with occasional opportunities to fly, and then six months as air observer, followed by pilot training, was in striking contrast to the meteoric rise of Albert Ball. Indeed in most ways they were totally dissimilar. Ball's dark, unruly mop was the extreme opposite of McCudden's flaxen thatch, smarmed down close to the scalp. Ball was instinctive and impetuous, the typical street fighter, prodigal of his energy; McCudden was measured, percipient, calculating. Ball was brash but introspective, McCudden modest but anxious to be sociable. Although Ball was mechanically minded, he had not served in the ranks or trained as a technician as McCudden had, and although both men were individualists and loved nothing better than hunting alone, Ball knew only one way to fight whereas McCudden knew many. In sporting parlance, if Ball was the gifted and dedicated amateur, McCudden was the seasoned professional. Yet it was the combination of Ball and his Nieuport which now grabbed the headlines, and when he was finally posted home for a rest on 4 October he had earned himself two bars to add to his DSO and MC, making him the first triple DSO in the British Army. His fame had gone before him and he went home to a hero's welcome, to be mobbed in the streets in his native Nottingham. Meanwhile McCudden, in his now obsolescent DH2, opposed from mid-September by the new German scouts, was struggling to survive.

Trenchard was much too alert not to know that the air superiority enjoyed that summer was ephemeral, and with the Germans, by the third week in July, suspending their Verdun offensive and concentrating the majority of their strength on the Somme, his demands for still greater expansion excited dismay at home. 'With regard to the number of pilots we have had and are asking for,' he explained, 'I admit the demand is enormous.' But he couldn't understand the protests. 'We are fighting a very big battle, and fighting in the air is becoming intense. The fighting will increase, I regret to say, not decrease, and it is only a question of keeping it up longer than the Hun.' Trenchard was again emphasising the numbers game, the war of attrition which, by the brutal arithmetic of casualties, the Germans must lose. 'If we cannot do that, then we are beaten; if we do it, we win.'

As successive assaults, in the months leading up to the final phase, gained little, and the blood-letting continued, Trenchard amplified his worries to Brancker: 'I must warn you now that in the next ten days, if we get fine weather, I anticipate a very heavy casualty list ... But what is to be chiefly remembered is that whatever we suffer, the Huns are suffering more ...'

The results of Allied bombing in this period – the delay and damage caused, and the effect on ground troops – may best be judged from the response of the German defences. The normal load for a bombing machine was two 112 lb bombs or eight 20-pounders, with escort machines often carrying a few 20-pounders for good measure, and there were some spectacular successes; but the Germans reacted so aggressively that although escorting DH2s, FE2b's and Sopwith 1½-strutters generally held their own, bomber losses increased.

The 1½-strutter, so called because of its short centre-section struts, was a two-seater originally ordered by the RNAS. Its Scarff Ring mounting, which allowed the observer in the rear seat to swivel and fire his gun in any direction easily and quickly, was the invention of a back-room boy in the Admiralty Air Department, Warrant Officer (Gunner) F.W. Scarff, RN. It was so successful that it was incorporated in other types of machine. Scarff also had a hand in producing the Scarff-Dibovsky interrupter gear for firing through the propeller arc, also used in the Sopwith.

*   *   *

The third and final phase of the Somme battle began on 15 September. Haig still believed that the elements of shock and surprise might achieve a breakthrough, and these elements were represented in a new weapon, the tank, of which thirty-six were now available. Impatient to deploy them, Haig ignored advice to wait until they had been delivered in greater numbers, making the same mistake the Germans had made with their Fokker *Eindeckers*. The plan was to keep the tanks clear of observation until the night before the attack, when they would move into position under cover of darkness. The RFC were to co-operate by night-flying over the lines to drown or camouflage the noise of the tanks moving up, and by shooting down all kite balloons whose observers might be in a position to spot the build-up.

The best weapons for destroying kite balloons remained the *Le Prieur* rockets, and the only squadron equipped with them on this part of the front was No. 60. The massed batteries protecting these balloons made rocket attack especially hazardous as the rockets could only be fired accurately in a steep power-dive. Early on the morning of 15 September Trenchard and Baring drove up to the 60 Squadron Mess in their Rolls-Royce and told the pilots who had 'gathered round' that the balloons must be destroyed before the ground assault commenced. He then called for volunteers. In deathly silence, according to Baring, three were chosen, and Trenchard spoke to each one. After he had wished them luck he revealed the true extent of what he expected of them: it was to be a suicide raid. 'Remember this. It's far more important to get those balloons than to fail and come back.' With this stark invocation resounding in their ears, the three pilots took off.

Their vulnerability had not been exaggerated. Two balloons were shot down, but the two pilots who returned had met fierce opposition and their machines were riddled, while one pilot was missing. Since German Intelligence had in fact been aware that tanks were to be used, it was the familiar story, in the air as on the ground, of a sacrifice in vain.

While much of the work of the RFC preserved lives indirectly, there were times when the saving was immediate and obvious, as during the opening assault on the 15th, when the crew of a BE2e of No. 34 Squadron on a contact patrol reported three knocked-out tanks, one ditched and lopsided in our own trenches, one upended against a tree, and one in flames straddling the German trenches. These losses left the attacking force exposed to a potentially murderous machine-gun barrage, and a weighted message bag was dropped to corps headquarters to warn them. Further reconnaissance, and a verbal report made after landing, averted a pre-planned frontal attack, which, it was said, 'would have resulted in the complete wiping-out of the attacking force'.

A contact patrol observer on No. 9 Squadron whose reports were models of accuracy and tactical acumen was Second Lieutenant T.E.G. Scaife, a 24-year-old South African farmer, born in Leicester but educated in Cape Town. Seeing about 50 British infantrymen pinned down by a German machine-gun nest, Tom Scaife and his pilot used their Lewis guns so effectively that the barrier was removed. Of these contact patrol crews it was written: 'They, alone, were the witnesses of the whole titanic struggle, and through their eyes the army commanders could follow the fortunes of their troops.' Air to ground communication was often by klaxon horn, which could be heard above the din of battle, and which asked the infantry to indicate their positions by ground signal. Scaife and others flew as many as eight hours on that first day, and failures of the ground troops to achieve a particular goal were often traceable to poor visibility hampering or grounding these patrols. If the work was unspectacular and the crews largely anonymous, they were at the vortex of the fighting and their exposure to danger was unsurpassed. Scaife himself, with his pilot, was shot down and killed on 26 September at the climax of the battle.

Every kind of show had its own particular perils; the grass seldom looked much greener elsewhere. Roderic Hill was a great admirer of the FE2b crews of 11 Squadron, with whom 60 Squadron shared an aerodrome, and whom they often escorted. Of the observers he wrote: 'They were not strapped in, and they had to move around their roomy cockpits, oblivious of their safety, standing up on their little boxes, firing now forwards, now rearwards over the top plane, wielding their Lewis guns in the icy blast as though they weighed no more than rapiers. They also operated the bombsight and released the bombs. Although sluggish and unmanoeuvrable, the machine was sometimes thrown about in combat, and then the observer sat on the floor, with both legs from the knees down hanging over the outside of the cockpit, gripping the edge with the back of the knees and at the same time gripping the gun with both hands to hold on.' At the best of times they had little more than a strong grip and a Lewis gun to hold on to, yet they claimed to have no fear of falling out. The airstream held them in.

FE2b's and d's were still flying offensive patrols, generally in pairs, and Lancastrian Sidney Attwater, now a pilot on 25 Squadron, records how he and his Lancastrian 'pal' Tom Mottershead, whose sustained courage had already earned him a Distinguished Conduct Medal (Attwater had a Military Medal from his earlier work as an observer), made a pact to stick together whatever happened. They had much else in common. Mottershead's fighting spirit was undimmed despite his maturity and his dependants – he was twenty-four, with a wife and baby son. Attwater had married while home on pilot training. They were reconnoitring a German airfield, inviting a scrap, when Mottershead began pointing down and signalling to Attwater to follow. He did so, down to 500 feet, and still Mottershead went on down, finally landing on the airfield. 'By the time I got down,' said Attwater, 'he and his observer had already opened up with their guns at the hangars, so we did the same. I know we used about 200 rounds of tracer, and one hangar was on fire. So I pointed up, and off we went.'

Back at base, and anticipating a reprimand for exceeding their brief, they resolved to say nothing of what they had done. But when the squadron commander sent for them and asked: 'What have you done with your ammo?', they had to own up. Threatened – tongue in cheek – with a court martial, they were given seven days' early parades, 'which meant nothing,' according to Attwater, 'because we were up in the air most mornings. But we felt much better for not just wasting petrol, but really having had a bash.'

Hearing some weeks later that Mottershead, transferred meanwhile to another squadron (No. 20), was in hospital, Attwater visited him to find him badly burned but remarkably perky. On a fighting patrol, his observer, Lieutenant W.E. Gower, had repelled one Albatros, sending it spinning down, but they had been set on fire by another, their fuel tank ruptured. Gower had played a fire extinguisher on Mottershead's clothing, and somehow Mottershead had flown the burning aeroplane home. In the inevitable crash-landing Gower was thrown clear, and he had helped to extricate his badly scorched pilot. Surgeons then began the fight for his life.

While Attwater was at his bedside a kite balloon was seen falling in flames in the distance, and Mottershead got out of bed to watch it from the hospital window – and got back in again when a nurse came in to scold him. He died next day, leaving Attwater to ponder whether his visit, and the episode of the balloon, had contributed. It seems not: his burns were too extensive for him to survive. The award of a posthumous VC underlined yet again the importance attached by the authorities to getting man and machine home. Clearly Tom Mottershead was one of the men whose desire to take the offensive inspired and even incited his fellows. Gower, who was one of them, was awarded an MC. Attwater, who was another, was later shot down on a dawn reconnaissance and taken prisoner; he survived into his eightieth year.

Throughout that summer the BE crews snatched a few hours from their corps duties to load up with bombs and distribute them over enemy airfields, railheads and sidings, protected more by the offensive patrols of the army squadrons than by direct escort. And long before the infantry attack on 15 September the bombers were at work. No. 27 Squadron, where the avuncular Sidney Smith, a founder-member, had succeeded the extrovert Borton, hit General von Below's headquarters that morning, together with rail centres and rolling stock, but their best work was done in the afternoon, after crews of 70 Squadron (1½-strutters) had reported forty trains on the lines in the Cambrai region, seeming to presage the arrival of an entire division. Eight Martinsydes took off, and three of them, seeing a train approaching Gouzeaucourt station, dive-bombed in turn. The first bomb stopped the train, bombs from the second machine blew up the rear truck, and the pilot then turned and dropped a 112-pounder on the troops as they evacuated the train. The third Martinsyde pilot hit an ammunition truck in the middle of the train, which blew up and started a succession of explosions in adjacent trucks. The remaining pilots hit trains and a supply dump nearby.

One of the flight commanders on 27 Squadron was the inventive Robert Bourdillon, who will be remembered as one of the architects of the CFS bombsight. He had meanwhile transferred to the RFC and qualified as a pilot. He studied the problems of flying in cloudy conditions, introduced more sophisticated methods of time-and-distance navigation to help his crews on long-distance missions in bad weather, and designed an effective 40-lb phosphorus bomb. Finally he pre-empted Leonard Cheshire by initiating target-marking attacks from low level to guide his fellows, becoming the first of the Pathfinders. His work was recognised by the awards of an MC and an AFC. (He survived to pursue a distinguished post-war career in medical research.)

Most of the day's air fighting took place above the region of Bapaume, which itself was bombed by BEs escorted by FEs. All the fighting took place behind the German lines. 'It was a terrific day in the air,' wrote Baring, and it was another year before so much flying was done again. Twenty-four German machines were brought down, against six RFC machines lost, with nine crew members missing. But four officers and a sergeant gunner had been wounded, all but one dying subsequently of their wounds.

The heaviest casualties that day were suffered by 70 Squadron, where an early morning patrol of seven 1½-strutters led by Guy Cruikshank was engaged in 'some of the bloodiest fighting of the day' (H.A. Jones). Cruikshank, a Gordon Highlander, and one of the pioneers of August 1914, will be remembered as the first Britisher to disgorge an agent successfully behind the enemy lines. He was 'a great and loved pilot,' according to Maurice Baring, 'with a sublime belief in his own invulnerability.' Another tribute spoke of him as 'one of the greatest pilots produced by the war'. He had been making a name for himself in the Sopwith two-seater as a scout pilot, with an ambition to try conclusions with Boelcke himself. When, unknown to Cruikshank, the opportunity came, Boelcke was patrolling alone in one of his new hunting machines, for which the Sopwith was no match. Yet witnesses of the spectacular duel between the two machines that followed, lasting a quarter of an hour, were enthralled by a mutual exhibition of flying skills. Eventually, after a lethal machine-gun burst from Boelcke, Cruikshank's machine disintegrated, and he and his observer fell to their deaths. The day's losses so distressed 70 Squadron that Trenchard sent Baring along to give a day's outing to any young pilots or observers whom the squadron commander deemed to be in need of a boost.

18

THE NEW GERMAN SCOUTS:
RICHTHOFEN'S FIRST:
CRITICISM OF TRENCHARD:
SMITH-BARRY GETS HIS WAY

O N 16 September, the first bulk delivery of the new Albatros and Halberstadt pursuit planes enabled Boelcke, having trained his men in the preceding fortnight, to plan a patrol on the 17th with a select few of his *Jagdstaffel 2*, five machines in all. Meanwhile the British were planning a raid on the same day on one of their principal objectives in the German rail communications system. Neither side knew of the plans of the other.

Beyond the Bapaume–Peronne road ran the two great feeder lines serving the enemy front, heading south from Cambrai. At Marcoing, six miles south-west of Cambrai, a branch line left the main Peronne line for Bapaume, and it was this junction, and the adjacent station, that the British chose, on the morning of 17 September, as the target for eight BEs of No. 12 Squadron, each carrying one 112-lb bomb and four 20-pounders, which meant leaving observers behind. They were escorted by six FE2b's of No. 11 Squadron. Taking off at 6 a.m., the formation had reached its operating height of 6,000 feet when a ground mist so hampered navigation as to rule out any chance of accurate bombing, and the formation returned.

By 09.30 the mist had cleared and take-off was again ordered. Similar conditions may well have delayed the take-off of *Jasta 2*; but however that may be, the scene was now set for tragedy on the one hand and prestigious victory on the other. It was a victory accomplished in machines that had only arrived at the front the previous day, flown by pilots, among them Manfred von Richthofen, who were eagerly awaiting their first clash with the RFC.

After forming up and gaining height, the British formation, soon to be reduced to six through various defects, crossed the lines at 10.30, in air that had become so clear that the cliffs of Dover were plainly visible. For some it was to prove a farewell glimpse of home; and the chances of survival – and of serenity – were not improved for BE pilot Robert Money when his petrol pump broke. But he still had his hand pump, and rather than abort he continued, as the good soldier-turned-airman he was. But as the pump was situated outside the fuselage, rather too far forward for comfortable working, he found the burden too great to enable him to keep in formation. Sickeningly aware that he was gradually losing height and speed, he found himself well adrift of the others as they approached Marcoing.

Ahead of him he saw the leader turning for home, evidently having dropped his bombs. There were three more BEs with him, but the fifth had disappeared. Money realised that he was going to be very lucky to get home; but it still did not occur to him to turn back. Ignoring Archie, which was becoming intense, he dropped his bombs and watched them fall; he was waiting for the last bomb-burst when he was startled by a crackle of machine-gun fire. The BE was involuntarily borne upwards, and in the next instant the engine stopped and he was enveloped in a cloud of smoke and flying fragments. Half the engine seemed to have gone, but by pushing the stick hard forward he managed to keep straight and level.

Again he heard the rattle of machine-gun fire, and looking up he saw one of the escorting FEs, having evidently hurried to his assistance, going down in a steep spiral, with two Huns on its tail. Cursing his own impotence, he got off a few rounds from his Lewis in the general direction of the hostiles, then realised it was hopeless. Another FE was going down, and he saw a third try to intervene although itself under attack. It seemed to Money that the air was thick with Huns.

Bunched together on the horizon, apparently out of harm's way, was the little group of four BEs, their escape apparently dependent on the sacrifice of the FE crews. (In fact, Moranes of 60 Squadron were about to arrive on the scene.) Meanwhile Money's emotions fluctuated between desolation and rage as Boelcke's five were joined by at least seven more enemy scouts, and the FE pilots, always vulnerable directly astern, fought a losing battle. Descending haphazardly earthwards, almost stalled, Money was the unwilling witness of their fate. Finally, almost as he crash-landed, he saw another BE, presumably the one that had been missing from the group, hit the ground nearby and pitch forward on its nose.

He was welcomed into enemy territory by the usual cliché: 'Well, the war is over for you!' The speaker was an officer, and Money was taken to a nearby Mess and given a drink, after which a doctor came and cleaned him up; he had suffered only superficial cuts and bruises. It was the base of a fighter unit, and they had witnessed the scrap. Several spoke English, and Money asked what had happened to the FEs. 'Two, three, four – finished,' they said.

'And the tractor biplane – the BE?'

'He too is finished. Boelcke himself shot him down.'

The figures were accurate: four of the six FEs and two of the eight BEs were lost. The pilot of the other BE, Second Lieutenant Aubrey Patterson, died a week later.

For the pilots of *Jasta 2*, other than Boelcke, this was their first victory against the RFC. One of them took pains to record particulars of his victim. It was an FE, and the pilot crash-landed in a field. Learning his trade quickly, principally from Boelcke, Manfred von Richthofen had crept up underneath the FE's blind spot, and he could not resist landing beside the wreckage of his victim. He was just in time to see pilot and observer being lifted out of their cockpits. The observer is said to have opened his eyes as Richthofen bent over him, smiled, and succumbed to his wounds. The pilot died on the way to hospital.

To celebrate this first of his victories, Richthofen wrote to a jeweller friend in Berlin and asked him to engrave a small commemorative silver cup with the date of the action and the type of machine. The jeweller obliged and forwarded the cup. He could hardly have imagined that this ritual would be repeated sixty times in the next few months – and indeed would have extended further had the supply of silver in blockaded Germany not run out.

Trenchard immediately sensed that the Germans had brought a new fighting squadron, or squadrons, into action on this front. These were not his only casualties that day, and he was quick to realise that the pendulum was swinging against him. The new German scouts, faster and more manoeuvrable, with their two fixed machine-guns firing through the propeller arc, and fighting in formation, out-classed anything the British had. But as yet their numbers were small, and Trenchard resolved to stick it out. He would not easily abandon his policy of aggression.

As for Richthofen, a cautious and calculating approach, a refusal to engage the enemy unless the circumstances were favourable, and the somewhat ghoulish collecting of trophies, rendered him less attractive as a hero to the British than to the Germans, but his methods made sound military sense. Yet he couldn't have succeeded as he did but for Trenchard's policy. 'Let the customer come to the shop' was Richthofen's motto. By operating over his own territory he faced no dangers from Archie, and with the prevailing winds in his favour he could never be trapped or caught out, as the British often were, on the wrong side of the lines.

In the month of September the Germans destroyed 127 British and French machines for the loss of twenty-seven, and although this partly reflected the natural advantages of defending, the air superior-ity of the Allies was put under serious threat. On 29 September Trenchard warned the War Office that he would be looking for a doubling of the number of fighting squadrons working with each army, and next day Haig backed him up, writing of 'the urgent necessity for a very early increase in the numbers and efficiency of the fighting aeroplanes at my disposal.' After paying glowing tribute to three summer months in which the RFC had maintained 'such a measure of superiority over the enemy in the air that it has been enabled to render services of incalculable value,' he warned that all but a few of the fighting machines at his disposal were 'decidedly inferior' to the improved machines of the enemy, leading to a marked increase in casualties and threatening a very serious situation unless adequate steps were taken. Whereas practically no German machines had crossed the lines in the first two months of the battle, they were now venturing up to the lines and across them. He then echoed Trenchard's conviction that 'it is the fighting far behind the enemy's lines that tells most.' Trenchard then put forward a statement of estimated requirements. When the massacre of the RFC that followed in the spring of 1917 earned the appellation of 'Bloody April', no one at home could say that they hadn't been warned.

Meanwhile the Allied armies, because of a break in the weather, were unable to exploit the undoubted advantages they had gained, at enormous cost. Even the RFC, which had fought a new type of warfare with courage and distinction, without rest and often with grievous losses, was so impeded by the conditions that army commanders had to report that the number and accuracy of air reports was 'not up to the usual standard'. In summary, a crescent-shaped area about six miles across at its widest point had been gained, but the battle, conceived as a diversionary attack to relieve the French at Verdun, had burgeoned and had seemed to promise a breakthrough that had not materialised. British casualties, killed and wounded, amounted to nearly 419,000, the French 194,000, with the grim consolation that the Germans, already outnumbered, lost 650,000. Taking 22 November, when winter finally set in, as the end of the battle, the RFC from 1 July lost 308 pilots, 191 observers, and 782 aeroplanes. German losses were less than half that number, yet the RFC still controlled the air above the battlefield. This they achieved by never forgetting their fundamental *raison d'être*; working for the army. By taking the fight to the enemy even when losses seemed prohibitive, Trenchard stuck to his principles, relying on the tenacity and resilience of his air crews. They never failed him.

Yet there was certainly criticism from within the Corps. The most outspoken, as already quoted, was Smith-Barry, who was contemptuous of the whole basic philosophy and psychology of the training organisation, quite apart from his reluctance to put half-trained men into battle. Trenchard openly apologised to his pilots for asking them to fight against a better-equipped enemy with obsolete weapons and machines, but he demanded it just the same. The BE2c remained the maid of all work, but employing it would have been suicidal but for the Moranes, the FEs and the DH2s, and finally the Nieuports, and their offensive patrols. Then had come the *Jastas*, of which by November there were seven, to disturb the equilibrium.

When Eric Routh, who had learned the hard way that summer with 34 Squadron under the analytical Major J.A. Chamier, was posted to 16 Squadron as a flight commander in November, again on BEs, he was introduced, as the composition of his flight, to one surviving pilot and one surviving observer. 'Reinforcements are on their way from England,' he was told. But when they came they proved to be worse than novices. Routh was allowed a period in which to train them, but their quality depressed him. There was one newcomer, he wrote, who 'looked more intelligent than most, but that is not saying a great deal'.

Born in Malta twenty-one years earlier of a naval family, Routh was mature enough to cope without being driven either to despair or drink, but he did occasionally find relaxation in the Mess with the adjutant, who provided a shoulder to cry on. '"Uncle" Davidson and I have a drinking bout. He put down eleven liqueur glasses of neat whisky, I beat him with twelve of brandy. I had the pleasure of seeing him carried to bed.' He added, with pardonable pride: 'I put myself to bed.'

Robert Money, from the comparative safety of POW camp, also found much to reflect on. He was especially critical of what he characterised as the 'flying for the sake of flying' mentality, even flying for the sake of kudos. It seemed to him that the RFC squadrons were often asked to do work of doubtful utility in unsuitable machines, something which he believed other nations eschewed. 'The British seemed to have less regard for air casualties than the French or the Germans.' He was trenchant, too, on the subject of throwing raw recruits into the fray. 'The practice we followed of sending pilots over the lines semi-trained – which cost us so heavily in lives and machines – was not followed by the French or the Germans, whose pilots had usually completed at least fifty hours in the air, were masters of their machines and had had some practice in navigation and air tactics.'

Ewart Garland, the Australian who had been so emphatic about the term Hun, was another BE pilot with few illusions – unless he imagined that his château billet on No. 10 Squadron was typical. Occupied that summer in artillery work, contact patrols, and bombing, he rated the bombing as mostly casual and random. It went on all day and every day along the whole length of the front, penetrating anything from ten to forty miles beyond the lines, each squadron looking after selected targets in a designated area. Strong headwinds remained a perpetual hazard, and Garland felt that higher authority took a sadistic pleasure in sending them out on suicidal missions, sluggish and overladen and at the mercy of machines which were twice as fast and twice as handy.

Garland himself had had only five hours solo when he was posted to 10 Squadron at the start of the battle: he had put up his wings eight days' previously. He shared a general cynicism among BE pilots about the faith placed by Trenchard in the scout pilots and their offensive patrols, believing that bombing by the BEs would be much more effective given close escorts. It was an eternal argument. 'Our fighter squadrons always went well into enemy territory,' he wrote later, 'deliberately provoking the Hun fighters to join battle. Our Higher Command held to the theory that this policy drew the enemy fighters away from our slow bombers and photo and observation aeroplanes; but we slow and more or less defenceless chaps disagreed violently with such policy, and urgently wanted our fighters to "look after us" on all our missions. I well remember how safe and happy we felt on the rare occasions our bombing formations were escorted by fighters, which buzzed all round us like hornets while we plodded along in fairly tight formations at half the speed of the fighters. On these happy occasions enemy scouts kept a respectful distance, and we usually got back unscathed. How it warmed our spirits to have the fighter boys with us!'

As Trenchard had feared, there was bitterness at the publicity now being accorded scout pilots. Twenty-five-year-old Lieutenant John Quinnell, an Anglo-Irishman who spent a year on No. 10 Squadron (and much later became an air commodore), felt that because corps work was unspectacular it was underrated. The scout pilots were magnificent and deserved their decorations, but he knew of two corps recce squadrons which got one decoration each at the end of six months of hard flying. 'All other breasts', noted Quinnell, 'were as bare as a sparrow's.' Although mentioned in despatches, he was not decorated himself until late in the war, and he complained that however conscientiously they worked they got no word of appreciation, yet they should have been sharing in the distinction and the glory. Their task was the prime one, yet it was made to seem subordinate. Weary, but too proud to ask for a rest, many corps pilots asked to be recommended for transfer to an army squadron.

Garland, while conceding that the scout pilots did great things, saw them as the darlings of the service, searching out the enemy high above the corps squadrons like knights of old, not to be bothered with escort work. He was happier with night bombing, which came to be regarded as a useful adjunct to the work of the BEs. It did not require escorts, and there was no interference from Archie, though there were dangers enough in the crude facilities for take-off and landing, the rough surfaces of aerodromes, and the primitive cockpit instruments available.

Throughout that autumn Smith-Barry continued to complain to Trenchard about the inadequacy of replacement pilots and to disparage the whole system of flying training. Whereas, in peacetime, young flyers had persistently begged for opportunities to fly, men straight from training school, although young and fresh, showed little enthusiasm for flying and had to be virtually ordered into the air. They rarely sought permission to go for a practice flight. S-B blamed the instructors: pupils were discouraged through being taught by instructors who lacked a sense of vocation and whose indifference was contagious. The mental attitude of the instructor – who often regarded his stint of instructing as a chore – was reflected in every pupil he trained.

One of S-B's hobby-horses was that a pilot under training should always sit in the pilot's seat, not, as was general, in the passenger seat, obliging him to make his first solo flight in an unaccustomed position. He wanted a standard type of machine, suitable for every kind of manoeuvre, and certainly not a type as inherently stable as the BE, which corrected most mistakes and gave the pupil a false sense of security. The pupil must learn to be master of both himself and his machine. As it happened, the ideal machine for practising manoeuvres was about to become available in the 100-hp Monosoupape-engined Avro 504J and later K.

S-B had another slice of luck at about the same time. The greatest fear of pilots was of spinning, and a great many lives were lost because the technical reasons for spinning were not fully understood and the corrective action was not known. It was a very lucky pilot who survived a spin. One who did, as early as August 1912, was a naval lieutenant named Wilfred Parke, who recovered from his spin accidentally by, as he put it, 'doing everything wrong'. His experience naturally aroused interest, but the control movements which brought about his escape, although analysed, were never confirmed for circulation to all pilots and instructors. The reluctance of pilots to experiment further, in the absence of parachutes, is understandable.

The pilot's instinct, when he got into a spin, was to pull back on the stick to bring the nose up: it went against nature to push the nose forward. This, however, with some application of rudder, must have been what Parke did.

A post-war investigation attempted to summarise what was known of the spin and the history of attempts to control it.[1] The first man to set down the procedure for getting out of a spin appears to have been Major Frank Goodden, test pilot at Farnborough, who, in August 1916, 'in view of recent accidents', spun an FE8, the last of the Factory's pushers, and summarised his method of recovery:-

1. Glauert, H., *The Investigation of the Spin of an Aeroplane* (Advisory Committee for Aeronautics, June 1919).

1. Switch off motor.
2. Control stick put central and pushed forward.
3. Rudder put in centre.

This, explained Goodden, resulted in a nose-dive, from which the aeroplane, having once got up speed, could easily be pulled out with the control stick pulled back slightly. Sufficient height was assumed.

Frank Goodden's test flights predate a scientific investigation carried out in 1917 by Dr (later Professor) F.A. Lindemann, who learned to fly to prove his theories. Several other pilots, including John Chamier and a New Zealander named Balcombe-Brown, made similar discoveries in the autumn of 1916, convincing a sceptical Smith-Barry. The work of another Hawker, Harry, Sopwith's test pilot, is referred to; but there is no mention of Lanoe and the DH2.

Meanwhile S-B's ideas had crystallised into a belief that his best course was to start a school for instructors, with the intention that all instructors should eventually pass through it. Only by standardising pilot training throughout the service could there be any real long-term benefit.

Finally Trenchard's patience cracked. 'Don't worry us any more with your complaints. If you think you can do better, go and do it.' But the irritation was as much counterfeited as real; he appreciated that Smith-Barry's *métier* was instructing. 'It's time you tried out all these ideas you've been pestering me with. I've told the training people, so don't let me or yourself down.' He was to take over the Gosport School of Flying, where he had previously served as an instructor under Ferdy Waldron, and the scene was set for the revolution in flying training which was to spread worldwide. 'The number of lives he saved', proclaimed Stanley Vincent, who later became his deputy at Gosport, 'is incalculable.'

19

THE BREEZE VERTICAL

'We were never far from our fears.'

S o wrote Thomas Traill, a pilot on 20 Squadron who, although only eighteen, had seen action as a naval cadet in the Dardanelles in 1915 and who, in a future war, would become an air vice-marshal. What were these fears?

During training, the fear of failure was paramount, eclipsing the fear of being killed or maimed. For most trainees, this was their first chance of measuring themselves against their peers in a man's world, and many who suspected they were unsuited to flying and had no aptitude for it persisted with their training until they were forced to abandon it, either by their instructors or because of an accident. Such accidents were all too often fatal.

Once posted to a squadron in France, the fears multiplied. Forced landings during training could be negotiated safely: the English countryside presented ideal surfaces for landing light aeroplanes. But forced landings in or near the front line might offer a choice between one maze of shellholes and another, often in a crippled machine. There was no such thing as a nice smooth belly-flop: all machines had fixed undercarriages, ready to snag on any declivity or protrusion. Engine failure, gun stoppages, navigation in cloud or bad weather, the incessant exposure to Archie, not to mention enemy scouts, the prevailing wind that always fettered the homeward flight, the long, unrecoverable fall to earth in a doomed machine, above all the 'flamer' – these were daily physical hazards, which most people succeeded in putting to the back of their minds. But added to all this was the abstract fear of fear itself, of letting the side down, of being found wanting. What held a man in the line, according to Traill, was the fear of being exposed as one who would leave his comrades to carry the can, with the burden of living with oneself thereafter.

Every man had his own reservoir of courage, which might be dissipated slowly, quickly, or suddenly: the difficulty, for squadron commanders, lay in judging the rate of evaporation. Doctors attached to operational bases were not necessarily skilled in monitoring flying fitness, and some squadron commanders were remote figures, but the best of them watched closely for that haunted look which was euphemistically known as staleness. Such paragons might send a man on leave whether it was his turn or not. There was an awareness from the top down of the effects of protracted combat flying, and in 1916 Henderson recommended the formation of a Special RFC Medical Board. But it was 1917 before flying fatigue cases were sent away for special study and treatment, and even then, when so many were weary, who could be spared? Experienced men had to be retained to protect the beginners.

The medical officer in charge of RFC patients at the General Hospital at Étaples, Captain Dudley Corbett, RAMC, listed the symptoms to watch for. They began with a general lassitude. Sleep did not come so easily, or would be troubled when it came, interrupted by nightmares, often hysterical: anyway it would cease to be refreshing. While airborne a man might recover his keenness, but he would take less trouble with himself and his machine and might fly erratically, attacking recklessly or not at all. He would be preoccupied and irritable beforehand and exhausted afterwards. Smoking could be so incessant as to become neurotic. Some, to keep going, relied on alcohol, but in Corbett's experience this was rare.

Tommy Traill was aware of men on 20 Squadron who had to prime themselves beforehand, and even take a bottle up with them. A stiff drink, they found, stiffened resolve. But Traill and his colleagues were too preoccupied with their own nervous tensions to feel compassion for those who couldn't cope. For Traill, the men who took to the bottle were infinitely to be preferred to those who shirked in the air but talked themselves into the scrap at debriefing. 'It was usually impossible to know what others were doing during a dog-fight,' conceded Traill, 'but you soon got to know these people. There were only a few of them.' Squadron commanders had the same difficulty, when making judgements on fitness to fly, in sorting the fake from the genuine. As for alcohol, 'we did have periodical binges when the weather permitted,' wrote one pilot, 'but ours was a pretty sober squadron, for we all knew that alcohol and flying don't go well together.'

Arthur Gould Lee, like Traill a future air vice-marshal, often referred in his letters home to squadron parties. 'Binge last evening – thick head. Sing-song round piano. But about ten o'clock, chaps on dawn patrol "sent" off to bed by their flight commander.' The inverted commas were Lee's: it wasn't an order. 'Another binge developed last evening.' And later: 'You ask about the frequent binges we have. But we don't have them that often . . . Otherwise there's not a great deal of drinking. I drink nothing but lime juice at meals, and the others do the same.' Again: 'The binge went on riotously until midnight, but I packed up at eleven because of the early job.' 'Rowdy binge 11.30 p.m. Sunday. But I'm on early patrol and felt I'd had enough to drink.'[1]

Robert Money, recalling a Mess party, wrote: 'I don't want to convey the impression that we drank excessively or regularly.' The heavy drinkers, he thought, were not to be found at the front. Life was eventful and exciting enough without stimulants. And for most of these youths, a single drink brought exhilaration, two and they were ready to smash the place up – which they often did. Money disagreed with the impression given later by the American Elliott Springs, in his book *War Birds*, of RFC men drinking themselves silly to anaesthetise their nerves. 'I'm certain that kind of thing didn't happen in 1915 and 1916.'

Gwilym Lewis extended this view to later years. 'A great thing is that there is practically nothing drunk but soft drinks, so that the Mess is always full of spirit without any artificial stimulants.' But

1. Lee, Arthur Gould, *No Parachute* (Jarrolds, 1968).

consumption varied, and there were exceptions. Of a colleague of whom he was clearly fond, a Canadian who made him laugh, he noted: 'He drinks too much.'

Parties were an occasion, sometimes started to relieve the gloom after losses. When they developed, the damage was to property rather than to person, though a raid on an adjacent squadron could get out of hand and result in real injuries. With alcohol so freely available, inevitably there were abuses, but over-indulgence was rare. 'Dawn patrol with a hangover?' wrote one pilot, 'No thanks!' But those not on the detail might be less abstemious. Jack Slessor admitted: 'We used to drink a good deal.'

Major F.J. Powell, MC, when commanding an SE5 squadron in 1917, thought the centre of his squadron was the bar. It was not something he discouraged. He always carried, when airborne, a small flask filled with rum. At altitude in winter his moustache would get frozen into a block of ice. 'A nip of alcohol had an immediate and glorious effect.'

Squadron life was a therapy in itself, something which men on 'rest' in England longed to return to, despite the dangers. They missed the camaraderie that is only present in a fighting unit. The flying itself could be enjoyable, and when it was over the freedom itself was intoxicating: one's time was one's own. Trenchard's policy of no empty chairs, old faces dissolving into new, checking any tendency to brood, was brutal but effective, and Mess nights, with uninhibited horseplay and the singing of traditional songs ('The Young Aviator Lay Dying' etc.), were invaluable for *esprit de corps* and for letting off steam.

Everyone was made aware sooner or later, in the loss of close comrades, that it could happen to them. But as in training, so in battle, a man would rather die than drop out. Labels like LMF – lack of moral fibre – were not yet known, and a loss of nerve was not classed as a crime. But the quitter, in addition to loss of self-respect, faced an uncertain future. If he had a regiment he would be returned to it, which was in itself a humiliation. If not, it could mean a transfer to the infantry.

The tradition that 'Flying will continue as usual', established at the outset, was doubtless a wise as well as a cherished one, but when it was applied to individuals there were dissentients. Surgeon Lieutenant H. Graeme Anderson, of the RNAS, learnt to fly himself to test his theories, and they proved contentious. 'If a pupil crashed and was apparently uninjured,' he wrote, 'he was ordered to go up again in another machine almost immediately. This was supposed to prevent loss of nerve, or, if known to be lost by the crash, [help] the immediate recovery of it. The author has seen the results of this method of treatment, and can say emphatically it is a method to be condemned . . .'

Bryan Sharwood-Smith (48 Squadron under Keith Park, and later knighted for his work in the Colonial Service), having narrowly survived a nerve-shattering dog-fight, was sent over the lines again within forty-eight hours. 'Such was the rule and a good one,' he wrote. 'Too much time for reflection was fatal.' But the reaction came a few weeks later, on home leave, when, after a chance remark by his sister, he broke down completely in front of his family. Yet the home leave did the trick: he had recovered by the end of it.

'I suppose most people live in a perpetual state of wind-up during a patrol,' wrote Bernard Oliver; and the actor Mervyn Johns said: 'I don't think there was a single moment when I was not scared to death.' But the impression that most men crossed the lines in a state of blue funk is not borne out by contemporary diaries and letters. The admission that they were often scared was general amongst RFC veterans, but a proper appreciation of mortal danger was essential for any chance of survival. The man who knew no fear was a freak.

According to John Quinnell, pilots sent back to England before they broke down had every chance of recovery, but if they broke down in France through being there too long they were seldom much use abroad. Two known exceptions were Harold Balfour, who was said to have gone 'loony' after a crash in a 1½-strutter but returned to do great things; and Ewart Garland. 'Bad weather meant a holiday,' Garland noted, 'otherwise one kept on flying to the limit of endurance and beyond.' Garland, like a good many others, was tested to destruction: understandably, he had a sudden breakdown at 10,000 feet and was given a staff job at Brigade Headquarters as a rest-cure. This was after he had been in action for eight months.

For Garland, as for many others, the monotony of staff work proved a short cut to rehabilitation. 'I have that deep down feeling that I ought not to have this soft job,' he wrote. 'My conscience pricks me when I am recording pilots' activity in action.' What he missed above all was the comradeship. Fed up with the staff and all its connotations of pomposity and red tape, he added: 'The sooner I fly again the better.' He got his wish, but not in a squadron in France: he was posted to a reserve squadron in England to help work it up to operational pitch.

While there were certainly men, like Cecil Lewis, whose confidence in their own survival was not misplaced, most, like Albert Ball, soon lost any illusions of indestructibility. Others had premonitions, and knew that their time had come. Norman Macmillan, who later gained distinction as an aviation writer, talked to his tent companion one summer evening of joining others in a walk into the local town of Cassel for a meal. 'No thanks, Mac,' was the reply, 'I've got some letters to write.' When Macmillan got back to the tent he was asked: 'If anything happens to me tomorrow, Mac, will you post these letters for me and see that my kit is sent off to these two addresses?' With that he turned in and fell into a deep and untroubled sleep. Next morning the crews of eight 1½-strutters were briefed to get photos of Menin railway station, which they knew would be a tough assignment. 'I'm sorry I couldn't get you an escort,' concluded the squadron commander. They got their photographs but were intercepted on the way back. Many suffered damage, and of the two who were shot down, one was Macmillan's tent companion. Letters and kit were posted as requested.

There was one sure way of escaping with integrity intact, and there were few men who did not know a pang of envy of those who profited from it. Convinced he had been shot through the arm and that he could feel the warm blood flowing, Tommy Traill was already envisaging the hospitalisation and the posting home when, on examination, it was found he had not been shot at all, but merely grazed. 'To go home wounded,' he admitted, 'would have been an honourable way out of immediate danger and a temporary relief from the conflict.' The conflict he was referring to was not so much the war but fear itself, above all the fear of burning, and, almost equally, the fear of human weakness, the fear of failing one's comrades.

Nobody, it seemed, could stand the strain indefinitely. 'Ultimately it reduced you to a dithering state,' wrote Gwilym Lewis, 'near to imbecility. You had to go out and do the job, you could never say frankly: "I am afraid, I can't face it any more." So you continually had to win battles over yourself and your fears.' The result, believed Lewis, was damage to the essential tissue of one's being.

Men blessed with a spiritual faith were the stronger for it, but organised religion gave solace to few. 'You never hear anyone talking religion,' said Lee, 'whether in the Mess or privately. We do have padres, and they occasionally hold services, but mostly they organise cinema shows and bury people. They can't even do much for anyone whose nerve is beginning to crack, the doctors come in on that.' Service padres were hopelessly under strength, few were resident, and Church parades were rare. 'I have been to Church this morning,' wrote Gwilym Lewis in a letter home, 'I attend when I can.' But no one was more fiercely critical of the padres. 'Most of these fellows who stand in pulpits I often feel I would like to get hold of, shake them thoroughly, kick them hard and tell them to go and have a look at the world as it really is, and then start talking about it.' One padre, unable to bear the distressing sequence of casualties and replacements – or perhaps discouraged by rejection – applied for a posting to a regiment in the line.

Innermost thoughts, never revealed, undoubtedly dwelt on more spiritual matters, but outwardly, more attention was paid to super-stition. Many carried mascots and were inconsolable if they were lost. Lee touched wood before a scrap. Prayers were a form of insurance, only heartfelt in moments of crisis. 'Why should God grant me any special favour?' asked Lee. 'The Hun I'm fighting may be calling on him too . . . How can anyone who has to fight believe in God, with all the mass killings? How can I call on God to help me shoot a man down in flames?'

Home leave could be confusing as well as therapeutic. There was a quiet satisfaction in seeing the crowds of holidaymakers on beaches in midsummer, yet it was a reminder of how remote the civilian was from the war, with no conception of what it meant to the fighting man. The underlying stoicism of the masses, and the pride in bereavement, were not easily divined. More visible were the profiteers, the strikers, the conchies, the people with cushy jobs for whom the war couldn't last long enough, bitterly resented by men for whom there was no escape from a return to danger and probable death. Yet that return could be strangely uplifting. Lee wrote of the sensation of coming home, of welcome and comradeship, of a feeling that this was where one belonged, not amongst the money-making and pleasure-seeking mob that one could not escape from in London. Communication might be limited, the eternal verities were seldom discussed; who they were, where they came from, what made them tick – none of this mattered. All that counted was whether the other chap had what it takes.

20

CLASHES WITH DOWDING AND TRENCHARD: THE DEATH OF BOELCKE: HAWKER'S DUEL WITH VON RICHTHOFEN

Arriving in France in October, commanding a new squadron of Sopwith 1½-strutters, No. 45, and impatient for a third crack at the enemy, was Willie Read. But it was not a happy return. At Candas on the Somme, where a second aircraft park had been established the previous year, there was snow on the ground when they landed, and as nothing had apparently been prepared for them, the aspect was bleak. Read had expected to be met by the commander of the wing they would be serving under, 'Stuffy' Dowding, but Stuffy was not in evidence. Candas happened also to be Trenchard's headquarters, and it was 'Boom' himself who came across to welcome him and his twelve machines. 'Boom asked if we were all right,' Read related afterwards, 'and I said we would be later.'

'Rations all right? Where are your tents?'

Trenchard's questions were rhetorical: it was obvious that none of these items had been provided. But he left without further comment. 'I think he twisted Stuffy's tail,' said Read. 'This was rather unfortunate as Stuffy and I were not very fond of each other.' Early in 1914 they had had a row at CFS, owing, according to Read, to Dowding's 'pugnacious temperament'. The self-willed

Read could be pugnacious himself, and they had nearly come to blows.

There were two Bessoneau hangars – canvas-covered, wooden-framed sheds capable of holding four machines each – on the perimeter, not enough to house the twelve Sopwiths, so in the absence of tents Read decided to quarter the men in the hangars and picket the machines outside, the obvious solution to a man accustomed to looking after his men. Then Dowding arrived. 'Turn the men out of the hangars', he ordered, 'and put the machines inside.'

'And where are the men to go?'
'Now you are being insolent.'

Dowding sent him some tents, but the incident rankled. 'Stuffy had his knife into me,' said Read, 'from then on.'

It was normal for a new squadron to be given at least a week in which to get acquainted with conditions before venturing over enemy territory, but 45 was ordered off at once by Dowding. 'On our first patrol of three machines only one came back,' bemoaned Read, 'and I lost my best flight commander, one Porter by name.' Read's anger and distress, at the start of what he had hoped might be a brilliant campaign in the Sopwith, may be imagined. To wing headquarters the missing men might be no more than names on a casualty list, but Read, like any good squadron commander, had made it his business to get to know all his crews. Porter, for instance – Leslie Porter – an Ulsterman, married with three young children, was a distinctive figure at the mature age of thirty-five, a pioneer in the motor industry in Belfast and a prominent figure in motor racing before the war. In Read's view he would certainly have gone on to command a squadron. His death in captivity, within a few hours of the action, was later confirmed. (Twenty-five years later his son David was luckier in surviving being shot down and captured.)

Struggling to launch raw pilots in an imperfect machine, Read suffered such severe losses in that first month that his squadron, as Smith-Barry's had been, was sent away to recoup. To add insult to injury, Dowding blamed their losses on inefficiency. But at least the transfer switched them to a different wing. 'I was glad to get away from Stuffy,' said Read. But he still found the control exercised over him by his new brigade commander, T.I. Webb-Bowen, irksome. Occasionally he led a formation himself, in defiance of the order that squadron commanders must not fly over the lines, and the operation reports reflected this. 'I was continually getting snorters from HQ for disobeying orders.' How was it possible, he argued, to keep in touch and direct and criticise his pilots and observers unless he took part in affairs himself? Pugnacious or not, Read was certainly head-strong, and instead of giving way he dug his toes in. Webb-Bowen used to visit the squadron with the object, Read felt, of finding fault, and he became very unhappy. He stuck it for six months and then applied to go back to his regiment. 'Boom was very annoyed with me for applying, and when he finally agreed he said: "In a few months' time you will ask me to take you back and I shall say no – as I have to everybody else so far."' But Read persisted, and in April 1917 he went back to the King's Dragoon Guards, reverting to captain, after a sad leave-taking from the squadron he himself had formed and led.

'I had another reason for wanting to go back to the regiment,' admitted Read. 'It looked at about this time [just before the Battle of Arras] as if we were going to advance and get the Bosch on the run, and by going back to the regiment I saw the possibility of getting a gallop with them.' But the gallop didn't come off, and for the rest of 1917 he watched with a wistful nostalgia as the corps machines circled overhead. Would Boom, for old times' sake, take him back after all? The time came when he decided to try.

A fresh hazard of air fighting, as formations got bigger and dogfights between opposing groups proliferated, was collision, and it was ironic that the man who had done more than anyone to develop team fighting should be one of its first victims. On 26 October 1916 Oswald Boelcke brought his personal score of victories to 40, but he was already admitting to his closest friend and colleague Erwin Boehme that he was feeling the strain. It was in this state that a moment's inattention or over-confidence could be fatal. Certainly when they took off again two days later, on the 28th, there seemed nothing in the opposition – two DH scouts of Hawker's squadron – to trouble the five Albatros pilots Boelcke was leading. Having recently captured a DH2, the Germans had proved in mock combat what they already knew, that their new machines were far superior. Yet the two DH2 pilots manoeuvred so cleverly that they must be given some credit for what followed: their names were Lieutenant A.G. Knight and Second Lieutenant Alfred McKay.

Six more German fighters arrived as Boelcke started his attack, and this may have led to confusion. Anyway, he and his friend Boehme dived for the same target, and neither saw the other. The horror of the German pilots, as Boehme's undercarriage struck Boelcke's upper wing, was fleetingly relieved as Boelcke dropped away apparently under control, but then they saw the wing break away, and as Boelcke fought in vain for control they knew that his death was certain. Boehme escaped unscathed, while Knight and McKay, who continued their manoeuvring, deserved their luck. In pursuance of the mutual respect and camaraderie that distinguished air combat, the RFC dropped a laurel wreath over the German lines next day, bearing the inscription: 'To the memory of Captain Boelcke, our brave and chivalrous foe.' Sadly, Knight was killed just before Christmas 1916, McKay a year later.

Boelcke had not merely inspired the German Air Force while he was alive, he had left behind an indelible legacy. Meanwhile the leading air tactician on the British side, whose motto of 'Attack EVERYTHING' still graced the notice board of 24 Squadron, remained in command. He still flew regularly if less frequently, and when he did he continued to take a subordinate role in the formation, lest he betray any hint of rustiness. The flight commanders flew almost daily, and he was content to follow them, usually replacing a tired pilot, and usually in a strange machine. It was a difficult time for DH2 pilots, called upon to face superior machines, their weaknesses known and their tactics rumbled. Experienced pilots were thinning out, and there was too little time to train the new ones or break them in properly, while their shooting was often abysmal. Hawker did all he could, but with demands for patrols unceasing he was forced to compromise. He could do little more than keep an eye on the general health of his pilots, and recommend them for leave if he felt they needed it, or to be sent home as instructors if he felt they had done – or had had – enough. He knew from personal experience that lack of leave had an effect on efficiency: reactions became slower, perceptions less acute.

He himself was feeling wartorn before the summer was out, without much hope of a rest. The approach of autumn removed a favourite form of relaxation: it was too dark after tea to play tennis. If at times he felt stale, he gained rejuvenation from the eagerness of his pilots and their high spirits at Mess parties and Mess games. When at last he did go on leave, on 5 November, with the Somme battle foundering in a sea of mud, his betrothal to Beatrice was unofficially confirmed. He expected to serve another two or three months in France and then be promoted to lieutenant-colonel and a staff job, when marriage would follow. Yet he found London depressing. Of The Empire Leicester Square, then a music hall and hitherto a frequent haunt of his wartime colleagues, he wrote: 'I didn't meet a soul I knew.' It brought home to him the shocking carnage of the past two years: either his contemporaries were dead or they had been promoted out of sight. Meanwhile expansion had changed the face of the RFC completely; no longer did everyone know everyone else.

Although by the time he got back to France the ground battle was stagnating, the DH2s were still penetrating enemy territory in support of Trenchard's determination to maintain air superiority over the lines. Hawker was soon back in action, and on 23 November he took off with two of his senior pilots on an offensive patrol. The leader, the tall, dark-haired, pencil-moustached J.O. (Jock) Andrews, a striking figure in his Highland forage cap, had joined the squadron a year earlier at Hounslow and, with Hawker, was the last surviving original. The third member of the patrol, R.H.M.S. 'Bob' (sometimes 'Sandy') Saundby, who would one day be 'Bomber' Harris's deputy at Bomber Command, had been on the squadron four months following distinguished anti-Zeppelin service in England. Quite simply, on patrols of this nature they were looking for trouble.

Over Bapaume at about 9,000 feet they spotted below them what Andrews, caring nothing for the niceties, later described as 'a few fat Huns'. It seems likely that these were a decoy. Above them an umbrella of Albatros scouts, led by Richthofen, was waiting to pounce. (Richthofen by this time was the leading living German ace with ten victories.) Andrews was about to abandon the pursuit of the obese two-seaters when Hawker dived past him, intent as ever on attack. A Hun scout followed, but Andrews drove him off, firing about twenty-five rounds at close range. Soon Andrews too had a Hun on his tail, 'pumping shells into his backside,' as he put it, and his engine (a pusher in the DH2), was hit. He had no option but to try to limp back over the trenches. He saw Hawker hesitate as though to assist him, and then, perhaps satisfied that his leader could look after himself, chase after one of the Hun scouts. The last Andrews saw of him he was scrapping with a hostile, apparently under control.

Soon afterwards Saundby saw Hawker in a circling fight with a German at about 3,000 feet, but by this time his own engine was out of action and he could do nothing to help. Knowing Hawker's skill, however, he wasn't unduly perturbed. He was not to know that his commander was pitted against perhaps the only pilot in the German Air Force with a reasonable chance of shooting him down in a duel.

Hawker's experience, and the manoeuvrability of the DH2, might well compensate for the overall superiority of the Albatros, but he could not manoeuvre indefinitely. Under the prevailing wind, every turn was taking him farther from the lines, and sooner or later shortage of fuel would compel him to run for it. For the moment, though, as he waved spontaneously to his adversary – who reciprocated – he was giving every indication of enjoying himself.

'We circled round and round like madmen,' wrote Richthofen afterwards, 'twenty times to the left, thirty times to the right . . . I had quickly discovered that it was not a novice that I had to deal with . . . it was clear to me that I was being tackled by a flying champion.' A group of German grenadiers were in no doubt that they were watching a duel between 'first-rate champions of the air'. Inevitably the time came when Hawker, despairing of pinning his man down, had to break off, and after a few stunts he began a sudden zig-zagging dash for the lines at low level. Richthofen followed, firing all the time, and victory for him seemed certain until his guns jammed. Hawker was only fifty yards short of the lines when, perversely, a single bullet from that final burst found its mark, and he fell, shot through the head.

Richthofen's pride in downing what he called 'the English Immelmann' was immense, and he concluded his account: 'His machine-gun was dug out of the ground and it adorns the entrance to my room.'

21

TRAINING, AND THE LACK OF IT

'Our so-called instructors were not flying instructors at all.'

AIR MARSHAL SIR HUGH WALMSLEY

T HE men who flew to France in August 1914 had all been trained, at their own expense, by professional flying instructors at one or other of the civilian schools. Having been taught to fly, and having gained their Royal Aero Club certificate, they reported to the Central Flying School to be passed out for their wings. This, according to Jack Slessor, was a perfunctory business, calling for no particular skill. The anxious candidate was asked some rudimentary questions about the theory of flight, the internal combustion engine, and the organisation of the RFC, while dual instruction consisted of a few circuits and landings, in which the instructor flew the aeroplane, with the pupil having his hands and feet on the controls 'to get the feel of them'. An occasional bang on the back to attract the pupil's attention revealed the instructor waving his hands to show that he had relinquished control. Afterwards the pupil was asked whether he felt confident in himself, and if he answered 'Yes' he was sent off solo. 'I do not remember,' recalled Slessor, 'anyone having the moral courage to answer "No" to that stock question, though I personally felt anything but confident in myself.' Yet the pre-war service atmosphere, with pilots allotted their own machine and flying almost where they chose, to visit other squadrons, to attend race meetings and similar events, landing where they could, soon bred skill and confidence.

On the outbreak of war, experienced civilian instructors were quickly absorbed into the service, but the rapid expansion that followed soon exhausted their capacity. Complaining that the situation with new pilots was unsatisfactory, Brancker reported that the right kind of young men were coming forward in gratifying numbers, but that the shortage of aeroplanes and engines was only equalled by the paucity of skilled pilots capable of imparting their knowledge and experience. Long waiting lists accumulated.

There were few branches of service tuition in which errors could be so catastrophic as in the training of pilots. This was before the days of flight simulators, and almost from the outset the syllabus exposed the pupil to the ultimate danger. Crashes could be especially costly for the pupil, who, in the flimsy machines of the time, occupied the front seat. Whereas the rear cockpit might remain more or less intact, the forward cockpit was often demolished.

There was no standard manual for instructors, no aptitude tests, and no instructors' schools. Most of the men recruited as instructors were home from the front 'on rest', and if many of them approached the task with a minimum of enthusiasm it is hardly surprising. They saw the posting as a come-down; yet it required courage to turn the controls over to a raw pupil, and it was certainly no rest for the nerves. They had to be continually on the alert, and they were overworked and over-stressed.

In Jock Andrews's experience, if the instructor wasn't on rest he was probably waiting impatiently to go overseas. There were even some who had been categorised as suitable for reserve squadron duties only. Their results were not monitored, they worked without a proper syllabus, and they looked upon their work as drudgery.

When Peter Portal went home after Christmas 1915 to learn to fly at Castle Bromwich, after his stint of observing, he was astonished at the ignorance of the majority of his instructors. Some were good, but some he thought disgracefully bad, and all were idiosyncratic, teaching in their own way. Most were competent pilots, but few had the technical knowledge or the qualities of character and temperament likely to inspire confidence in others. Morale amongst the pupils was correspondingly low, and when Portal graduated to CFS he found the ambience even worse, the rot starting at the top. 'Certain senior officers refused to fly certain types of aeroplane.'

The best instructors, not surprisingly, were those who had graduated pre-war and had war experience as well. Tom Mulcahy-Morgan, before his return to the front for a spy-dropping role, soon forgot the fatigue of the retreat and actually enjoyed instructing, finding his keenness revived by it. 'There are great compensations in instructing,' he wrote. 'One sees progress daily and feels there is a visible result for work done.' Channel-Islander Henry Brock found the much maligned BE8 Bloater 'a good school machine', but he was critical of the lack of efficient control from the front seat, which, as Smith-Barry objected, left the pupil to attempt his first solo from an unaccustomed position.

Perhaps not surprisingly, in view of his humanity, Willie Read made an ideal instructor. 'From the start Read treated his pupils,' wrote one of them, 'with a degree of friendliness that was altogether charming. He let his pupils do all the work, making corrections only when necessary.' The result was 'nerves nil, confidence max'. In the paternal care of this notable live-wire, pupils progressed in an atmosphere of serenity.

Unfortunately, natural tutors like Mulcahy-Morgan, Brock and Read were rare. Not every seasoned flyer was correspondingly gifted. 'Our so-called instructors were not flying instructors at all,' wrote Hugh Walmsley (a future air marshal). 'They were chaps who'd survived a tour in France and come home for a rest. The only rest they could be given, because there was such a shortage of pilots, was to go to a reserve squadron as a flying instructor.' Many of these men found the exhaustion of a day's instructing more than a night's rest could restore.

A compensation was the preservation at home stations of the peacetime attitude to 'social' flying: borrowing a machine to fulfil some social engagement. Ewart Garland's instructor, having promised that he would send him off solo that day, announced that he would start by fulfilling an assignation. 'First of all the instructor went with me and did a few stunts over Worthing and landed on the wet sand. We stayed there for twenty minutes while he talked to his girl and while the crowd gazed on the machine and us with awe. Then we went back to the aerodrome and landed and he got out and after a few advices I started alone.' This liberal attitude was extended to 'Huns', an appellation for pupils born of the Teutonic-like protective helmets they were ordered to wear.

Some instructors, because of the strain they were under, only aggravated the fears of their pupils. Such reported invocations as 'Shove her nose down, you bloody fool, do you want to kill us both?' were hardly calculated to inspire confidence. Vernon Brown, later to become a leading test pilot and accident investigator, learnt to fly on a Vickers Gunbus at Joyce Green: the machine had no dual control, so the instructor sat on the fuel tank behind Brown with his hand on Brown's shoulder, though it was Brown's hand on the joystick. 'Right rudder, you fool!' Brown would hear him shouting. 'Now pull her up!' And then: 'Look out! You'll go through the floor if you do that!' Such irascibility hardly made for relaxed flying. But Brown passed his test. 'You appear to be a perfectly good pilot,' he was told at CFS. 'You can be an assistant instructor here.' With fifteen hours solo on various types he started teaching others to fly.

Brown's experience typified a tendency to keep back the bright boys from one class to teach the next. Some doubted if this was sound in principle: the last men you wanted as instructors, it was said, were those to whom flying had come easily.

Instructors found it difficult to gauge whether a man had the essence of it in him or not. Even on a reserve squadron there was a unit as well as a personal pride, which drove men on. Some of those who took longest to go solo made the best pilots. But the reverse was also true. Robert Money's ambition was to be the first on his course to go solo, and he achieved it. Of the last one to go solo he wrote: 'I don't think even then he thought he was fully competent, but he hated the idea of being left behind.' Three days later he was killed.

What were the ideal characteristics of a wartime pilot? The high spirits and resilience of youth came high on Trenchard's list. They could not all be eighteen or nineteen, that would be too restrictive,

[213]

but they should be under twenty-five, and unmarried. There were exceptions, but marriage was reckoned to have an inhibiting effect. Athletic, alert, cheerful, even happy-go-lucky, the paragon would also reveal initiative and a sense of humour. A desirable weakness might be a lack of imagination. The greatest strength was an incurable optimism. 'It's the other chap who gets the chop,' said trainee Gerald Dixon. 'It never entered my head that I was going to get killed.'

However desirable extreme youth might be, it posed accompanying disciplinary problems, though these were generally viewed with indulgence. 'They treated us like schoolboys,' said John Chrispin, a pupil at Old Sarum, 'which we virtually were.' Sent to Hendon to collect a new machine, Chrispin conceived the notion of deliberately mistaking the GWR line out of London, which would take him past a small field next to his uncle's house at Wantage, for the LSW line to Salisbury. After 'force-landing' in the field he reported his whereabouts by telephone, promising to fly off next morning. But overnight the wind changed, and he nearly killed himself on take-off, just squeezing between two trees. Back at Old Sarum, his CO, Major E.J. Fuller, one of the 3 Squadron originals as a second lieutenant, came out to meet him. 'Glad to see you back. What happened?' As Chrispin told his story, Fuller had to turn away to hide his amusement. All he said was: 'Be more exact with your map-reading.' On another occasion Chrispin, on a cross-country training flight, decided to fly to Huddersfield and land in one of his mother's meadows on a farm on the edge of the town, which delayed his return. He later learned that Fuller and the chief instructor, a man named Ruxton, had been pacing anxiously up and down, fearing for his safety. 'Shall I go and play hell with him, sir?' Ruxton asked Fuller when Chrispin eventually arrived. 'No,' answered Fuller resignedly, 'as long as he's safe it doesn't matter.'

Maurice Kay, sent from CFS to pick up a new Sopwith scout at Coventry, got fed up with waiting for better weather as advised and set out of his own volition. Caught in a mist as he crossed the hills between Cheltenham and Cirencester, he flew through the branches of a tree at 80 m.p.h. 'My machine lurched and I thought I was going to nose-dive to earth.' He didn't, but his left lower wing was badly damaged and half his undercarriage was gone. The engine was vibrating alarmingly, but somehow the Sopwith kept flying. He made a perfect landing back at Netheravon, despite a missing wheel, a cracked wing, three cylinders out of action, and a badly chipped propeller. Everyone was amazed that the machine had held together, the old hands hardly crediting that it could have flown at all. 'The commandant was awfully pleased', boasted Kay, 'and told me to write an account, that he thought it was a very fine effort, and that he would forward the account to higher authority as a record.' Nothing was said about his decision to fly south against expert advice. Much was forgiven of a press-on type, and of extreme youth. The same indulgent attitude was prevalent in France. 'I should always like to be eighteen,' wrote Gwilym Lewis. 'You can do just what you like and no one considers you responsible for your actions.' Perhaps this was fair. Manhood was not reckoned to be reached until twenty-one.

Pupils went through fevers of self-doubt in the course of their instruction, many having to summon up reserves of courage to continue. One sensitive young pilot, barely free of his mother's apron strings, kept a diary – anonymously – in which he noted when he was booked for flying. One such entry carried the comment: 'I got one of those spasms of wind-up and dodged it. I do not think I shall ever make an airman. I'm on tenterhooks all the time I'm up – and I shall be in France next month so God help me.' He was thinking of going to the adjutant and asking for a transfer to observer.

Over the next eight days the saga moved to a climax. On the Saturday he knew he was down to fly, but when he got to the hangars someone had rubbed his name off the board, and he kept out of the way. 'Then began a day's torture, my mind being in a ferment all the time. The struggle was on as to whether or not I should chuck up flying and apply to be transferred as an observer.' At last he decided to go and ask his instructor, a man named Stewart, to wash

him out, but Stewart wasn't in his office, and in a trauma of indecision he 'wobbled away'. It did not help that 'Poor old Barradale
has been killed in an RE8 this afternoon.'

The weather clamped next day and he played solo-whist, but it
cleared up later. 'About 6.30 they started to fly, and I was down at
the hangars three times looking for my instructor, and feeling wind-
up for fear that I should find him. But I didn't.' That night he played
solo again. Next day Captain Stewart sent for him, and when he
told of his lack of confidence, Stewart promised to have a word
with the CO, and added something about getting him transferred to
scouts.

Two days later: 'Captain Stewart saw me after tea and said that
he had seen the CO (which I doubt, as the latter would have sent
for me), and that he had said I could either carry on or go back to
my regiment. This was a bit of sarcasm, because Stewart knows jolly
well I haven't got a regiment. I knew he was determined to stop me
when he mentioned scouts.' He was damned if he wanted to be an
observer, 'only I shall probably kill myself on these RE8s.' Yet he
felt he had far better kill himself than resign his commission. That
would mean total humiliation.

An unnerving experience with Stewart at the controls with a dud
engine 'put the wind up Stewart as well'. In the next two days Stewart
took him up to 5,000 feet, the highest he'd been, and then to 10,000
and 12,000, but 'height jiggers me . . . If I had been solo I should
have crashed as sure as eggs are eggs.' He told Stewart this, and
asked him to take him up high regularly. 'I finished up the night in
the ante-room, writing up this diary, and reading. I also refused to
play solo as the mater doesn't wish me to gamble.' Here was another
young man of eighteen still answerable to mother.

As the war progressed and manpower became stretched, suitable
candidates for training became rarer, and almost anyone medically
fit was considered. It became not unusual for gun-shy trainees, especially once they had been commissioned, to employ all manner of ruses
to delay posting to France, knowing how difficult it was to get them
reduced in rank and sent to the trenches. Stewart would have met
some of these, which would explain his cussedness. But eventually

he accepted that this particular (anonymous) pupil was genuine and let him go.

The need for pilots became so urgent that below average pupils might be given the benefit of the doubt, often with tragic results. Instructional hours were reduced, and trainees might be required to go solo before they had attained a proper proficiency. This resulted in so many accidents that Australian Francis Penny, after a spell as an observer on 12 Squadron, was required, on starting his pilot's course, to contribute a lump·sum for the purchase of wreaths for those killed, on a *pro rata* basis: trainees two shillings and sixpence, administrative officers five shillings, instructors seven-and-six. The weighting against instructors was logical – if they did their job properly they wouldn't have to pay up. Those not on the flying roster were liable for duty as pall-bearers.

Trainee pilots awaiting advanced instruction in combat tactics, air firing and formation flying were liable to be diverted overseas to fill empty cockpits, the intention being that the squadron should train them. But preoccupation with urgent tasks generally meant that training, where it existed at all, was sketchy. 'Many went out with as little as five hours on their service machines,' wrote Second Lieutenant Harold Seymour. 'The two lads I crossed the Channel with and talked to on the boat were both shot down before I had been over the lines.' Seymour was lucky in that his CO made newcomers fly behind the lines for a fortnight before sending them on patrol.

The demand for replacements at the front remained insatiable, and although senior instructing staff were not unconscientious, and many did what they could for their charges, decisions on postings were outside their control. Some made a strict rule that, irrespective of personalities, if a pupil had not gone solo after a fixed period he was automatically turned down. Undoubtedly this saved many lives. Pupils aiming to be scout pilots were transferred to heavier types if they didn't adapt quickly.

Arthur Gould Lee was another of the lucky ones. A major crash in training so lengthened his learning period that he accumulated many more solo hours than the average. He had been kept in England long enough to learn properly, and he believed it was no accident that, where so many fell in their first few weeks, he survived.

Gerald Dixon, on his first solo at Catterick, 'had absolutely no idea what to do. Only a natural aptitude saved one from catastrophe.' He insisted that, although he *learned* to fly, he was never *taught* to fly. Under the pressures of the time, perhaps this was inevitable. Yet even on his first solo he felt no fear: he was far too busy keeping the machine in the air. Many others remember their first solo as among the most exciting moments of their lives, anyway in retrospect.

Perhaps the casual approach taken by many instructors was relaxing for the pupil. 'Off you go,' F.C. Ransley was told, 'tootle around the perimeter of the aerodrome two or three times and try some landings. An ambulance is handy if you crash.' The tradition that 'flying will continue as usual' applied equally to pupils. Provided they were uninjured, it was still thought good psychology to send them up again straight away after a crash.

On-the-squadron training varied, but, as already indicated, was frequently minimal. Eighteen-year-old Harold Tambling, with thirty-one hours solo, felt his training at home had been sound. He had progressed to the F2b Bristol Fighter, and he found it a revelation. But on joining 22 Squadron, which had just been re-equipped with the type, he had what he called 'a very cursory interview' with his commanding officer, Major L.W. Learmont. Leonard Learmont had a distinguished career ahead of him, but at that stage he seems to have been overwhelmed by his problems. 'You'd better take a plane up and see how you feel,' he told Tambling. Next day Tambling was allotted an observer – Flight Sergeant W. Organ – and didn't realise at first how favoured he was, since Organ was an experienced man and therefore in great demand. Two days out of three they were over the lines on various tasks, generally with four or five others. Tambling had had some formation flying practice in England, but none on the squadron, and they flew in a sort of gaggle, never very close: this allowed them to weave about when they were Archied. There was no particular briefing beforehand, and no tactical discussions;

they were just given a line to patrol. In a scrap it was every man for himself.

Tambling developed no particular friendships – the turnover inhibited this. 'We hardly knew each other, there was a completely new squadron every few weeks.' There were no high jinks, everyone was too preoccupied, and they weren't encouraged to get together. He didn't drink, nobody did, so far as he knew, and he didn't even feel the baby of the squadron – there were others of a similar age, with a similar lack of experience. The one fellow he thought might become a friend was killed while practising air-to-ground firing. It was accidents like this, and the frequency of patrols, which inhibited a full training programme. But he had great confidence in the Brisfit, and the actual flying he thoroughly enjoyed.

Despite occasional victory claims their casualties mounted. Tambling recorded in his log book, in a period of under three weeks, five crews either prisoners or dead, one pilot killed on the aerodrome, and five wounded, one of whom died. The squadron ambulance juddering across the grass to collect casualties from crippled machines became a familiar sight. Consistent with the average, Tambling was shot down himself within a month of arrival, on a dawn patrol which started badly. Of six machines detailed, the leader had engine trouble and had to abort, and the deputy leader had to turn back half-way to the line. The remaining four pressed on and had just about reached the limit of their patrol when Tambling saw the machine on his right stagger and burst into flames.

He heard Organ firing the Lewis behind him, and he tried a few speculative bursts from the front Vickers at the scarlet, wasp-like machines that buzzed around him, but then he felt the Bristol shudder as it was hit and they started to slew round in circles. He couldn't correct the slide, and as they descended he knew he was being fired at continually as fuselage and wings took a peppering. He was thankful now for the experience of Organ, whose accurate return fire was keeping their assailants off their tail. Organ's coolness protected them from total destruction until they struck a tree as they neared the ground and the machine was thrown on to its starboard wing-tips, cushioning their fall.

[219]

Miraculously, neither man had been hit or badly hurt, and soon a party of Germans, who had been following their descent, arrived in a truck and took them prisoner. Separated from his NCO observer, as was the custom, Tambling never saw him again. He was taken to the Officers' Mess for a meal and interrogation: he couldn't tell them much because he knew so little.

More rewarding, perhaps, was his own self-examination. It had been his first real scrap, and he had been totally green. He had arrived on the squadron simultaneously with a change of aeroplane, from FE2b's to Bristol Fighters, which reversed the positions of pilot and observer, and of the engine in relation to both, calling for major adjustments in outlook and tactics. Yet he knew of no attempt to develop their confidence and skill. They had simply flown north until they could see the coast, then flown back again, that was their patrol. Later Tambling concluded: 'We were simply looking for trouble, and this time we got it.'

The experience of C.B. 'Ben' Lefroy, a test pilot at St Omer, was that 'there were a lot of boys who shouldn't have been out there at all – they just didn't know how to fly'. He blamed this on the corners that were being cut for the sake of expansion. Lee deplored 'sending fellows out to fight when they haven't even learned to fly . . . newcomers had to be pushed out on patrol before they'd found their feet'.

The failure to impose strict training programmes on new squadrons as they arrived, and to organise routine training programmes on all squadrons in France, surely amounted to culpable if not criminal negligence. Certainly Harold Tambling, like Oscar Greig before him, blamed his downfall on the lack of squadron training. Squadron and flight commanders, although under pressure to fulfil commitments, cannot be held blameless; but the pressure came from the top. As always, whatever the army demanded, Trenchard felt duty bound to provide. Whether such a degree of compliance was always essential remains controversial.

In the army or fighting units, squadron and flight commanders had little option but to take the men sent to them on trust. They may well have felt it was too late for more than local familiarisation, backed up by experienced leadership. In any case, they may have argued, by far the best training was battle. 'New pilots arrived untrained in formation flying and had to be initiated in action,' recalled Lee. 'Of four new pilots who arrived in mid-June 1917, none had been given proper training in formation flying.' For a long time there was no school anywhere for scout pilots – they arrived at squadrons raw.

There was more chance for the preparation and training of crews in the corps squadrons, where instruction was given in camera work, gunnery, and liaison with batteries. Challenging as the work was, it was more a matter of routine. By giving a raw pilot an experienced observer, and vice-versa, new men could be introduced to the job without any great loss of efficiency.

22

WATERSHED

I F the year 1916 disappointed as a turning point, stimulating a scepticism, cynically voiced in the trenches, that the war would last for ever, it nevertheless qualified as a watershed. The year had begun with the Fokker scourge, forcing the RFC to resort to measures to reduce casualties that brought a shrinkage in operational capacity instead of the planned expansion. Yet, as recorded earlier, the Fokkers had never mustered more than fifty machines in front-line service at any one time, their period of ascendancy had not contributed decisively to any ground campaign, and it had been ended by the advent in the spring of the DH2, the FE2b, and the Nieuport. The RFC then became an expanding force again, with a brigade attached to each of the five British armies in the field.

Partly because of unseasonable weather, the Somme battle had ended in stalemate. It had virtually destroyed Kitchener's volunteer army; yet the loss of life had not been totally futile. So far as such slaughter is susceptible to sober analysis, certain minimum objectives had been achieved. First, the critical situation at Verdun had been relieved. Secondly, the enemy had been kept fully occupied at a time when the French were on the verge of collapse. Thirdly, in the retrospective view of the official RFC history, the campaign had 'dealt a blow at the morale of the enemy troops from which they never recovered'.[1]

The Allies had shown their preparedness to continue a war of attrition to the point of exhaustion. For the enemy, this dictated policy revisions which, unless they proved outstandingly successful, doomed them to eventual defeat.

By the beginning of the Somme battle, the air situation had been transformed. Corps machines photographed the German trenches 'without once being attacked by the Fokkers', noted General Rawlinson. Artillery co-operation had become an essential part of the battle scene, aided by the Sterling wireless transmitter, weighing less than 20 lb and now in general use. Bombing was more concentrated and had been extended to the hours of darkness. Contact patrols fed an up-to-date picture to army commanders. And Trenchard's doctrine of unceasing and relentless offensive had driven the German air force back to its own side of the lines. This was the positive side. Against it had to be set the heavy and often disproportionate losses that resulted for the RFC, in the ratio of four to one against those of the enemy.

Between July and December 1916 Trenchard lost 499 pilots and observers killed or missing and another 250 wounded or injured and put out of action. A further 250, for various reasons – unsuitability, physical or nervous debility – had been removed from strength. Meanwhile, by September, Germany was fast bridging the numbers gap and producing superior machines with better trained pilots. Prospects for the early delivery of the new British scout machines on order – the Bristol two-seater and the SE5 and Camel single-seaters – were scant, as Trenchard well knew, hence his pleadings for acceleration. As for his complaints about the quality of his reinforcement pilots, Brancker, in his reply, did not spare him. They were paying the price for too-rapid growth and for rushing new squadrons into the line prematurely. Trenchard was unabashed. ('We are fighting a very big battle.') There was no escape from casualties.

Trenchard's warnings, amounting to forecasts of impending

1. Jones, H.A., *The War in the Air* (The Clarendon Press, Oxford 1928–1937).

catastrophe failing the reinforcements he sought, reached a new fervour that winter. Germany too was beginning to realise the importance of taking the offensive in the air, and the DH2 and the FE2b were outclassed in their turn by the new Albatros and Halberstadt scouts. More and more Jastas were forming – twenty-five in all by the end of the year. On 16 November, in a further appeal to the War Office, Trenchard asked for another twenty of the new scout squadrons to protect his corps machines, in addition to those already agreed, making a ratio of two scouts for every corps machine at the front.

Production capacity at home was slowly improving to cope with these demands, and by late summer a rapidly expanding labour force had already reached 60,000 engaged in the manufacture of aeroplanes and another 20,000 in building aircraft engines. Yet British production, in quantity and quality, still lagged behind the German and the French. The combined Allied total, however, outnumbered the German. This accounted for the latter's policy of husbanding their resources and concentrating them where and when local superiority was needed. 'Our fighter squadrons,' ordered Hindenburg, 'which are far from numerous must not be equally distributed over the whole front . . . They must be grouped sometimes here, sometimes there, so as to prevent the enemy's observation for a few hours at least, and make our own observation possible.'

Political changes that autumn promised a greater energy in the prosecution of the war. In Germany, Ludendorff's position was strengthened. In Britain, Lloyd George succeeded Asquith as prime minister. One of his first appointments was that of industrialist William Weir, formerly director of munitions in Scotland, to the crucial post of controller of aeronautical supplies in the Ministry of Munitions. He also appointed Weir to a seat on the Air Board. Henderson, for his part, recognising that the Royal Aircraft Factory had failed to keep pace with design progress and had become a political and industrial liability, terminated O'Gorman's contract as superintendent and appointed one of Weir's men in his place.

Criticism of Trenchard's doctrine of the offensive continued, but he remained unmoved. The aeroplane was basically an offensive weapon, not a defensive one, even against other aeroplanes: he did not see this doctrine as being impaired in any way by his losses. It was a doctrine not perhaps seriously challenged until the advent of radar.

Since taking over command of the RFC in the field in August 1915 Trenchard had pursued his policies unimpeded except by material and personnel defects and shortages, winning Haig and the army over to a belief in and indeed an implicit reliance on air support. Above all was the success of the corps squadrons, of whom Rawlinson wrote that 'his experiences in the battle had brought home to him the enormous importance of aeroplane and artillery co-operation.' He went on to emphasise the necessity for maximum development of this branch of aerial warfare.

From the tentative and underrated probings of August 1914, air power had become a factor in all military engagements. As industry on both sides responded rapidly to the need, aeroplanes became more numerous, more reliable, and flew faster and higher. Advances in technology, in weaponry and fire-power, and in communications and surveillance, threw mounting strains on individual airmen. In the RFC, the human element, far from being eliminated, remained paramount. This found its expression in the emergence of public heroes, but it was equally true of the daily round. And in the campaigns to come it was the RFC, and on the ground the BEF, who were to bear the brunt of the fighting.

Of Trenchard, Professor Trevor Wilson, in his book *The Myriad Faces of War*, has written: 'He gave the RFC determined leadership and a clear sense of direction. He won for it the admiration and devoted support of the army command...'[1]

If the second panegyric had been truly won in the skies, it could not have been achieved without Trenchard's dynamism.

1. Polity Press, Cambridge, in association with Basil Blackwell, Oxford, 1986.

PART II

From Bloody April 1917 to Final Victory

NORTH SEA

Dunkerque

Calais

St Omer

Ypres

BELGIUM

BRUSSELS ■

Lille

② 4 April: RFC begin air offensive to free (subordinate) British battle area of hostile aircarft. Artillery bombardment begins. 9 April on: British and Canadian infantry take Vimy Ridge.

Vimy Ridge

Loos

Vimy

Douai

Mons

Maubeuge

Arras

Bapaume

Cambrai

Le Cateau

Doullens

① Shaded area shows ground given up by the enemy to consolidate defences and hamper British communications and supply lines, meanwhile distancing RFC from its objectives.

Abbeville

Somme

Albert

Péronne

Amiens

St Quentin

Roye

③ 16 April: main attack by French meets immediate and disastrous opposition, breakthrough fails, French morale shattered, mutinies follow. Pétain replaces Nivelle.

Noyon

Chemin des Dames

Compiègne

Aisne

Soissons

Rheims

F   R   A   N   C   E

Oise

Marne

④ In April as a whole, newly designed RFC machines fail to materialise, or are mishandled, losses escalate. RFC suffer worst setback of the war. Haig obliged to maintain pressure on enemy to protect French army.

Seine

PARIS ■

Disaster on the Hindenburg Line
March/April 1917

– – – Frontiers of 1914
▬▬▬ Limit of German Advance

0   10   20   30   miles   50

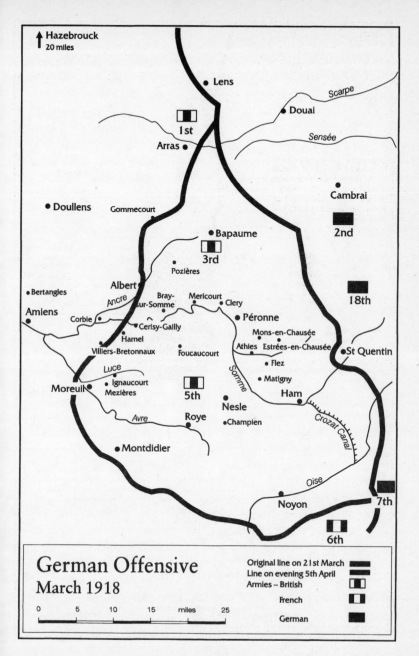

German Offensive
March 1918

Original line on 21st March	▬
Line on evening 5th April	▬
Armies – British	⬛⬜⬛
French	⬜
German	⬛

0   5   10   15   miles   25

1917

1

A NEW GERMAN WAR-WINNING STRATEGY: THE RFC OUTFOUGHT AND OUTCLASSED

T HE hectic war of movement in the late summer of 1914, when the German dash for Paris and a quick victory had been so narrowly frustrated, had preceded two years of largely attritional warfare. Thus, at the end of 1916, the combatants still confronted each other across an unbroken front 350 miles long, stretching from the Channel ports to the Swiss border. It was a line that had altered little over the years, despite the costly attempts by the Allies to push the invading German armies back whence they came. And it was the Allies, still territorially deprived, who were now planning yet another massive frontal assault, with all that this meant in human suffering and slaughter. To the Allied Command there remained no other practical means of inflicting on the enemy the final and overwhelming defeat from which a just and lasting peace might be dictated.

The Germans were equally committed to a war of attrition. But they no longer believed in outright victory, not anyway by military means. Unrestricted submarine warfare, a strategy which they openly declared on 1 February 1917, was to be the route to victory: all shipping in the Atlantic war zone was to be sunk on sight. Meanwhile, as a direct result of their losses on the Somme, they were preparing to give ground, pulling back substantially but secretly, and constructing a new defensive line, devised by Ludendorff (but designated the Hindenburg Line by the British), well behind their existing defences. In justifying this withdrawal, Ludendorff wrote:

'The Army had been fought to a standstill and was utterly worn out.'
Frightful as the cost had been, this was the achievement of the Somme
battle. It had forced the Germans to change their strategic plan in a
way which risked direct American involvement in the war.

The new barrier, stiffened by man-made strongpoints, would take
all possible advantage of existing natural obstacles. The Germans
would be fighting on ground of their own choosing, with a network
of communications that would give greater economy in logistics and
manpower, incidentally freeing fifteen divisions for the reserve. The
whole edifice would constitute a fortress of such impregnability as
to repel, with decimating losses, all attempts to invest it. Deadlock
in the land battle, and a Britain starved out by the U-boats, would
produce a compromise peace in which Germany would be permitted
to hold on to her conquests. Such was the new strategy, and it seemed
a reasonable gamble that any American reaction would come too
late to affect the outcome.

Evidence that such a defensive line might be in preparation was
first elicited by air observation in October and November 1916, but
it was not until 25 February 1917 that six Sopwith Pup pilots of 54
Squadron brought back irrefutable evidence that German troops
were withdrawing in stages to a new line from Lille to Metz. Captured documents, and the interrogation of prisoners, gave confirmation, enabling an unopposed British advance to begin on 17
March over ground deliberately devastated by the enemy to provide
an obstacle in itself.

The plan for the 1917 Allied offensive was the brain-child of a
new French commander-in-chief, General Robert Nivelle, who had
earned a big reputation for his 'creeping barrage' tactics – the separate but simultaneous progression of infantry and artillery – during
the second phase of the Battle of Verdun. He succeeded Joffre, who
had been relieved of his command after the blood-letting on the
Somme. Joffre's plan for a cautious, step-by-step advance with
limited objectives was anathema to Nivelle, who favoured a single
decisive blow at maximum strength. Lloyd George, who had
succeeded to the British premiership that December, was also
calling for a more energetic prosecution of the war. Despite the mis-

givings of the French High Command and the objections and apprehensions of the British C.-in-C., Douglas Haig, Nivelle's persuasive
advocacy of his plans enthused the newly-formed British War Cabinet. They agreed to place him in overall command, over the aggrieved
Haig's head, on the grounds that France, as the country that had
borne the brunt of the fighting so far and was still suffering occupation, should have the final say.

Haig would have preferred to attack farther north, in Flanders,
where one of his objectives would have been to clear the Flemish
ports and deny their use to the U-boats, and this was his ultimate
intention. The Admiralty were warning that with the U-boats in
control it might become impossible to hold the Channel crossing and
therefore to continue the land war. But any major offensive clearly
had to be an Allied venture, and Haig, after considering resignation,
gave way.

By this time Britain had five armies in France, holding the line
from Lille south to Peronne. The First and Third Armies were on
the Arras front in the centre, the Second was to the north, and the
Fifth and Fourth to the south and extreme south in that order.

A serious obstacle, of which Haig was well aware – and on which,
in November, he had expressed himself trenchantly – was the ascendancy over RFC hardware of the new German *Jastas*, which were
increasing in strength. Haig was no student of air strategy but he
believed in the air. Briefed by Trenchard, who had been warning of
the expected inferiority for many months, he expressed the opinion
that the RFC could not be ready to support a major offensive as
early as April, the projected date. 'Our fighting machines', he wrote,
'will almost certainly be inferior in number and quite certainly in
performance to those of the enemy.' Supremacy in the air, he protested, could not be looked for in April, and might even pass to the
enemy. Trenchard had stressed that new types of machine – namely
the Bristol Fighter, the SE5, and the Camel – which it was expected
would prove superior to the German, were not yet available. Meanwhile, however, his policy of maintaining the offensive, even in
adversity – indeed, especially in adversity – would be pursued. Trenchard would argue the RFC's case vehemently and persistently at

the highest level, so much so that in December the Army Council formally approved expansion of the RFC to 106 active squadrons and 95 reserve, plus two night-flying squadrons. But this was only the projection, and meanwhile, whatever the odds against, Trenchard – rightly or wrongly – would not plead the RFC's shortcomings as an excuse for delaying the land campaign.

Haig was right about quality; but in fact the RFC, with twenty-five squadrons on the Arras front alone totalling 365 aircraft, nearly twice as many as their adversary, had the advantage in quantity, and Trenchard was relying on this – and on the resilience of his crews – to offset the quality gap. He was well aware, though, that half the German aircraft were scouts, vastly superior to his own in speed, climb and armament, and that this was going to mean heavy casualties for the RFC.

Forecasts of three to four months as the average active service life of two-seater crews, and two and a half months for single-seater scout pilots, were soon to prove over optimistic, greatly underestimating the numbers of newly-trained pilots and observers likely to be needed in the next twelve months. Just when the training organisation at home under Jack Salmond was laying down new minima of flying experience before exposure to active service in France, inability to cope with the manpower demands of the squadrons was to lead to these minima being drastically curtailed. Casualty replacements, as hitherto, could only come from the drafting-in of inadequately-trained beginners.

Air operations, hampered by the weather, continued in a desultory fashion through the worst of the 1916–17 winter, though with a disproportionate increase in the activity of the German Air Force, which was seeking to reassert itself and to cover the withdrawal to the Hindenburg Line. The size and scope of this move took the Allies by surprise. German superiority was soon to be increased by a new and faster Albatros with an improved ceiling, the DIII, and the new *Jastas*. (Richthofen, who was awarded the *Pour le Merité* or Blue Max, Germany's highest award, in January, was now commanding his own unit, *Jasta 11*.) The principal change, first marked in December, was the more venturesome behaviour of German pilots, who no longer restricted their depredations to their own side of the line. In December alone, of twenty-seven British machines shot down, seventeen fell on the British side, a hitherto unheard-of proportion. The only RFC aircraft now capable of meeting the enemy on equal terms or better were the newly-delivered Sopwith Pups of 54 Squadron, complementing the Pups of Naval 8, which had been on loan to Trenchard since September. One captured enemy flying man, who had good reason to regret their introduction, threw a revealing light on Hun attitudes. 'We don't like Pups,' he said, 'but we don't worry about BEs unless they get in our way, and that's the end of them.'

The Pup, a light-weight tractor biplane, was nimble and sturdy but, although it had the advantage of being able to turn inside the Albatros, it was inferior to it in all other respects – speed, armament, rate of climb. The forerunner of the Triplane and the Camel, its delay in production, caused by a lack of official enthusiasm, meant that it was obsolescent by the time it arrived. A second Pup squadron, No. 66, arrived in March 1917, but pilots soon found that to live with the Albatros they had to use all the cunning and expertise at their command. The Tripe, although flown exclusively by the RNAS, reached the front in February, but the Camel, produced as an antidote to the Albatros, did not come into operation until June. There was some prospect, though, that a squadron each of Bristol Fighters and SE5's might be operational some time in April.

Assigned the subordinate role of creating a distraction in the north to divert German reserves while Nivelle broke through on the Aisne, the BEF was given no specific long-term objective. Its primary task was to capture the high ground at Vimy Ridge, three miles north of Arras and inconveniently on the wrong side of the line. This was an enemy stronghold, with well-embedded guns strategically placed. There was also a vast programme of air registration of enemy batteries and defensive positions to be accomplished beforehand. Most vulnerable, as always, were the photographic sorties, when pilot and observer tended to become engrossed in scanning the ground. One who was engaged in this task was 19-year-old Oscar Greig, flying an FE2b (Farman Experimental 2b) 'pusher'. Greig had matured from the callow youth who, fourteen months earlier in a Vickers

Gunbus, had lost his nerve temporarily after a horrific spin, just when he had been in line for a decoration that, as he noted in his diary, 'would please Mummy so'.

His new appointment as a captain and flight commander on 25 Squadron began badly when he sensed that his squadron commander, Major R.G. Cherry, resented him as an intruder: he had wanted to promote one of his own men. When Greig had to report that that individual, on posting home, had absconded with squadron equipment, he was even more unpopular. Another contentious point was Cherry's refusal to allow his crews to wear safety-belts, on the grounds that in a crash they would be thrown clear of their cockpits, instead of being crushed by the rear-mounted engine when it plunged forward, as it was wont to do. Greig had always worn a belt in the Gunbus and he didn't fancy being thrown out. He was aware, too, that Cherry was trying to get rid of him, and the final snub came when Cherry went on leave just before Christmas and left a lieutenant, not Greig, his senior flight commander, in charge.

Greig had been flying FE2b's in England and had grown to like them. He was disappointed on his first flight with 25 Squadron to find that under active service loading they just wallowed along, without the sense of liveliness and buoyancy to which he'd been accustomed. He wondered what Major Cherry's experience was, and he enquired of his senior lieutenant: 'Does Major Cherry ever fly these things?' 'No,' was the reply. In this Cherry, who held the Military Cross, may have been inhibited by Trenchard's policy at that time of conserving experience.

There were certainly squadrons where the avuncular commanding officer, running the squadron from a desk, was highly successful, and other squadrons where a commander who led his men in the air was seriously overburdened; but Greig didn't see Cherry as the avuncular type. Nor was he a disciplinarian – not, anyway, where flying discipline was concerned. Greig had been away from the front for fourteen months, much had changed in the meantime, and he was anxious to learn, but there was no practice flying, no ground instruction, and no rehearsal of communications systems. Especially important, but in Greig's view neglected, was communication between pilot and pilot in formation. Greig himself, as a newly-appointed flight commander, might well have sought to change this, but he was inhibited by Cherry's attitude towards him.

The task on 24 January was to photograph important rail communications in preparation for the attempt to capture Vimy Ridge. In the FE2b the observer operated the camera, which was fixed to the outside of the cockpit. Behind him, slightly elevated on the petrol tank, with engine and radiator immediately at his back, sat the pilot. He had a magnificent view forward, but could see nothing behind or below. The observer – in this case Second-Lieutenant J.E. MacLennan – had a front Lewis gun and another, mounted between him and the pilot, which, by standing up somewhat precariously, he could fire upwards and rearwards over the top wing. The FE was slow and not easy to manoeuvre, and although it had proved a match in the previous year for the Fokker monoplane, it was totally outclassed by the new German scouts. Thus, when Greig set off that morning for the Vimy Ridge area, he was leading – with streamers on his struts and tail to identify him – a formation of two groups of three. In each group, the leading machine carried a camera and the other two, for all their inadequacy, would attempt to provide close escort. There would also, more or less simultaneously – so they were told – be offensive patrols around and above them, and several other scouts patrolling the area. As it happened Greig was not worried: he had been lulled into a false sense of security. The New Year had begun quietly, he had crossed the lines eight times in the previous few days, and he had not seen an enemy plane. But these things could change overnight. What he didn't know was that Richthofen had made his first flight in the latest German fighter, the Albatros DIII, the previous day, had shot down an FE8, and would be looking for custom.

After climbing to 10,000 feet approaching the lines, Greig asked MacLennan in sign language – made necessary by the noise of the Beardmore engine, recently boosted to 160 hp – if his escort was in place, and MacLennan shook his head. This was disturbing. Greig was flying his usual machine, deliberately selected as one of the slowest, yet he had outpaced them all. He fired a green Very light as the signal to close up and waited until MacLennan nodded the OK before setting course. MacLennan, too, was apprehensive: he was due to go on leave next day.

From his high seat Greig studied the terrain ahead, looking from the map to the ground, pointing the machine directly up the line of the area they were to photograph, noting landmarks ahead and keeping the machine on an even keel. MacLennan was leaning over the starboard side of the cockpit, looking through the camera sights and just starting to take the exposures. Neither man noticed that their escort had again dropped back. They were not being bothered by Archie, which was often a warning of fighter attack, but Greig thought the gunners were probably holding their fire until he had penetrated more deeply. In the next moment he heard machine-gun fire and saw a rash of bullet-holes appear in his left lower wing like the first raindrops in an April shower. So absorbed had they been in their task that they were taken completely by surprise.

Turning steeply towards the attack, nearly jettisoning the unsecured MacLennan, Greig tried to get the enemy plane in front of him, at the same time looking in vain for his escort. Another burst of fire, this time from the starboard side, silenced his engine and pierced his right ankle, knocking his foot off the rudder bar. Continuing to circle, trying to catch sight of his attacker, he was saved again and again by the bulk of the engine behind him as bullets poured in.

He was below 2,000 feet when the firing stopped and he headed at once for the lines, which were only three miles away. He was half-way there when MacLennan pointed dramatically upwards. A very fast scarlet biplane, after a murderous burst of fire, skidded over the top of them, so quickly that there was no time to use the back gun, and the front gun had jammed. Greig tried everything to restart the engine but it only spluttered and he had no choice but to land straight ahead, somewhere between Vimy and Fresnoy, avoiding the innumerable shell-holes by chance. Both men had bullet-holes in their leather coats, and MacLennan, like Greig, had been wounded. Germans were running towards them from all directions but they just had time to ignite the incendiary torch they carried and set the machine on fire. There was no hope of escape and, when they raised their hands in surrender, bayonets were sheathed. A German officer who arrived shortly afterwards was pleasant and courteous and returned Greig's salute.

Greig was afterwards to rate his thirty-seven days on 25 Squadron as the most unpleasant of his war service, but at least he was remembered kindly by one new sergeant observer, H.G. Taylor, a Machine-Gun Corps veteran of the Somme whose first attempt at a reconnaissance sketch Greig had described as 'bloody marvellous'. And at least the final day was a memorable one, especially in retrospect when he learned that the man in the speedy scarlet scout had been von Richthofen himself. But for that he might have escaped.

It was the lack of on-the-spot squadron training, he believed, which caused his downfall. But in being shot down by the Red Baron he was in good company, and unlike all too many of his fellow victims he had escaped with his life. He may well have reflected that, despite the mischance of captivity, Mummy would not be displeased.

The tribulations of 21-year-old Eric Routh, begun after he had been appointed a flight commander on the rump of the massacred 16 Squadron (BE's), were exacerbated in the New Year. His flight was taking shape, but the quality of the intake exasperated him. Why was it that the hamfisted and the irresponsible all seemed to come to him? He assessed one of them as moderately good, another as having potential – supposing he survived those fateful first few shows – a third as altogether too nervous, a fourth as a good talker but a poor listener. Even when they were sent up merely to fly round the aerodrome for familiarisation they were apt to get lost. One who did not return was seen to collect an obliging Hun escort; seeing that he was flying solo, with no one to man the gun, the Hun pilot headed him off every time he tried to turn for home, finally motioned him to land on the German side, and alighted beside him to claim him as his own. Another newcomer, sent up with an observer, disappeared altogether. All had been warned not to cross the lines, but no one had seen a machine brought down, so after forty-eight hours Routh was writing to their next of kin, hoping they too were prisoners.

Born in Malta of a naval family, Routh was more worldly-wise than most young men of his time. Typical was the incident when the adjutant, a man of middle age, took him on in a drinking bout to cheer him up and had to be put to bed after eleven shorts to Routh's twelve. Next morning Routh was the one with the clear head. 'Sergeant Dangerfield has gone up with Lance Corporal Webb and has not returned. I told him to be careful not to lose himself. God knows how these people were brought up.' But his judgement of Dangerfield, for all his faults, was sound: he was a survivor. 'I expect he's sleeping the night at some comfortable chateau.' And so it proved.

Routh went on leave on 2 March, returning on the 17th to find that 'several pilots have been done down by Huns'. 16 Squadron was attached to the Canadian Corps, and the main work of cooperating with the First Army in preparation for the Vimy push had fallen to them. Of one of the missing men Routh wrote: 'I specially told him to practise sharp turns, but he would never do it. And I specially warned him never to dive straight away from a Hun – which he was seen to do. He would have been perfectly all right if he'd kept his head.' The observer, whom Routh had liked 'very much indeed', was a married man. 'He was a very stout fellow. I am sorry for both of them.'

He badly needed a pick-me-up. 'I went to Bethune this afternoon and had more champagne than I ought to have had. It did me a lot of good.' Certainly it seems to have done him no harm: next morning he did three hours 20 minutes' observing for the guns in the Vimy area, bringing back valuable information, and another hour in the afternoon. His spirits were restored, and when his former commanding officer on his previous squadron, No. 34, John Chamier, wrote and offered him a job as an instructor at Brooklands, he decided against it. 'It would become boring after a time.'

With formations of enemy scouts, six or eight strong, continually patrolling the lines ready to pounce, there was no chance of boredom for the corps squadrons or anyone else. One of the most desperate clashes occurred on 9 March during an offensive patrol by nine FE8's of 40 Squadron. Old Etonian Leonard Tilney, aged twenty-two, had just taken over the squadron from the forty-year-old actor Bobbie

Loraine. The FE8 was the latest and last – already obsolescent – pusher-type fighter of Royal Aircraft Factory design, similar to the DH2. Only two squadrons were equipped with it. Its top speed was 94 m.p.h. and it mounted a single forward-firing Lewis. On this sortie, one machine was forced to turn back with engine trouble (100 hp Monosoupape), but the remaining eight were swooped on by five Albatros DIII's led by Richthofen. Four were shot down and the other four forced to land in a damaged state, a catastrophe which persuaded the authorities to re-equip the squadron with Nieuports. A few DH2's which tried to help lost one of their number.

Outclassed though they were, the squadron had fought to the death, very nearly achieving the impossible by shooting down the Red Baron himself. With petrol pouring into his cockpit from a pierced fuel tank and his engine riddled, he looked a certainty for a 'flamer', but, mercifully for him and tragically for his future victims, he force-landed safely.

Something of what the half-tutored men of Routh's squadron were facing was recorded by another newcomer, Second-Lieutenant Gerald Jamieson. Jamieson crossed by sea to Boulogne on 7 March, joined the squadron next day, flew that afternoon on reconnaissance, and got 'Archied like the deuce'. On the 10th he did his first counter-battery shoot, and 'did it rather well so was sent up in the afternoon to do another'. The men who proved useful always got the bulk of the work. On the 11th, 12th and 13th he was taking photos, sometimes twice a day. On the 14th he was attacked by two Albatri and only escaped by stalling and spinning, from 9,000 feet down to 500 – but not before his aileron control had been shot away, his observer had been wounded, and he himself had had a narrow escape. 'My pipe in my pocket was shot clean through by three bullets.' Then on the 15th: 'My observer died overnight. My nerves in a terrible state.'

On the 16th he was up with a new observer to show him the lines, then in the afternoon on a shoot. 'It proved quite successful.' On the 17th they were attacked by two of the new Halberstadts and 'managed to bring one of them down on his side'. He was up twice on the 18th taking photos and patrolling, and during a shoot on the 19th he got eight OK's (the code for a hit) from the gunners and got the credit for the destruction of a Hun battery. On the 20th he was taking photos seven miles into Hunland and only just got back after his engine was hit. On the 21st, after helping to install a new engine in the morning, he did an air test and a patrol in the afternoon, when 'nerves started to be groggy'. Yet on the 22nd: 'Tried flying again, nerves all right. Took some photos in the afternoon, quite successful.'

Jamieson had been up for two-and-a-half hours doing a shoot on the 23rd when he met an Albatros. 'My observer got an explosive bullet in his leg. Unconscious all the way home. Poor old Gay got shot down.'[1] But they were claiming two Huns between them. On the 24th, with his third observer, he was up for two-and-a-half hours registering targets. 'Plane had nine holes from Archie, one right through the strut.' He had to fly back low over the Hun trenches, 'could see them firing at me, let them have it too'. He was patrolling for another two hours in the afternoon. 'We lost one machine. My wounded observer getting well in hospital.'

During a three-and-a-half-hour shoot on the morning of the 25th on two Hun batteries he had a scrap with another Halberstadt. 'He beetled off to his lines afterwards at low altitude. Got a few shots into him.' Only the caution and inexperience of the average German pilot saved Jamieson and countless others in this period. Then on Monday the 26th: 'It rained all day. Went into Bethune.'

It was the first day since he arrived on 7 March that he hadn't flown, mostly twice. Clearly he had performed rather better than the average beginner, but his contribution, although immense, was not untypical. He was only remarkable in that he had been lucky enough to survive. Yet the ground offensive, and the air offensive proper that was to precede it, was still to come.

One man who was actually enjoying it all, if his letters to his family back in Gomshall, Surrey were to be believed, was observer George Downing, of 57 Squadron (FE2d's, with the new 250 hp Rolls-Royce engine). Norman McNaughton, Downing's pilot, was

1. Second-Lieutenant F.H. Gay. He died of his wounds.

of the fearless, daredevil type and they made a good team. With three others of their squadron they ran into five Hun machines and chased them off. Five minutes later they met another batch. 'My pilot dived straight at one of the beggars, and when I was quite close I fired 60 rounds right into him and had the tremendous satisfaction of seeing it depart in flames to Mother Earth. After that it was glorious sport, we fought four different Hun formations for 1½ hours.' Of another perilous incident he wrote: 'What a thing it is to have a man like that for a pilot, because he simply laughed! Guess I'd go anywhere with him.'

Items about colleagues who'd been killed or had had limbs amputated were mixed, in his letters, with typically boyish family jokes and facetious comments. No doubt, in a later idiom, he 'shot a line', though he and McNaughton were clearly in the thick of the fighting. On one patrol they were about ten miles over Hunland when Downing spotted through the glasses a formation of six Huns about 1,000 feet below them. 'Of course that was good enough, so Mac and I dived right into the middle of them, shooting right and left, followed by the rest of the formation. Our machine swung right on top of a Hun and I pumped about 50 shots into him. It was rather a rotten sight, the machine turned upside down and the unfortunate Hun fell out from his bus about 5,000 feet up, so I rather expect he hurt himself . . . We did not have much time for sympathy, as there were several Huns which required attention, and I managed to hook down another in the course of the fight. So altogether it was rather a good day for this child.' To this he added, surely tongue in cheek: 'I hope you won't think this job is risky but it is quite the reverse really, only one must make it sound a little exciting sometimes.' It didn't need much literary skill.

Men like McNaughton and Downing, working as a team, kept the German airmen from too arrogant an assertion of their superiority, and both were awarded the MC. Then, in June, Downing was sent home on a pilot's course. One could almost have wished they had stayed together. He had scarcely arrived at Castle Bromwich when he heard that McNaughton, with a new observer, had been shot down in combat; both men had been killed. Soon afterwards he noted: 'I see poor old Erlebach is killed. That just about finishes poor old 57 of the original lot.'

A job as an instructor, which his family favoured, was mooted when he qualified, but he decided it was 'quite time I interviewed Brother Bosch again', although 'I expect the mater will not be so pleased'. Here was another mother, like so many, torn between pride and apprehension. 'By the time you get this I shall have started strafing Brother Bosch again. Don't worry about this child. He's going to look after himself. I expect my luck will carry me through.'

George Downing had gone to France with 57 Squadron in December 1916, and on 6 November 1917, after a year as full of incident as any young man could wish for, or perhaps wish to avoid, his luck ran out, and he was posted missing, believed killed. His death was later confirmed.

Teamwork was equally important in the corps squadrons, more than doubling the chances of survival. One of the No. 5 Squadron pilots working with the First Army, flying a BE2e, was Second-Lieutenant Charles D. Smart; he was partnered as observer by a Lieutenant Hendry. On 1 March Smart noted in his diary: 'Things getting very hot round here, we had a machine shot down on each fine day during the last fortnight – I do wish my leave would come along.' He had hoped that his younger brother George, who had preceded him into the RFC and was now flying Nieuports on 60 Squadron from an adjacent aerodrome, might have got leave at the same time, but it hadn't worked out. Both were well-built six-footers in their early thirties and had been directors of their father's cotton mill firm in Manchester before volunteering for flying. George had begun as a sergeant pilot but had been commissioned in the field for gallantry.

One day when Hendry was not available, Smart was given an air mechanic named Tyndal as observer: it was Tyndal's first show. There was often a shortage of observers, but rarely of air mechanic volunteers: their reward, when they flew, was the princely sum of an extra two shillings a day. The trip was a testing one, 800 yards beyond the Hun front line. 'Did not fancy the trip with an inexperienced man as gunner . . . I made Tyndal kneel at his gun the whole time.' Tyndal seems to have taken it well, and fortunately they were not molested. Fiercely Archied three days later on a photo recce, showered with wood splinters, with his rudder jammed, and with a large hole in his aft fuel tank, Smart was 'all the time in fear and trembling in case the machine should catch fire'. But he got back safely, and on the 9th he took Tyndal again, a sure sign that the young air mechanic had made the grade. Next day, 10 March, Smart went on his much-desired leave. But not for long. 'March 11/1917. Arrived home 6am, telegram arrived 5pm recalling me. Do feel pleased.' He had not been vouchsafed a single day.

The losses No. 5 Squadron were sustaining in preparation for the Canadian assault had clearly inspired Smart's recall, but Ewart Garland, a young Australian on 10 Squadron, also working for the First Army, went on leave two days earlier and escaped the recall. Garland had well-heeled friends in London, in particular a business associate of his father, Sir Arthur du Cros, chairman of the Dunlop Rubber Company in the UK: Garland's father was head of the Australian company in Melbourne. With the du Cros family, who treated him like a son, he lunched at the Ritz with Bonar Law, Lady Curzon and Mrs [sic] Astor, enjoyed the river at Maidenhead and the sea at Brighton, and met, in their company, actresses Fay Compton, Binnie Hale and Vesta Tilley. He had been born in Canada of an Irish father and an English mother and was no prude, but he was shocked by the squalor of the London streets, which he found degraded by hordes of prostitutes who openly solicited servicemen of all nationalities and ranks. Much the same, he supposed, as in Paris, which a friend had described as 'one vast brothel'.

Unspoiled and highly literate, Garland made few friends in wartime London, outside the du Cros family. 'I don't smoke, I don't gamble, don't play cards, don't go with "bad women"! These things seem to be necessary to be in the swim.' His best companion was his vest-pocket Shakespeare, which went everywhere with him – especially over the lines, in case he was captured.

Charles Smart, after his hasty return, was back with his original partner, Lieutenant Hendry, and they were soon in action. On 21

March a Hun got behind them threateningly, and Hendry took off his gloves and goggles and manned the gun. 'The Hun got right above us and then put his nose down and I thought to myself "Now for it"', wrote Smart, but seeing Hendry's reaction the German pilot wavered, pulled his nose up, and streaked off home. 'Some of these Huns are poor chaps . . . Hendry is a good chap and I like flying with him. He was worth watching with his steady Scotch eyes glued to the sights of his gun . . . I think he was a bit disappointed when the Hun turned away. I'm afraid I can't say that I was.'

On the 22nd Smart went, by tender, up to the old lines which the Hun had recently vacated, giving him a reminder of the gulf between his recent experience and that of the infantry, of which he had once been a part. 'Our shell-fire is truly terrible.' There was not a piece of flat ground anywhere, the trees were mere stumps, and worst of all, the dead, German and British, were still lying about in their hundreds from the previous July. 'I wonder what the mothers of these poor chaps would feel like if they could see their sons thrown about in heaps like so much garden rubbish. One can see from each man's attitude that he was carrying on his job when killed . . . Here and there a superior pair of boots show where an officer has fallen . . . I was glad to get away from this place.'

The RFC had 120 machines shot down in March, half of them on the British side of the lines, a sure reflection of the way the air battle was going. The hesitancy of many of the German scout pilots was disappearing as they gained in experience and confidence. In addition, many machines and a number of pilots and observers were lost in accidents. It had been impossible for Trenchard to husband his resources for the offensive, as he would have liked, and a recurring problem was that the RFC, unlike the Army, had no reserves to call upon.

When Garland returned from leave he found he had been transferred, with several others of his squadron, to help reinforce the overworked and undermanned 16 Squadron; it was one of the first squadrons to be increased to three flights of eight, twenty-four machines in all; yet they were still flying the outdated BE. The base at Bruay was very much a front-line aerodrome – a contrast to Garland's chateau billet and surroundings at 10 Squadron. The quarters were rough and ready, the Mess was like a canteen, and the casualties were so frequent there was hardly time to get to know anyone. The occasional loss at No. 10, always of an acquaintance and often of a friend, had made a greater impact. Curiously enough he was joined shortly afterwards by three pilots from 5 Squadron, among them his fellow diarist Charles Smart.

For the first time Smart found himself taking photographs, and he thought it 'a poor game, it is highly dangerous and it doesn't give one a chance of telling any tales ... The route you have taken is recorded on the photographic plates with the same clearness as the track of a snail is marked upon the wall up which it has climbed.' He was not altogether surprised that morale in 16 Squadron was not all it should be. 'The people in this squadron have fairly "got wind up" about crossing the lines, not without reason perhaps for a great number of machines have been shot down.' He found a wry amusement in a sort of anachronistic Catch 22: they were told not to cross the lines without an escort – yet no escort was provided for numerous jobs which could not be accomplished without crossing the lines. In his diary he quoted a stanza that seemed apt:

> Mother may I go to swim?
> Yes my darling daughter.
> Hang your clothes on a hickory limb –
> But don't go near the water.

2

THE BEGINNINGS OF 'BLOODY APRIL': BAPTISM OF THE BRISFIT

WITH the attack on Vimy Ridge scheduled for 9 April, Major-General Sir David Henderson, Director-General of Military Aeronautics at the War Office, felt constrained, at the beginning of the month, to justify the heavy and disproportionate RFC losses of February and March. The German retirement to the Hindenburg Line, he declared, had greatly extended the penetration necessary for all forms of reconnaissance and artillery cooperation. Types of machine in which great hopes had been vested, the Martinsyde 'Elephant', the FE2d and the Sopwith 1½-strutter, had not fulfilled expectations, the DH2 was outclassed by the new German scouts, and the arrival of the next generation of fighting machines, the Bristol Fighter, the SE5, and the Camel, had been subject to various setbacks, not least in engine production (partly owing to industrial disputes and wildcat strikes). Nevertheless a squadron of Bristol Fighters, No. 48, reached France on 8 March and was acclimatising, and a squadron of SE5's, No. 56, was about to leave for the front. Meanwhile the RFC, as an army corps, was obliged to meet army requests whenever feasible, thwarting any notion of conservation before the battle.

Henderson added one vital point that he rightly proffered in Trenchard's support: the work of the RFC was not to be measured in statistics alone. Against the record of positive and productive work

– of reconnaissance, artillery cooperation, contact patrols, and the bombing of enemy communications, strongpoints, and troop concentrations – the German Air Force was primarily engaged in the negative and defensive task of trying to shoot down British machines. Disproportionate as the RFC losses might seem, they should be measured against the losses amongst the German ground forces to which the RFC decisively contributed.

Scandalmongering at home, in the House of Commons, and in the Press, while adding not a single new machine to the order of battle, threatened instead to undermine in advance the morale of pilots and observers bound for the front. But one young Australian, Francis Penny, volunteering, after starting his pilot training, to help fill dead observers' shoes, got his discouragement *en route*. Crossing the path at Boulogne of a pilot on his way home, he mentioned that he was on his way to No. 12 Squadron. 'I've just come from there', he was told, 'and in the last month we've lost 20 pilots and observers, either killed or taken prisoner. I reckon you'll last about six weeks.'

No one had warned more vehemently of the likely inadequacies of the RFC for the planned spring offensive than Trenchard himself. And no one could have been more brutally frank with his crews about the odds they would have to face in the coming weeks. He continued his familiar 'gather round' invitations when visiting squadrons and at the same time he would ask what was most needed, Maurice Baring would 'make a note', and action would be taken. But at the beginning of April, on a visit to 25 Squadron (FE2b's and d's), he told the assembled crews that if they refused to fly the FE2b's any more it would be hard for him to take any action: he thought that every time they went up in them they were virtually committing suicide. The machines were obsolete, and he regretted he couldn't supply them with new ones. The best he had been able to do was to get them a few FE2d's (with the Rolls-Royce engine); but until new types were available he would rely on them to do their best.

The plea worked: when volunteers were requested for a photo reconnaissance of Vimy Ridge, everyone stepped forward, and Major Cherry chose three. Despite forming their customary 'ring o' roses' when attacked, two were lost, one to Richthofen.

The air offensive that was due to start on 4 April was no more than a progression from the costly preparatory work of previous weeks. And there was plenty of action from 1 April. Already, as observed by another diarist, Major A.S.W. Dore of 43 Squadron, Vimy Ridge was almost invisible under a blanket of shrapnel from British guns. Ignoring the Archie, and dodging a cloudbank, 34-year-old Alan Dore looked down on an area already pitted with water-filled shellholes. But when he led a formation of six 1½-strutters in the afternoon, they were driven back by snowstorms. Bad weather was the one obstruction that Trenchard's crews could not surmount.

Very much the old man of the squadron, Alan Dore had been a major in the Worcesters but had learnt to fly, started at the bottom on BE's with 13 Squadron, and joined Sholto Douglas's 43 Squadron as one of his flock. Working his way up, he had recently replaced a man of similar age, A.J.L. Scott, as flight leader. Jack Scott, a successful barrister before the war, and a friend of Winston Churchill, was 'rather a ham-fisted pilot', according to Douglas, and after breaking both legs in a crash he limped on sticks much as Smith-Barry had done. He had to be lifted in and out of his machine, but after serving with 43 Squadron as a flight commander he had graduated on merit and by sheer force of character to command 60 Squadron on Nieuports.

For air crews within reach of a town it was still possible to enjoy a night out, and the austerity that was emerging in England had not yet dulled the cuisine – or the cellars – in France. Farmers were still working their land almost up to the front line, spasmodically under shell fire. That evening another of Douglas's flight leaders, Captain D.C. Rutter, gave a dinner at Auchel for a twin celebration: his birthday and the award of an MC. 'A jolly evening,' noted Alan Dore. At ten o'clock next morning six of the party, led by Dore, set out to photograph a section of the Hindenburg Line. 'At 5,000 feet, with clouds above and below us,' recorded Dore, 'we saw some Huns.'

Presently Dore noticed a flight of what he took to be Nieuports apparently coming to join them, and when he heard his observer start firing he shouted at him to stop. But the red belly and fish-tail of an Albatros scout diving on another of the Sopwiths convinced him his observer was right. The attacker, as he afterwards discovered, was Richthofen. The Sopwith under attack, piloted by Lieutenant Peter Warren, disappeared into the clouds, apparently under control, but later Dore heard that a Sopwith had been seen to land east of Vimy. 'Hope they are prisoners and unwounded,' he wrote. He learned later that Warren had indeed survived as a prisoner but that his observer, Sergeant Renel Dunn, a 19-year-old former Oxford University student, had died of his wounds. This was Richthofen's thirty-third victory, and Dunn was the fifth fatality in what was to become infamous in the annals of the RFC as Bloody April.

Jack Scott had despatched three Nieuports from 60 Squadron to patrol the lines and help any reconnaissance machines in trouble, and these must have been the Nieuports seen in the distance by Dore. Outstanding among the Nieuport pilots was a comparative newcomer named Billy Bishop, one of a stream of Canadians who were to prove themselves unsurpassed as air fighters. (Ewart Garland, who had had the task of training some of them while he was 'on rest', wrote of one of them: 'Like all the Canadians he is very quick and seems adapted to the air.') A week earlier Bishop had chalked up his first moral victories: now he was the only one of the three Nieuport pilots to survive the subsequent clash with Richthofen's *Jasta*.

That same day Charles Smart was over the lines early to observe for a battery that he cursed for wasting the best part of an hour – and the best of the weather – through not reaching its agreed position and putting out ground strips and erecting its wireless mast until eight o'clock. Nevertheless he managed to observe 24 shots for them, 'and did quite well although no OK's were registered'. When his air mechanic observer passed him a note saying 'I feel kind of seasick,' a malady from which many observers suffered in silence, Smart scrawled back 'afraid you'll just have to stick it.' The delayed start meant that the airsick mechanic's ordeal lasted three hours 10 minutes.

There was no respite for Gerald Jamieson, the young man who had flown daily from 7 March to the 25th, often twice, lost two observers, and somehow recovered, for the moment anyway, from severe attacks of 'nerves'. How long, at this pace, could he last? On 1 April, starting at 6 a.m., he flew twice in the morning, a counter-battery shoot and a photographic mission, and then did a patrol in the afternoon. On 2 April he suffered engine failure and only just limped back over the lines, and on the 3rd he managed to take some photographs in the afternoon despite the rain.

An urgent request reached 16 Squadron that day from the Canadian ground forces for fresh photos of the ridge before plans for their attack, due to be launched on the 9th, could be finalised. The air offensive proper was scheduled to start along the whole British front next day. The task fell to Garland, as the senior man in his flight after the flight commander. His determination to get his photographs was only equalled by the eagerness of the Huns to prevent him, their scouts diving on him again and again, firing incendiary as well as ordinary bullets. (Often represented as being contrary to various Hague Conventions – which outlawed expanding bullets – their use was reckoned to be a cad's trick, and there were pilots, Mannock among them, who wouldn't use them, but both sides did.) Finally, when his observer's one-and-only gun jammed, Garland virtually hurled his machine at each attacker in turn in the hope that the pilot would choose to avoid certain death in a collision. Between attacks he dived, side-slipped and stunted, trying never to present a stable target. He must still have been doomed in the end had not five FE's come to his rescue. There were forty holes in his machine when he got back, but the photos looked good and were rushed to Canadian HQ by motor-cycle. He learned only much later, from the Canadian commander, General Julian Byng, in person how vital these photographs had been.

The air offensive duly opened on the 4th, the declared objective being to draw hostile aircraft away from the immediate battle area so as to leave the sky free for the corps squadrons. Of the original 'contemptibles', two were commanding squadrons in the front line – Willie Read, still running 45 Squadron under protest, and Harvey-Kelly, brashly confident in the superiority of the French-built Spad 7 with which his new squadron, No. 19, was equipped: it came to be regarded as the best French design of the war. Veterans Josh

Higgins and Gordon Shephard were commanding brigades. Other squadron commanders with names to conjure with included Arthur Tedder and Sholto Douglas (1½-strutters, 70 and 43 Squadrons respectively), and the ebullient Jack Baldwin, 55 Squadron, operating Geoffrey de Havilland's new nimble high-altitude Rolls-Royce-engined bomber the DH4, in which great hopes were vested. (Twenty-five years later, flouting 'Bomber' Harris's orders, Baldwin, as an air vice-marshal, was to take part in the first 1,000-bomber raid.)

The programme was timed to synchronise with a massive five-day bombardment by 2,800 guns, after which, on 9 April, the infantry would go over the top. But as had seemed all too likely in the previous forty-eight hours, artillery cooperation was greatly hampered by low clouds and rain. Despite this, as Garland noted, 'the air was thick with British machines.' Jamieson was among the lucky ones in finding a clear patch. 'Two trips, two shoots, successful,' he recorded; but some did not get off the ground at all. Alan Dore, noting 'a very stormy day, low clouds', flew over to his old squadron, No. 13, and found 'a few familiar faces amongst the men', but only two officer survivors of his era.

Smart, still attached to 16 Squadron, was booked for a shoot on the 5th, but noted: 'Quite hopeless owing to thick mist and low clouds.' It took him and others like him all their time to find their way about, but he did stay to witness what he called 'a fine bombardment by our guns'. Visiting the battery, a Canadian one, that afternoon, he was told by the major that the Hun 'will never stand the bombardment we are going to put up'. Smart concluded: 'They were certainly making things hot for Fritz.'

Elsewhere, throughout the five days, Fritz was making things even hotter for the Brits. Garland was lucky when taking photographs without escort when he spotted two of his BE2 colleagues briefed for the adjacent sector being attacked by three Albatros scouts in turn. Both went down in flames. 'One was Whitaker and the other Knight, who was with me yesterday. Both had observers.' All four men were lost. Garland managed to get all his photos, then 'scuttled back over to our side' as the Huns turned towards him. 'I came back safely but felt a bit off seeing those two go down in flames.' Next day, to his unashamed joy, he was transferred back to his first love, No. 10, as a flight commander, where his welcome was ecstatic. '*Quelle guerre!*' He was 20.

On 5 April Baring noted, somewhat tardily, 'Fighting in the air has begun.' It did in fact begin that day for the Bristol Fighters of 48 Squadron, which had arrived in France exactly four weeks earlier, giving them ample time, it seemed, to work up. Sooner or later they had to be blooded, to see what impact they could make on the air battle. The Brisfit was a sizeable machine for its time, 26 feet long and with a 40-feet wing span. The two crew sat back to back, the pilot with a synchronised Vickers, the observer with a Lewis mounted on a Scarff Ring with a swivel seat, firing on the flanks and to the rear. It was the observer's wide field of fire that was regarded as the bullpoint, especially as the Brisfit was erroneously thought to have inherent structural weaknesses which prohibited aggressive man-oeuvring. In any case a full understanding of the employment of the Brisfit in combat could hardly be arrived at except in action. The experience was to be dearly bought.

It was perhaps inevitable that the flight commander chosen to lead the first patrol should be a man who had already made a name for himself, a man whose fame in England eclipsed even that of Albert Ball. Over a period of many months, from January 1915 until September 1916, a total of 39 Zeppelin raids had been mounted against England, killing 439 people and injuring nearly a thousand, and the bearded commander of airships, Captain Peter Strasser, a fanatical believer in airships as a war-winning weapon, had mustered, for the night of 2 September 1916, an armada of sixteen for what he called 'the climactic raid', a decisive blow against Britain's capital city. All that threatened to hinder them over London was a mobile anti-aircraft force and half a dozen frustrated pilots in obsolescent machines – BE2c's – both rendered impotent by the height advantage that conferred virtual invulnerability on the raiders. Yet a young man named William Leefe Robinson, 'Robbie' to his intimates, had given Londoners the most spectacular heavenly conflagration of all time, witnessed by hundreds of thousands, by overcoming the odds stacked against him and shooting down the army airship SL11 over Cuffley, the first airship of any kind to be shot down over Britain. The sight of their comrades' incineration, cheered to the echo by Londoners, had so appalled the remainder that they turned tail.

A man who could do that, it was assumed, could do anything. Now here he was, seven months after his famous exploit, entrusted with the task by his commanding officer, Major A.V. 'Zulu' Bettington (from Cape Colony), of leading the first-ever Bristol Fighter patrol against the enemy.

Cynicism over the true worth of Leefe Robinson's feat was general in the RFC in France. Provided you could get the height, anyone could shoot down a Zeppelin: it was merely a matter of being in the right place at the right time. The hazardous part was finding one's aerodrome – or any aerodrome – and getting down afterwards, with the aid of a few flares in an otherwise darkened world. It was a predicament that led to many crashes, some of them fatal. But did its surmounting warrant a VC? Wasn't it a fact that once the psychological barrier had been removed, admittedly by Robinson, the feat had become commonplace – rather like, in a later age, Bannister's four-minute mile? Those unacquainted with the full story resented the publicity accorded the home-based hero, and wondered what qualified him to take command of a flight of the new Bristol Fighters in the front line.

In fact, Leefe Robinson was no stranger to France: he had flown with No. 4 Squadron in BE2c's as an observer before sustaining a shrapnel wound in May 1915 which had proved to be a 'Blighty' one. Recovering, and learning to fly, he had begun the lonely work of Zeppelin-chasing at night on Christmas Eve 1915, and persevered with many setbacks until his triumph of September 1916. But survival in the skies beyond the lines in April 1917 demanded special qualities of cunning and resource, not necessarily similar to those required for Zepp-chasing. Robinson had trained hard on the Brisfit in England, the work-up period in France had seemed adequate, and there is no doubt that he was better equipped to lead than most newly-arrived pilots: but this still fell far short of the ideal. Yet someone had to do it, and, to Zulu Bettington, Robinson must have seemed the obvious choice.

What followed was no fault of Leefe Robinson's: but blame must surely be attached to those who chose the route for this first offensive patrol. It seems that they were actually seeking a showdown with Richthofen: if so, they were notably successful. They met Richthofen where they would expect to find him, near Douai, where his *Jasta* was based. They hoped to give him a nasty surprise. But the tactical assessment that the Brisfit would be best suited to operating in close formation for mutual protection, like the FE2b, basing both offence and defence on the observer's gun, proved disastrously mistaken, and four of the formation of six were shot down, two by Richthofen. A fifth was badly shot about but got back along with the sixth. It was some consolation that Leefe Robinson, forced to land with his engine put out of action, survived with his observer to be taken prisoner. As a baptism of fire for the Brisfit, however, it was calamitous.

Richthofen was dismissive of the quality of the new British machine and pronounced his Albatros far superior; but after some technical and tactical adjustments, the Brisfit was to prove him culpably wrong.

No. 48 Squadron was not the only one to suffer in those first few April days. Heavy losses were also sustained by the Nieuports of 60 Squadron (ten in three days, all to *Jasta 11*) and the FE2d's of 57; in neither case could inexperience be blamed. A bombing offensive, beginning on 5 April and aimed at forcing the enemy to withdraw anti-aircraft defences and aeroplanes from the front line, also suffered costly setbacks. Good news came on 6 April when the United States declared war on Germany. Bad news was the loss of four Martinsydes: but they shot down two Halberstadts, and two of the pilots survived as prisoners.

The faster, high-flying DH4's of 55 Squadron made a good start in their first show by scoring direct hits with 112 lb bombs on an assembly point at Valenciennes and then, when swarms of Albatros scouts pursued them, outdistancing them comfortably. Daylight bombing was rarely granted close escort, but it was often loosely accompanied, or supported by offensive patrols, whereas the DH4's at high altitude were expected to take care of themselves. But any notion of invulnerability was quickly confounded when they lost three out of four in a raid on 8 April. Nevertheless pilots soon rated the DH4 the best bomber of the war and observers liked it for its dual control. A drawback was that pilot and observer were separated by the fuel tanks and were too far apart to communicate verbally.

An innovation was the night attacks by FE2b's of 100 Squadron armed with one-pounder quick-firing pom-poms, especially effective against ground targets; they succeeded in wrecking hangars and buildings on Richthofen's aerodrome at Douai, keeping Richthofen out of the air for a day or so.

Escort work, according to Alan Dore, remained 'a ticklish job'. Detailed to lead five 1½-strutters to protect six BE's bombing a rail junction at Don, Dore saw nothing of the bombers. As happened far too often, something had gone wrong with the timing. Returning against a near-hurricane, the Sopwiths were pinpointed by Archie and chased by fifteen Hun scouts. 'Our formation of five is well closed up and gunners ready. Just before crossing the lines they dive at us. Both my guns are jammed. I see one get on to my tail so stall and go down in a spinning nose-dive . . . We cross the lines separately . . . Thornton and his observer Blackburn fail to return.'[1]

Resentment and indignation amongst pilots at the obsolescent machines they were given to fly was not always suppressed. Returning from a deep penetration to bomb Tournai rail junction, a flight commander on 45 Squadron (also 1½-strutters) boiled over. 'Some say Sopwith two-seaters are bloody fine machines, but I say they're more bloody than fine.' At the time the brigade commander, T.I. Webb-Bowen, was visiting the disgruntled Willie Read to tell him that his request to return to his regiment had at last been granted by Trenchard. Webb-Bowen overheard the remark and had the man removed to Home Establishment forthwith. Yet Read, who was shortly to be succeeded by Major H.A. van Ryneveld, a South

1. Second-Lieutenant C.P. Thornton and Lieutenant H.D. Blackburn, killed in action 5 April 1917.

African, could not but be sympathetic. From October 1916 to early May 1917 the squadron lost twenty-three pilots killed and five wounded in exchange for three hostiles destroyed.

Balloon-busting, which exposed its practitioners to withering machine-gun and rifle fire, not to mention 'flaming onions' – balls of fire projected upwards in string-of-onions succession – was attempted by the Nieuports as part of the air offensive, but rapid reaction by enemy winchmen frustrated many attacks, and the ratio, in the space of four days, of five aeroplanes shot down for five balloons destroyed, with the balloon crews – but not the Nieuport pilots – escaping by parachute, was discouraging.

On 8 April Smart noted: 'Tomorrow the infantry go over to take the Vimy Ridge. Good luck to them, they have been marching past the aerodrome towards the lines all day, all of them looking very pleased with life and ready for anything.' Undoubtedly this readiness for action could be blunted over a period, but airmen, like soldiers, generally got a boost, rather than the blues, from the prospect of action. Even Garland's rejoicing at returning to 10 Squadron was tempered by regret. 'The pity is that tomorrow is the "push" and now of course I shall miss it.'

In the five days of the preliminary air offensive, from 4 to 8 April, the RFC lost 75 machines in action and 105 pilots and observers – 19 killed, 13 wounded and 73 missing. It was a destructive period, too, for accidents, partly because of the many inexperienced pilots on the squadrons and the stress they were under, 56 machines being wrecked. The wastage on some squadrons, particularly of observers, was catastrophic. 'Of the observers who came out with us from England – eighteen in number – not one remains,' wrote Dore of 43 Squadron. He added: 'We have eight of the original pilots left.'

On the eve of the attack, and the last day of the preparatory air offensive, Trenchard, despite acute bronchitis, toured the front-line in an RE8, with Baring tagging along behind in a BE. They visited eleven squadrons and talked to all the pilots. No. 56 Squadron, the first SE5 squadron, had arrived at Vert Galand that day, under an energetic organiser in Major R.G. Blomfield, born in Sydney, Australia. Harvey-Kelly, the squadron's first CO, had laid the foundations so well that the dapper 'Dickie' Blomfield found himself commanding some of the best available pilots, led by three experienced flight commanders. He himself was going to be the majordomo, fostering rather than leading.

By means of shrewd exchange postings, Blomfield enhanced the general expertise of squadron personnel. He assembled a group of musicians with London orchestral experience and inveigled a culinary wizard who before call-up had been a chef at the Ritz. Demanding high standards in all departments, he set out to mould his squadron into an élite force.

But first there was much to be done. The untried SE5's needed many modifications to make them combat-worthy, and during the working-up period in mid-April one young pilot was obliged to apologise to his parents for his slackness as a correspondent. 'I haven't written because we've been busy altering our machines. Dawn till dark we were hard at it.' This was the 18-year-old Maurice Kay, who as a trainee had disgraced and distinguished himself simultaneously by ignoring expert advice to stay on the ground, only to redeem himself, after crashing through the branches of a tree, by skilfully controlling his crippled machine and miraculously surviving.

Another young pilot, who had long pleaded to be allowed to get back to the fighting, was so disillusioned with the basic SE5 that he followed Trenchard from one airfield to another and begged for a Nieuport for lone forays. His publicity value in attracting recruits was such that he had been permitted to join 56 Squadron for one month only: his name was Albert Ball. At first, Trenchard prevaricated.

Ball had no illusions of indestructibility. He had told his father: 'No scout pilot who does any serious fighting and sticks to it for any time can get through.' But there was no doubting his delight at being back. 'They're giving the Ball', he said, 'another run.'

*   *   *

The Battle for Vimy Ridge duly began on 9 April, in abominable weather, with the promised attack by the Canadians. 'Infantry went over at 5.30 a.m.,' noted Smart. He was sent up to spot the flashes of enemy guns and advise the Canadian battery commander. 'Terrific wind blowing and as bumpy as Satan.' It was too much for his observer, who passed him a note saying he felt sick and wanted to go home. 'I passed him a note back reminding him there was a war on and telling him to think of the poor devils below.' But after ninety-five minutes Smart had to return for a change of observer. 'This chap was the real thing, he felt very sick in the bumps but did not say anything about it. We had a great time . . . and had the satisfaction of seeing several active enemy batteries strafed and silenced, thus making things easier for our infantry . . . Rumour has it that we have taken 10,000 prisoners and 16 guns, hope this is true.' The Canadians had indeed seized a section of Vimy Ridge, though only after three hours' heavy fighting. Near Arras, in the centre, the Third Army, by pushing the Germans back three-and-a-half miles, had achieved the biggest gain in two-and-a-half years of trench warfare.

Smart rated this day one of the worst for flying he'd known. Yet: 'I managed to do four and a quarter hours after having breakfast at 6.30 a.m. and lunch at 5 p.m. and nothing in between. Am on the early morning stunt tomorrow, shall be doing the same job again. Our shellfire today was worth seeing, the enemy lines were simply seething with bursting shells . . .' And Dore wrote: 'All along the Vimy Ridge a white line of bursting shrapnel told me that we had reached the summit. Below us the contact and artillery machines swept backwards and forwards like shuttles . . . Looking round I see some men on a road and wagons behind. Descend and shoot right into them receiving a few bullets in return.'

Other pilots, undeterred by the snowstorm, but often forced down to 300 feet, located targets for the artillery hour by hour as Smart had done, but they weren't all as lucky as he was, and casualties were heaviest among the corps machines. Yet enemy batteries continued to be registered and trenches photographed. 'Despite inferiority,' recorded Baring proudly, 'the work of the army was done and thousands of casualties saved.'

The RFC was pulling its weight despite the weather and the ever-present deterrent of flying through the barrage they were master-minding. Garland noted: 'Our own gunfire was a definite hazard . . . it is no exaggeration to say that the sky was thick with shells . . . Our planes had to fly in the thick of the shell fire for as much as three hours on end, not to mention enemy action aimed at our planes.' And Dore wrote: 'Once I felt the concussion of a big howitzer shell pass so near that the whole aeroplane shuddered as though struck. Later I actually saw a shell come up and pass by me on its way to the Germans.'

Smart was out of bed next morning at 4.40 and in the air at six. But after locating two active batteries: 'We ran into a most awful snowstorm, turned west and flew for ten minutes at a height of 600 feet absolutely blind . . . I got most horrible "wind-up" for there is a lot of high ground about here . . .' He force-landed as soon as he could and was told he'd just missed a chimney stack. 'The wind was huge and I had to get two Tommies to hold on to each wing-tip.' When they got tired, however, 'over she went, fortunately without doing any damage.' Examining his machine when he got back to the aerodrome he found it had been peppered with machine-gun fire and that his observer, especially, had been within inches of mortal injury.

Enemy small-arms fire, Archie, poor visibility, and high ground, were all familiar hazards, but there was nothing more intimidating than the unavoidable necessity of flying through the aerial minefield of 'friendly' shells. 'After a completely dud day and no flying,' wrote Smart on 12 April, 'we were all sitting in the mess at 6 p.m. when the CO rushed in and said "The Huns are shelling the Pimple."' This was a small hill recently taken during the push. One machine from each flight was ordered up and as Smart was first for duty in his flight he ran down at once to the aerodrome and ordered out his machine. 'It was raining hard and a thoroughly miserable evening, however we had to go.' When they reached Arras they were faced with an unforgettable sight: all guns on both sides in the district were firing away at frenetic speed. 'The whole ground, particularly on the enemy's side, was simply reeling with bursting shells, these together with the gun flashes presented a wonderful sight, there seemed to be millions of spots of flame spread all over the countryside and it must have been as near hell as possible for those down below.' It was equally hell for those up above. 'The air was just stiff with flying shells and we got no end of bumps from them as they passed under and over us.' To some extent Archie was predictable, but the barrage was haphazard, and the BE's of 16 Squadron did not escape unscathed. 'One C flight machine was struck by a passing shell, both pilot and observer being killed.'

Next morning Charles Smart was transferred back to 5 Squadron. 'Everyone was very glad to see me and I was jolly glad to get back.' But euphoria was cruelly truncated. 'I got the afternoon off and walked over to 60 Squadron where I got an awful shock being told that George was shot down over Arras last Saturday. Poor old chap, he hasn't had much of a run. The news has depressed me terribly.'

George Smart had been shot down in flames on 7 April by Richthofen, who recorded that his victim had 'tried to escape six times by various tricks and manoeuvres'. Burnt to death, he was buried in a shell-hole close to the wreck of his Nieuport, with his broken propeller for a headstone. But when Charles returned after ten days' compassionate leave and tried to locate the grave he found the ground torn up by artillery fire and all traces of it eliminated. Charles applied for transfer to a scout squadron, thinking to avenge his brother, but he was still wanted where he was.

The dud day mentioned by Charles was a blessing for some. 'It has given us a rest, which has been much needed,' wrote Eric Routh, the harassed C Flight commander of 16 Squadron. Essential tasks could be attended to. 'We buried poor MacKenzie and Everingham.'[1] They had been shot down over ground taken during the push. 'Mac was looking most peaceful and quite normal, being shot through the back (probably died instantly or unconscious), but Everingham looked as though the end had not come quite so peacefully. He was not shot, but badly broken by the fall.' They had spun down from 4,000 feet: it was this agonising last minute or so that all but the

1. Second-Lieutenants Keith Ingleby Mackenzie and Guy Everingham, shot down by Manfred von Richthofen on 8 April 1917. MacKenzie was eighteen.

most unimaginative had experienced in morbid daytime fantasies or in nightmares, and it explained the difference between the death-mask of unconscious pilot and sentient observer. 'They were buried', recounted Routh, 'close to what was left of the machine. All around were hundreds of dead bodies, our own and the Huns. One dead man was leaning up against a tree, another had a cigarette in his mouth with a box of matches in his hand and looked very much alive, like a waxwork. Burying parties were at work, but it was a lengthy and tedious process.' Dore, too, taking advantage of the blank day, climbed the famous ridge. 'You could hardly put a pin's point between the shell craters . . . Devastation and mud . . . Ground littered with dead or portions of dead.' Reaching the crest, his party were immediately shelled, and Dore took cover in a trench. 'Realise I have lost the art of taking shells complaisantly.' It was better to be airborne after all.

Visiting 56 Squadron, Trenchard had tea with Blomfield and his star pilot, Albert Ball. He was so delighted to hear Ball speak with mounting respect of the SE5 that he gave in to his earlier request. 'He is giving him two machines,' noted Baring, 'the SE5 for his ordinary work and a Nieuport for his lone enterprises.' The squadron, still busy with refinements, expected to be ready to start patrolling within another few days.

Trenchard's visits sometimes met with cynicism from the men at the sharp end. He did sometimes reveal a capacity for stating the obvious. 'Boom came and inspected us today and talked a lot and told us all the work we had done previous to the 9th had been the cause of the success of the attack on the Vimy Ridge, this was stale news as we all knew that, and so does everyone else with brains.' Thus spake the long-suffering Routh. 'He also complimented us on the amount of flying, more especially in the rain and snow. He told us he was sorry we had casualties and that our machines were not quite all that could be desired, but "a working machine will never have a chance against a fighting scout".' It was a subject, wrote Routh, with some bitterness, 'on which we were all agreed'.

Routh was still going on about his *bête noire*, Sergeant Dangerfield, who had not returned from an evening patrol. 'Every time he's been out to the lines he's failed to return through some reason or other – either lost his way or had a forced landing. He is without doubt the most unreliable man I have.' Yet Routh had learnt to respect the man's ability to turn up like the proverbial bad penny, and he was quite upset when he had to report Dangerfield missing. It was no great surprise when, a week or so later, he was named as a prisoner. He had got down all right, as before.

With the capture of Vimy Ridge consolidated, ground patrols pushed vigorously forward, and on 13 April the weather improved. It was also a Friday, and it was not a lucky day for the RFC. Those who suffered most were the RE8's, the 'Harry Tate' as it was dubbed in rhyming slang, the machine ordered in 1915 to replace the BE range. It embodied most of the long-awaited two-seater improvements, pilot in the front cockpit with synchronised gun, observer behind with swivel gun, more powerful engine, faster speed and rate of climb. But from the beginning, production was dogged by misfortune, after which early models revealed a marked tendency to spin. Modifications in design were slow to impress and the machine acquired an evil reputation, which it was only just beginning to live down.

But now came a setback. Soon after eight o'clock that morning six RE8's of 59 Squadron set out on a photographic mission which called as always for accurate flying and a steady progression. Good support was being given at this time by three RNAS squadrons, flying Sopwith Tripes or Pups, but no close escort was detailed, reliance being placed on offensive patrols by FE2d's, Spads and Bristol Fighters. Two of the FE2d's were shot down, the Brisfits saw nothing, and the Spads were late. Intercepted by six single-seaters led by Richthofen, all six RE8's were shot down, ten of the twelve crew men being killed.

3

'BLOODY APRIL' – THE CLIMAX: BALL, BISHOP AND MANNOCK: MANFRED VON RICHTHOFEN

O N 16 April, along a 50-mile front on the river Aisne, 80 miles south-east of Arras, General Nivelle launched his controversial spring offensive, the massive assault that he had promised would destroy the enemy's forces and achieve a breakthrough that would win the war. Haig, Pétain and others believed that Nivelle had exaggerated his prospects and underestimated the enemy's strength, and this was almost certainly true; but security leaks arising from the distribution of plans down to unit commander level destroyed the vital element of surprise. Warned of the Allies' plans, the defenders were well prepared and enemy gunners in fortified positions inflicted frightful casualties when the French advanced. The eager *poilus*, buoyed up by forecasts of a virtual walk-over, were shocked into a dismay that quickly degenerated into demoralisation. There was a whiff of betrayal in high places, further setbacks precipitated widespread mutinies, and Nivelle was discredited. Within a month he had been succeeded as commander-in-chief by Pétain, with Foch replacing Pétain as chief of staff. The leading mutineers were executed, negative concepts were suppressed, and Pétain began the task of averting a complete collapse before rebuilding could commence. Meanwhile, Haig, one of the few privy to the truth about the mutiny, had to redouble the diversionary pressure.

Four days of bad weather on the British front so hampered the work of the corps squadrons that artillery preparations for a renewal of the offensive were delayed, but after an improvement on the evening of 20 April a full day's air cooperation on the 21st allowed the preliminary bombardment to begin. Despite their losses, 16 Squadron remained heavily engaged, and Eric Routh, led by senior flight commander J.P.C. 'Jock' Mitchell, took off with a young observer named MacKenzie (no relation of the pilot Ingleby Mac-Kenzie they had recently buried). After registering enemy trench junctions they penetrated more deeply to take photographs. 'On our way back we were attacked by three Albatros destroyers, two went for Jock and brought him down in flames, and the third went for me. I was hit in the hand by the first burst, but what with MacKenzie firing and my twisting and turning he did not get on to me again, though he had already succeeded in putting a bullet through my engine, camera and petrol tank.' Routh landed safely beyond Vimy Ridge but realised that the Albatros pilot was still firing at him. The chivalry of earlier years was by this time wearing thin, but even so Routh registered surprise: relations, he reflected whimsically, were becoming less than courteous.

'Directly we landed I shouted to Mac to get his gun on the Boche again, which he did from the machine and drove him off.' The Canadians were also firing 'for all they were worth'. Someone quickly bandaged Routh's hand. 'Poor Jock was not so fortunate as I was and I'm afraid is dead with his observer Rogers. One of them jumped out at about 500 feet, both were killed.' Routh added: 'I am afraid Mac is rather upset at the whole thing, and is rather shaken, but it made me laugh to see him after half a glass of neat whisky, it made him awfully tight and he was most amusing.'

The battle-hardened Eric Routh, as we know, could hold his liquor. But soon afterwards a minor accident when loading a French bomb ended his service with 16 Squadron after 126 days. The youthful MacKenzie's nerves did not recover.

Routh had been extremely lucky to survive so long. According to Garland, 10 Squadron had lent eight crews to 16 Squadron and only two had returned. 'If Durrant and I hadn't been posted back to No. 10,' wrote Garland, 'there's little doubt that we'd have been done in.'

Another victim of 'Bloody April', Lieutenant Norman Birks of 29 Squadron (now re-equipped with Nieuports from DH2's), had something to say on the subject of chivalry. The German sergeant pilot who shot him down visited him in hospital and apologised for continuing to shoot when Birks's machine was crippled and on the way down. 'If I'd left you alone you'd have got back over the lines,' was his excuse, which Birks agreed was true. Birks added: 'Until about 1917 it was considered "not quite the thing" by both sides to continue firing on a machine which was incapacitated. But this sense of chivalry was rapidly disappearing.' Boelcke, 'our brave and chivalrous foe,' for one, was credited with such acts of mercy. Routh would have agreed that the gloves were off.

When infantry attacks were finally launched on the morning of 23 April, there were 48 single-seaters patrolling the area, including 20 Sopwith naval Triplanes, 14 Nieuports (29 and 60 Squadrons), and, for their baptism of fire, seven SE5's of 56 Squadron. There were also 24 two-seaters – 1½-strutters, FE's, Armstrong-Whitworths, and RE8's – on line patrol, all aiming to keep the skies clear for artillery spotting and contact patrols. But with fighting continuous and fluctuating as the enemy counter-attacked, and enemy planes interfering when they could, requests by air observers for the lighting of flares on the ground to reveal forward positions were met with understandable reluctance and were mostly ignored. 'This', as the army commander reminded his corps commanders that evening, 'makes effective artillery support almost impossible.'

A combined reconnaissance and bombing operation, meticulously planned, got through unscathed, but there were losses amongst the FE's, and on the eve of the battle a Spad formation, bemused by identification problems (easy enough in the now crowded skies), mistook a group of hostiles for friendlies and suffered accordingly. Of eight DH4's of 55 Squadron setting out to bomb an ammunition dump, two crashed even before they reached the lines, and although the remaining six got through to their objective, they were savagely attacked on their way home, and before they could shake off their assailants they had lost one pilot killed and three observers wounded. Yet the Tripe pilots were asserting their superiority wherever they were engaged, the pilots of the Pups, recognising the strengths and limitations of their mounts, did useful work, and the Brisfit crews, revising their tactics, more than held their own. News of the SE5's, too, with their 150 h.p. Hispano-Suiza engines, was eagerly awaited.

The SE5, even more than the Brisfit, had had a disastrous inception. Owing to an unsuspected fault in the wing-tip structure, the prototype had broken up in mid-air, killing test pilot and spinning expert Frank Goodden. The resultant mood of despondency called for positive measures, and after remedial action had been taken Roderic Hill, replacing Goodden, set out to restore faith and confidence in a 20-minute display of handling and aerobatics especially for the benefit of the apprehensive pilots of 56 Squadron.

Diving, zooming, spinning, corkscrewing and looping, directly above their assembly airfield at London Colney, he demonstrated the reliability and robustness of the basic type, and the power of the 150 h.p. Hispano-Suiza engine, for all to see. The machine was armed with a synchronised Vickers firing through the propeller arc and a Lewis mounted on the upper wing. The many imperfections that remained had all proved susceptible to modification at squadron level, and at last the SE5, whose ancestry went back to Geoffrey de Havilland's SE2 in 1914, was ready.

In the months that followed, 56 Squadron, especially after the 200 h.p. Hispano-Suiza was introduced into their SE5A's in mid-June, were to eclipse all other scout squadrons in terms of victories; but on this first foray their pilots sighted nothing. Then Ball, patrolling alone soon afterwards in his Nieuport, picked out a pair of Albatros two-seaters and at once initiated his favourite form of attack. 'When I get to close quarters I generally pretend I am going to attack from above . . . then suddenly I dive under the machine, and if I am lucky I empty a drum into his petrol tank and he goes down.' One of the two-seaters escaped out of range, but Ball emptied half a drum of Lewis into the other and it staggered and began to go down. He followed it, still firing, and watched it crash. No one got out.

It seems that the surviving Hun had noted the red spinner that Ball always displayed on his propeller: anyway he reported the characteristic method of attack, giving due warning that the English-man Ball was back in business.

Fifteen minutes later Ball glimpsed another two-seater as it disappeared into cloud and dived after it. But in his eagerness he overshot, presenting the German with a fleeting but point-blank target. The German escaped, and back at Vert Galand Ball found the wings of his Nieuport were so riddled they had to be changed.

The first fortnight of Ball's permitted month in France had already expired, so he had only a fortnight to achieve an ambition he had conceived of passing the record of the Frenchman Georges Guynemer, which stood at thirty-seven. He was out to make up for lost time, and he was off again two hours later, this time in his SE5, and again his wonderfully keen eyesight, or his instinct, found him a target others had missed. Stalking a white Albatros two-seater at 12,000 feet, and closing in under its tail, he had barely begun firing when his Lewis jammed.

Landing at the nearest aerodrome, he cleared the stoppage and within minutes was back on patrol. Above Cambrai he sighted five green-painted single-seater Albatros scouts, patrolling with justifiable arrogance, masters, as their pilots reasonably believed, of the sky. Ball's tactics against scout formations seldom varied: he dived immediately on the leader, opening up with his Vickers from close range. By the time the formation had recovered from the shock, one green Albatros was falling in flames. The others fired at him, but they had lost their leader, and as Ball turned to face them they cleared off home. Perhaps they too had seen the red spinner.

Testing his controls, Ball soared away and circled over Cambrai. He sighted another Albatros two-seater and made his usual feint attack, then pulled down his Lewis in Nieuport style and trimmed his machine tail-heavy to leave both hands free. He fired half a drum, then had to break off to avoid collision. He chased the pilot down through the cloud layer, but when he saw him crash-land safely he left him alone.

That night he wrote excitedly to the eighteen-year-old land girl he had met and fallen in love with only a fortnight before leaving England. 'Have got my first two Huns. I had three flights and managed to bring down one. This I did in my Nieuport. Next I went up in my SE5 . . . I got five shots in my right strut, four in the wings, and two just behind my head. This was done by five Albatros scouts. But I got one of them and set it on fire . . . Poor old chap inside.'

Ball's success gave a timely fillip to 56 Squadron, where the youngest pilot, Maurice Kay, not in the least overawed by his seniors, or by the enemy, was acclimatising well. In his letters home he gave a vivid picture of squadron life, in the air and on the ground. 'Ball has done himself great credit, making himself an even bigger name. Yesterday we did a lot of fighting, I had two flights. Had to give up each time with my man in my sights when my guns jammed.' Gun stoppages were a nightmare at first in the SE5, but Kay was philosophic. 'No matter, I put the wind up both . . . It was good fun – and the excitement was terrific!'

Kay continued: 'Things are going very well indeed . . . While I write this the piano is going strong, everybody is making quite a noise, I am thoroughly enjoying life. It is great fun . . . I must say again how ripping it is out here.'

This naive exuberance was checked only momentarily by bad news of a family friend in another squadron. 'Poor Heyworth, who is officially missing, is I'm sorry to say feared to be killed . . . He was seen to go down in a nose dive. It is very sad!! He was a good fellow!!!' Then he added, more soberly: 'I wouldn't say anything to Mr Heyworth about Heyworth being killed, when we only know he is missing.' (In fact, Heyworth had survived as a prisoner.)

Bad weather in the next two days gave Ball a chance to put the final touches to his hut, dig his garden, and tread in a few plants. Then, quite unselfconsciously, out came his violin. 'The chaps do laugh,' he wrote. His garden too, he said, always caused 'a lot of sport. When I am happy I dig in the garden and sing.'

Another succession of combats on the 26th brought him a third victim with 56 Squadron. 'It was dark when I returned', he wrote, 'and everyone thought I had been done in. You see, they do one or two jobs each day and I lead them, but during the remainder of the day I go up in my Nieuport and have a try by myself. This is the only way to get them. Just keep at them all day.'

The pace at which Ball was living, however, was bound to catch up with him, and in his letters home he confessed to a tiredness close to exhaustion. Often he went straight to bed after the evening patrol. This was in marked contrast to a future ace whose ambition was to overtake Ball one day: the Canadian Billy Bishop. Hearing that the short cut to a squadron at the front was as an observer, Bishop had volunteered. Undeterred by his experiences and injuries in the underpowered and unreliable RE7 and a subsequent grounding, he recovered to take a pilot's course under Garland and volunteer again for France, arriving to join 60 Squadron in March 1917. Like Ball an individualist, he differed in harbouring a personal vendetta against the enemy, perhaps because of what he had seen during his army cooperation work in the RE7. He revelled in spending seven hours or more in the air each day, and never seemed to tire: he was in his element. 'Far from affecting my nerves,' he wrote, 'each combat becomes more and more enjoyable.' And later: 'I had found the one thing I loved above all others. To me it was not a business or a profession but just a wonderful game.' Yet he resembled Ball in his aggression, his love of stalking alone, and in being no more than an averagely proficient pilot. He crashed so frequently while training that one of his instructors was heard to say: 'Get out of that bloody mess, Bishop, you ought to be flying a Harrod's bedstead!' But he was soon given a roving commission by Jack Scott, just as Ball had been. He also displayed qualities of leadership, and on 25 April he was promoted to flight commander.

If Bishop at 27 belied the theory that a scout pilot was too old at 25, a man in his thirtieth year, with defective eyesight, could hardly hope even to qualify as a pilot, let alone aspire to greatness. Yet this was the description that fitted Edward Mannock, a recent recruit to 40 Squadron (Nieuport 17 Scouts). Born, like McCudden, into a non-commissioned service environment but into a less stable family, Mannock knew deprivation as a child and had to take menial jobs on leaving school at 15. He later attained white-collar status but sacrificed it when he found office work depressed his spirit, becoming a telephone linesman. A cable-laying contract took him to Turkey, with good prospects, but when he realised in August 1914 that his work would benefit Turkey's ally Germany he downed tools. He was reviled and humiliated, and at the request of the Germans he was interned. Then, after breaking out of camp to get food for sick companions, he was punished with solitary confinement. When at length he was repatriated under an exchange of prisoners, he sought revenge.

Inspired by the exploits of Albert Ball, he applied for pilot training. 'You're too old,' he was told; but he had already made a study of the tactics of air combat, and he talked his way into a medical. An infection contracted in childhood had left permanent damage to one eye, but he is said to have kept the fault hidden by turning up early at his medical board and memorising the eye-test chart. Yet his colleagues have vouched for his exceptionally long sight.

Towards the end of his training, during which his maturity, leftist bias and half-Irish loquacity marked him out as a potential leader, he had the good fortune to be taught and befriended by McCudden, who by this time was working as a fighter instructor on an advanced pupils' course at Joyce Green. This was one of the first such courses. 'He was older than us', said a fellow pupil on his initial training course at Hounslow, 'and he was a thinker, and certainly no fool. Some of us learnt quite a lot from him on politics . . . Good chap, used to play the violin and sing mock opera with bogus Italian words . . . I never met him again. I got shot down, he became the ace of aces.' Thus when Mannock arrived in France in April 1917 to join 40 Squadron under Major Leonard Tilney, an Old Etonian who at 22 was eight years his junior and radiated the enthusiasm of youth, he was not quite the raw novice expected.

Indeed he was not what the squadron expected at all. An inch over six foot, with dark-brown hair and deep-set blue eyes, he was ten years older than most of them, yet as a new boy he was not expected to have opinions. In a community notorious for its studied reticence he talked, it was thought, too freely, and his self-educated, radical outlook irritated some. His intense hatred of the Germans, too, whatever the cause, was distasteful to men who were fighting a strictly impersonal war. In contrast, in his first few flights he showed no great eagerness to get to grips with the enemy. Unlike the boisterous Bishop, who went out of his way to seek action and gained almost immediate popularity with all ranks on 60 Squadron, Mannock met something approaching hostility.

Mannock was an idealist. He was fighting for social change as well as for military victory. But he was no rash, hot-headed youth. Too many novice pilots, he believed, were lost unnecessarily in their first weeks of combat. He had resolved on a cautious beginning. It was an attitude that was easily mistaken for cowardice. 'My feelings very funny,' he recorded after first crossing the lines, 'I had the wind up, I don't mind admitting.' He was still trembling after he landed, which did not go unnoticed. 'Now I can understand what a tremendous strain to the nervous system flying is.' Fear, then, was something to be reckoned with, something to be overcome.

Back with No. 10 Squadron at the chateau, Ewart Garland was getting his game of tennis again after patrols. But he was soon making nostalgic references in his diary to old friends wounded, missing, or killed. 'Poor old so-and-so,' 'Poor little so-and-so,' and so on. 'Directly we got back from the funeral,' went one entry, 'Bulmer and I went up . . .' On 26 April he noted: 'Someone in the squadron is brought down pretty well every day now.' But the 'playing fields' attitude amongst flyers, he believed, persisted, German pilots being referred to almost affectionately as 'the old Hun'. He found it interesting to talk to a couple of wounded Huns who had themselves been brought down: how did they feel? 'They were both only 19 years old, and said they had no desire to fight.' Nor , if it came to that, thought Garland, did he. He commented later: 'It seemed natural enough to me at the time, just turned 20, to refer to the German prisoners as "only 19"'.

On 28 April the infantry attack was renewed, with good communication at first between ground and air. But as soon as the enemy counter-attacked, the infantry, as before, stopped lighting flares, and reports from the air of their progress dried up. Meanwhile the enemy pilots, aided by low cloud, and concentrating on the weakest vessels, destroyed or severely damaged twelve corps machines, of which ten were BE's. Leading his flight, Ball shot down an Albatros two-seater, but this was an isolated riposte.

'Bloody April' rose to an awesome climax as the weather on the 29th improved and the air fighting intensified. The day began with a scrap between six grey Albatros scouts and an offensive patrol of three SE5's of 56 Squadron, led by flight commander C.M. 'Billy' Crowe, with Canadian Jack Leach and Maurice Kay in tow. FE2d's of 57 Squadron joined in, but lost one of their number almost at once, pilot and observer surviving to be taken prisoner. They were more than avenged when Leach got on the tail of an Albatros that was chasing Kay and set it blazing, the pilot, rather than waiting to be consumed in the fire, plummeting, arms and legs whirling, into space.

Leach had seen Kay flip into a spiral to escape the Albatros and had assumed he was safe. Sadly, there were to be no more letters home from the boyish Maurice Kay. The last act of the doomed Albatros pilot, unseen by Leach, had been to shoot him down.

At Vert Galand, Harvey-Kelly, commanding 19 Squadron, had been asked by Wing HQ to put up a Spad section to scout for Richthofen, who had been spotted leaving Douai. A and B flights were already out on offensive patrols, and there was no way of contacting them, so C Flight, which had just returned from an abortive dawn patrol under sub-leader W.N. Hamilton, was called upon. Hamilton's companions were to have been two young second-lieutenants named Applin and Harding, but the prospect of getting to grips with the Red Baron was too attractive for Harvey-Kelly to miss, and Harding was stood down. Then Applin was delayed, leaving Harvey-Kelly and Hamilton flying in tandem.

Richthofen, of course, was not alone, and soon his flight of six red Albatros scouts was sighted and joined by the remaining five grey ones. Reinforcement was on the way, too, for the Spads, Richard Applin having chased bravely after them and located them at 5,000 feet east of Douai.

When six naval Triplanes hove in sight, Harvey-Kelly, despite his lack of height and the odds against him, did not hesitate. Vigorous action could turn the tables: that was their best chance. And the

Triplanes would be along in a moment. No sense in waiting for them: that would give the enemy time to think. He followed his golden rule: get your blow in first.

Going for the rearmost Albatros, he signalled for Hamilton to aim for the centre, a manoeuvre designed to prevent the leader attempting to gain a height advantage. Applin followed. But the odds were too great. Richthofen zoomed before diving on Applin, whose Spad exploded and broke up. He was Richthofen's 49th victim. Harvey-Kelly, too, was surrounded, his final executioner being the German ace Kurt Wolff. Only Hamilton, who was shot down by the Red Baron's younger brother Lothar, lived to tell the tale. Harvey-Kelly survived for three days but died in a German hospital.

The absence of any news of the three Spads and their pilots cast a gloom over Vert Galand. The loss of the lovable Harvey-Kelly, the first RFC man to land in France, severed one more link with the armada of August 1914.

Earlier that month H-K had told Trenchard that the current stock of German pilots were like 'floating meat', and it seems possible that he had reached the stage of over-confidence which was one of the most dangerous for experienced pilots. Trenchard might perhaps have divined this from the remark. But H-K had acted entirely in character. His expectations that the Triplanes would come to his aid were well founded, and at least one of the enemy formation was shot down. Later, Billy Bishop, escorting the FE's of 11 Squadron on photo reconnaissance, spotted one of the enemy scouts and dived on it out of the sun. Firing in bursts of three, he watched it go into a spin before bursting into flames. If this went some way towards avenging Harvey-Kelly, the afternoon, during which Richthofen recorded his 50th and 51st victims and completed five in one day, went, like the rest of April, overwhelmingly to the enemy.

Although Richthofen's Circus proper had not yet been formed, the four *Jastas* based at Douai, the 3rd, the 4th, the 11th and the 33rd, were combined on 30 April to form a single group, capable of operating *en masse*, and were promptly dubbed 'Richthofen's Circus' by the RFC. Simultaneously, smaller enemy scout formations sought targets at low level over the battle front, while two-seaters spotted for the German artillery and machine-gunned Allied trenches. 'Bloody April' thus ended with the future course of air fighting firmly delineated. But with Brisfit and SE5 pilots gaining in experience and confidence, and with the introduction of the Camel, together with the gradual replacement of the BE's by the RE8, the superiority the Germans had enjoyed that spring was at an end. Never again, even in the crisis months of 1918, was the RFC to be so afflicted or to suffer such casualties. These amounted, in April alone, to 151 machines brought down, as against 119 German, with 316 aircrew dead or missing. The dead included those who, although mortally wounded, regained the Allied lines.

The expectation of life of a newly-arrived pilot in April 1917 had fallen to seventeen days, and an accusing finger was inevitably pointed at Trenchard. Although he retained the unqualified support of Henderson and Brancker, and certainly of Haig, there were voices, both in Parliament and in the RFC hierarchy, which questioned his policy of aggression at all costs and asked whether his pursuit of it were not both obdurate and profligate. 'Is the work being done, even in wartime,' William Joynson-Hicks, MP for NW Manchester, wanted to know, 'at too great a sacrifice?' Harold Balfour, unnerved after being shot down and crashing into the lip of a crater on Vimy Ridge ('he is said to be temporarily "loony" ', wrote Alan Dore), later dubbed Trenchard's policy 'aerial attrition', and wondered whether a little more subtlety might have reduced casualties and served the army just as well.

Sending 'untrained lads' over the lines was inexcusable on any grounds, in the judgement of Brigadier-General P.R.C. Groves, an energetic RFC staff officer who had distinguished himself in operations in the Middle East. 'It was a squandering of resources, especially in an aerial arm where efficiency and survival depend upon adequate skill.' Keeping formation, clearing gun jams quickly, out-manoeuvring the enemy, engaging him from the best angle, breaking off combat when necessary, knowing how and when to shoot – these were some of the essentials listed by Groves. But he was writing in retrospect. Of more immediate significance was the stand taken by Lionel Charlton, then serving in the Directorate of Military Aeronautics at the War Office – and the response of the brass hats to it. To Charlton, one of the RFC's original flight commanders and holding a DSO, to detail men for action in France when they could only just about fly, and knew nothing beyond that, seemed little short of murder, and he resolved to put his foot down. He made it a rule that no pilot should be sent to France who could not satisfy him or one of his assistants that he was qualified in every possible way. Translating this resolve into action on the spot, he cancelled the posting of three youths who were patently undertrained. Despite his seniority, in less than half an hour he had been overruled – presumably by Henderson, under pressure from France.

A strong supporter of Trenchard was Jack Slessor, then a flight commander on 5 Squadron. He applauded him for not reverting to the defensive, despite intense pressure, thus avoiding the mistake made by the French at Verdun. 'The essential point', wrote Slessor, 'is that the requirements of the army in reconnaissance, photography and artillery cooperation must always be met.' Although the Germans had air superiority they had been hotly engaged east of the line over their own aerodromes, and Slessor knew of no instance of a photograph being required and not being obtained, or of a shoot being left undone, despite continual harassment from enemy machines. This was a proud boast, but it cost many lives. And having said all that, Slessor still suspected that some of the most arduous and hazardous work, such as photography, which always drew fierce opposition from the Germans because they knew its importance, was superfluous, and that cover twice a week was all that was strictly necessary.

Fred Winterbotham (who later made his mark in Military Intelligence), joined 29 Squadron (Nieuports) under Major H.V. Champion de Crespigny that April and noted that pilots were arriving and disappearing daily. But he did not blame Trenchard. 'The RFC was of course subject to orders from Army Command, who seemed blithely unmindful of the tremendous losses of highly trained pilots and valuable aircraft which the air photography entailed, and which the Germans were anxious we should not carry out.'

Inevitably there were mutterings within the squadrons against

Trenchard, but he still inspired a fierce loyalty amongst his crews. One of his youngest pilots, 18-year-old Bertram Wood, another recent arrival on 29 Squadron, wrote on 8 April: 'It does make me wild to see articles in the papers running down our Flying Corps on account of the casualties. If you only knew the work we do compared with the Hun, you would realise how ridiculous this is.' Bert Wood, or 'Woodie', of Grimsby, whose lucky mascot, a Lincoln Imp, adorned an inter-plane strut of his Nieuport, had quickly absorbed the ambience of sympathy with the infantryman which informed all RFC thought. Despite his fair-skinned, almost effeminate good looks, and his aura of aestheticism as the naturalist and poet he was, he proved a dashing and skilful pilot and a brilliant patrol leader, credited with eighteen victories after three months in France, with an MC for his air fighting and a Bar for his low-level strafing. A career which must surely have led to even greater honours was later cut tragically short in a flying accident while he was engaged in the air defence of London. He had left his lucky mascot on his machine in France, where it survived.

Trenchard, in his own defence, could point to his continual pleadings and warnings of lack of resources throughout the second half of 1916, and again in 1917, of which the last had been a mixture of recrimination and despair. 'You are asking me,' he had told the Air Board, 'to fight the battle this year [1917] with the same machines I fought it with last year. We shall be hopelessly outclassed.' Nothing could have been clearer than this. He had continued: 'Something must be done. I am not panicking, but the Hun is getting more aggressive. I warned you firmly as far back as last September, and the Chief [Douglas Haig] warned you in November, and I warned the Air Board personally on 12 December. All I can say is there will be an outcry from all the pilots out here if we do not have at least these few squadrons of fast machines I have asked for as absolutely necessary.'

The Air Board, set up on 11 May 1916 under Lord Curzon, a former Viceroy of India and a member of the inner Cabinet, was seen as a forerunner of an Air Ministry. It had naval, military and Parliamentary representatives but no executive powers. It had since been strengthened and reconstituted under Lord Cowdray, and it now included: Godfrey Paine, the Fifth Sea Lord, first commandant of the Central Flying School and one of the earliest of naval flyers; Sir David Henderson, Director-General of Military Aeronautics; William Weir, Controller of Aeronautical Supplies; and Percy Martin, Controller of Petrol Engines; with Major J.L. Baird as Parliamentary Secretary. It functioned principally as a Ministry of Supply, helping to eliminate competition between the two services, but it was many months before its efforts were reflected in France, and meanwhile the supply position remained acute.

It was at the December 1916 meeting of the Air Board, which Trenchard attended, that the Admiralty had agreed to lend four additional naval squadrons to the RFC 'at this moment of great emergency'. They were to prove invaluable, but they were not enough. All Trenchard could do was brace himself for the inevitable casualties. They had to be expected, and they had to be ignored. The 150,000 casualties suffered in the Arras battle by the army were more than enough justification. No sacrifices were too much for these men.

For the RFC, one of the most poignant losses in the ground battle was that of the massive figure of Colonel C.J. Burke, of the Royal Irish Regiment, known to every participant in the Channel crossing of August 1914, which he had led (although pipped on the post by Harvey-Kelly), as 'Pregnant Percy'. Promoted beyond routine operational flying, and hearing that the Royal Irish were short of officers, Burke had insisted, in the summer of 1916, on returning to his regiment. He was killed leading his men on the first day of the Arras offensive, 9 April 1917.

4

PARCELS FOR PRISONERS

THE puritanical disdain of Bob Smith-Barry for anyone he suspected of making preparations against possible capture was generally regarded as idiosyncratic. Most men took a more fatalistic view. But Smith-B, or S-B, as he was commonly known, having borrowed a machine from one of his flight commanders, had been scandalised to find a package neatly stowed in the cockpit containing all manner of comforts, from silk pyjamas to cigarettes. 'One of my pilots is preparing to be a prisoner!' he had exclaimed, and he had scattered the contents of the package irascibly across the sward. But on most squadrons, crews carried an irreducible minimum of razor, toothbrush, soap, and a wallet of francs.

On a long-distance bomber squadron towards the end of the war, Willie Read had a batman who volunteered to become proficient on the Lewis gun solely to accompany and succour his 'gentleman' on bombing raids. A valet in peacetime, he always went aboard with a little suitcase 'in case we land the other side, sir.' Food and drink while airborne and something extra for emergencies seemed no more than prudent husbandry.

Spartan if not harsh conditions were expected in captivity, but the initial greeting was often surprisingly friendly, especially when aerial adversaries met on the ground. One of the crew of an 18 Squadron two-seater bomber badly shot up over Bruges was observer-turned-pilot Robert Ingram; he managed to land on the beach at Ostend. 'For three days we were the guests of a German squadron and were extraordinarily well treated. It has come as a great surprise.' One of the German pilots turned out to be an ex-Dulwich schoolboy and a graduate of Merton College, Oxford, and he offered to drop letters from Ingram over the lines, addressed to his CO and his girl friend. They got the letters. But a Belgian who saluted him on his way into captivity was 'very badly roughed up by the Germans'.

Maurice Marcus Kaye, also of 18 Squadron, was pulled out of his burning FE2b by his observer, Sergeant F. Russell, although both had been quite badly wounded. They had been escorting a photographic machine west of Cambrai. While Russell, as was customary, was whisked away separately, Kaye found himself being driven to hospital in the company of the man who claimed to have shot him down, one Wolter Niesen.

Niesen kept calling to the driver, '*Langsam, langsam*', to spare Kaye's injuries on the bumpy road. Grateful though he was for this consideration, Kaye soon realised that Niesen had a more selfish motive: he wanted Kaye to sign a statement that it was he, Niesen, who had brought him down. Kaye obliged, only to discover, much later, that he had been Niesen's first and only victory, and that his signature would qualify Niesen for the coveted *Ehrenbecher* or cup of honour. But thanks to Niesen and a German surgeon – and not least, in the first place, to observer Russell – Kaye's life was saved. 'In POW camp the Germans were strict but they treated us with respect,' recorded Kaye, 'and we got our [Red Cross] parcels.' Segregation between prisoners by rank meant that Kaye never saw his rescuer again.

As related earlier, Arthur Whitten Brown, shot down near Aachen with his pilot Harold Medlicott, was completely incapacitated by his injuries, until a series of operations, eight in all, set him on the road to rehabilitation. 'I have been in three hospitals,' he wrote, 'and received the kindest treatment and consideration.' Both men had made contingency plans for escape; Medlicott was later shot dead in the attempt. Brown's post-war achievement with John Alcock in making the first direct air crossing of the Atlantic in 1919 is commemorated in a statue at Heathrow.

Second-Lieutenant J.E.P. Howey, one of several observers who got their machine down safely on the German side after their pilot had been killed, said of his captors: 'They were all as kind as possible.' He was taken to the Mess, his damaged ankle was put in a splint, and he was given food, drink and a smoke. One of the pilots who shot him down landed nearby, shook him by the hand, and cheered him up by assuring him he had had no chance.

Canadian test pilot Ben Lefroy, after transferring to a squadron, crashed in no man's land and lay there unconscious, a target for both sides. When he came to, a German was bending over him. 'Can I have a cigarette?' asked the German. After rummaging in Lefroy's pockets he pulled out a silver cigarette case, took one for himself, gave Lefroy one, lit both, then closed the case and put it back in the Canadian's pocket. His rummaging had disclosed Lefroy's identity. 'I bet you wish you were in Vancouver now.'

The first responsibility, on being shot down, was to destroy the machine, using the incendiary torch always carried. Lieutenant G.W. Armstrong, intercepted by six scouts during a bombing raid on Roulers, was shot down despite the spirited return fire of his observer, Hubert Pugh-Evans, who kept firing until they actually hit the ground. The crash-landing was successful until the machine ran into a ditch, which turned them over. As with Eric Routh, the German pilots continued firing on them throughout, 'churning up the ground on all sides like a plough'. Armstrong was trapped but Pugh-Evans got him out, and between them, with German soldiers running towards them, they set fire to their BE2c.

Edward Pennell, earlier a pioneer pigeon dropper when he was working with agents in 1915, and now flying a Martinsyde of 27 Squadron, bombed the railway junction at Hirson from 1500 feet, climbed back to 14,000, and then had mechanical trouble and lost height alarmingly. After nursing his engine as best he could he force-landed alongside a wood, which he judged was on the Allied side of the lines. To his horror he saw a gaggle of troops, patently German, emerging from the wood. With his torch inaccessible, he set fire to his fuel tank with revolver and Very pistol, under the noses of the Germans, who watched the blaze apathetically. Then from the wood came a second group, whom Pennell recognised as *poilus*. He had landed on the right side after all! The Germans, dumbly indifferent, were the prisoners of the French.

'My lovely plane,' he moaned, 'which I had burnt! I felt like weeping!' 'Biffy' Borton, his monocled squadron commander, was almost choleric – until Pennell suggested he might have done the same in similar circumstances, to which Borton had to agree.

Second-Lieutenant E.L. Edwards, an observer on 43 Squadron, shot down in a 1½-strutter on a photo recce after his guns had jammed, was immediately surrounded by enemy infantry; neither he nor his pilot had any chance to burn their machine. But they steadfastly refused to answer any questions about their role. For this they suffered a period of solitary confinement. Indeed the obdurate Edwards resolved to make life as difficult as he could for his captors, and later he was awarded 108 days' solitary for disobeying an order and insulting the commandant. He was repatriated after the war.

Interrogation on capture could be searching, accompanied by threats, and it wasn't unusual for a prisoner to get fourteen days' solitary for giving unreliable information. Few prisoners could tell the Germans much anyway, because they knew so little themselves.

Harold Tambling, a Cornishman whose father was an Admiralty overseer on the Clyde, wrote, after his capture, to a Glasgow firm of outfitters with a list of requirements that included shirts, collars, underwear, socks, gloves, pyjamas, towels, and silk ties. The manager thanked him for his order and said he was sending the goods by parcel post in two packages. 'You'll notice prices have increased a little, but the quality is keeping up the old standard. Things are going on here much as usual, business is very good with everyone.' The men in the trenches would surely have read this with incredulity. The packages duly arrived.

Second-Lieutenant H.C. Wookey, a Brisfit pilot in 11 Squadron, shot down near Cambrai in October 1917, was court-martialled and sent to a criminal prison, his crime being to have carried propaganda leaflets, which the Germans declared to be illegal. This was, perhaps, an indication of the effectiveness of this type of warfare, so often ridiculed. Eventually the British Government, after threatening reprisals, effected his release, and he followed the usual route via Brussels and Karlsruhe to Holzminden. To avoid further such incidents, the practice was abandoned, the prevailing wind being utilised to carry these leaflets into enemy territory by balloon.

Lancastrian Sidney Attwater, whose exploits with posthumous VC winner Tom Mottershead are recorded elsewhere,[1] had no chance when, on a dawn photo recce in an FE2b, with an aircraftman second class named Leigh whom he knew as a good gunner, he met the Richthofen Circus. 'Leigh got one down,' said Attwater afterwards, 'and so did I, but there were no clouds to hide in.' The next thing he remembered, some German girls were giving him a drink. When he looked round for his gunner, he 'saw the old bus burning like mad.'

It was a relief when he spotted Leigh. His face was badly gashed and one eye looked damaged beyond repair; but otherwise he appeared to be in one piece. The area was packed with Germans, who marched them off. As a POW, according to Attwater, he 'had a pretty rough time'.

A prisoner who had an even rougher time was Lieutenant A.D.G. 'Grey' Alderson, of 3 Squadron. Shot down in March 1918 and seriously wounded, he was plied, when barely conscious, with questions he couldn't answer. Eventually the interrogation officer gave him a pen and a postcard, to write a message home. With great difficulty he managed to scrawl: 'I have been captured by the Huns, will write, Love, Grey.' When the interrogator returned an hour later, Alderson was told he was going to be court-martialled.

Orderlies came in and arranged a table and chairs in the centre of the ward, and he was guarded by two sentries instead of one, both fondling fixed bayonets. What could he possibly have done? A stamping of feet and a clanking of swords heralded the arrival of a German general and his staff. After the charge had been recited in German

1. *The Royal Flying Corps in France: from Mons to the Somme* (Constable, 1994).

it was translated by the interrogation officer. Alderson had insulted His Imperial Highness Kaiser Wilhelm II by his use of the term Hun.

The bemused Alderson was quite unable to follow the proceedings, no notice was taken when he tried to protest that he had intended no insult, and eventually he lapsed into a coma. Suddenly the general, in a frenzy of rage at his apparent indifference, strode over to his bed, called him a *schweinhund*, tore the postcard into fragments, and threw them in his face.

Alderson's worst deprivation was that they had confiscated his pipe. Transferred to a hospital in Douai, he was subjected to excruciating pain in the wagon, which was callously driven, he believed deliberately. His wounds had not been treated, and he feared they would fester. But in Douai Hospital a nurse spoke to him with transparent kindness in perfect English. She talked of happier days when she had been at school in England; she had only returned to Germany from a sense of duty just prior to the outbreak of war. Alderson was the only prisoner in the hospital; all the others were wounded German soldiers. They called him *der flieger*, treated him as one of themselves, and shared their food parcels with him.

Still he received no treatment. But the nurse was engaged to the senior surgeon in the hospital, and she pleaded with him to do what he could to save Alderson's life. An immediate operation was performed, and he recovered.

An even more critical operation, on a wounded patient who looked and was no more than a boy, this time in a prison camp hospital, was not so successful, despite the most devoted attentions of the German surgeon. The story was told forty years later by the man who had been in the next bed, formerly Second Lieutenant R.F. Glazebrook, who, like so many others of his time, had hitherto resolved not to inflict his war experiences on his family. 'I will never forget the German doctor bursting into tears when his patient died,' he recalled, 'and how he cursed the warring nations for sending their children to war.'

*   *   *

Perhaps the most famous British prisoner was William Leefe Robinson, and it seems that he was made to suffer for it. He had been responsible for the death of a German hero in the airship commander Herbert Schramm. He planned escape from the beginning, his attempts landing him in solitary confinement. Transferred to camps where security was stricter, he ended up in Holzminden, where he was harried and even persecuted. He became the focus of the malevolence of a notorious camp commandant in Karl Niemeyer, who is said to have used every instrument of cruelty against him short of physical violence. Robinson got home safely a month after the armistice, but in his weakened state he succumbed to the influenza virus which claimed millions of lives immediately after the war, 150,000 in the United Kingdom alone.

The contrast between Harold Tambling and his Glaswegian gents' outfitter, and the harsher treatment meted out in camps under men like Niemeyer, was stark. And as the Germans themselves felt the stranglehold of the blockade, conditions in the camps deteriorated. Ewart Garland, by then back on a bomber squadron, was one who realised, by the end of the war, that he had badly misjudged the conditions in these camps. 'I was soon engaged in picking up Allied POWs straggling and staggering along the roads a few days after the armistice. Many died of exhaustion and all were skeletons.'

These men still had to face a final interrogation by MI9 on their return to the UK: they had to show that their capture was genuine, that they had not wantonly given themselves up. From this it can be inferred that there were some who did. If anything discreditable was unearthed, the perpetrators were sent for short sharp shock correction at a so-called Patriotic School.

It was not until 28 July 1919 that Harold Tambling was 'presented with the compliments of the authorities', the writer, loftily impersonal, being '*commanded by the Air Council to inform him that his statement regarding the circumstances of his capture by the enemy having been investigated, the Council considers that no blame attaches to him in the matter*.'

For men like Harold Tambling, after months of airborne hazard and years of incarceration, this could only come as an affront.

5

CHARLES SMART AND ALAN DORE; VON RICHTHOFEN THE UNSURPASSED; MANNOCK REHABILITATED; 'REMEMBER BALL'

JUST as the RFC could only function in France under the protection of the ground forces, so the army itself depended on a secure home base; and this security had come under increasing threat from Germany's espousal of unrestricted submarine warfare. Starting with a modest pre-war force of some twenty U-boats, the Germans, on the outbreak of war, had begun an urgent construction programme, and by early 1917 they had built up a sizeable fleet. From 31 January, one outgoing British and Allied ship out of every four leaving the UK was doomed never to return, while the crews of American and other neutral ships were refusing to sail to British ports. A million tons of Allied shipping was sunk in the month of April alone, a rate which spelt defeat if it were allowed to continue. But with the introduction of the convoy system in June 1917, long resisted by the Admiralty because of their strategic preference for offensive rather than defensive measures, and with the help of new anti-submarine techniques, backed up by intensive RNAS patrols, losses were dramatically reduced. A shortage of escort vessels weakened the new system at first, and it was not until the end of the year that it became fully effective, but eventually, with the growing support of the American Navy, maximum protection was given. Soon new ship construction was keeping pace with losses, and before the year was out the Allies were sinking U-boats faster than Germany could build them. But in May 1917, as Haig and his army commanders, complemented by Trenchard, planned for an Allied summer offensive that must inevitably be dominated by the British, the outcome of the war at sea, and therefore the security of the BEF in France, was still in doubt.

Haig's plan, which had been gestating for many months, aimed to end the stalemate on the Western Front by breaking out of the Ypres salient, capturing the high ground on the eastern flank, and, by advancing north to take the Flemish ports of Ostend and Zeebrugge, denying them to the U-boats. He would then be poised to drive the Germans out of Belgium. Meanwhile, to divert attention from his preparations in Flanders and from the French collapse, and to buy time while the French recovered, he renewed his action on the Arras front. Trenchard too was working on proposals for the redistribution of his forces for the summer offensive, but the RFC likewise was still deeply involved around Arras. Although there were factors which fostered genuine hope for improvement – the new machines and their air and ground crews were rapidly acclimatising – the lowering skies of April did not immediately dissolve into a sunlit May.

One man who could attest to this was Sergeant-Observer H.G. Taylor of 25 Squadron, the man whose first reconnaissance sketch had been described as 'bloody marvellous' by Oscar Greig. Formerly a machine-gunner on the Somme, where he had faced death every second, not knowing when it might come, he was grateful for the stand-down periods when he could count at least on a few more hours to live. Returning from leave on 1 May to be met by a host of new faces, replacements for those killed or missing in his absence, he found that his best friend on the squadron, an observer like himself, had died from his wounds after a raid the previous day and that he was to act as a pall-bearer that morning at his funeral. Furthermore, he was to take the dead man's place as observer to a Lieutenant Berry King, a Jamaican, aged twenty-six; King had somehow escaped injury and was to be given no rest. It was a further shock, though, to be briefed that same afternoon to take off on a bombing raid with King that evening in a formation of six FE2b's.

Standing up in the open cockpit of the pusher, facing the tail, where attack generally originated, held no terrors for Taylor, for all its apparent insecurity: he felt perfectly at home. Their target was an ammunition dump, and they had dropped their bombs and were on their way home when they sighted a formation of nine Albatros scouts, with two other hostiles in attendance. Three of the Albatris immediately dived on Taylor's machine and within seconds he had stopped a succession of bullets which 'blew one thigh to pieces and paralysed one arm'. Bullets were brushing his hair, his gun was smashed, and their fuel tank was pierced, blowing petrol all over the nacelle. By this time Taylor was slumped on the cockpit floor, bleeding profusely. Then came oblivion. He did not know it, but his principal assailant had been the German ace Kurt Wolff, the conqueror of Harvey-Kelly. The shock of hitting the ground revived him briefly: they had crash-landed on Arras racecourse, and somehow King had again escaped injury.

Losing consciousness again, Taylor woke up on a stretcher amongst masses of wounded infantrymen on the floor of Arras Cathedral, which was doing duty as a casualty clearing station. The only way the surgeons could save his leg was to leave it permanently stiffened, and pieces of bullet were still being removed from his thigh fifteen years later. In his old age the leg was amputated.

There was still no rest for Jamaican-born Berry King: he was airborne again forty-eight hours later, accompanied by his third observer in five days, named as 'Trumpeter Lawrence', which suggests that volunteers had been called for to fill the gaps. If so, it was first time unlucky for 29-year-old James Lawrence, of Cupar, Fifeshire, and third time unlucky for King. Returning from a similar raid on the same target, they had no chance when their machine caught fire and nose-dived out of control.

Charles Smart, also back from leave, was sent to St Omer to learn to fly RE8's, a move to which he strongly objected. 'No end of experienced pilots have killed themselves on their first trip in these machines.' And of his conversion training he was similarly dismissive. 'The course of instruction consisted of a three-minute lecture from a man who stuttered and a seven-minute flight as a passenger . . . I cannot say I like the machine, it is much too heavy and cumbersome, more like a flying steamroller than an aeroplane.' But he was not so prejudiced as to fail to appreciate its speed advantage – 105 m.p.h. against the 90 m.p.h. plod of the BE2e.

The renewal of the infantry attack, scheduled for 3 May, was preceded by intensive air cooperation with the artillery, accompanied by the bombing of aerodromes and other military targets by Martinsydes, DH4's and FE's, the latter bombing by night as well as by day. There was also a pre-planned assault on enemy kite balloons. While the artillery put down an extra-special barrage on the German trenches, Nieuport pilots of 40 Squadron began a hedge-hopping approach to the balloons, surprising the winch crews before they could haul the balloons down. Eight balloons were caught out by the ruse, four were destroyed and the remainder damaged, without loss to the Nieuports, although many were hit.

Despite clear skies, bomber and corps crews alike reported less opposition than previously, partly because of a change in enemy tactics, which concentrated their fighters into massed formations at set times, generally morning and evening, leaving periods of comparative inactivity of which advantage was taken. Another factor was the departure from the front on 1 May of Manfred von Richthofen. Postcard portraits of him were being circulated throughout Germany, newspapers featured his exploits, and wherever he went he was mobbed. He had become a propaganda pawn, his name a byword, and the German High Command may well have felt that his loss would be a staggering blow to morale. In any case the landmark of 50 victories called for some gesture, and they prevailed upon him to cooperate in producing a book on his exploits.

Representations of Richthofen as a cold, calculating killer who exposed himself to as little personal danger as possible, selecting easy prey while leading strong formations that amounted to a personal bodyguard, fail to give him proper credit for professionalism. No doubt compared with Mannock, who generously passed opportunities (or the credit) to underlings when he himself had enemies at his mercy, he was vain and acquisitive. He is said to have been jealous even of the success of his younger brother Lothar, though 'even' may be redundant here, since jealousy between brothers is not uncommon.

But however that may be, in the context of the battle he was fighting, the elder Richthofen was unsurpassed. He combined the hunter's instinct with the alertness of the hunted.

The German Air Force was generally outnumbered, hence the need for economy. Its pilots scrapped only when they had the advantage, and preferred, as Richthofen himself had put it, to 'let the customer come to the shop'. All the great RFC patrol leaders stressed the importance of seeking the advantage before attacking, and of not being ashamed to live to fight another day. Also, as the fighting progressed, they concluded that the initiative in any attack must always lie with the flight leader. Formation-keeping during combat, rather than individual pursuit of targets, was mandatory. 'The natural consequence of this order', as Sholto Douglas later observed, 'was that it was usually the flight commander who shot down the enemy machine.' As the formation leader he was usually the most capable, and with his flight behind him to protect him he could concentrate on the job in hand. This, in simple terms, was Richthofen's method, but it did mean that his absence left a bigger gap than that of the average patrol leader. Lothar, whom he left in charge, was possibly the greedier killer (he was already credited with twenty victims), but his devil-may-care temperament was less suited to the group philosophy.

Manfred's flamboyant arrogance and apparent immunity might be resented, but the painting of the machines of his *Jasta* bright red, and the variety of patterns and hues of other *Jastas*, had a definite psychological effect. 'A good deal of harm was done', wrote Slessor, 'by pilots returned wounded or time expired to the UK, nerves not at their best, talking wildly about the famous Red Albatros circus and their deeds.' As with the Fokker Scourge two years earlier, new pilots arrived with an exaggerated fear of the enemy. The circus would rarely attack, in Slessor's experience, except in superior numbers, and even a well-handled RE8, with its gunner swivelling a Lewis in the rear seat, could cause a formation to break off. Nevertheless the techniques adopted by Richthofen, other things being equal, became standard in the Allied air forces. Only McCudden, and later Mannock and one or two others, could compare with him.

This is not to devalue the inspirational aggression of men like Bishop and Ball. In a force whose ethos it was to take and maintain the offensive they were an essential part, as confirmed by the new pilots on 56 Squadron, who, like the unfortunate Maurice Kay, responded eagerly to Ball's leadership. 'Captain Ball is surpassing his previous efforts and has already accounted for six Huns off his own bat,' wrote a young pilot named Roger Musters. 'He came back the other day with a huge hole right through the tail of his machine. He got out and immediately got into another machine and was off again. He really is a marvel.'

On the evening of 2 May, when twenty-five RFC scouts went out to seek their German counterparts over Douai, most of the individual combats were indecisive, but Ball shot down an Albatros two-seater and watched it crash. It put him ahead of Guynemer, with thirty-eight victims, and that night Trenchard visited Vert Galand to congratulate him. The feat was riotously celebrated in the Mess that night; but Trenchard was alarmed by Ball's expression of utter fatigue, and he feared he was burning himself out.

'Would you like two weeks in England?'

Ball shook his head. There was work to be done, and at least he would stay until his allotted month was up. The party that followed helped to revive his spirits, and soon he was back at the top of his form. 'Everyone is very pleased,' he told his Land Army girl-friend Bobs. 'I am now one in front of the Frenchman ... Just longing to be with you again, and when I have made my total 40 I will come. I have only two more to get.' This was on 3 May. Four days to go.

The infantry attack that began that morning was fully prepared for the tactics of counter-attack that both sides now favoured, based on lessons learned in the Somme battles, and this led to suitable RFC squadrons being employed in a new role. They were to scour the ground from low level in advance of positions taken in the initial assault and report any obvious enemy concentrations to the artillery. But with both sides employing similar tactics the battlefield became too chaotic for lucid description, though there were exceptions, notably among observers in the 1½-strutters of 43 Squadron. They spotted enemy troops massing for a counter-attack on Oppy, taken that morning but hidden from the artillery by the Vimy Ridge – and were rewarded for their vigilance by being ordered to go out and stop them.

The Sopwith 1½-strutter was already obsolescent, being outclassed above 10,000 feet by the new German scouts, but it was useful at low level, and by increasing the size of their formations from three to five, closing up, and improving their shooting, they had some success in their new role. They were described by Alan Dore, also returned from leave, as 'the tanks of the air'. 'At 11 o'clock we learn that Huns are massing at Mauville Farm. Flying low I cross at 1,500 feet with a missing engine. At Neovireuil I dive to 600 feet and fire with front guns at Huns. I can see into the trenches and village. Dare not go lower. Engine hardly takes me over the ridge. My other four machines do finely.' Unimpeded by engine trouble, they fired their guns from between 50 and 300 feet. 'Other low-flying attacks on isolated bodies of men', notes the official history, 'were made by the same squadron in the afternoon.'

Another man in his thirties, Charles Smart, still for the moment flying a BE2e, with the faithful Hendry (now awarded an MC) as observer, also found himself over Oppy, on a contact patrol. 'We had to go up and fly amongst the shell barrage and spot our infantry flares to see where they had got to. The shell fire was simply terrible.' A heavy ground mist and the smoke from bursting shells forced them down to 900 feet in order to see. 'Shells were whipping through the air in thousands, bumping us about all over the place.' Nevertheless they marked the position of one of the flares and dropped a message over Division Headquarters before returning to the lines. 'Just as we got over Oppy we got an awful bump and a crack, one of our own shells carried away the right lower wing-tip leaving it hanging in shreds of canvas and wood. I thought all was up but found I could still fly the machine by keeping the stick right over on the left-hand side.' With gentle handling Smart managed to crawl back to his aerodrome and land. 'This is the worst trip I have had up to now and I feel more than a bit shaken.'

He didn't expect to be flying again that day – but was told to take up two observers one by one in an RE8 to give them the feel of the gun position. 'Orders are orders so I had to go up.' Next day he began his new career in RE8's by acting as escort to a machine on photography. He had done his sixty-first and last show – and very nearly his last show of all – on BE's. Two-thirds of these had been with Hendry. He was getting adjusted to the new machine and noted: 'RE's do climb fairly well, we got to 8,500 feet in twenty minutes.'

'The fine weather continues,' noted Dore on 4 May, 'and gives us all a great amount of work.' Enemy activity, too, increased, and Ball shot down an Albatros two-seater. Flying was curtailed on the 5th, partly because of thunderstorms and partly to give the crews a rest, but it did not stop Ball going out in his SE5 at six o'clock that evening. Crossing the lines at 8,000 feet, he spotted two Albatros DIII scouts 1,000 feet above him, heading across his path. Climbing to get above and in front of them, he deliberately exposed his tail to tempt them, and the Germans accepted the bait. By timing his next manoeuvre, a steepling figure of eight, to a nicety, Ball turned the tables on them completely, getting underneath one of the surprised enemy pilots and pulling down his Lewis. While he was changing a drum the German spun away, but Ball rapidly overtook him, and with bursts from both Vickers and Lewis at point-blank range sent him spiralling down.

Now he had to cope with the pilot of the second Albatros, who had closed in and started firing. So determined was the German to avenge his comrade that he was developing a head-on attack which threatened the end for both men. With the Hun hurtling straight at him, Ball held his ground, firing his Vickers, yet still the Hun came on. As the two machines closed, Ball sat there as though paralysed, his thumb frozen on the gun-button. A week ago his sense of preservation would have saved him. Now it was blunted.

The shattering, mutilating shock of the inevitable collision was something his senses seemed to absorb. He was awaiting the long spiral into oblivion when he found he was sailing on with reduced velocity into an empty sky. The collision had taken place solely in his imagination. At the penultimate moment he had shot the German down.

He descended to 3,000 feet to get his bearings, and there beneath him, not 400 yards apart, were the mangled wrecks of the two machines whose pilots had set out to destroy him. 'Flushed in face, his eyes brilliant, his hair blown and dishevelled,' wrote the recording officer afterwards, 'he came to the squadron office to make his report.' He was so overwrought that he found dictation impossible, and for a long time all he could do was mutter incoherently. 'God is very good to me ... I was certain the Hun meant to ram me ... God must have me in his keeping.' It was midnight before he could sleep, and he was up again at four, but mercifully the weather was bad and he was able to busy himself in his garden.

The squadron went on an offensive patrol that evening, and Ball went with them, but he had chosen to fly in his Nieuport, and he could not keep up with the SE5's. Yet he took on four red Albatros scouts over Douai, dived straight into them with his customary verve, broke up the formation, and shot down one of them, watching it crash near a cross-roads. The others recognised his red spinner and made off.

Earlier that day, 6 May, the commander of 9th Wing, Cyril Newall, had called for a full report from Blomfield on all Ball had done with 56 Squadron. This was to include: his combat reports; what other pilots had seen him do; the condition of his machine on returning; any confirmation of machines destroyed; and any other points Blomfield might think of. The request arrived on 7 May, Ball's thirty-first and last day in France, if the month was to be adhered to. Although Trenchard's offer, on 2 May, of two weeks in England is hard to reconcile with a fixed stay of one month, it seems likely that Newall had it in mind to relieve Ball and that he was seeking material on which to put him up for a further award. Since he already had a triple DSO and the MC, the award in prospect must surely have been the VC. Many people were asking why the award hadn't been made already.

Mannock, with two other pilots of 40 Squadron, had his first scrap with a Hun early that morning, 7 May. Between them they drove an intruder off, but it was only a decoy: lying in wait were the scarlet scouts of Richthofen's *Jasta 11*. Mannock did as much as anyone to shake them off, but he got separated from the others, and he was the last to return. His colleagues feared he must have gone down and they had time to reflect that he had fought his corner, and to regret their coolness towards him. Thus when he landed he was greeted with unaccustomed warmth. All was forgiven and he was 'Mick' to them now. Then at nine o'clock that same morning seven pilots of 40 Squadron, Mannock among them, took off in an attempt to repeat their balloon-strafing success of five days' earlier. As before, an artillery barrage was put down on adjacent enemy trenches and the Nieuports hedge-hopped to the lines. This time, with surprise less likely to be achieved, four more Nieuports were briefed to patrol overhead while twelve naval triplanes gave top cover.

Leading the attack was a new flight commander with a reputation for pugnacity, W.E. Nixon, himself only twenty. At a colourful briefing he directed each of his pilots on to individual balloons. Mannock's target was on the extreme left of the line, where the enemy fire was even fiercer than before, and Mannock found himself peering through an inferno of tracer as he raced towards his target. Holding his fire, he was convinced that if his engine kept going he couldn't miss. After emptying an entire drum from his Lewis he pulled up over the top and saw his balloon writhe before spurting smoke and flame. Ducking his head below the cockpit coaming, he rammed the throttle open and headed for home.

All the strafing pilots sustained damage to their machines and all wrecked them in forced landings or crashed them back at base except Mannock, who somehow achieved a smooth landing. But when his rigger showed him the damage to his plane he shuddered. In his diary he wrote: 'I don't want to go through such an experience again.' He was shocked, too, when he learned that Nixon, trying to divert an attack by German scouts, had been shot down, a victim of Lothar von Richthofen. But Mannock had had a good day.

The habit of the German scouts based at Douai of patrolling in strength morning and evening issued an implicit challenge to the SE5's, and in the absence of the Red Baron – which was known – planned interceptions were encouraged by Wing HQ. A morning patrol on 7 May failed to make contact, but that evening ten SE5's of 56 Squadron, with six Spads of 19 Squadron, tried again. Also airborne in the vicinity were a few Pups and naval Triplanes. One of the SE5 pilots was Cecil Lewis, and he described vividly the tall voluminous peaks of thunder-cloud, fraught with valleys and ravines, that they were obliged to thread their way through. In these conditions it was impossible to keep together, and when Ball, leading the SE5's, sighted the scarlet wings of *Jasta 11* and urged his pilots into action, his three flights, chocolate-coloured in contrast, became separated, while all but one of the Spad pilots lost touch completely. An eerie light, bilious in the west but darkening in the east, pervaded the scene, and visibility was worsening. Soon it began to rain. Nevertheless the skirmishing was bitter and there were losses on both sides. One such was Roger Musters, the young man who had written so enthusiastically that Ball was 'a marvel'. The remaining SE5's reformed over Arras, where another dog-fight started.

Ball emerged safely from the resultant mêlée and fired another attack signal which glowed brilliantly in the gathering dusk. Then he chased a red Albatros into cloud. Almost certainly the pilot was Lothar von Richthofen. Flight commander Billy Crowe, of 56, spotted them and followed Ball into the cloud. When he came out on the far side, both Albatros and SE5 had vanished.

That the two met in combat seems certain, and that they could have shot each other down more or less simultaneously is feasible. Lothar is known to have force-landed soon afterwards with engine failure, possibly resulting from a clash with Ball. At about the same time, Ball was seen to crash.

According to a message dropped later at Vert Galand, Ball had been shot down by 'a worthy opponent' – Lothar von Richthofen – and no doubt the Germans believed it. But the claim is irreconcilable with Lothar's own account of the scrap, which identifies a triplane as his adversary. An alternative claim that Ball was shot down by a machine-gunner mounted in the tower of a church in the village of Annoeullin, a mile or so from the crash, also gained some credence. But neither of these claims was supported by eye-witnesses.

A young German lieutenant stationed at Annoeullin, Franz Hailer, heard the sound of engines and saw an aeroplane emerge from the cloud. It was flying, he said, upside down. It then disappeared behind a row of trees before crashing into rising ground. 'We examined the wreckage,' wrote Hailer later, 'and we all came to the conclusion that the aircraft had not been shot down from the air or by anti-aircraft fire, as the dead pilot had no marks or scratches and had not been wounded.' This was hardly conclusive, as the machine had been wrecked and the engine may well have been hit. Hailer himself had gained the impression, when Ball flew over, that his propeller had stopped.

The mystery that veiled the exit of so many of the aces also shrouded Albert Ball. It seems likely that he was alive when he over-flew Annoeullin, and that he was killed when he crashed. 'The doctor couldn't find any bullet wounds on the body,' said Hailer, 'although the back and one leg were broken.' Could it be that, in cloud con-ditions colourfully described by all who flew that evening, Ball was a victim of turbulence, or of losing orientation? It seems a possible explanation.

But whatever the truth, Albert Ball was dead, and the VC that was probably in the pipeline was awarded posthumously. More sig-nificantly, the spirit of aggression that he personified had become the lodestar of the RFC, and later of the RAF. Many fighter pilots of World War II were brought up on a slogan from World War I:

> He must fall,
> Remember Ball.

'In the ranks of the great fighter pilots,' said the Official History, 'Albert Ball yields place to none'. He had forty-four confirmed vic-tories, perhaps many more, and he was still not 21 when he died. He was quite irreplaceable. But it is curious that the day of Ball's death should have coincided with Mannock's coming of age as a scout pilot.

6

THE GOTHAS AND THE SMUTS
REPORT: 'SPORTING AUDACITY'

A GREAT many pilots were arriving in France from the UK in this period, including some who, like Mannock, could soon be said to have arrived in more senses than one. Among them was a former Norwich schoolboy named Philip Fullard, an outstanding sportsman and scholar who had played centre-half for Norwich Reserves on the one hand and won an Exhibition to Brasenose on the other. Learning to fly at his own expense in 1916 at the age of 19, he gave up his Exhibition to join the RFC. Because of his exceptional flying skills he was soon made an instructor, and he was still under twenty when he was posted to France. Although familiar with the Sopwith Pup, he found himself, with the bizarre logic of the services, joining No. 1 Squadron on Nieuports, a machine with which pilots arriving from the UK were totally unfamiliar, since there were none available in reserve squadrons at home. Within six weeks of his arrival he saw eighty-four pilots pass through the squadron, many of them because they couldn't cope and were posted elsewhere, but all too often because they became casualties almost before they had unpacked their kit. Fullard, who harboured no false modesty, had boasted, to reassure his parents, that the RFC 'would not let a dud man go to scouts', but he himself found the Nieuport unwieldy after the Pup. The biggest drawback, undoubtedly, was the lack of prior training on the type.

For all his natural abilities, Fullard had learnt that success had to be worked for, and, in No. 1 Squadron under Major A. Barton Adams, he found himself amongst kindred spirits. By exploiting the Nieuport's strengths and allowing for its limitations, by a meticulous attention to armaments, and by developing a discipline in formation flying that was in itself a deterrent to attack, even by superior numbers, they succeeded despite the marked superiority of the Albatros DV and the Fokker Triplane, both of which were introduced that summer. Fullard scored his first two victories in May 1917 and five more in June, and he was soon promoted to flight commander. Nine more in July and twelve in August brought him an MC and Bar, and with confidence and compactness as their watchword, every pilot in Fullard's flight gained five victories or more. He suffered a blank September through breaking a blood vessel while stunting a Nieuport on test, but another fourteen that autumn brought him a DSO and took his score to forty-two. He then broke a leg playing football and had to be sent home when the injury didn't mend.

Looking back on his six months with No. 1 Squadron, Fullard admitted to neither stress nor strain, and he insisted that any good instructor ought to make a good scout pilot, a somewhat singular view. He attributed his success – again in unorthodox fashion – not to superior marksmanship, nor to getting in close, nor to surprise, nor to luck, nor to an aggressive nature, but to sheer flying skill. (Compare with McCudden's: 'Good flying has never killed a Hun yet.')

The squadron's loss when Fullard went home has been compared to 24 Squadron's when they lost Hawker. Letters to relatives written by squadron commanders were inevitably couched in appreciative, even fulsome terms, but in Fullard's case there were no sorrowing parents to be soothed; yet Barton Adams wrote: 'No. 1 Squadron will lose its finest and most stout-hearted pilot . . . He was the "crack" pilot in France.'

Attempts to reset the broken leg failed repeatedly, ending Fullard's operational career, and eventually the leg had to be plated. Meanwhile – as contemporaries might perhaps have been consoled to hear – he completely lost his nerve for flying.

Not all the men reaching scout squadrons in France were embryonic Fullards, however, and it was distressing for both pilot and squadron when their unsuitability was recognised. A young man named Stuart (L.S.) Campbell, posted to 56 Squadron, had already experienced a similar rejection. He was waiting at CFS for a posting to France when he was instructed one night by his flight commander to take up a BE12, fly to Bath and return. He had no experience whatsoever of night flying and the BE12 was a single-seater, so there was no place for an instructor or observer. 'It was a bitterly cold night with heavy storm clouds,' wrote Campbell, 'and when over Devizes I ran into a murderous snowstorm. The only sensible thing to do was to turn back whilst the lights from the Upavon sheds were still visible.' This he did, to be told by the flight commander that he was 'not suited to being a night-flying pilot.' This, it seems, was his qualification for posting to a crack scout squadron. But it was soon apparent at Vert Galand that he wouldn't make a scout pilot either, and his fate was to be transferred to 27 Squadron on Martinsydes. 'Its role was long-distance daylight bombing,' recorded Campbell, 'and it was, without question, an absolute death trap when up against fast-moving Albatros scouts.' In its ceaseless war against enemy communications the squadron was averaging three raids per day, but escort by the Pups of 66 Squadron met with such remarkable success that after a dismal April not a single Martinsyde was lost in May. The Pup was chosen because it was slow enough to stay with the Martinsyde, a somewhat dubious distinction; indeed, once the Martinsyde had dropped its bombs it was actually the faster. Nevertheless by timing their supporting action to a nicety the Pup pilots generally fought off interception.

Eighteen-year-old Gordon Taylor, one of the Pup pilots guarding the Martinsydes, was an Australian. Despite a nervous wreck of an instructor at Netheravon whose sole aim was to send his pupils off solo as soon as possible so he didn't have to fly with them, killing in the process the compatriot Taylor had travelled with from Australia, Taylor himself, a natural flyer, was at home in the air from the start. He soon resolved that if he survived the war he would make flying his career.[1] No. 66 Squadron was formed at Filton, Bristol, where

1. Which he later did, to become, both solo and with fellow Australian Charles Kingsford-Smith, a pioneer of trans-oceanic and air route flying. Both were knighted.

Taylor 'gained some measure of fame,' it was said, 'by flying under Clifton Suspension Bridge.' It was further said that the squadron commander, Owen Boyd, 'turned a blind eye to the incident, feeling rather that the reputation of his squadron had been much enhanced.'

Under flight commander J.O. 'Jock' Andrews, formerly a stalwart of 24 Squadron with Lanoe Hawker, VC, Taylor prospered. Determined to put his trust in the Pup or perish, he looped it six times over Filton and satisfied himself and others of its structural integrity. A mock duel with Andrews at 6,000 feet earned him the appointment of deputy flight leader, and with the judicious Andrews leading he actually enjoyed the cerebral challenge of outsmarting the Hun in an inferior machine. When Andrews went home in July with a DSO to add to the MC he had won on DH2's, Gordon Taylor, having himself won an MC, replaced him. The B Flight commander went home at about the same time: his replacement, on a three-week attachment, was Jimmy McCudden.

The attachment was intended as a refresher course: after four months as a fighter instructor at Joyce Green, McCudden sought and was granted an opportunity to bring himself up to date on the latest trends in air fighting, ostensibly for the benefit of his pupils, although he was also looking ahead to his third tour of operations. Dispassionate, astute, and analytical, McCudden had appreciable fighting experience, but this was confined to two-seaters as an observer and to the DH2 as a pilot. His only operational experience in a tractor scout came that summer in his personal Pup, the machine in which he toured training stations to lecture and demonstrate. In this he joined Home Defence squadrons in chasing after the Gotha bombers, which mounted their first big raid on London on 13 June. On that raid, in broad daylight, 162 civilians were killed and 432 injured, and of 92 machines which went up to intercept, none got close enough to do any damage.

In the clamour for improved home air defences that resulted, Haig was forced by the War Cabinet to transfer two of Trenchard's best fighting squadrons, No. 56 to Bekesbourne near Canterbury and No. 66 to Calais, to cover both sides of the Dover Strait. Trenchard strongly resented this misappropriation, as he saw it, and would have refused it if he could. In one of his pep talks to his pilots he delighted them with the opinion that 'it does politicians good to be bombed occasionally.' On paper he pointed out that, to be effective, any system of defensive patrols would require a far greater effort than could feasibly be mounted, and that the most effective counter would be to clear the enemy from the Belgian coast, which happened to be one of the main objectives of Haig's coming offensive. This would increase the distance the Gothas had to travel and oblige them to traverse territory occupied by the Allies. He also correctly forecast that the Gothas would simply turn to attacking towns and bases behind the British lines. After a fortnight or so of useless patrolling the detached squadrons were returned to normal duty, whereupon the Gothas at once resumed their assault on London. This led to renewed demands by the Cabinet: first, for two first-class fighting squadrons, as before, and second, for a reprisal bombing raid on Mannheim, a diversion Haig had already rejected after the June attack. Haig promised to send two scout squadrons at once, but he warned that the fight to establish air supremacy prior to the summer offensive had already begun, that it would be the severest test yet, and that his entire campaign depended upon it and would be seriously jeopardised by both demands. Whether or not his predicament was overstated, the Cabinet settled for a single Sopwith Pup squadron, No. 46, which was released in turn after seven weeks. They abandoned the Mannheim project for the moment.

More significantly, the concept of an independent Air Ministry, already urged by Winston Churchill and others as a logical coordinator of the competing demands of the two air services, was flushed into focus by the attacks on London and the desire for reprisals, leading to the appointment of the South African statesman and visionary Jan Christian Smuts to enquire and report. Smuts, who had acted as the South African representative at an Imperial War Conference in April 1917, had since been co-opted by Lloyd George to the War Cabinet. In the meantime a project for the provision of forty long-range bomber squadrons to attack German cities sent Trenchard scurrying to northern France in search of possible bases, though he was doubtful of the wisdom or practicality of either project. The unobtrusive and farsighted David Henderson, as Director-General of Military Aeronautics, and as the RFC's first leader, joined Smuts as an adviser.

Henderson, whose training manual published in 1907 on the acquisition of information about the enemy ('The Art of Reconnaissance'), had replaced his own earlier manual on Field Intelligence, recognised the aeroplane as a fresh challenge, and he learned to fly in 1911 at the age of 49 to study and report on its practical applications. A graduate of two Scottish universities, he combined a quiet persistence with a rare quality of gentleness, together with an indifference to personal aggrandisement. Perhaps because of this, his contribution to the birth, first of the RFC and later of the RAF, has been underrated. Trenchard called him the true Father of the Air Force.

McCudden left for France on his refresher course in mid-June and found himself on the same airfield as 56 Squadron. He had visited them twice when they were at Bekesbourne and renewed acquaintance with an old friend from his days with 29 Squadron, G.H. Bowman, now a flight commander, and he rated them the best outfit he'd seen. The atmosphere created by Blomfield, with his international orchestra and cuisine, was unique, while the pilots were an exceptional bunch, and the new SE5A, to which the pilots were converting, was proving noticeably faster, with improved ceiling. Although McCudden's record of five confirmed victories might appear modest, it had been achieved in a difficult period, recognised by his MC, MM and *Croix de Guerre* awards, and Blomfield invited him to join one of 56's sorties under A Flight commander Captain P.B. 'Bruce' Prothero, promising to get him transferred 'as soon as a chance arose'. .

The red-haired Prothero, as McCudden soon discovered, was an extrovert. A true Scotsman, with a burr hard to decipher after a dram or two, he insisted on wearing a kilt at all times. When he returned from a patrol his knees would be blue from the cold 'and the hair thereon would stick out like bristles on a hog', according to Canadian colleague V.P. 'Versh' Cronyn. One day Cronyn asked him why he punished himself in this way, to which Prothero replied: 'You wouldna have me taken prisoner in disguise, would you now, laddie?' Sadly he was shot down and killed five days later, his place being taken by Gerald Constable Maxwell.

Another vacancy for a flight commander was in fact already imminent, through the impending transfer of Captain Ian Henderson, MC, only son of Sir David Henderson, to instructor duties. Still only 20, Henderson had seven victories.[1] Thus McCudden, after a final sortie with No. 66, some more Gotha-chasing, and ten days' leave, returned to France on 14 August as the new commander of B Flight.

Despite the vital work of the corps squadrons, it was the scout pilots protecting them who caught the public imagination, and this was exaggerated by a system of decorations which rewarded the spectacular rather than the routine. The achievement of scout pilots was readily measured in their scores, whereas corps pilots were less easy to assess one against the other, while qualities of leadership were in less demand. The contrast in recognition caused much bitterness, as was inevitable, and Trenchard deplored it, yet the life of a scout pilot tended to be shorter, providing justification. A higher level of physical and mental fitness was required of scout pilots, for whom sudden and frequent changes of altitude were commonplace, and they had to be imbued with a spirit of aggression – a burning desire not merely to get to grips with the enemy, but to bring him down 'in the greatest possible numbers'. This competitive instinct, the ambition to shine above his fellows, was accepted as a vital ingredient. No one put his finger more imaginatively on the temperament of RFC scout pilots than Trenchard's opposite number General von Hoeppner, who wrote of their '*sporting audacity*'. They too had to suffer at various times from inferior machines and unpopular policies. Enough has been said in praise of the men of the corps squadrons to emphasise their worth; but the fighting squadrons got the best of what was going, both in mechanical and human terms.

When McCudden joined 56 Squadron he was amongst equals. Half a dozen of the pilots had more victories than he did. Men

---

1. Ian Henderson was killed in a flying accident in Scotland on 21 June 1918.

like 'Beery' Bowman, so called because of his florid complexion, Constable Maxwell, Dick Maybery, Arthur Rhys Davids, Leonard Barlow and the Canadians Reginald Hoidge and 'Versh' Cronyn would have stood out in any company. Compare this with the experience of flight commanders in corps squadrons, many of whom were struggling, as Eric Routh had done, with demonstrable inferiority in both man and machine. Jack Slessor, still not twenty, returned to France on 1 May 1917 to take over A Flight of No. 5 Squadron on RE8's, which he was flying for the first time and which to his surprise he 'rather liked'. 'Pember is a rotten bad pilot,' he wrote, 'he will have to go home if he crashes again.' 'Pember twisted off his tail fin and bent his axle again. I wish the CO would get rid of him.' 'Hodges destroyed another RE8 and retired to hospital, he will have to go now, thank Heaven.' His replacement was 'a good fellow but a rotten pilot – he did in his centre section today on his first flight.' 'Hanman seems a footling person . . . lands badly.' There was grief for a pilot shot down in flames, and a complaint of a lack of protection. 'I don't know what's the matter with our Tripes and scouts these days.'

There were still compensations in the occasional day off. 'Went to Amiens with Joyon and Duncan and Owen, had a great time. Amiens rather a good spot. Lunched at the oyster shop and dined at the Grand and filled in the time with Charley's Bar.' A guest night in the Mess two nights later improved morale – but the quality of the new pilots remained abysmal. 'The flight is in ghastly shape now.' Pember, having weathered all Slessor's disdain, and having finally transgressed by losing formation, had fought well when attacked – but had been lent to 10 Squadron, Garland's unit.[1] 'Hanman is still in hospital, and Lomas is going home. Nerve all gone to pot, fainting in the air etc.' Slessor, inevitably, was getting all the flying he wanted and more. As for the unfortunate observers, there were only two qualified men left.

In mid-July Slessor noted: 'Two new pilots just rolled up. Not bad but not up to much.' But next day: 'The new pilots are pretty bad.

---

1. E.H. Pember, formerly of the Royal Artillery, survived to be promoted to Lieutenant, but was killed in action on 30 September 1917.

One got into a spin and nearly killed Stone.' Stone was one of the two surviving qualified observers, already badly shaken by three similar escapes. Duncan, one of the men who had accompanied Slessor to Amiens, 'crashed badly amongst the transport lorries getting off. The other new pilot, Ashton, wrote off 8683. Stone with him again. I think his nerve has gone badly now. No wonder, he has had five bad crashes, all with new pilots.'

It was going to be a long time before Smith-Barry's revolutionary training methods, begun early in 1917 at the Gosport School of Flying, would be reflected in new arrivals at the front. As late as 1918, Gerald Dixon, during pilot training at Catterick, had never heard of Smith-Barry or his teachings. Meanwhile, raw pilots continued to arrive at the squadrons, filling empty chairs but driving harassed flight commanders to distraction. A more mature newcomer, Fred Winterbotham, posted to Nieuports on 29 Squadron, complained of 'pilots arriving and disappearing daily'. But after seeing action he commented, as others had done before him, on 'the strange *détente* between those who fought in the air'.

7

'HALF A PARACHUTE IS BETTER THAN NO PARACHUTE AT ALL'

T HE principal reasons advanced by the British for the failure to incorporate parachutes in the equipment of aeroplanes in the First World War were:-

1. That pilots, given a means of escape, would be tempted, when under threat, to abandon their machines prematurely.
2. That although it was right for the crews of kite balloons to be offered a means of escape because they were vulnerable and couldn't hit back, aeroplane crews were equipped to defend themselves.
3. That the parachutes available were altogether too bulky for stowage in the tiny cockpits of the time, and too complex and cumbersome for external fitting; that their weight (28 lbs) would have detracted from aircraft performance; that they would have become entangled with the tailplane or some other obstruction on release; and that they were unreliable anyway.
4. That most fatal crashes occurred on take-off and landing, or when stunting at low level, when height was insufficient for a parachute to open.

Whatever one may think of the slur on the fighting instincts and resolve of pilots implicit in the first excuse, the other three scarcely bear examination. Many of the machines shot down were so poorly armed as to be almost as vulnerable as kite balloons; urgent priority could surely have been given to the design of parachutes for aeroplanes and of cockpits to accommodate them; while the last excuse could only have been advanced by men whose knowledge was confined to training units in the United Kingdom.

There is no doubt that the RFC authorities were almost pathologically opposed to the notion of parachutes in aeroplanes, and that they went so far as to discourage efforts to develop them. A pilot's job was to stick to his machine. Curiously enough there is also little doubt that a kind of macho bravado existed amongst pilots which scorned the safety angle and stifled any concerted pressure for the development and issue of parachutes, either from squadron and flight commanders or from the pilots themselves.

Tom Mapplebeck, brother of Gibb, who flew at the time of the Fokker scourge, said he 'never thought about parachutes'. Harold Tambling, of 22 Squadron (FE2b's), said the same. 'Puggy' Shone said: 'We never thought about parachutes seriously as part of our equipment, because the additional weight would have affected the performance of our aircraft, and we accepted that the powers that be really believed that it might affect our morale if we were equipped . . .' Harold Balfour denied that there was ever any controversy about parachutes in the squadrons in which he served. Hugh Walmsley said he loathed the idea of parachutes, because of the discomfort they inflicted on the wearer; even when they were introduced in the mid-1920s he didn't wear them. Jack Slessor recalled: 'The first time I really thought about a parachute was in about 1924, I suppose when I was told I was going to have one.'

Against this, there were pilots who vilified the authorities *at the time* for failing to provide them, others who sought to procure their own. Among the more vociferous was Arthur Gould Lee. Arriving in France in May 1917, he was moved to sympathy with colleagues and enemies alike when he saw them in unrecoverable situations three miles up but with plenty of time to get out. Although he conceded that there was no room for a parachute in the tiny cockpit of his Sopwith Pup, he cited many other types, particularly the more vulnerable, where a parachute should have been mandatory. Why weren't machines designed from the beginning to take parachutes?

Lee believed that every pilot would have sacrificed a little in performance for a chance of escape *in extremis*. So far from weakening resolve, it would, he thought, have been a great boost to morale: 'To know you had a sporting chance from a break-up or a flamer would make you much braver in a scrap.' The same point was made by the inventors of parachutes.

The use of a parachute to retard a fall from a height had long been envisaged, but one of the first to pursue its practical application in the twentieth century was Edward Maitland, the veteran airship and balloon pioneer of the original No. 1 Squadron at Farnborough. Maitland became so concerned for the safety of his balloon crews if war came that he made a parachute descent himself from a balloon as early as 1908, and he continued for many years to study and experiment with parachutes for lighter-than-air craft, making the first descent from an airship in 1913.

Parachute descents from aeroplanes were made before the war in Britain, France and America; but it was as a life-saving device in kite balloons that the parachute became a recognised wartime accessory, the first suitable British parachutes being designed by the firm of C.G. Spencer. Spencer himself made a demonstration jump from an airship at the Royal Naval Air Station at Kingsnorth on 17 December 1914, an experiment so successful that 'it completely changed the views of all who saw it'. The airship positioned itself as directed by Spencer, who jumped from 1,000 feet. The parachute opened within 100 feet and Spencer came gently and safely to earth despite a brisk wind, landing almost exactly where he had intended. Soon afterwards his firm were invited to tender. Thus when the operation of kite balloons in France was taken over by the RFC, they inherited the C.G. Spencer Static-Line (Automatic) Parachute.

Another inventor, retired railway engineer E.R. Calthrop, was meanwhile developing a more sophisticated and practical model. This was both smaller and lighter. No doubt he had an eye to profit, but he expressed a noble intent: 'To Reduce the Unnecessary Wastage of our Airmen'. Despite pre-war rebuffs from both the Admiralty and

War Office when he offered to test his parachute in their presence, he persisted. In October 1915 Mervyn O'Gorman, the flamboyant Superintendent at Farnborough, proposed to the Directorate of Military Aeronautics that an experienced balloon jumper be engaged to carry out experiments with a Calthrop parachute, but a Minute from the Assistant Director, enquiring of Henderson, the Director-General, whether experiments were to be continued, was annotated emphatically: '*No, certainly not!*' This uncompromising negative was still being quoted a year later to stifle further initiatives.

Much of the blame for this attitude has been assigned to Trenchard, though Henderson was the one who expressed it so forcibly. Yet it is surprising that Trenchard didn't campaign for an urgent programme of research and development. He seems, at least, to have had no part in the shameful declaration by the Air Board on parachutes for the RFC.[1]

It is the opinion of the Board that the present form of parachute is not suitable for use in aeroplanes and should only be used by balloon observers.

It is also the opinion of the Board that the presence of such an apparatus might impair the fighting spirit of pilots and cause them to abandon machines which might otherwise be capable of returning to base for repair.

Here it was at last, in plain, brutal language: the RFC, and presumably the RNAS, could not be trusted with parachutes. This was to turn the whole question on its head. What about the pilot himself returning to base for repair, an outcome which a parachute might achieve? Few machines in which a pilot dived from a height to his death were repairable; why not at least try to save the pilot, and the observer if one were present? The salvaging of the machine was not and never was crucial, except perhaps when a test pilot might stay too long in a vain effort to preserve a prototype. Apart from the human reasons for putting life before hardware, once a pilot had got

1. *The First Great Air War*, by Richard Townshend Bickers (Hodder, 1988).

past his first few shows his value became immense and his replacement infinitely more difficult than the replacement of his machine.

Encouraged by Maitland, Calthrop persisted, and he resumed trials of his parachute at the naval air station at Polegate. By 21 August 1916 the Admiralty were pronouncing the trials 'most satisfactory', and they proposed to adopt the 'Guardian Angel', as Calthrop named his parachute, for use in kite balloons and airships. The tests were all made from an airship, first with weights, then with dummies, and finally with a volunteer parachutist, Sir Bryan Leighton. Leighton jumped from 9,000 feet, the parachute cushioning him and opening in two-and-a-half seconds. In a personal report to Commodore Murray Sueter, Head of the Admiralty's Air Department, Leighton observed: 'I am quite sure I could do the jump from a BE type of aeroplane' – but the offer was ignored. Maitland believed that the Guardian Angel 'represented a distinct advance on the Spencer', but his report was more reticent than Leighton's, recommending the parachute as 'a thoroughly reliable one and fit to be taken into use for lighter-than-air craft of all descriptions (aeroplanes and seaplanes excepted) forthwith.' Nevertheless the Spencer type was retained for kite balloon work. It had become familiar, and it was also thought that the Calthrop might deploy too near to what might be a burning balloon. So Calthrop was disappointed again.

His persistence seemed about to pay off, however, when the Guardian Angel was used in the first British military live descent from a heavier-than-air craft, by Captain Clive Collett, a 30-year-old New Zealander in the RFC, in an experimental flight in a BE2c from the test flying and research establishment at Orfordness. After twenty drops from the same machine using dummies, Collett made his jump from 600 feet on 13 January 1917.

A report on Collett's jump, by Vernon Brown, who was one of the pilots involved, makes it clear that the Guardian Angel, as then constituted, demanded skilful piloting to ensure a safe exit by the parachutist, the dummy drops having disclosed that canopy and rigging lines were liable to snag in the tail skid unless a banked turn was being flown. This was scant reassurance for a pilot and observer jumping from a crippled machine, and once again Calthrop was disappointed. An alternative prototype, designed by a Captain Mears, was similarly rejected.

Less than a month after Collett's historic descent, an extract from a Minute addressed to the Secretary of the Air Board settled the matter: 'The heavier-than-air people all say that they flatly decline to regard the parachute in an aeroplane as a life-saving device which is worth carrying in its present form.' The crux of the matter lay in the last four words: further development was needed. But the Air Board gave no lead, basing their inaction on factors which reveal a breathtaking callousness:

1. Safety was not really considered important.
2. The ignorance and prejudice of pilots, and the fact that a good proportion of accidents occurred on landing, take-off, and stunting close to the ground. [This was the desk-bound Home Establishment attitude again.]

Not only were the Board antipathetic to parachutes for the RFC, they were also dog-in-the-manger about letting anyone else have them. In March 1917 the Board considered an application from the Russian Government for '100 Calthrop's Patent Safety Guardian Angel Parachutes', but this did not influence them to change their stance. 'In view of the opinion of the Naval and Military Flying Services that this device has little chance of being used in aeroplanes, it was decided in the first instance to enquire for what purpose the Russian Government required the parachutes.' This question, bordering on impertinence, was soon answered: the parachutes must be adaptable for both airships and aircraft. At this the Board consented to an order, not for a hundred but for twenty, with the proviso that 'the Russians should be informed that the Board could not agree to their being supplied for aeroplane purposes, for which they were not considered suitable for the British Air Services.'

Trenchard himself was far more sympathetic to the introduction of parachutes for his crews, and he suggested that trials should be conducted in France, asking for twenty Calthrop parachutes for this purpose, but this was refused. Yet when he asked for twenty parachutes for dropping agents behind the lines he got them. If this was a ruse to go ahead with the trials against orders, there is no evidence that they ever took place.

One of the early RFC pioneers, however, took up the fight. This was Charles Longcroft, who was already a major when he took part in the Channel crossing of August 1914. He had taken a leading part in some of the earliest reconnaissances, led No. 4 Squadron, and finally commanded a brigade. Mild in manner, but clinical in mind, and no respecter of persons, he told his seniors: 'I and my pilots keenly desired parachutes.' To the objection that parachutes would impose too great a strain on the pilots themselves he replied that their principal use would be to escape from a burning machine, surely sufficient compensation for any minor inconvenience. As for the notion that pilots might jump prematurely, he simply did not believe it.

Soon afterwards, on Maitland's recommendation, a Parachute Committee was formed, which included representatives of the Technical, Airship, Supply and Air Inspectorate Departments, the Establishment Branch and the Kite Balloon Section; but practical difficulties with the models available persisted. One progress report opined that 'half a parachute was better than no parachute at all'; but it was also said that unless an aviator had confidence in his equipment it was more likely to disturb his peace of mind than to enhance it.

Pressure for more rapid progress was about to be applied from an unexpected quarter: in the last summer of the war, the Germans started using parachutes. They had previously introduced them for their airship crews, but their weight reduced altitude, the airship's most effective defence, and they were withdrawn. The aeroplane type was named after its developer, Otto Heinicke, whose parachute was similar to British models. It was packed in a sack strapped to the pilot, and a 50 lb break cord attached to the machine was designed to jerk the canopy out of the sack once the pilot was clear of the tail surfaces of the plane. Air could be spilled from the canopy on landing. The parachute was by no means foolproof, nor was it universally fitted, and escapes from crippled or burning aircraft did not always succeed.

Major-General Sir David Henderson, Director-General of Military Aviation: according to Trenchard 'the true father of the Royal Air Force.'

Ian Henderson, MC (7 victories), son of Sir David. He was killed in a flying accident in June 1918.

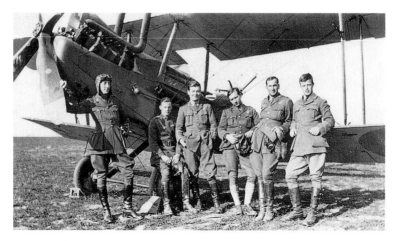

Charles Smart and Jimmy Larkin first and second from the left, Hendry fourth, in front of an RE8. 'We now call ourselves the Circus.'

Alan Dore, 34, formerly a major in the Worcestershire Regiment, then observer, pilot and squadron commander in the RFC.

George Downing. Of his pilot he wrote: 'Guess I'd go anywhere with him . . . It was glorious sport!'

Left: 'They're giving the Ball another run.' Leaving for France, hatless as always, to join 56 Squadron, 7 April 1917.

Above right: The youthfully enthusiastic Maurice Kay. 'Ball has done himself great credit . . the excitement was terrific!'

Right: P.B. 'Bruce' Prothero always flew in a kilt. 'You wouldna have me taken prisoner in disguise would you now laddie?'

No rash heroics for Jimmy McCudden. He stalked
his prey, but could be content to fight another day.

P.G. Taylor (later Sir Gordon) with his air mechanics. For him, flying
became a vocation, hence the knighthood.

Eric Routh (21) of 16 Squadron (BE's). 'Why was every ham-fisted pilot sent to me?'

Oscar Greig. Rated his 37 days on FE2b's of 25 Squadron 'the most unpleasant of his service,' worse than his subsequent capture.

2nd Lt R.F. Glazebrook, when a prisoner, witnessed how a dedicated German surgeon broke down when his young RFC patient died.

William Leefe Robinson, VC. First man to destroy a Zeppelin over Britain – but he suffered for it later as a prisoner.

Edward 'Mick' Mannock. 'He planned every attack like a chess player.'

W.A. 'Billy' Bishop. 'To me it was not a business but just a wonderful game.'

Starting on his 19th birthday, J.T.P. Jeyes developed a successful partnership, in RE8's, with an observer from his old school.

Arthur (later 'Bomber') Harris. 'With your favourite mechanic, you were just a team together.'

Gwilym H. Lewis (12 victories) in his SE5A. 'Everything is spoiled at the time by being so frightened.'

All on this page flew with 56 Squadron, and, according to McCudden, were 'as splendid a lot of fellows as ever set foot in France.'

Arthur Rhys Davids (centre), Keith Muspratt (left) and Maxwell Coote (right).

Leonard Barlow   Dick Maybery

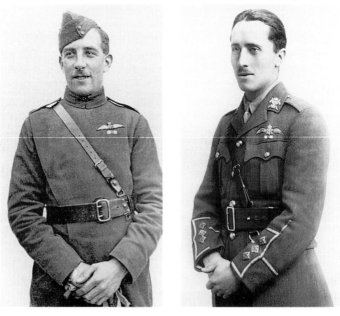

The most publicised escape was that of Ernst Udet, the second highest ranking German ace, who owed his life to Heinicke's invention (as, later, did Hermann Goering). Udet jumped on 29 June 1918 following a clash with a French Breguet, though after unfastening his safety-belt and standing up in his seat he was blown aft and his parachute harness snagged on the forward tip of the rudder. With the strength of desperation he broke off the rudder tip, only to find himself tumbling over and over, convinced that his parachute had failed. He was down to 250 feet when it opened, and he sprained an ankle on landing. Yet he would surely have endorsed the view that 'half a parachute was better than no parachute at all'.

Curiously enough, neither the French, nor the Americans, who might have been expected to provide this kind of luxury – if luxury it was – for their pilots, had produced a practical parachute by the war's end. After the final plunge of the American ace Raoul Lufbery on 19 May 1918, when witnesses saw the pilot jump to escape the flames and plummet to earth, Colonel Billy Mitchell, the American air commander, commented: 'If he had had a parachute he could easily have been saved.' But the US Government still refused to issue the parachute, thus far imperfect, that they were developing. Yet the British, goaded by the protection being afforded their enemies, seemed about to move swiftly at last. The greatest proselytiser was a former Royal Marine, by then in his forties, Major T. Orde Lees, who risked his neck in a number of spectacular jumps, none more so, in November 1917, than from the top of Tower Bridge. His frequent visits to France eventually brought, on 16 September 1918, the following declaration from the Headquarters of the RAF in the Field: '*All single-seaters are to be fitted with parachutes forthwith.*'

By this time the Camel was regarded as obsolescent, so it was decided to convert only SE5A's and Sopwith Dolphins and Snipes. Orders were to be placed – with Calthrops – for the requisite number of parachutes. The two-seaters were not forgotten: the Brisfit and the DH4 and DH9 bombers were also to be adapted for parachutes. The Armstrong-Whitworth and the RE8, for the same reason as the Camel, were not.

All this sounded positive and expeditious. But other points in the

Headquarters letter of 16 September on the Adoption of Parachutes suggested that much was still to be done. The weight of the parachute was, if possible, to be reduced – but not if it meant reducing the size of the canopy. All parachutes were to be fireproofed. Because of the number of man-hours required to pack and repack, service and maintain the Calthrop parachute, experiments were requested with a view to simplifying the design. Trials were requested to determine the difference in performance between fitted and non-fitted machines. And so on. Clearly all this would take months. 'Forthwith' was an idle boast.

Nothing more was achieved before the Armistice, and it is implicit in subsequent events that the notion of parachutes in peacetime did not appeal and was pigeon-holed. It was not until the mid-twenties that the Irvin Air Chute, a free-fall type of American design, was introduced.

Sholto Douglas was only one of many who later learnt 'to my disgust' that it had been official policy 'to deny us the use of parachutes'. He wrote of the great comfort it would have been to have had such a means of escape, not to mention 'the saving of many men from horrible deaths.'

8

OVER AND UNDER MESSINES

A LTHOUGH spasmodic air fighting over the Arras front continued into June, Trenchard, by the first week in May, had already worked out the redistribution of his forces in support of Haig's long-gestating Flanders offensive. The objectives of this offensive remained as Haig had devised them: to break out at what he considered the enemy's weakest point, the Ypres salient, protect his eastern flank, and advance north to the Belgian coast. Few shared his optimism that the campaign would succeed as planned, but major offensive action of some kind had to be undertaken that summer, if only to buy time while French morale recovered from the mutiny. The magnitude of this catastrophe was still a well-kept secret, not only from the enemy, but also from the British War Cabinet. But if Haig failed to act decisively, the French collapse might be total. There remained the frightening possibility that the BEF would be stranded by the U-boat campaign, which still demanded urgent attention. In any case, for Haig to keep his armies idle, and abdicate the initiative to the enemy, was unthinkable.

These were the factors that determined Haig's strategy for the remainder of 1917, from the preparatory Battle of Messines (7 June), to the main assault at 3rd Ypres (beginning 31 July). Various subsidiary battles were to follow in August and September, culminating in the final reckoning in October and November at Passchendaele.

Essential to the launching of the main offensive was the prior capture of the dominating heights of the Messines ridge, rising in places to 260 feet, from which British preparations could be monitored by the enemy. For Trenchard, as for the BEF, the planning for this preliminary operation took precedence.

The RFC now had forty-five squadrons in action in France, plus five naval squadrons on loan, a total of 881 aircraft in all. Of these, some 300, a third of them fighters, were earmarked for the Messines front. Of the naval squadrons, three were Sopwith Triplanes; but in the RFC squadrons there was still a dearth of modern machines. There was only one SE5 squadron, No. 56, only one complete Brisfit squadron, No. 48 (though No. 11 was soon to join it), and only one DH4 squadron, No. 55. Squadrons that had been raised to twenty-one machines and sometimes twenty-four for the Arras battle had had to revert to eighteen because machines to replace those lost or damaged beyond repair were not forthcoming. The RE8 now outnumbered the old BE2 by two to one, but there were still five BE squadrons operating daily. For much of that summer, Nos 43, 45 and 70 Squadrons were still flying the outmoded Sopwith two-seater, re-equipment of all three squadrons with Sopwith Camels not being completed until September. It was to the pilots and observers of these three squadrons that Trenchard particularly addressed himself on his final round of visits before the Battle of Messines.

As always he was brutally frank. After praising them for their successes, he told them he knew only too well that their machines were outclassed by the latest enemy fighters. He promised he was doing all he could to get them better equipped; but meanwhile, knowing of his efforts and of his sympathy with their predicament, he would rely on them to do their best. This meant, he stressed, that they must go at the enemy with all their might to achieve the vital task of keeping the sky clear of enemy aeroplanes, not merely over the lines but far behind them, to a depth of some 10,000 yards. Once again Trenchard was appealing to the aggressive instincts of his pilots to bridge the quality gap, of which they were only too well aware.

What was the reaction to Trenchard's apology and exhortation? There were always cynics and critics. Few were more critical than

Arthur Gould Lee, but of Trenchard he wrote: 'He is a fine man, with a terrific personality, who knows how to impress and inspire us. To have a few words of praise of our work was an enormous encouragement. Trenchard is a leader after the hearts of service pilots, and although we don't like some of the things we have to do, such as Distant Operational Patrols in obsolete machines, everyone in the RFC looks up to him as a great commander.'

The RFC's primary tasks at Messines, in simple terms, were for the corps machines, under the protection of the fighting squadrons, to give the maximum help to the British artillery in registering targets and directing fire, and for the fighting squadrons to prevent the German Air Force from registering our own battery positions. So successful were they that when the bombardment proper opened on 31 May the corps squadrons enjoyed almost complete freedom of movement and were rarely attacked. Of thirty-three machines reported missing in II Brigade between 15 May and 9 June, twenty-nine belonged to the army wing and only four to the corps wing.

The preliminary bombardment of the Messines ridge, which had begun on 21 May, was much more concentrated and detailed than for previous battles. For the RFC, cooperation with the artillery included finding the targets and directing the fire for the 2,400 field guns that had been assembled on a ten-mile front. Among specific aims was the obliteration of the barbed wire entanglements fronting the German trenches to clear the way for the advancing infantry. Graphics and charts carried by the corps pilots proliferated so alarmingly that Charles Smart (RE8's, No. 5 Squadron), complained, on 2 June, that he would have to take a secretary up with him. 'It nearly drove me frantic trying to remember where each lot of ground strips were situated and whose turn it was to fire and on which target.' He lined things up eventually, but admitted it was a very worrying business. 'Archie does not help you much in the thinking line either.'

Day bombing, mainly by the Martinsydes of No. 27 and the DH4's of No. 55, helped to hamper and divert enemy air activity, the Martinsydes with Pup escort and the DH4's from high level, but it was the night bombing of the FE2b's of 100 Squadron that inflicted the most damage. The DH4's also flew photographic reconnaissances up to 21,000 feet. But as Trenchard had foreseen, the Sopwith two-seaters were outclassed, and they suffered accordingly. Eight machines of 45 Squadron on a photo recce were challenged by five Albatros scouts, with more German pilots joining in as the scrap evolved. The Sopwith crews did not need Trenchard's blandishments to fight for their lives, and one of their attackers was sent down in flames. But two of the Sopwiths were lost, a third was forced down behind the lines, and two more were so crippled that they were wrecked in forced landings.

Exceptional skill was often shown, of necessity, by the FE2b crews, but they were up against it when seven of No. 20 Squadron were attacked by fifteen Albatros scouts. One of the pusher pilots was mortally wounded by the red-painted leading Albatros, but another, after a running fight, got in a burst at close range that pulverised the Albatros, which broke up in mid-air. Lieutenant Harold Satchell and his observer, Second-Lieutenant T.A.M.S. Lewis, had shot down the German ace Karl Schaefer, whose score had reached thirty at the time of his death.

Meanwhile a system of eavesdropping on the signals of intruding enemy machines by army intercept stations, fixing their position and notifying the fighting squadrons, had proved so successful in previous months that many similar stations were established solely for the purpose of reporting the movements of hostiles. The hope that these messages might be transmitted direct to airborne machines was never realised for lack of equipment, but alternative signalling methods proved adequate, and interception rates were greatly improved.

Other tasks of almost equal significance were discharged daily once the battle started. Contact patrols, working low over the heads of the infantry in the attack area, sought continually to report progress to the relevant headquarters, often returning to deliver fresh instructions in weighted and streamered bags. Yet there were still times when the ground forces showed a frustrating reluctance to reveal their positions. Equally important were the persistent machine-gun attacks on enemy airfields, transport, and troops. This low-level ground strafing, which had been begun successfully at Arras, developed at Messines into an established part of air support for the advancing ground forces, to be used extensively in July and August at 3rd Ypres and subsequently. But it exposed its practitioners to withering fire.

Alan Dore, who had taken command of 43 Squadron after the solid Sholto Douglas injured himself when hitting a horse on an emergency take-off (the horse it was that died), despatched seven two-seaters at 4 a.m. on 7 June to strafe troops and transport behind the Messines Ridge. 'The dull rumble of guns reaches me as I see them off in a grey light. It is a dangerous mission. Then telephone messages come through ... One [Harriman] is down with petrol tank shot through ... D'Arcy is wounded and lands his machine in splinters. Rutter comes back not at all.' At one point Harriman had almost despaired of surviving, while D'Arcy, although wounded, had shot down a balloon and damaged another. 'D'Arcy goes on long after he is wounded and lands in a faint.' Rutter, one of the flight commanders, who had treated Dore and others to dinner two months earlier to celebrate his birthday and the award of an MC, had been one of the last three remaining of the original thirty-six officers of 43 Squadron. 'His loss is another link snapped.'

Nieuports of No. 1 Squadron, Sopwith Pups of 66, FE8's of 41, and a Spad and an SE5 from 19 and 56 respectively, all joined in the low-level mayhem. The strafer in the SE5 was Second-Lieutenant Leonard Barlow, born in Islington and about to celebrate his nine-teenth birthday. He dived at a German aerodrome and peppered the hangars from twenty feet, spotted a nearby train and hosed it with both Vickers and Lewis (having wired them up so they could be fired from the same button), and riddled rolling-stock in the nearby station yard. He still had enough ammunition – and aggression – to perforate the sheds of a second aerodrome on his way home. Of an ingenious turn of mind, he was known as the gadget king.

The most spectacular weapons employed for the actual taking of the ridge were the mines that had been laboriously laid by tunnelling companies over many months under the German front line, to depths of up to a hundred feet. Twenty-one of these were planted at inter-vals, and the nineteen that were successfully detonated at 03.10 on 7 June aggregated nearly a million tons of high explosive, the boom being heard 130 miles away in London. Ten thousand Germans are believed to have been killed, and 7,000 more were stunned and captured. The Allied infantry were able to advance rapidly, and by 09.00 they had seized the ridge. For once the German casualties were heavier than the British, and next day an enemy counter-attack was repulsed. Yet Messines, although brilliant in conception and execution, was still no more than a local success. Several days before the engagement ended with a final push on 14 June, Trenchard was already bent on consolidation for the main struggle ahead.

Addressing his brigade commanders – there were now five of them, one for each of Haig's armies – on 10 June, Trenchard wrote: 'I would ask that as far as possible you do your best to point out to your Armies that it is of the utmost importance that the Flying Corps should avoid wastage in both pilots and machines for some little time.' Nothing could have been more revealing of the dependence of Trenchard and his brigadiers on the restraint and good sense of the various army commanders. He continued: 'My reserve at present is dangerously low, in fact, in some cases it barely exists at all, and the supply from home is not coming forward sufficiently freely to enable us to continue fighting an offensive in the air continuously.' In this respect, as he was careful to remind them for their own use, they were worse off than the infantry. 'As we have no reserve squadrons it is necessary to do everything to avoid losses.' But as always with Trenchard, there was a sting in the tail. 'It is of the utmost importance, however, that the offensive spirit is maintained in the Flying Corps.' Take it easy on the one hand, but keep up the pressure on the other.

Proud of their successes at Messines – and mourning their losses – pilots and observers felt they hardly needed this form of cajolery. Equally extreme, perhaps, was the conclusion of an X Corps staff officer in a memorandum on *Lessons of the Battle*, though it sounded harmonious to an airman's ear. 'The success [at Messines] was due to a great extent to the excellent work of the artillery which made the work of the infantry exceptionally easy as there was practically no wire left.' Clearly the work of the corps squadrons, mostly RE8's and BE2's, favoured by good weather and the suffocation of enemy interference by the army squadrons, had been decisive. The RFC had achieved its primary task.

There was still room for individual initiative, and it was a scout pilot, during the build-up to the battle, who conceived one of the most daring exploits of the war. This was Billy Bishop, of 60 Squadron. Fred Winterbotham, of 29 Squadron, based on the same aerodrome, and also flying a Nieuport, records that 'a boisterous young Canadian' asked him, on the evening of 1 June, 'can I join your patrol tomorrow?' This was the dawn patrol. It had been a favourite ploy of Albert Ball to get in an extra patrol in this way, and Winterbotham agreed without further thought. Bishop, who had already cleared his exploit with his squadron commander, Jack Scott, arranged an early call, pulled his flying suit over his pyjamas – normal practice for the dawn patrol – and took off with 29 Squadron just before four o'clock. It was a misty morning, with a drizzle of rain, but when they were well over the lines Winterbotham caught a glimpse of Bishop peeling off steeply and diving down towards Cambrai.

Bishop's plan was to make a lone surprise attack on a German aerodrome at the moment when they were rousing themselves for the business of the day. He hoped to do spectacular damage. After losing himself for a time in cloud, he found himself overflying a German airfield well inside hostile territory, but found to his chagrin that it was deserted. His luck soon changed as he sighted a second aerodrome, which was pulsating with early morning activity. This was Estourmel, on the outskirts of Cambrai.

Several machines were already lined up in front of the hangars with their engines running, just as Bishop had imagined they might be. He counted six Albatros III's and a two-seater. Diving to 200 feet, he began machine-gunning the line of aircraft, but was challenged at once by a barrage of small-arms fire from the perimeter defences. Turning back on a reciprocal course, he saw one Albatros already starting a take-off run. Dropping to 60 feet, he caught it with a 15-round burst just as it left the ground and saw it crash.

Meanwhile a second Albatros was already airborne and Bishop pursued it. The accuracy of his shooting was already legendary, but this time he missed. Yet the virulence of his attack so disorientated the German pilot that he crashed into a tree.

Two more Albatros pilots took off in opposite directions, intent on trapping their tormentor, and Bishop, still under withering small-arms fire, had no alternative but to stay and fight. Here the agility of the little Nieuport served him well. He had to climb to 1,000 feet to engage them, but he shot one of them down and the other withdrew, giving Bishop a chance to escape.

Bishop was no automaton, and the tension of the previous minutes had left him dazed and nauseated. Also he had run out of ammunition. When a formation of hostiles suddenly appeared directly above him, he unshipped his gun – which was now useless to him – to gain speed, then dived at full power for the lines, braving the inevitable barrage. When he landed back at base, the hundred or more bullet holes in his wings and fuselage were eloquent of all he had faced.

Bishop's subsequent report was forwarded by Jack Scott to Wing Headquarters, who lost no time in spreading the news. Although there could be no witness to corroborate a lone attack of this kind, Bishop's personal account was accepted, and Trenchard called his exploit 'the greatest single show of the war'. A Military Cross had been gazetted seven days previously, a DSO was already in the pipe-line, and on 9 August, more than two months after his lone raid of 2 June, Bishop was told by Trenchard of the imminent award of a VC.

The lapse of time suggests that Bishop's claim was carefully checked and confirmed, though it is not clear how this could have been done, and some air historians have never been wholly convinced. Of the fifty-one VCs awarded to airmen in two World Wars, Bishop's, based on personal evidence only, uncorroborated by witnesses, or by Allied or especially in this case by German records, is unprecedented. More brashly self-assertive than most of his squadron colleagues, and sometimes accused of hyperbole, even of 'bullshit', he was nevertheless immensely popular with seniors and juniors alike, and this, and the support of Jack Scott, and of Trenchard himself, was crucial. But it is worth noting that Bishop's claims throughout his career enjoy formidable verification – from his Combat Reports, from Squadron Records, from Official Communiqués, and from his letters home.[1]

A Bar to his DSO followed him when he returned to Canada on extended leave on 1 September 1917, by which time his official score was forty-seven. And he would be back.

1. Philip Markham, *Historical Research Section of the Friends of the Canadian War Museum, Ottawa, Ontario.*

9

SUNNY DAYS IN JUNE: THE COLD AT HIGH ALTITUDE

A PLEASING picture of the hot, sunny days of June 1917 has been painted by the author Norman Macmillan, a pilot on 45 Squadron. He recorded how a grassy path led uphill from the hangars at St Marie Cappel to a little footbridge, emerging into a sizeable meadow surrounded by trees. Tents lined the eastern and northern perimeters of the meadow, and the Mess marquees, one for each flight, dominated the western side. When pilots and observers were not on duty they lazed on camp beds in the shade of the trees, drowsily aware of the hum of bees and the calling of birds, with camp dogs, panting in the heat, sprawled at their feet. Sometimes the heady resonances of summer were smothered by the rumble of a homing flight from some sister squadron or the muffled booming of distant guns. It was totally unreal, yet it was better to savour the moment than to dwell on what Macmillan called 'that other life', the life that lay behind them and might or might not lie before them. It was folly to think about that.

Only that morning they had been patrolling above the battlefront in their Sopwith two-seater scouts (1½-strutters) at 12,000 feet, photographing an amorphous world of scarred and cratered earth, with a farrago of explosions blinking menacingly at them the while. Yet the pall of smoke that defied the naked eye would have been partly penetrated by their cameras.

Through recurring casualties, and the departure to Home Establishment of seasoned survivors, Macmillan had become one of the squadron's senior pilots, and he cooperated enthusiastically in taking care of newcomers, giving them conducted tours of the lines, sending them off with an experienced observer, and positioning them next to the leader on patrol, with one or more protecting machines behind. But in spite of this paternalism, it was still the tyros who formed the bulk of the casualties. Nothing changed that. But if they could survive those first precarious weeks, a longish career could follow.

This was certainly the experience of Charles Smart, whose dedication to the task in hand was enhanced rather than diminished by time. Smart had been engaged on several trench-bashing shoots in the Oppy area, a German strong-point six miles north-east of Arras on which a second infantry attack was planned, the first having failed after heavy fighting. 'I understand the attack on Oppy comes off tomorrow evening,' noted Smart. 'I have put myself down for the contact patrol job, I must see the show through . . .' His narrow escape over this same target six weeks earlier, when his wing-tip had been shredded by a 'friendly' shell, was to prove insignificant compared with what lay in front of him now.

The attack was launched at 19.10 on 28 June under cover of the usual shell barrage, and Smart, with Lieutenant Currie as observer, took off at 19.30 with instructions to call for flares by klaxon horn at 20.00 to find out how the attack was going. He was also to drop messages from Corps Headquarters. 'I did not like the look of the weather as we took off,' he wrote afterwards, 'but of course the job had to be done at all cost.'

At about 19.50 the storm Smart was expecting broke. 'In a few seconds I was fighting for my life with every muscle and sinew in my body. The gale was like a mighty whirlwind, lightning flashed and rain came down like a deluge, clouds and thick mist came up and blotted out everything. My machine bounded up and down like a mad thing and was quite out of control most of the time. Our job simply had to be done so I dropped down to 400 feet till we could just see the ground . . .' They crept along a road through their own shell barrage, but could not call for flares as they could see nothing.

Six times they flew back and forth along this road, until a break in the mist just as they crossed the lines finally fixed their position – and brought a blizzard of machine-gun fire. 'Currie thumped on his klaxon horn and as if by magic a row of red flares appeared on the ground below us right along the line of our objective. Currie nearly went mad with excitement . . .'

Their next task was to find their pre-arranged dropping stations, where flares would be lit to guide them, drop their messages, and fight their way back to their aerodrome. There they found that the gale had demolished three hangars and the machines inside them and ripped off the roof of the Mess, while a thunderbolt had dug a hole in the aerodrome four feet deep. The ground was so waterlogged that as soon as they came to a standstill their machine sank up to its axles. Amidst general astonishment that they were still in one piece, they were hauled out of their machine, revived with an egg flip (egg, brandy and milk), and driven at breakneck speed to Corps Headquarters to report.

Back at the aerodrome they learned the good news that the commanders at all three dropping stations had telephoned to know if they were all right. The bad news came when the squadron commander, Major E.J. Tyson, asked if they felt equal to doing the same job again in a few hours' time, taking off at 03.45. 'Of course we said "Yes", although personally I felt as if I never wanted to see an aeroplane again . . .' By the time they had calmed down they decided it was too late to go to bed, so they sat up smoking until it was time to go up again. Fortunately the storm had abated and they were able to report that the infantry were still hanging on.

'I got to bed at about 6 a.m. quite exhausted,' wrote Smart. But at nine o'clock they were awakened by an orderly with the message that Gordon Shephard, their brigade commander, wanted to see them. Surely not another show? 'The General was awfully nice and said the usual thing about upholding the honour of the Flying Corps etc.' So all was well. The General Officer Commanding also congratulated them, saying that 50 per cent of the success achieved was due to No. 5 Squadron RFC. Oppy was only a small show, as Smart realised, with limited objectives that were not as it happened attained.

He was told by Major Tyson that he had been recommended for a decoration, but he didn't expect anything to come of it. Personal congratulations also came from the divisional commander, who told Smart that their messages were the only news that came through from the front line that night, that the phone wires were all cut, and that the barrage was so fierce the runners could not get through. The general also recorded his astonishment that a machine could be kept in the air in such weather. Smart's MC came through a fortnight later.

The episode, both in the air and on the ground, was a stark reminder that the summer months, although they might be idyllic at times, as Norman Macmillan recorded, could not always be relied on for campaigning. The weather could sometimes turn nasty. It was a threat, though, that had to be ignored if a major breakthrough was to be attempted that year.

The preliminary bombardment that was due to begin on 8 July was itself delayed, bad weather restricting flying until the 11th. Every delay brought the autumn and winter nearer. Meanwhile Haig, who had not yet received acceptance of his plans from the War Cabinet, was being pressed, as already recorded, to release squadrons for home defence. With nearly a million Allied soldiers crammed into the Ypres salient, the Germans could not but be aware of the impending attack, and they assembled in similar strength. Also based at aerodromes opposite Ypres was the newly-formed Richthofen Circus, a hunting group of four *Jagdstaffels* the essence of which was mobility, individual *staffels* being capable of being switched at short notice to sensitive areas. Richthofen, whose presence at the front had been rated by Ludendorff as 'worth three divisions', had returned in mid-June, and the old magic was beginning to work. The task that faced him was to prevent the RFC from regaining control of the air before the battle commenced.

On the morning of 6 July he was out with his *staffel* when he spotted a formation of FE's. They were fighting FE2d's of 20 Squadron, and they were engaged at once by up to forty German fighters, led by Richthofen. Four Sopwith Tripes of 10 (Naval) Squadron were providing top cover for the FE's and they drove down four of the hostiles without loss to themselves; but although the FE's fought tenaciously they suffered losses, two being shot down and the observer being wounded in a third.

The streamers that denoted the leading FE acted like a magnet to Richthofen, but he was up against a skilful flight commander in Captain Douglas Cunnell and an experienced gunner in Second-Lieutenant A.E. Woodbridge, who had already driven off several challengers. Recognising Richthofen's scarlet Albatros, and knowing he would have no chance against its superior armament if he let it get close, Woodbridge opened fire early in the hope of driving it off. Richthofen had not even flipped off his safety-catch when he was struck by what he would have called a lucky hit on the left side of the head. As the Albatros spun viciously earthwards, Richthofen instinctively switched off his engine to prevent a fire, meanwhile fighting for orientation. Temporarily blinded, he pushed back his goggles, but he was falling through a veil of darkness from which there seemed no escape.

Richthofen had sent so many good men to their deaths that he knew no one was indestructible. But as he gathered up his energies he was suddenly conscious of light and shade, and finally of colour. He was down to 2,500 feet, but his comrades were protecting him from further indignity and he managed to get his Albatros down. He was still barely conscious when they rushed him to hospital. The wound refused to heal quickly, and this put him out of the reckoning for a few weeks at least, during which the struggle for air supremacy over the battlefield would be fought. If Woodbridge's hit was a fluke, it was a significant one.

Six days later, on 12 July, as the weather cleared, air activity of an unprecedented intensity developed over the Ypres front. Although the Allies had a numerical advantage, the Germans were doubling and trebling the strength of individual formations, and British casualties were inevitable. Among them was Douglas Cunnell, whose gunner (Lieutenant Albert Bill, not Woodbridge this time) got an Albatros before flying the FE2d back to base when Cunnell was killed. Yet German losses generally exceeded the British. Enemy pilots thought twice before crossing the Allied lines, but the RFC's overall task, as at Messines, of keeping the skies clear for the corps machines, and denying reconnaissance access to the enemy, had yet to be achieved.

In pursuit of the desired ascendancy, an air battle was fought on 26 July near Polygon Wood, five miles east of Ypres and two miles behind the lines. A typically massive German hunting formation was matched by an equal number of RFC single-seaters, so that an estimated ninety-four fighting machines became locked in combat at various levels. The *casus belli* was a flight of German two-seaters, lurking on the German side at 5,000 feet, waiting for an opportunity to cross the lines and reconnoitre the Ypres area. Three thousand feet above them, thirty protective Albatros scouts were being challenged by seven of the new DH5's, tractor replacements for the outmoded DH2 pushers. Five thousand feet above them in turn, ten Albatros scouts were fighting off thirty British scouts of various types. Higher still, up to 17,000 feet, seven naval Triplanes were slugging it out with another ten Albatros scouts. None of these exchanges, however, was decisive, but the engagement must be accounted a defeat for the British. While they were absorbed in the mêlée, four of the German two-seaters sneaked across the lines and completed their reconnaissance.

More successful was a deliberate enticement the following day in the same area, when eight of the FE2d's of 20 Squadron crossed the lines in close formation to set a trap for the Circus, to be sprung by a posse of avenging fighters drawn from British squadrons within reach. It was typical of the self-confidence of the crews of this pusher squadron that they embraced the idea with enthusiasm. Circling nose to tail as was their wont for mutual protection, they held off a swarm of some twenty Albatros scouts while simultaneously luring them towards the fighters. SE5A's and Triplanes both scored victories, more than offsetting their own losses, but the day was won by the FE crews themselves. Mounting three Lewis guns to a machine, two for the observer and one for the pilot, they claimed six hostiles destroyed, with some justification. Two were seen to go down in flames, a third broke up in mid-air, and three more crashed, while the only casualties sustained by the FE's were a wounded pilot and observer.

[333]

Slowly the squadrons were recovering from 'Bloody April' and all it entailed. The Australian Francis Penny, whose pilot training had been interrupted when he had been shanghaied to help fill empty cockpits on 12 Squadron as an observer ('I've just come from there,' an informant had told him, 'I reckon you'll last about six weeks'), had lasted long enough to be sent back eventually to England to complete his pilot training. He had just about qualified when another urgent appeal, this time for pilots, sent him scurrying back, again to 12 Squadron. In his absence, RE8's had replaced the BE's, and this was not the only change: the array of new faces was daunting. Yet in many ways life with the RFC in France continued to be comparatively luxurious.

No. 12 Squadron had a new commander, Major C.S. Burnett, who was accustomed to having a whisky and milk before breakfast. The milk had to be fresh, not condensed. Penny, reckoned, as an Australian, to be accustomed to cattle, got the job of acquiring a squadron cow, and after fitting up a vehicle as a cattle truck he began scouring the countryside. Eventually he found a farmer willing to sell a likely looking animal. A nearby cavalry regiment provided suitable fodder, and an airman who admitted to having worked on a farm was appointed cattleman and milkmaid. Fresh milk in the Mess was much appreciated – and the major got his whisky and milk.

Meanwhile the Germans, copying the night bombing of their aerodromes by the FE2b's of 100 Squadron, reciprocated in kind, sometimes with dire results. But at 12 Squadron the only casualty was the cow, which was reported missing. Very sensibly, she had decided to make her way back to the more peaceful atmosphere of the farm. Next morning Penny remounted the cattle-truck, and he and the airman/farmer set off in pursuit. They found the cow grazing happily by the roadside, and with some difficulty persuaded her back into the truck.

A contrast which the infantry did not have to endure was that between the summer temperatures at ground level and the cold at higher altitudes. Frank Ransford, commissioned in 1914, was another recruit from the trenches, and by July 1917, after transferring, he was posted as an observer to FE2b's. He tells of reporting for orders on summer mornings in full flying kit – thigh boots, lambswool leather coats, fur caps, mouthpieces, goggles and scarves, essential protection in open cockpits, but unbearably sweaty on the ground. Not all transferred infantrymen took kindly at first to the vertiginous peculiarities of the FE, but Ransford settled quickly. 'I take my seat in the front edge of the nacelle, facing my pilot, as I am responsible that no one dives on our tail . . . I sit there as easily and comfortably as if I am sitting in a deck chair.' Perched right on the edge of the nacelle at 100 miles an hour at perhaps 12,000 feet, anchored to nothing, holding on to nothing, he experienced no fear of falling out. Every succeeding flight made him feel more at home and increased his confidence in pilot and machine. But for all his care with guns and ammunition, he was under no illusions about the FE's vulnerability, and spoke of 'the joyful sight of an escort', seldom granted.

Yet another recruit from the infantry, Lieutenant A.D. Light, had seen the army order that all RFC applications must be forwarded, whether recommended or not, and he told his brigadier his nerve would fail him if he stayed in the trenches much longer. It was an escape route for officers that was rarely available for other ranks. The brigadier knew his man and gave him a good report, and although he was told he was too old at twenty-six, he joined 48 Squadron under Zulu Bettington that summer as an observer, after a spell at the School of Aerial Gunnery at Hythe. Within a week of his leaving the line his replacement was killed, and he was lucky, too, in joining 48 Squadron. Although said to be too old in 1917, he flew as an air gunner in flying boats more than twenty years later in the Second World War.

10

THE PRANKS OF SIBLEY AND SHONE

N o. 48 was a truly remarkable squadron. After its disastrous start, it had quickly acquired a reputation commensurate with its status as the first Bristol Fighter squadron. Besides the inimitable Zulu Bettington, the three flight commanders were all distinguished in their way. New Zealander Keith Park, at 25, was described by contemporaries as 'like a Greek god', and he was revered by those who flew with and alongside him; but he might perhaps be said to have his greatest days to come, as AOC 11 Group in the Battle of Britain. Brian Baker, then just 20, and dubbed by contemporaries, for reasons now obscure, 'the corporal-major', also had a brilliant career ahead of him. But of the third flight commander, Samuel Sibley, 'Squibs', as he was known, it might be said that, even among the giants of 48 Squadron, he was something special. As for his nineteen-year-old observer, P.N.M. 'Puggy' Shone, he was incomparable.

Haig's plan for developing his campaign inland from the Belgian coast, once the Roulers–Thourout railway link was in Allied hands, meant the transfer of a number of squadrons to support the British Fourth Army in that area, and one of these squadrons was No. 48. Already suffering from shell shock, Shone, as an infantryman, had re-applied for the RFC in the spring of 1917, directly he heard that anyone who had been turned down on minor medical grounds and still wanted to transfer could do so. Shone had slightly defective vision in one eye. 'Sorry I can't give you a choice between pilot and observer,' he was told in France by a certain Major H.O.D. Segrave, later to be associated with speed records on land and water, 'but we're very short of observers, so that's what you'll have to be.' 'I don't mind,' replied the accommodating Shone, 'as long as I get in.'

Returning to England to report with eighteen others to the Gunnery School at Hythe, he was thrown around in an Armstrong-Whitworth FK8 'Big Ack' for ten minutes, only keeping in by holding on to the Scarff Ring. Of the eighteen trainees, nine were lifted out after their ordeal in an appalling state of air sickness and returned to their units. But not Shone. He was posted to 48 Squadron. Park's regular observer was on leave, so for a time Shone flew with him ('a delightful man,' was his verdict). When Park's observer returned, Sibley, on Park's recommendation, asked for Shone.

Sibley had joined 24 Squadron in its early days at Hounslow under Hawker and served with him in France – a worthy apprenticeship – until a crash, in August 1916, interrupted his career. To Puggy Shone, he seemed out to make up for lost time.

Sitting back to back in a Brisfit, with no artificial aids to intercommunication, pilot and observer had to have an understanding, and Sibley and Shone worked out their own code of taps and signs for various tactical situations, so that eventually they became instinctive. They soon became not merely close friends but, in Shone's words, 'an absolute team'. Sibley taught Shone how to handle the Brisfit, lest he be incapacitated. 'Come on, Puggy,' he would say, returning from a patrol, 'you take over.' Shone eventually turned down the chance of a pilot's course to stay with Sibley.

The main job of a Brisfit squadron at that time was the offensive patrol, and in the summer of 1917 they would be off the floor by 4 a.m. and formed up at about 14,000 feet by the time they reached the line, when they started looking for trouble. 'We nearly always got it, within a very short time.'

They were doing a daily average that summer of one long OP and one short OP, the former involving a penetration of about twenty miles, the latter about five. The average life of a pilot/observer combination, during the fighting in May/June/July for what was euphemistically known as air supremacy, was twenty hours. Before their partnership was broken, Sibley and Shone had done 150. Long before then, according to Shone, the RFC, with the help of the RNAS, had regained the ascendancy.

'We knew exactly what we would do in any and every dogfight,' boasted Shone. But he admitted that he had very little recollection of what actually happened. Two bangs on the back of Sibley's flying helmet was Shone's signal that he had spotted hostiles. Sibley then led his flight into the best possible position for attack, and when Shone fired a red light, it was every man for himself.

Team work was the main but not the only factor. Armament for the Bristol was a Vickers for the pilot firing through the propeller arc and a Lewis for the observer; later a second Lewis was fitted. Shone angled his second Lewis at approximately 45 degrees to the ground, as it often happened when they met an enemy formation that two hostiles would dive together at their tail, the first firing from about the same level, the second continuing the dive until he attacked from somewhere below. Shone found he just had time to fire at the one coming straight for him and almost simultaneously loose off a burst at the chap underneath. By loading his guns – they all filled their own drums – with tracer he made sure the hostiles could see they were being fired at. It had a most salutary effect.

Something of the temperaments of these two men may perhaps be gauged from their nicknames. They had no illusions, but they enjoyed themselves, off duty and on. Grounded because of the weather, they went into nearby Dunkirk for a meal and some shopping. Sibley stopped by a fruit stall. 'Look, Puggy, I've got an idea. All those blasted Huns who sit out on the promenade at Ostend with their girl friends – I really don't think we can allow that to go on.' It was a scene they had glimpsed many times as they photographed the coastline to prepare for the amphibious landing that was planned. 'Let's get a big bag of oranges, and one day when we've got some broken cloud on the way back from a show, we'll come down nice and low over Ostend and throw these oranges at them. What do you think?' 'Squibs,' said Shone, 'it's a brilliant idea!'

Within a few days the conditions were favourable, the oranges were ripe, perhaps a shade over-ripe, and Sibley came down to fifty feet parallel with the promenade. Rows of Germans and their girl friends were socialising happily when suddenly Shone stood up and began hurling oranges at their feet, one after another as fast as he could. 'We watched these chaps falling off their chairs, jumping up and rushing into the cafés behind them, their girl friends in pursuit, convinced they were the victims of some frightful new weapon. Why we didn't crash, because we were laughing so much, I really don't know.'

Later they played a similar trick on a German aerodrome. They got hold of an old football, painted it bright red, attached long streamers to it, waited for reasonable cloud cover, and dropped it from 500 feet on a line of Albatros scouts, some with their engines running. Their aim was accurate, the football behaved like a bouncing bomb, and there was a gorgeous moment of chaos as mechanics ran for cover and pilots tried to taxi their aeroplanes clear. It would have been easy enough to give them a few bursts with a machine gun for luck – but that would have spoiled the joke.

Chivalry, according to Shone, was not quite dead: messages dropped in metal canisters asking the fate of missing men nearly always got a reply, dropped from machines sent over at maximum height. And there was still at least one pilot/observer combination too squeamish to shoot down a machine in cold blood. On their way back from a show, in broken cloud, Sibley and Shone, to their amazement, saw an unarmed enemy two-seater training machine emerging sedately from the sanctuary of cloud, pilot and instructor looking in the opposite direction, completely oblivious to their peril. 'I tapped Squibs, but he kept on an absolutely level course. He made a gesture, and I knew what he meant. It was our duty to shoot the plane down, but we couldn't do it.'

The same thing happened again a few days later, only this time the German crew had got lost over the Allied lines. 'Sibley motioned them down and we landed at our own aerodrome with our capture. We gave the crew a jolly good lunch and plenty to drink before notifying wing headquarters.'

It was not that life on this part of the front was significantly easier than elsewhere. Photographing the whole coastline from Nieuport to Ostend and beyond had been a major and precarious task, quite apart from their offensive patrols. Confidence in their machine and in each other was a part of it, but their keen sense of the ridiculous did not always protect them from fear. 'There was no tour of duty,' noted Shone. 'You went on until you'd had it. You did not admit to your closest friends that you'd got to the point where you doubted if you could go on.'

Early in September Sibley's flight was involved in a tremendous scrap. Two Brisfits were lost and Sibley's machine was in a sorry state, main spars splintered, ailerons, rudder and elevator damaged, engine running roughly. Only superb handling by Sibley got them back. As they passed Ostend and neared the trenches Sibley alerted Shone and pointed down, indicating that, once they had crossed the lines, he would have to attempt a landing on the beach. On touching down the fixed undercarriage collapsed and the Brisfit somersaulted, finally coming to rest upside down. 'I undid my safety belt,' said Shone, 'turned on my back and undid Squibs's belt for him, and he gently slid out.' Bruised and bludgeoned, they crawled away and sat exhausted on the beach. 'Sibley then made one of the absolutely classic remarks of World War I. "You know, Puggy", he said, "the trouble with this war is that it's so bloody dangerous."'

Not surprisingly, the crash reactivated Shone's shell shock. His older brother Geoffrey, a pilot on 56 Squadron, was killed on 19 October, and he realised that his nerve had gone. He was reduced to instructing his batman, when calling him for the early morning long OP, to wake him up with two stiff whiskies. 'Without them I wouldn't like to think what I might have done.' Soon afterwards, in another fierce engagement, their machine was crippled again, and they had barely crossed no man's land when they crashed. Under fire at first from all sides, they were rescued by one of their own batteries. Sibley recovered quickly but Shone spent the next ten months in hospital and convalescing. On 14 February 1918, with a new observer, Sibley was shot down and taken prisoner, but both men survived the war.

*　　　*　　　*

Less spectacular, but still of prime importance, was the work of the corps machines. Lieutenant John Theophilus Percival Jeyes joined 21 Squadron on RE8's on his nineteenth birthday, 3 June 1917. The experienced observer he was given to get him started was soon posted home, to be replaced by a beginner, Second-Lieutenant M.L. Hatch; they soon discovered that they were both old boys of Oundle School. Maurice Hatch was the senior by several years and had actually been Jeyes' school prefect, but he gave Jeyes great encouragement by showing confidence in him and acknowledging him as skipper. 'We soon found that we could work together in the air,' wrote Jeyes, 'which was a great thing for us both.' Jeyes believed that boys from an engineering school like Oundle had a better chance of coping with the practical side of aviation than boys from the more illustrious colleges. (Against this, the record of Old Etonians in the RFC seems exceptional.)

The routine of artillery cooperation remained much the same, with wireless playing a much larger part than in the early days. After their various pre-flight checks and procedures came the task of getting airborne from their small airfield, with Jeyes holding the machine down low over the grass and pulling up swiftly to avoid the hop poles beyond. Even near the front line, French peasants were always at work. Jeyes would then circle while Hatch unwound the trailing aerial and made a check call to the wireless station on the aerodrome. If he reeled out the aerial too quickly it would snap, and they would have to land to repair or replace it – a tricky procedure when they had bombs on board, as they often had. The work of fixing the aerial would take about fifteen minutes, and then they would have all their pre-flight checks and procedures – and the take-off – to go through again. It would then take about an hour, with the loads they carried, to get to 7,000 feet.

On the way to the lines they would start calling the battery they were to work with, and the battery would put out ground strips to acknowledge that they were ready for action. For the next hour or more they would be monitoring and directing the battery's fire, which meant continual manoeuvring of the machine so they could see the battery's shells bursting. So absorbed did they become in their work

[341]

that they sometimes forgot how vulnerable they were, and reminders from Hun machines and Archie could shock them into sudden awareness. But thanks to the fighting squadrons, and to their own growing competence, the two ex-Oundle schoolboys continued to work successfully together. 'We used to think we were being overworked,' wrote Jeyes, 'especially after Dawn Patrols and two other patrols in the same day, lasting approximately three hours each patrol and usually getting attacked by Hun aircraft, and always ack-ack at us when we were photographing enemy lines and unloading 25 lb bombs on them . . .

'When flying in formation, and one [machine] is shot down and the others left, it is really frightening to carry on . . . But one soon forgot one's fears and got busy with immediate problems.' They survived all vicissitudes, mostly together, for the rest of that summer and far into the autumn and winter, being posted home at last in January 1918, the only known instance of a team of Old Boys 'Playing for the School'.[1]

Before the end of July 1917, two more squadrons, Nos 11 and 22, had completed conversion from FE2b's to Bristol Fighters, and 70 Squadron had swapped their Sopwith two-seaters for the first of the RFC's Sopwith Camels. Although the Camel was inferior in speed and rate of climb to some of the later German models, the gyroscopic forces produced by its 130 hp Clerget rotary engine gave it an ability to flip round to the right with an extraordinary turn of speed and complete a full circle while other machines were turning only 90 degrees, disconcerting for enemy pilots to say the least. Everyone loved the Camel once they had mastered its peculiarities, but it remained, in essence, 'a fierce little beast'. A switch in training from an Avro to a Camel could be altogether too abrupt, resulting in many accidents, and not until the cockpit of trainer Camels was modified in 1918 to take an instructor behind the pupil was the death rate among the latter reduced.

Meanwhile the new machines had played their part in redressing

1. Maurice Hatch also flew frequently with Second-Lieutenant Basil E. Catchpole, MC, DFC, later a flight commander on this Squadron.

the imbalance of March, April, May and June, so that the Fifth Army was able to record by the end of July that the enemy 'has shown less individual activity and does not cross our line as often as he used to'. The large formations in which he had begun operating had been repeatedly repulsed, nearly always on the enemy side of the lines, while counter-battery work, supported by air reconnaissance, had actually caused a further postponement of the battle, because the enemy had been forced to withdraw many of his batteries and time was needed for our own forces to adjust. Haig knew well enough that the establishment of ascendancy in the air was a vital contribution to the battles ahead, and on 28 July he passed his 'very hearty appreciation' and 'best congratulations' to Trenchard. Three days later he began his Flanders offensive.

11

THE THIRD BATTLE OF YPRES: 'ALL
FOR TWO SHILLINGS A DAY'

AIG'S attack, aimed north-east from the Ypres salient by
Gough's Fifth Army on a front of seven and a half miles,
with the French First Army on his left and Plumer's Second
Army on his right, opened at dawn on 31 July, the British Government having finally approved Haig's plans on the 20th. The results
of the first day's fighting were encouraging, much of the first German
defence system being overrun, but the pre-arranged plan for RFC
cooperation was negated by low cloud and rain. The problems of
the air observers were exacerbated by the infantry's failure to light
flares when requested by klaxon horn to do so, and many corps
machines were hit and put out of action through crews having to
sweep over at low level to try to identify uniforms. Fifty-eight contact
patrols were flown in the course of the day by the corps squadrons,
and only by dogged persistence did they succeed in keeping pace
with the general progress of the attack.

Typical of their tenacity were the crews of the RE8's of No. 6
Squadron. The pilot of the machine entrusted with the initial patrol
was killed, and the observer of the relief plane was wounded. The
long-stop detailed was a newcomer, Second-Lieutenant Nicholas W.
Wadham, for whom this was his first experience of action. His Canadian observer, Harry Quigley, wore the ribbons of the Distinguished
Conduct Medal and the Military Cross, but these awards had been

won first as a private in the Canadian Infantry and second as an officer with the Canadian Engineers, and his experience as an observer was less impressive. Wadham set off in some trepidation, but at least his observer was likely to be cool under fire.

With cloud down to 500 feet over the battlefield they had to fly under it, and they had been over the lines no more than minutes when an 18 lb shell drilled what Wadham called 'a perfectly neat hole' through the peak top of his engine cowling. Understandably, he was 'extremely frightened', but the reaction of his battle-hardened observer astounded him: he 'appeared to think it was the best joke in the world'. Totally unconcerned, he rallied Wadham and actually kept him over the lines for another two hours, giving him agonies of suspense but teaching him an operational equanimity he might never otherwise have acquired, and they came back with a valuable report. 'I gradually came to see the affair', noted the chastened Wadham, 'more from his point of view. That shell', he concluded, 'must have gone right through the prop without touching it and then over the top plane, for nothing was hit except the cowling.' It was a bizarre example of reverse synchronisation. 'No wonder Quigley thought it funny.'

The army squadrons, too, were impeded by the weather, and the patrols they attempted proved abortive. They reverted to bombing and harrying aerodromes and communications centres. This change of tactics, dictated by the conditions, was anticipated only just in time, fighting squadrons being up most of the previous night fitting improvised bomb-racks and 25 lb bombs, generally four to a machine, with little idea what the result might be to the airworthiness of the machines. The Spad pilots were spared the gamble because it was found impractical to fit bomb-racks to their machines, but not so the pilots of the newly delivered SE5A's, who found themselves, with much misgiving, putting the experiment to the test in battle.

Few matched the verve and aggression at any time of the head-strong Lieutenant R.A. 'Dick' Maybery, of 56 Squadron. Twenty-two years old and a native of Brecon, he had begun the war in the cavalry and was known as a dead shot. His combat report for this opening day has been widely quoted. Taking off at 04.45, Maybery crossed the lines at 500 feet 'underneath very thick clouds', just as Wadham had done. The smoke from the artillery barrage made it impossible to see ahead, so he steered south-east and came down to 200 and then to 30 feet. Sighting Courtrai, he headed for the Circus aerodrome at Heule, but was spotted and attacked by two Albatros scouts. He tried to frighten them off with a few gun-bursts, but combat, in his heavily loaded machine, had to be avoided. He saw a Spad machine-gunning a ground target that was invisible to him, suddenly realised he was alone, sighted Courtrai again in improving visibility, found the aerodrome at Heule, zoomed to 200 feet, and circled the 'drome to pick his spot. 'I then flew east, turned and came back along the line of the southernmost sheds and dropped my first bomb, which hit the third shed from the east and exploded. This caused immense excitement . . .' Turning first to the left, he flew along the line of the easternmost sheds and dropped another bomb, which hit the first shed from the south and exploded. He next flew straight at the sheds at the town end of the aerodrome and dropped his third bomb, which went through either the roof or the door of another of the sheds: he could see smoke, and he felt and heard the explosion.

He had one more bomb to drop, and as he came near, approaching this time from the north, a machine-gunner opened up at him from the rear of the sheds. He pulled the bomb release, but nothing happened. He was still looking for the explosion when he found his bombing run had taken him close to the railway station at Courtrai. This seemed a worthwhile target and he pulled the bomb release again, hopefully. This time the bomb fell away and exploded between a goods train and a shed.

He had no bombs left, but he was not quite finished with Heule aerodrome. The same machine-gunner fired at him, and another whom he could not locate, but he silenced the former, and the latter evidently thought it best not to reveal his position. He then flew twice across the aerodrome, so low the second time that he actually brushed the ground with his wheels as he fired both guns at the sheds.

Incredibly, he was still not finished. Flying straight on to Cuerne, another Circus aerodrome, he machine-gunned the sheds before attacking, as opportunity targets, two military-looking horsemen, witnessing their dishevelment when their horses bolted. An attack with both guns on a column of infantry 200 strong scattered them to the verges of a road, and after changing drums he attacked them again. Sighting a German two-seater at 200 feet, he zoomed without being seen and shot it down, seeing it crash. 'Only one man got out.' Not until he ran out of ammunition for the Lewis, and the Vickers jammed, did he recross the lines and return.

Many other pilots reported similar experiences, among their targets being aerodromes, transport and troops. In giving their own troops a helping hand, three pilots and one observer were killed, two two-man crews were shot down and taken prisoner, and the pilots and observers of four more crews escaped with wounds. Despite the conditions, twenty-three combats were recorded and eight victories claimed.

Yet Trenchard's doctrine of the offensive, and his constant theme that the aeroplane was not a defensive weapon, was still not fully understood by army commanders, or by their subordinates, who did not appreciate the RFC's achievements in depth because they could rarely see them, and they called for local protection whenever a strafing German intruder appeared. Trenchard was obliged to pre-pare a paper for circulation among the General Staff clarifying the role and limitations of the aeroplane in battle.

Haig's remark to Trenchard, before the Battle of Neuve Chappelle in March 1915, that 'If you can't fly because of the weather I shall probably put off the attack', suggests that the 1917 Flanders offensive might never have been begun if the weather in the remainder of that summer could have been foreseen. 31 July had been bad enough, but the first four days of August were marred by continual rain, stormy and unsettled conditions followed, and counter-battery work, reconnaissance, and all forms of patrolling, on which the ground forces now relied so heavily, were impeded if not choked altogether. The battle area, already churned up by the preliminary bombardment and with its drainage systems mutilated, turned, in the words of Haig's subsequent despatch, into 'a succession of vast muddy pools. The valleys of the choked and overflowing streams were speedily transformed into long stretches of bog, impassable except for a few well-defined tracks, which became marks for the enemy's artillery.' For the Allied soldier, to leave these tracks was to court death by drowning, a fate that befell men and pack animals alike. 'In these conditions,' as Haig himself wrote, 'operations of any magnitude became impossible.' The fine weather that Haig relied on for the ground to recover came too little and too late, and the succession of minor battles of the next few months developed into a war of attritional slaughter. Nearly all the ground gained was eventually lost, the prior condition of the capture of the Roulers–Thourout rail link for the opening of the Nieuport offensive was never fulfilled, the main German line was not even reached, and criticism of Haig for persisting right through to November has since been widespread. Meanwhile the RFC, still an integral part of the Army, fought and suffered with it.

Pilots whose patrols were rendered sterile by the weather usually sought to contribute something positive by coming down low on the return flight to strafe enemy trenches. This form of harassment was becoming routine, but the crews, too, were vulnerable. Alan Dore records how men in the Allied trenches witnessed the end of a Sopwith two-seater of his squadron, No. 43; they saw the tail come off and the observer either jump or fall out. Dore motored out to the front next day to recover the bodies. 'We buried their poor mangled remains amid the desultory shell-fire that always greets you near the trenches.' The pilot's name was Second-Lieutenant L.A. McPherson, and his observer, or more accurately gunner, was a second-class air mechanic named Frederick Webb, another two-shillings-a-day volunteer. A study of squadron records reveals how vital to the work of the RFC these largely anonymous and unhonoured volunteers were.

The same squadron, still under Dore, and still waiting for their Camels, registered – despite heavy losses – a remarkable success in mid-August in a subsidiary attack on Hill 70, near Lens, before the Ypres operations proper were resumed. After the night and day bombing of aerodrome and communications targets on 13 and 14 August by Armstrong-Whitworths, Martinsydes and DH4's, Dore noted: 'Tomorrow [15 August] is the day of the attack. For several days past we have been preparing for it. I attend the conference at Canadian Corps Headquarters [First Army] ... We are to try to spot counter-attacks and send out machines to fire at troops from the air.'

Dore took off with the rest of his squadron for an advanced landing ground at 04.45 next morning, his crews being employed all day in groups of three at a time, watching the zone through which the enemy must pass to counter-attack. Their brief was to look for movements, to machine-gun any congestion of enemy infantry, to engage enemy artillery, and to attack any intruding enemy aeroplanes. Dore could see at once that the attack was going well, but he could also see several of his machines on the ground, 'two having evidently collided'. He landed and managed to recruit a doctor for the injured men. Of the rest of his squadron he recorded that one of his flight commanders, Captain Collier, had had his fuel tank perforated but had got home on his gravity tank with a wounded observer; Hood had dived at and fired on some enemy guns; Veitch after many adventures had strafed a battalion, a battery, and various smaller groups; and best of all, an observer named Croll, flying with a Lieutenant Thompson, had identified the signs of an enemy counter-attack. This, believed Dore, was the RFC's first success of this kind. The bad news was that 'Maplestone returned wounded in the foot; Hargreaves made a good landing but died a few minutes later; Moore and Snelgrove did not return.' Both, it transpired, had been killed.

These casualties, in the words of a First Army report, 'were slight in comparison with the value of the work done by the squadron'. Eighteen flights, at 1,000 feet or under, were flown by 43 Squadron that day and a total of 5,000 rounds fired, an enemy two-seater was destroyed in combat, and a pilot named Gedge, attacked by twelve single-seaters, drove one down out of control. The outstanding success was the frustration of the enemy counter-attack. The General Officer Commanding First Army thanked Dore personally, and

Trenchard wired his congratulations. Soon afterwards Dore went on leave, his first for four months. 'Very glad to get away after the strain of the last few days.'

Other squadrons successful that day included No. 40, still flying Nieuports and operating from the same advanced landing ground as No. 43; their orders were to go up in pursuit of low-flying enemy machines that had been sighted and reported by wireless from one of the strategically placed observation stations. One of their flight commanders, recently promoted and awarded the MC, was Mick Mannock. Two of the hostiles were destroyed, three shot down out of control, and many others were damaged or driven off. It was directly attributable to the work of 43 and 40 Squadrons that the corps machines remained unmolested all day.

The RE8's of 16 Squadron, now under Peter Portal, DSO, MC, also earned high praise, first for their work in engaging hostile batteries and infantry concentrations, secondly for providing up-to-date photographs of the enemy lines, and thirdly for their contact patrols. 'Perfect liaison was maintained and we were instantly informed of the situation.'

The main battle that ensued on the Ypres front – of Langemarck, as it was known – failed in its objective, but the RFC bombed their targets successfully, strafed enemy troops remorselessly and recorded movements accurately. RE8 crews particularly distinguished themselves, the counter-battery work of No. 9 Squadron standing up exceptionally well to subsequent analysis, while the observers of 7 and 21 Squadrons showed no fear of interfering Albatros scouts, destroying two and possibly three on the first day without loss to themselves.

It was an RE8 crew – of 59 Squadron – who were called upon, at seven o'clock on the evening of 18 August, to register a vital target for a siege battery, at a point where the enemy wire defences had been insufficiently cut, holding up the advance. This particular crew, like many others, had taken time to settle down, mutual appreciation only coming from experience of each other in action. On their first flight together, the pilot had actually reported his observer, through a misunderstanding, for failing to open fire. 'As we taxied across the aerodrome,' wrote observer Lieutenant Richard F. Sheraton, 'the pin on the left wheel sheared through and the wheel came off just as we were leaving the ground.' Sheraton saw it happen and warned his pilot, Lieutenant John A. Craig, but the reaction of both men was the same. 'It was vitally important that the shoot should be proceeded with, since dusk was approaching and there would be no further opportunity that day.'

After a successful shoot – the area was captured next morning – Craig and Sheraton returned to face what seemed a certain crash landing. Twice Craig circled the aerodrome in preparation, giving time for the assembly of an anxious but ghoulish crowd. 'The whole personnel of the squadron appeared on the aerodrome,' wrote Sheraton, 'since the RE8 was notoriously nose-heavy and prone to catching fire.'

Darkness was falling as they approached, heightening the drama. 'I felt our sole remaining wheel touch terra firma, and everything went quite smoothly until the axle dropped and cut into the soil. Immediately this happened, the whole world appeared to turn upside down and the plane went over on its back.' There was no fire, and both men scrambled out unhurt, but they had given the ghouls a run for their money.

'On 30 August,' concluded Sheraton, 'our Brigade sent a letter in acknowledgement of the work which Craig and I did on the 18th, when we continued our flight to range the enemy guns after losing a wheel taking off.'

12

'THE OBSERVERS OUT HERE ARE VERY PLUCKY CHAPS'

Captain Leslie Horridge, No. 7 Squadron

T HE shortage of experienced observers, mainly because of their vulnerability in combat, was often acute, and those who volunteered to fill vacancies inevitably took time to adjust. 'Starting out one morning with a new observer who had only that day arrived at the squadron,' wrote Brisfit pilot Frank Ransley of 48 Squadron, 'we had no sooner crossed the lines when we met an unusually heavy barrage of anti-aircraft fire which took me all my time to dodge. As soon as I had a chance I looked round to the back seat to see how my new observer was taking things. He was on the floor in a faint.'

Turning back to base with the idea of getting a seasoned replacement, Ransley felt a tap on the shoulder from a still pallid observer who was nevertheless pointing eastwards, anxious to redeem himself. 'Once more the anti-aircraft fire let us have it,' recorded Ransley. 'I looked round and the poor chap had fainted again. This time I took him right back to the aerodrome.'

Either the man was unsuited to aerial warfare, decided Ransley, or he should have been given his baptism of fire by degrees. Had it not been for the disproportionate casualty rate of observers, no doubt he would have been. 'I always had great sympathy and admiration for the observers in two-seaters,' Ransley wrote later. 'They not only had to face the perils of war but also the possibility of having to put up with the vagaries of a bad pilot.' This particular volunteer left the squadron the same day – without, according to Ransley, having unpacked his kit.[1]

From the earliest days, preparation for the specialist role of observer was patchy, and recruitment came mostly from volunteer infantry and gunnery officers already serving with their regiments at the front. Opportunities to transfer to the RFC were advertised, and the rule was that all applications must be forwarded to Headquarters. The chance to fly, and to escape from the Flanders mud, were among the attractions. Many of the aces started their careers in this way. They found the work frightening initially but intensely rewarding, particularly when cooperating with the artillery, giving them the satisfying feeling that they were assisting in hitting back at the Hun.

One might have thought that Archie would hold few terrors for men who had experienced bombardment in the trenches, but Leslie Horridge, who had faced both, did not agree. 'In an aeroplane there is always the feeling that it is a personal matter. They are not firing at a line of trenches but at you.' Sergeant-Observer H.G. Taylor had made a similar point. 'In the trenches you face death every second, not knowing when it might come . . . In the air you could see death coming.'

Highlander Jock Andrews had progressed from regimental officer to observer before becoming a pilot on DH2's with Hawker. Even as an observer he had relished the relaxed discipline and easy cama-raderie of squadron life; but for him, as for many others, this did not compensate for the feeling of inferiority inherent in the relative status of pilot and observer. There was no formal training for observers until 1917, such training as was offered was sketchy, and there was no career structure; for men like Andrews it was simply a step towards becoming a pilot. Promotion was negligible, the pay was less than that of the most recently arrived pilot, and decorations and mentions in despatches for observers were rare. The ironic conse-quence, as it seemed to Andrews, was that as soon as an observer became really proficient he went off to train as a pilot.

1. Frank Cecil Ransley, OBE, DFC, *Croix de Guerre*. He died in December 1992.

The meagre training available to observers meant that they learned their trade the hard way, in action over the lines. The coveted 'brevet' had to be earned. Once earned it could not be forfeited: it virtually amounted to a decoration. Robert Ingram, who had had a year in the trenches, completed 62 hours' flying before he was graded as a qualified observer and could proudly put up the half-wing. Ten flights over the lines was an absolute minimum, according to D.R. Goudie, in addition to the passing of various tests, the most important being a 'practical', under the critical eye of the brigade machine-gun specialist. Like pilots they enjoyed no simulated training, and many probationary observers didn't live long enough to qualify. 'We went up with an experienced pilot,' wrote E.D.G. 'Ted' Galley, 'and that's all the instruction we got.'

Some men felt perfectly at home almost immediately. After his first trip up the line, with a pilot named Cooper, Bob Ingram wrote to his family in Wimbledon, 'I can't tell you how I loved it. With a man like Cooper one feels as safe as in a bath chair on Wimbledon Common.' But he would not always have the admirable Cooper for a driver. Others acclimatised less readily. Quartered over the lines by ugly black clusters of Archie, they panicked. Airsickness, too, was a problem, causing some to be sent straight back to their regiments.

There was a reversal of roles when an observer became more settled: he would be expected to accompany a new pilot to the lines and familiarise him with the topography. Sometimes the new man would be apprehensive, sometimes over-confident. On one such indoctrination, according to Galley, the following conversation took place.

'What's that over there?'

'That's a Hun.'

'Good – that's what we're after!'

And the newcomer, determined to start his career in spectacular style, made straight for it. Nothing Galley could do would stop him. Fortunately it was only a harmless two-seater, which soon sheared off.

If Galley thought over-confidence was the worst fault, he changed his mind when a new pilot proved too nervous to take evasive action, flying dead straight with a Hun on their tail. Twice Galley was shot down in this way. The second time he was injured, but it got him home on a pilot's course.

Other recruits from within the BEF were the volunteer rankers, mostly air mechanics, whose extra two shillings a day was doubled to four shillings when they were graded 'proficient'. (Officers got a flat daily rate of flying pay of eight shillings.) A few of these men, McCudden among them, graduated to pilot, and many were decorated, but here again there was no career structure, and the prospects of advancement were poor. Yet neither corps nor army squadrons could have functioned without them. Charles Smart's diary entries are full of commendations of these men, and their casualty rate was high.

Recruits from the UK were often snatched from pilot training to fill empty observer cockpits. At the School of Aerial Gunnery at Hythe, they were liable to be handled roughly. O.L. Beater, a captain in the Royal Dublin Fusiliers, was scandalised by the slackness of discipline in the RFC, volunteers doing much as they liked when not flying. Many of them were 'noisy and obscene, their minds and language at an extremely low ebb'. When Beater's turn came for a trial flight, the pilot did his best to make him air-sick. The stench of burnt castor oil and doped fabric was nauseating enough anyway, and soon half his course had been rejected. But Beater qualified, spent many months with Trenchard's bombing force near Nancy, made and lost many good friends, won the DFC, and went home on a pilot's course – to be returned eventually to the artillery as 'hopelessly dud'.

Many of the methods of recruiting observers involved deception. D.R. Goudie, volunteering for pilot, was determined to resist a transfer to observer, but he was told he was medically unfit for pilot because he was long-sighted. He might misjudge his height on landing and possibly kill himself, or wreck the machine, or both. Yet he was also told that after six months in France as an observer he could come home and qualify for his wings. In the course of that six months, it seemed – if he survived it – his long-sightedness would undergo a miraculous cure.

Like Beater, Goudie found much at Hythe to alarm him. One evening in a Folkestone hotel, a popular rendezvous for airmen, he met a man with a Charlie Chaplin moustache and a rubicund nose who got so drunk that he fell down the stairs and they had to put him to bed. Next morning Goudie was horrified to see last night's Chaplinesque drunk, now apparently sober, waiting to take him into the air. At 2,000 feet, without warning of any kind, there was a sudden inrush of air, he felt himself being whirled around helplessly, he was not strapped in, and after hanging on desperately to the bracing wires from inside his seat he felt himself being forced through the floor of the cockpit, or so it seemed, and he waited resignedly for the end. After the landing he asked the pilot if he had been looping the loop and he agreed that he had. Goudie showed commendable understanding. First, the pilot was undoubtedly bored with his job. Secondly, because observers must expect to be thrown all over the sky in a scrap, such risks had to be taken.

The task of observing had originally been rated more important than piloting: one was merely the driver, the other the grand inquisitor and interpreter. In the German Air Force, too, initially, the observer was usually the captain, the pilot an NCO. But in time it was found that in most machines the pilot was better able to position himself correctly, whether for watching the fall of shot when working with the artillery, for the taking of photographs, or for the general exercise of aerial judgement. Thus over the years the observer in most types of machine became little more than a glorified look-out and gunner.

There was one other function that an observer might be called upon to perform, and that was to land the machine when the pilot was incapacitated. 'We always teach the observer something about flying,' wrote John Morris, of 49 Squadron, 'so that if the pilot is knocked out, they can save themselves and perhaps the pilot if he is only wounded.' In some machines there was a spare joystick and rudder control in the observer's cockpit, but this was not universal, and the contortions required to recover control of machines where the pilot had collapsed over the controls were often extreme. Yet there were many occasions when such contortions were successful.

Curiously enough, although more than one pilot was awarded the VC for getting a crippled machine back to the Allied lines and making his report, no such recognition was accorded an observer. No observer received the top award.

If observers came to reflect that it was a pilot's air force, they still had pride in their work and in the confidence placed in them. The tribute to their pluck by Leslie Horridge, paid during the Somme battle, was well deserved. Horridge's sympathies were aroused by the clumsiness of a fellow BE pilot. 'They have to go up with people like my friend of today, and if the machine crashes, they are the people who get it worst.'

Second-Lieutenant J.E.P. Howey, whose force-landing and capture have been related, said: 'I had a fight with two German aeroplanes at 10,000 feet . . . a shell burst very close to us . . . then the aeroplane started to come down head first, spinning all the time.' They were flying in a BE2c, and looking round from the front cockpit Howey saw his pilot, a boy named Claude Kelway Bamber, with a terrible wound in his head, 'quite dead', and realised that the only chance of saving his own life was to step over into Bamber's seat and sit on his lap, where he could reach the controls. 'I managed to get the machine out of that terrible death plunge, switch off the engine, and make a good landing . . . Poor Bamber, he was such a nice boy and only 19.' (According to records he was born in Bengal and was twenty.) Howey had badly damaged an ankle, and after fifteen months as a prisoner he was moved to Switzerland and subsequently repatriated.

Another captured observer who told his story later was Lieutenant W.O. Tudor-Hart, of 22 Squadron (FE2b's). His pilot, Captain G.W. Webb, was wounded when they were attacked by hostiles six miles on the German side of the line. Tudor-Hart was still firing when his pilot collapsed and the FE fell into a dive. He stood up, grabbed the joystick, and turned for home, but from his forward position in the cockpit he couldn't reach the rudder pedals. The machine settled into a steep turn and they lost height, but Tudor-Hart retained enough control to land without injuring himself or his pilot. Sadly Webb died of his wounds.

An unnamed pilot, in an appreciation of an observer named Brown, equally anonymous at first glance, wrote: 'A pilot never feels more lonely than when he is doing a difficult show, and he feels he cannot depend on the man in front of him to be cool and yet quick as a cat in the handling of his gun. One never worried about that sort of thing with Brown.' The Brown named so casually was Arthur Whitten Brown, later to navigate John Alcock across the Atlantic.

One of the most moving tributes was paid by Tommy Traill of an observer named Jones, 'an almost fearless man . . . I never knew his Christian name.' Traill knew absolutely nothing about Jones, where he came from, whether he had a family, what he did when they weren't flying. 'As far as we *did* know each other, we trusted each other completely.' Jones had a hot, potentially violent temper, no great sense of humour, and appeared to have no friends.

They were on a Bristol Fighter squadron, their job was to find and destroy German aircraft, and they never talked of anything but their fighting tactics and how to improve them. But their attachment was strong. 'Jones and I formed the habit, nothing said on either side, of shaking hands when we crossed the lines on the way home after a fight.'

Jones's preparations for a crash-landing in a severely damaged machine, obviously based on experience, involved a drill all his own. 'This was to unship his gun from its mounting and throw it over-board, so that it couldn't fly around and hit either of us. And then to sit down on his little seat facing aft, fold his arms, and relax. He really was a wonderful man.'

On their last flight together, Jones gave Traill the agreed emergency signal for hostile aircraft by tapping him on the top of the head. Traill kicked on left rudder, pushed the stick left and hard forward, and ducked. He heard a stuttering burst, felt a blow on his left shoulder, a bullet scorched past where his head had been a moment earlier, piercing his windscreen, and his controls were damaged. Jones shouted that he had 'got one of them', then suddenly it was over, and Traill coaxed the crippled Bristol back towards the lines. When he looked behind him, Jones was still sitting quietly on his little seat, his head resting on the butt of his gun. He hadn't unshipped it. 'I put my hand on his shoulder. I knew he was dead.'

Teamwork between pilot and observer or gunner was vital if either were to survive. Traill and Jones had lasted longer than most. Pilots soon rejected an observer in whom they had no confidence, but observers had no such choice. The contrast excited the sympathy, even the disgust, of 35-year-old Harold Wyllie, OBE (Military), a pilot who employed his skill as an artist (his father was the well-known marine artist W.L. Wyllie, RA), with the help of a carefully chosen observer, to map the German trenches from low altitude and circulate the results to the army. He got a frightful rocket from Trenchard, at the army's behest, for not going through 'the proper channels', but Trenchard added: 'That's the spirit! I'm too delighted for words!' Wyllie's euphoria was dulled soon afterwards when he watched a newcomer side-slip, stall, nose-dive, and crash, killing himself and his newly appointed observer, who happened to be a friend of Wyllie. Afterwards Wyllie wrote: 'He was a rotten pilot and should never have been allowed to carry a passenger.' And of the observer: 'He was one of the best fellows who ever lived and a valuable life thrown away by sheer bad flying.'

Being paired with a ham-fisted, timorous or over-confident pilot was a chance the average observer had to take. Many would find a congenial partner and be happy to live or die with him – or at least to survive until their own pilot's course came through. But a shocking number died as Wyllie's friend had died.

'It is generally admitted,' concluded a medical analysis of nervous instability in some 200 flyers, 'that an observer has a far greater strain placed upon him than a pilot . . .' Lack of confidence in a partner in the air was bad enough for a pilot: for the peace of mind of an observer it was paralysing. Another instance quoted was when a stricken machine was falling from height. Whereas the pilot was fully occupied in trying to recover control, the observer had nothing to do but sit there transfixed, anticipating the end. Even eventual escape might leave him devastated. 'Observers', it was contended, 'generally break down sooner and to a much greater degree than pilots.'

Supporting the theory that, because of their greater impotence, observers generally suffered the greater anguish, Gwilym Lewis related how a pilot in a single-seater Morane had his controls shot away at altitude, spun 'for several minutes', survived the crash, but went out of his mind.

Again and again pilots returned with wounded or dead observers, often unmarked themselves. The Jamaican Berry King, for whom third time was to prove unlucky, was an example. The figures quoted earlier by Alan Dore bear striking testimony. At the end of the first week of April 1917 ('Bloody April'), of the original complement of eighteen pilots and eighteen observers assembled in France in mid-January to crew the 1½-strutters of 43 Squadron, eight pilots remained – but not one observer. They had all become casualties, for one reason or another.

Whether men were flying as qualified observers or as gunners, their vulnerability was much the same. They were volunteers, and there seems to have been no penalty attached to failure other than the blow to personal pride. What is remarkable is that so many of those who survived stuck it for so long.

13

McCUDDEN AND 56 SQUADRON: RHYS DAVIDS AND VOSS

W HEN Jimmy McCudden returned to France as B Flight commander of 56 Squadron, his reception was wary. The squadron's patrol area, opposite Richthofen's *Jagde-schwader*, or hunting group, was one of the toughest on any front. Yet in three months the squadron pilots had scored a hundred victories, a unique achievement, and many of them were established aces. Some were ex-Sandhurst, many were ex-public-school, and McCudden was an ex-ranker: there were adjustments to be made on both sides.

A great deal depended on McCudden's first attempt at leading his flight. Of the five pilots who constituted it, Barlow had especially distinguished himself by his pioneering low-level machine-gunning attack at Messines. Keith Muspratt, erstwhile instructor and future test pilot, had learnt to fly at 16 in his holidays from Sherborne School: one of his pupils had been the incomparable Arthur Rhys Davids, also now in McCudden's flight. A few months earlier 'RD', athlete and classical scholar, had been head boy at Eton: he had gone into action almost straight from those legendary playing fields, and had earned for himself, in the scrap when Ball was shot down, the encomium from Blomfield that 'here is another Ball'. Completing the flight, specially selected for their personal qualities, were Canadian Verschoyle Cronyn ('Versh'), and Englishman Maxwell Coote

– 'as splendid a lot of fellows', according to McCudden, 'as ever set foot in France.'

At 6 a.m. on 18 August they took off in their SE5A's to mount the early patrol. Almost at once they sighted a formation of four enemy reconnaissance machines, 6,000 feet below them, heading south. Soon they recognised the stubby silhouettes as Aviatik two-seaters.

McCudden gave the signal to attack, but then his guns jammed and he had to land to clear the stoppages. It was a wretched start. But his professionalism was equal to it. He cleared the stoppages and rejoined his flight in time to help Barlow shoot down one of the two-seaters before protecting him from eight avenging Albatros scouts, destroying one of them before leading Barlow back over the lines.

There were no rash heroics from McCudden. They had been hope-lessly outnumbered. And he had a healthy regard for the Hun. 'The more I fight them the more I respect their fighting qualities.' But on the enhanced performance of the SE5A he was euphoric. 'It was very fine', he wrote, 'to be in a machine that was faster than the Huns, and to know that one could run away just as things got too hot.'

Breakfast that morning was an animated meal, with McCudden's swift return to the fray after his initial setback heartily endorsed. 'I hope', said one of his pilots, 'that your first Hun with 56 Squadron will be the first of 50.' McCudden, flying a really efficient fighting machine for the first time, did not dismiss this sentiment as fanciful.

He shot down a second Albatros on 19 August and a third on the 20th, though this one upset him strangely. He felt no sentiment for the enemy, but he had become so inured to the seeming invulner-ability of enemy aircraft to the guns of two-seaters that he was caught off his guard when this third Albatros exuded a flicker of fire and then tilted earthwards in a candle of flame. With pulses throbbing and hands a-tremble, he thought he was going to be physically sick. All he could think of was the fellow human being in that holocaust. 'Poor devil,' he thought, 'Poor devil'. Such squeamishness was not typical of him, and he told himself it had to be eradicated. It was unprofessional.

In less than a week McCudden established himself as a flight commander of rare tactical ability, providing just the right mixture of caution and aggression, always mindful of his responsibility to the less experienced. Meanwhile in his spare time he was developing a talent for stalking enemy reconnaissance two-seaters, increasing the speed and ceiling of his machine by various modifications, biding his time, choosing his moment, often surprising his prey at 20,000 feet and beyond, where they thought they were safe. He planned these interceptions as meticulously as he organised the patrols of his flight. Studying the Hun's routine, he would announce: 'If there's nothing doing up the line I'm going after the 11.30.'

Curiously enough, within two days of McCudden's arrival at 56, Richthofen, too, returned to duty. But he had come back too soon. On 28 August he wrote: 'I have just made two patrols. They were successful, but after each one I was completely exhausted.' Dizziness and air-sickness assailed him, and early in September, after recording his sixty-first victory, he consented to taking convalescent leave. It was during this break that he completed his book, *The Red Air Fighter*. Efforts were made to stop him returning to duty, but he was adamant that he must do so. 'I should consider myself a despicable creature if, now that I am loaded with fame and decorations, I should consent to live on as a pensioner . . . while every poor fellow in the trenches, who is doing his duty as much as I am, has to stick it out.' This was strikingly similar to attitudes in the RFC. But he was not well enough to resume his role of Ringmaster until mid-November.

McCudden resembled Richthofen in that he always weighed up the situation carefully before attacking, although Rhys Davids noticed that once he was committed he fought brilliantly, with complete disregard for his own safety. His machine, though, was rarely hit, and he very rarely lost a man from his flight.

Whereas McCudden, like Richthofen, could be content to live to fight another day, Maybery and Rhys Davids would take on any odds. Of Maybery, in the squadron's early days, Blomfield wrote: 'He and Captain Ball and Lieutenant Rhys Davids did more harm to the morale of the German flying corps than any other fifteen pilots between them.' After one of Rhys Davids' more reckless forays he was urged to be more cautious, and he admitted, in a letter to his mother, Caroline Rhys Davids (D.Litt.), that he had taken 'four times the risks I ought to have done'. But his resolve to go more carefully collapsed when he got into a scrap. 'You are a different man. At least, you aren't a man at all . . . you are a devil incarnate . . .'

His friendship with Maybery had blossomed when they were transferred to England in June to meet the Gotha threat: he fell in love with Maybery's seventeen-year-old cousin. There were many sides to his nature. Brought up in orthodox fashion, he confessed to having religious doubts, 'but one simply does not get the time to think them out'. The only man in the squadron of a similar sensitivity was Cecil Lewis. 'Sometimes, returning from a patrol,' wrote Lewis, 'we would break off and chase each other round the clouds, zooming their summits, plunging down their precipitous flanks, darting like fishes through their shadowy crevasses and their secret caves; such pleasure lay in this that never did we seem more intimate . . .' After landing they would stroll to the Mess arm in arm, with no hint of self-consciousness in their friendship. 'Sometimes we used to walk at night down to the stream in the valley. He would quote some line of half-forgotten poetry. I would take it up . . . At such times the war was quite forgotten.' Could this quiet, contemplative boy, marvelled Lewis, really be a war hero?

There was no stronger contrast in temperament than that between Rhys Davids and McCudden. Yet they maintained a working relationship. McCudden treated Rhys Davids' volatile nature with a mixture of grudging admiration and stern reproof. RD 'would have chased the Huns over to the Russian front if I had let him,' wrote McCudden, and the younger man had cause to be grateful many times to his leader. But the gratitude was not one-sided. McCudden could still feel clumsy and inferior in company in the Mess, and any assumption of social superiority was swiftly checked by RD, who shamed his colleagues into accepting McCudden for what he was.

Many of the air aces, McCudden and Richthofen among them, built up their scores on two-seaters, but not RD, and by September he had won the MC and Bar and was famous as 'Eton's boy hero'. 'If one was ever over the salient in the autumn of 1917,' wrote

McCudden, 'and saw an SE fighting like hell amidst a heap of Huns, one would find nine times out of ten that the SE was flown by Rhys Davids.'

The weather for the remainder of August remained so unseasonable that only minor ground operations were attempted, the whole Ypres area having deteriorated into a quagmire. It was during this hiatus that Haig transferred the overall direction of the main advance to the Second Army under the more patient and methodical Plumer, with the Fifth Army under Gough in support. When the weather improved in September, and the ground began to dry out, the offensive was resumed, but with more limited objectives and on a narrower front.

Bombing by day and by night, contact and counter-attack patrols, low-flying attacks on enemy reinforcements, artillery observation, and air reconnaissance, aided by the use of parachute flares at night to illuminate enemy movements, all contributed materially to a run of comparative success in which twenty-six RFC squadrons were directly involved. And it was during the Battle of the Menin Road Ridge (20–25 September) that one of the greatest air battles was fought. Again, the principal participants on the British side were 56 Squadron.

In Richthofen's absence, his twenty-year-old pupil Werner Voss, flying one of the new Fokker Triplanes, had begun to challenge his supremacy. Richthofen called him 'my most redoubtable competitor'. The 'Krefeld Hussar', as he was known (he had joined the militia in 1914 and fought on the Russian front), had thirty-nine victories, and in the week Richthofen went on leave he added another eight. Unlike his master, but like Ball and Rhys Davids on the British side, Voss would attack whatever the odds. Indeed he believed it was easier to fight six machines than two: bigger numbers got in each other's way. The Fokker triplane, diminutive, light, sensitive, but not easy to fly, had a fantastic rate of climb and could turn on the proverbial sixpence in the right hands – and Voss's were undoubtedly the right ones. It was not particularly fast, but in designing it Anthony Fokker had sacrificed speed for manoeuvrability. Richthofen was not greatly enthused by it, but for Voss it became an obsession, an extension of his personality. The star of the Circus was no longer the Baron and his scarlet Albatros but Voss and his silver-blue *dreidecker*.

Air activity fell off in the next few days as the Allies prepared for the Menin Road attack, but it resumed with increasing intensity from 20 September. Voss was due to go on leave on the 23rd, but he took off that morning from his aerodrome at Heule, spotted a DH4 on a reconnaissance mission, and promptly shot it down. That was his forty-eighth. As the day advanced, opportunities increased, and Voss resolved to fly one more patrol before going on leave. He needed two more victories for fifty.

Taking off at 18.05, with wing-men on either side, each flying the sturdy Pfalz DIII fighter, he headed for the front. Climbing through a broken layer of cloud, they found themselves sandwiched in clear air between the lower cloud layer at 1,000 feet and an upper layer at 9,000. Horizontal visibility was good, and large numbers of aeroplanes were seen. Among them were two flights of SE5A's of 60 Squadron led by Captain K.L. 'Grid' Caldwell, returning from a patrol. (To Keith Caldwell, a New Zealander, every machine was a 'grid'.) Caldwell's formation had been broken up, and the rear flight now consisted of Captain Robert Chidlaw-Roberts and Lieutenant Harold Hamersley. Both were embryo aces. Hamersley was keeping an eye on a formation of Albatros scouts when he spotted a Fokker triplane, accompanied by a Pfalz. Avoiding the Pfalz, he put his nose down and dived on the triplane, opening fire as he did so. Chidlaw-Roberts followed.

They were treated to a sequence of manoeuvres by the triplane that astonished them both. Reversing the position in some miraculous way, the triplane pilot put a burst into Chidlaw-Roberts' rudder and drove him and Hamersley back towards the lines.

Grid Caldwell, setting off in pursuit, felt sure the man in the triplane must be Werner Voss. He then saw that two flights of SE5A's of 56 Squadron had taken up the challenge. Although their numbers had been reduced from eleven to seven by previous skirmishes (four had been forced to turn back), they comprised two flight commanders

(McCudden and Bowman), Maybery, Muspratt and Rhys Davids; and two 'ace' Canadians, Reg Hoidge (twenty victories) and Versh Cronyn.

Voss had lost height in chasing Chidlaw-Roberts and Hamersley, so that McCudden was able to build up to what he called a 'colossal speed' as he tore into the attack. He had no fear of the SE breaking up. Slightly to starboard of Voss, with Rhys Davids to port, he was aiming to box the triplane in. But Voss saw the danger, abandoned the chase of the two crippled SE's, whipped his tail-plane round sharply, like a goldfish in a bowl, and turned through 180 degrees to face his attackers, firing as he came. McCudden, with bursts from the triplane's twin Spandaus ripping through his wings, was left with a sense of bewilderment.

Zooming out of the dive, with Muspratt and Cronyn following, McCudden sought to line up a second time. But again the triplane flicked round, coming out on a reciprocal course. This time Muspratt's engine was shot up so badly he had to force-land, his machine a write-off.

The Pfalz pilots, too, had been unable to live with the triplane. 'That left Voss in the middle of six of us,' wrote Bowman later, 'which did not appear to deter him in the slightest.'

Cronyn too had been hit: falling oil pressure turned his attempt to zoom into a feeble climb. Voss saw this and whipped round as before. Attacking from abeam, he gave Cronyn a perfect silhouette of his new three-decker, wings stepped down from the top, with comic whiskered face painted on a black cowling. Then the bullets came. Three months earlier Cronyn might have attempted to run for it, but he was too old a hand now. He dived just enough to turn in under the triplane and prevent its getting on his tail. Soon one of the others would drive it off.

Cronyn lost count of the number of turns he did to keep under the triplane. Half the time, without knowing it, he was flying upside down. When Voss came in for the kill he put his machine into a vicious spin, and when he flattened off he saw with intense relief that Voss was busy with the others. Petrol was pouring from his left cylinder block and spraying into his face, his engine was missing

[367]

badly, and he made for home. His machine too was a write-off.

Chidlaw-Roberts, Hamersley, Muspratt, Cronyn, all experienced scout pilots, all forced down within minutes, with two machines written off. Voss had reached his fifty victories. How long could he keep it up?

The triplane was quite capable of outclimbing the five remaining SE's. Voss could escape whenever he wished. But he did not choose to do so. Plunging, hovering, climbing, corkscrewing, he was proving his theories by gaining protection from pilots cramped by the risk of collision, and of shooting each other down. But he was gradually being driven west, down to 2,000 feet, near the British lines.

A red-nosed Albatros appeared and began guarding the triplane's tail. McCudden counted eleven more enemy scouts high to the east, but six Spads and four Camels were daring them to interfere. Suddenly McCudden saw his chance; but no sooner had he fired than up came the triplane's nose towards him and he saw the red-yellow flashes of the parallel Spandaus. Hoidge saw the opportunity for a simultaneous attack but with a twist of the tail Voss evaded them both.

While the other SE pilots held the ring, Rhys Davids dived repeatedly at the triplane. Each time Voss skipped out of the way. Once, in dodging RD, he came up broadside on to Bowman. It was Bowman's first chance and he shoved his nose forward excitedly. But the German kicked on full rudder, skidded sideways, and got in a devastating burst at Bowman, who stared in amazement. He didn't think such manoeuvres were possible without buckling control surfaces or stalling and spinning. Yet he had one consolation. He had given Rhys Davids the chance to lock on to the triplane's tail.

RD would never have got there, thought Bowman, had Voss not been distracted. There was no doubt he was vulnerable now. RD was not quite able to straighten up behind the triplane, but it was good enough. He fired from a hundred yards range down to seventy, emptying an entire drum.

For once the triplane held its course. There could be only one explanation. The pilot was either unconscious or dead.

It is not surprising, after such convolutions, that discrepancies should exist between the German and British accounts. What is unique is the reverence in which Voss was held by the pilots who faced him that day. 'As long as I live,' wrote McCudden, 'I shall never forget my admiration for that German pilot, who single-handed fought seven of us for ten minutes.' (Bowman and Hoidge put it at twenty.) 'His flying was wonderful, his courage magnificent, and in my opinion he was the bravest German airman whom it has been my privilege to see fight.' Bowman wrote: 'It was not until later that we heard that it was actually Voss in the triplane. Our elation was not nearly so great as you might have imagined.'

The chivalry so often ascribed to World War I pilots scarcely extended to the heat of combat, but admiration for a fallen enemy did. It was Rhys Davids himself who expressed the general regret at the death of Werner Voss. *'Oh, if I could only have brought him down alive!'*

14

COMBAT – EXHAUSTING BUT EXHILARATING: SMART AND HIS 'CIRCUS'

T HERE was a poignant postscript to the Voss fight: it marked the end of the career of Versh Cronyn. 'When I got out of the machine,' he recorded afterwards, 'the relief from tension was so great that I practically collapsed. For a minute or two everything went black ... I could hear someone asking, "Where has he been hit?" ... I wanted to laugh because I had managed to get down without crashing, but instead of laughing I started to sob ... Perhaps shell-shock would best describe my condition.' When he tried to relate what had happened he found himself stammering incoherently.

He asked for a fortnight's leave, thinking his depression would lift, but the medical officer grounded him and, feeling an outcast, he was posted home. Showing neither understanding nor sympathy, Major Blomfield said little more than 'Sorry I can't recommend you for promotion'. It was left to Major W.D.S. Sanday, the successor to Harvey-Kelly commanding 19 Squadron (Spads) on the same aerodrome, to catch up with him one day and take him by the arm in a most friendly manner. 'When you are better and return to France,' he said, 'I would be very glad to take you on my strength.' What a contrast, thought Cronyn. This man who went out regularly with his squadron and had the DSO and MC would be glad to have him, whereas Blomfield, who might take a machine up on test occasionally but never on patrol, and for whom he had flown thirty-four OP's in two-and-a-half months and been credited with seven or eight possible victories, could find nothing to say to him.

The effect of combat on the individual varied widely. Cronyn, joining No. 56, like Maybery, during its short sojourn at Bekesbourne, was given no instruction or advice on air combat or tactics. 'We will patrol the Menin–Roulers road area,' he was told by Bowman, his first flight commander. 'Don't take on what you can't finish and for God's sake keep a tight formation.' On his second patrol he found himself over the lines with four others surrounded by what seemed the entire German Air Force. In fact there were eighteen of them. 'After the first few moments it was born in on my consciousness that this was the real thing, that those vicious cracks were passing bullets aimed at me by the enemy, with everyone for himself, that the gun buttons on the control stick were there to be pressed, and to stay alive one must exert all possible skill in manoeuvring.' Somehow Bowman had extracted them from the mêlée without loss.

Later, in the Mess, animated and glass in hand, they might relive the action, and some discussion of tactics might follow. Cronyn never knew fear in the air because he was much too busy. 'The tense period was while waiting on the ground, or at night in bed thinking, when the fear shakes got me . . . These shakes are a strange thing. I was not conscious of fear but for no apparent reason I would just start trembling all over. We all had this condition at times . . .

'The toughest time for nervous strain was when called for the early bird flight. Little would be said, with no jokes, while we gulped a cup of coffee.' It was when the take-off was delayed, according to Cronyn, 'that their stomachs did queer things and we even got the shakes. One by one we would get up and walk away.' Cronyn wasn't actually sick, but others were. 'The tension was really beyond description. Yet once in the plane we felt we could cope . . .'

While few could stand the men who whistled unconcernedly while waiting for the order to take off, there were men like Ball and Maybery who seemed impervious to tension. 'It must be marvellous to have the sort of guts Ball had,' wrote Arthur Gould Lee, 'to be completely without fear, to attack regardless of the odds, not giving a damn whether you're killed or not. Most of us like to try to go on living even when we have to risk our skins fighting Hun scouts far better than ours.' Yet when, on patrol with other 1½-strutters, he sighted eight Albatros scouts, 'I began to tremble with excitement, all tensed up for the coming scrap ... Swooping down on an enemy formation from a great height was a madly exhilarating feeling.'

Many others, like Lee, felt 'that tingle of excitement before action.' But of the action itself, 'things happen so fast I have only a hazy notion of what followed.' Of his first victim, Lee wrote: 'I came down closer and closer, holding my fire. My heart was pounding, and I was trembling uncontrollably, but my mind was calm and collected.' His coolness surprised him. 'You are scared before you start, but once in it you don't feel excitement or fear, you fight in a sort of daze. When it's over, and you find you're still alive, you feel both exhausted and exhilarated ... The thrill was felt later when celebrating in the Mess.'

Charles Kennedy Cochran-Patrick ('Pat'), DSO, MC, thought by Trenchard in July 1917 to be the equal of any pilot then at the front, and who later commanded 60 Squadron, recognised the blood-lust in his own reactions. 'The excitement of it all was in my blood ... I was at 7,000 feet, coming down in a giddy spiral, shouting at the top of my voice.' 'Pat' had a reputation for being phlegmatic – but he didn't feel cool when on another man's tail, and there was always the dread of the clack of machine-gun fire from behind. Of an imaginary but all too typical newcomer he wrote, with some feeling: 'He sees blood and goes blind and straight with all his attention on the machine appearing at his mercy. Then, God help him, there is another hostile machine about. He is attacked and shot down before he knows anything about it.'

Bert Harris wrote: 'I think most fighter pilots in France were troubled by sore necks, trying to look both ways at once, trying to keep an eye on your own tail in a scrap – if you didn't you'd had it ...' The trouble, he added, was that 'once you were in a dogfight you really saw very little except the fellow you were after.'

'For many,' wrote Lee, 'it took a long time to realise that, whatever one's marksmanship, the only way to get your Hun in a dogfight was to get in really close before firing. The problem was to do it before someone did it to you.'

There were other apprehensions, even worse than the thought of the chap on your tail, which could cause Lee's goggles to mist up from the perspiration of fear. This was especially so in a dogfight. 'I levelled out, sweating from sheer funk. It's odd how the risk of collision frightens you more than the risk of bullets.'

Norman Macmillan was one of those to whom the tingle of anticipation was familiar. 'The intensity of concentration was so great that the mental attitude became detached from all emotions.' Sometimes, when still hyped up after a patrol, he and his squadron colleague Ray Brownell, a Tasmanian who had won an MM as a soldier at Gallipoli, would go out again on a voluntary patrol in search of hostiles.

McCudden's squeamishness at seeing another human being, enemy or not, falling in flames, and his shock, when closing for the kill on what he thought of merely as an enemy machine, to realise that 'there's a man in it', were shared by Lee and many others. Once, as though in a reflection in a mirror, Lee saw practically his double, and it was borne in upon him that Hun pilots and observers were simply the reverse of the coin. 'Although we often get to very close quarters in our dogfights, our scrapping is impersonal. We don't hate each other.' And Ball had written, of an enemy 'flamer', 'poor old chap inside'. But some did seek revenge, often for the death of former colleagues, and a wild but diminutive Australian named 'Jerry' Pentland (twenty-four victories), returning in a Spad of 19 Squadron from a kill, announced: 'I got the bastard stone cold.' Captain W.E. 'Moley' Molesworth (eighteen victories), wrote: 'Your first Hun in flames gives you a wonderful feeling of satisfaction.'

There were many who revelled in their role of scout pilot, anyway for a time. But for most, their nerve would fail them in the end. Even those with a natural flair for the job, the born scout pilots, if such existed, like Ball and Rhys Davids, soon tired of the slaughter. 'Oh, won't it be nice when all this beastly killing is over,' wrote Ball to his girl friend. 'I hate this game, but it is the only thing one must do just now.' For Rhys Davids it was 'a tedious war' that had stymied his scholarship to Balliol. With youthful ambivalence, in a letter to his mother, he saw his work as 'an absolutely superb game' while at the same time 'hating the whole damn business'. He told Cecil Lewis: 'It's a job. We ought to try to do it well. But when peace comes we'll do better.'

Courage and skill as a scout pilot did not necessarily imply integrity or reliability, or the sensitivity of a Cecil Lewis. 'The worst bounders', wrote Tom Tillard of No. 3 Squadron, 'sometimes make the best flyers.'

It is difficult to imagine that the crews of the corps squadrons, the BE2's and the RE8's, can have taken much pleasure in combat. But the evidence is that some of them did. Since they had to expect it, may have been their attitude, they might as well enjoy it. The excitement of fighting for the ultimate prize, their lives, took hold of them. Yet there must have been many, like the actor Mervyn Johns, who admitted to carrying on for months in a state of blue funk – and are all the more to be respected for it.

'The shoot was going fairly well,' wrote Charles Smart of an artillery cooperation show in an RE8 on 12 August 1917, 'and we were well over the lines, and like fools both of us were gazing at the target, when suddenly there was a terrific burst of machine-gun fire and four Hun machines dropped through the clouds right on top of us. I at once put our machine into a vertical bank and fell like a stone about 500 feet, then I pulled her out straight again and we made a running fight of it back to our lines. The Huns were fairly out for blood and dived on us time after time. Short [Smart's observer] kept his head well and worked his gun like steam. The odds were all against us for each German machine is armed with two machine-guns firing through the prop so we had eight guns against our one.

'Bullets simply zipped all over the place and I never thought we could get clear. I did a series of very steep spirals and S-turns and managed to get back to our lines, where our Archie started. The shells came much nearer to us than to the Huns but it had the desired effect, for the Huns left us.' They then carried on with the shoot. 'It was a most exciting fight and I thoroughly enjoyed it while it was going on though I must say after the Huns had left us my knees felt a bit wobbly.' When they got down they found more than thirty bullet-holes in their machine, 'the nearest one went through about six inches below my seat.' Relief at his escape was overridden by annoyance. 'I would give half of what I am worth to have brought one of the beggars down.'

As it happened, such a sacrifice was unnecessary. 'The CO of the battery we were shooting with reported to the squadron that we shot a Hun machine down badly damaged. He says he saw it fall out of the fight and had not the least doubt but that it was in serious trouble.' A week later, on the eve of Smart's last flight with Short, who was going home to learn to fly, Smart noted: 'We have just heard that we are officially credited with bringing down a Hun machine during our fight on the 12th ... Good!'

Such confirmation from the front line was not unusual. Recording a victory by a colleague in his diary, Smart wrote: 'The fight was seen by thousands of men in the trenches and the excitement was great. The machine that landed in our lines came down with a great crash and both man and machine were smashed into little bits. Smith, the pilot, managed to land his machine safely ... from where he departed in an ambulance amidst cheers from the assembled multitude.' There was no squeamishness from the men in the trenches, who had little enough to cheer. Nor was the cheering any less jubilant on the German side when a British machine came down.

A week after converting to RE8's, Smart recorded how photographic sorties from No. 5 Squadron began to be accompanied by an escort from within the squadron. Of the five RE8 crews detailed, three were to take photos and two to act as escort. Smart was one of the latter: with him as gunner he had an air mechanic named Smith. They had reached the limit of their patrol, and photos were being taken, when 'twelve Hun scout machines came right through us and a real ding-dong scrap followed.

'A Hun dived at the machine I was guarding and I had to do something, so I pushed my nose down with the engine full on and dived at him, firing my gun like fury. At the same time a Hun dived at me and my gunner engaged him with the rear gun.' Glancing at his air speed indicator Smart noticed that the needle, which registered up to 140 m.p.h., was stuck against the maximum, 'so we must have been going some. Down we swirled for about 2,000 feet, both guns firing and making no end of noise at both ends. Anyhow my machine made it so hot for both Huns that they broke off the fight and cleared east.'

All the RE's were attacked, one by four Huns at a time, but 'the Huns got more than they expected'. The German pilots had probably mistaken the unfamiliar RE8 for their old Aunt Sally, the BE2: the silhouettes were not dissimilar. Anyway they withdrew and the photographic mission was completed. Smart wrote: 'It was a glorious fight. I have never been through anything quite so exciting, machines were whizzing about all over the place like mad swallows, the air resounded with the pop! pop! pop! of machine guns, and tracer bullets could be seen flying in all directions. No one in our crowd was hit but the machines were pretty well shot about. We now call ourselves the circus, and rightly so, for have not five RE8's engaged twelve Huns on their own pitch and licked them hollow? First-class Air Mechanic Smith behaved splendidly right through the show, he just sat on his seat like a block of wood and fired his gun like steam so long as there was anything to fire at.

'It is strange how little fear enters into one during a fight, I never thought of being hurt, my only desire was to kill a German and I feel sure I would have rammed a Hun machine if I could have got near enough to do it. As for handling a machine, one can do simply anything when there is a scrap on.

'You cannot compare fighting on the ground with fighting in the air. [Smart, of course, had experienced both]. The two are in about the same ratio as tiddlywinks and big game shooting for excitement. Perhaps I should not say this if I had been in a bayonet charge.'

Smart relished escort work, and two days later he was 'out with the circus again'. Herbert 'Jimmy' Larkin, his flight commander, an Australian, had been christened Captain Barnum, and Smart, as his second in command, was dubbed Mr Bailey. Larkin, after being wounded at Gallipoli, had transferred to the RFC and was later to make a reputation on Sopwith Dolphins as a 'cool, calculating killer'.

The crews rotated, taking the two jobs in turn, and Smart, who had earlier described photographic work as 'a poor game', highly dangerous and with no chance of cheating (since the photos told all), had become resigned to it. 'Photography is a good job when you don't get hurt.' It usually lasted no more than one and a half hours, as against the two and a half and more of artillery work, and there was an incentive for doing the job properly: provided they got their photos first time they were finished for the day.

Like the infantry, they rarely saw the scout squadrons that were supposed to be clearing the air for them. But on an artillery shoot that summer, on two enemy trench points, after Smart had had to transmit MQHA (cease fire, hostile aircraft) several times and retire to a safe distance, four Nieuports turned up and mixed it with the German formation. 'They disappeared into the clouds all fighting like Kilkenny cats.' Smart was able to continue the shoot.

Then it was back to escort work. 'In a fight the excitement is intense. It is only after you land that you realise the risks you run. When you are about two miles above the earth you never seem to think of the fact that if anything happens to you or the machine you have got those two miles to fall before you reach your natural element. And when you do reach it you will hardly be in a state to appreciate it.' Not once in his diary does he mention a parachute.

Was Smart's insouciance in battle typical? Were all the corps observers as cool under fire as Lieutenants Hendry, Short and Currie and Air Mechanics Tyndal and Smith? When Smart was drafted to Home Establishment after ten months on active service he wrote: 'Glad I am going home for I feel just about done in, but still I am more than sorry to leave all the good fellows out here. I am proud to have been a member of No. 5 Squadron RFC, which has done some great work while I have been with them. All the men in the squadron with perhaps two exceptions have been real men and worth knowing.'

A week after writing this, on 26 September 1917, Smart concluded his diary with the following lines:

> *Married to Helena May Irwin.*
> *My word! This is a dangerous war.*

15

SOME TRAGIC NEWCOMERS: NO NEWS OF RHYS DAVIDS

H AIG's initial objective, to secure the ridge east of Ypres, still lay only partly realised, and after the successful Menin Road sub-battle he renewed the assault, on 26 September, in a second sub-battle at Polygon Wood. Overnight, the FE2b's of Nos 100 and 101 Squadrons, having concentrated earlier on German aerodromes and rail centres, dropped nearly five tons of bombs on villages where enemy troops were billeted, and on communications. Low cloud next morning hampered but did not prevent the work of the corps squadrons, and enemy counter-attacks were quickly detected from the air and repulsed. As a result of these sub-battles – there was a third, at Broodseinde on 4 October – Haig's Second Army now stood on the crest of the Ypres ridge.

For the RFC, the most notable features of these battles were first, the development of night bombing, and secondly, the increased employment of the fighting squadrons in harassing and sometimes scattering German infantry with light-weight bombs and machine-gun attacks, over and behind the battlefront. Night bombing, especially of aerodromes, was also practised by the Germans, but it did not amount in total to more than a seventh of the tonnage dropped by the British. And although the German Air Force was extremely active over the front in early September, it was forced back as the month advanced, the fighting squadrons keeping the skies clear for the corps machines, and the infantry free from undue harassment.

Meanwhile, in an effort to make good the disastrous losses of March–April–May, amounting to some 1,270 machines, the two aircraft parks, at St Omer and Candas, worked non-stop to feed over a thousand aeroplanes to the front-line squadrons in the month of September, enabling the flights of most squadrons to revert to eight machines each. For squadrons on artillery cooperation, each flight was able to maintain two machines in the air continuously from dawn to dusk. But the quality of the machines, standardised or reconstructed by the depots, was not always matched by the crews, expansion further diluting expertise. It was rare for pilot and observer to be of equal competence and fully familiar with the ground area: one or other was likely to be a novice. These novices often performed admirably, but their casualty rate was high.

John Worstenholme, a newcomer on No. 6 Squadron, was the pilot in one of a pair of RE8's on the morning of 21 September, the second day of the Menin Road battle, their mission to take photographs over Poperinghe. He was given an experienced observer named Frank McCreary, formerly of the South Lancashire Regiment, and they returned safely from what was his first mission. Afterwards, trying to relax, Worstenholme rehearsed what he felt had been 'some pretty tense experiences'. To begin with, he had lost the other RE8 in cloud. The sky had been stippled with machines, hostile as well as friendly, but neither this nor the fact that they were on their own had deterred them from trying to get their photographs. Worstenholme reflected, as he lay on his bed, that his experiences were probably commonplace and that pilots from his own squadron and every other squadron must get far more excitement daily, while scout pilots would already have forgotten about it. Yet every incident in the flight remained vivid in his memory and he couldn't sleep for thinking about them.

It wasn't that he was disturbed by the dangers that must have been present. He was insensible to them. 'I just lay there longing to be in the air again, and wanting to relive all those moments.'

That afternoon they were sent off again, to rendezvous over the same target with other RE8's to take more photographs. In extremely poor conditions he and McCreary managed to get their pictures, and 'I got a very good welcome from my CO, although I pranged his aircraft on landing.' His mind was still insulated from the more terrifying aspects of wartime flying.

Four days later, while on a contact patrol at 5,000 feet in cloudy conditions, Worstenholme's machine was attacked by a fighter out of the mist and he was knocked unconscious. McCreary was badly wounded in the hand, the machine started spiralling, and the enemy was following them down. McCreary had never flown an aeroplane before, but he *had* been shot down before, and as the RE8 nose-dived he brought it under control.

The RE8 was pointing towards the lines, but the enemy pilot attacked again, this time from astern, and McCreary had to relinquish control, face towards the tail, and open up with his rear gun. While he was doing this the RE8 fell into another dive, which he tried to control, but meanwhile he had driven the enemy off. Reasserting control, he found he had climbed to 6,000 feet.

Not knowing how to work the throttle, McCreary glided downhill until he was a mile from his aerodrome, but at about 200 feet he realised he was again losing control. The machine stalled and crashed, but it fell into an isolated clump of trees which cushioned the impact, and McCreary, seriously hurt but thankfully alive, was picked up by Australian troops and taken to hospital, where he 'gave a perfectly good reconnaissance report' to the General who visited him. His clear-headed display earned him an MC. But there were no more magic experiences to be relived for young John Worstenholme, whose wounds proved fatal.

The RFC was facing a familiar problem, that of preparing new pilots and observers for something for which there could never be adequate preparation. An extension of the training period would help, but perhaps no more than marginally: the moment of truth still had to be faced. More reprehensible was the continual drafting to squadrons in France of men who had not even completed the minimum of training laid down.

Jack Wightman was an 18-year-old from Coventry who had been rated the best pilot they had turned out at his training school, a distinction which may have cost him his life. Chosen to fly Bristol Fighters, he was unexpectedly sent to France to join No. 11 Squadron on 26 August 1917. 'He left England in a remarkably short time,' according to his brother, R.L. Wightman. 'I think he was sent out too quickly. He was not even sent to Scotland for a fortnight's gunnery course.' This was the kind of short cut that was still being taken, under pressure from France. Wightman was presumably selected as an outstanding pupil.

'The weather was atrocious for the first few days in France,' wrote the surviving brother, 'and no flying was possible. Then he was sent over the lines for an hour alone.' This would have been his familiarisation flight, when he would have been accompanied by an experienced observer, who evidently gave him a thorough indoctrination, as they were 'archied'. 'Next morning he went over again with three other planes under a captain.' This would have been his flight commander: the squadron was doing its best for him. 'They were met by a squadron of enemy planes. Jack went for one of them, but was soon outnumbered by about five to one, and his machine was last seen by another officer in flames.

'He had only been in France nine days and he was not quite 19 . . . It is so terrible I can hardly write about it. I shall be joining a cadet school myself soon, but I shall not take the RFC if I can help it.' Lost with Wightman was Second Class Air Mechanic John Heedy: neither man has any known grave.

The grief of relatives was not a subject likely to influence the hierarchy, although squadron and flight commanders – and in special cases Trenchard himself – did their best to write letters of condolence and tribute. There were times, though, when they were overwhelmed, or when they themselves were casualties, or when little or nothing was known. Plaintive letters pleading for information about loved ones could draw a blank from a much-changed squadron personnel, leaving relatives even further distraught. Yet casualty lists seem only to have stimulated recruiting among the young, and few would-be RFC men needed the encouragement of women distributing white feathers – as they did – to any young man of military age not in uniform. Some, like Ronald Ivelaw-Chapman, a future air chief marshal but then aged 17, went down on their hands and knees and prayed that the war would last long enough for them to train and fight. 'We schoolboys', wrote Bryan Sharwood-Smith, a Brisfit pilot on 48 Squadron by 1918, 'were fearful that the war would end.'

Night bombing, one of the features of RFC operations that autumn, developed so widely in 1917 that night flying in all types of machine came to be recognised as both feasible and desirable, forming a part of the repertoire of most squadrons. While the corps crews on the Ypres front were fully occupied in daylight, with no spare energy for night flying, corps and army crews elsewhere were given orders for night raids on targets where damage and harassment were judged to be helpful to the main offensive. Sopwith Pups of Gordon Taylor's squadron, No. 66, attacked German aerodromes at dusk, undeterred by the inevitable night landings. Brisfit crews on the Nieuport front did the same, Puggy Shone actually carrying a 16 lb bomb on his lap. 'If it got within ten miles of its target,' said Puggy, 'I'd be surprised.'

They were sometimes alerted to intercept German bombers returning from England. One morning Brian Baker emerged from his Nissen Hut in his pyjamas and announced, in his ebullient manner: 'I've got to go up!' He pulled on his flying kit over his pyjamas, took off, and was back within twenty minutes, shouting 'I got it!' Three others claimed a share in this victory, Baker's observer and the crew of another Brisfit. Four hours later Sibley and Shone, on an OP, saw parts of the wreckage still sticking out of the water, 50 yards off shore between Nieuport and Ostend.

The latest single-seater, the Sopwith Camel, hitherto regarded as unsuitable for night operations, was also employed, as the BE2's had been, for night interception. Camel pilots of a reserve squadron at home, and of the recently equipped 70 Squadron in France, climbed, unsuccessfully at first, to meet the challenge of the Gothas. Bombing raids on Gotha bases were also mounted by Martinsydes, DH4's, and FE2b's, and by the RNAS from Dunkirk, forcing moves to new aerodromes.

Most significant of all on the bombing front was the formation on 11 October of the Forty-First Wing, arising from the Gotha raids and the demand for reprisals. The forty long-range squadrons committed to the strategic bombing of German industrial targets, as originally mooted, were unlikely, as Trenchard knew, ever to materialise, but he had already chosen a suitable base at Ochey, near Nancy in north-eastern France, within range of Mannheim and other suitable targets. The two leading RFC bomber squadrons, Nos 55 (DH4's), and 100 (FE2b's) were transferred to the new wing, together with a naval squadron of Handley-Pages which had been operating at night from Coudequerke, inland from Dunkirk: each of these latter machines was capable of carrying fourteen 112 lb bombs, six times the load of a DH4. This was the beginning of the Independent Force, as it later came to be known. The 'Smuts Report' (Chapter 6) had meanwhile advocated the creation of an independent Air Ministry, and the amalgamation of the RFC and the RNAS into a single independent Service was soon to be accomplished.

The second feature of the succession of minor battles that autumn was the proliferation of low-level strikes on troops and other targets in and near the front line. Sometimes these attacks were substituted for operations farther afield that had been rendered impossible by the weather; but by the start of the Broodseinde sub-battle in October the single-seater fighters had become the fighting advance guard of the infantry.

All three Sopwith two-seater squadrons, the 1½-strutters, had meanwhile been rearmed with Camels, and it was in a Camel of 45 Squadron that Norman Macmillan, now a flight commander, 'rattled away at troops, transport, trenches, and, in the open, guns and gunners, anything that offered a target.' Pilots flew in pairs, they didn't carry bombs, just twin machine-guns, and for Macmillan, at least, 'these low-flying jobs were full of excitement', though many disliked them. 'You were shot at by friend and foe alike,' complained Fullard. Yet, hugging the contours, they were safe from aerial attack.

The exhilaration of seeing the ground rush beneath them, sighting some spontaneously selected target, perhaps a gun battery, splaying the whole emplacement with bullets, the gunners flattened and helpless, lent an illusion of invulnerability. 'Things flashed into view, were fired on, passed behind and were forgotten with the next target that loomed up.' Much of the time they would be flying through a tunnel of fire. Bullets spewed at them from all angles, the concussion of exploding shells threw their Camels about crazily, and although often unaware of it they were repeatedly hit. Simultaneously, in kaleidoscopic profusion, they caught glimpses of grey-clad troops hurling themselves into open shell-holes, trying to claw their way into the camouflaging mud. Terrified horses galloped into obscurity, dragging half-capsized wagons behind them, columns of marching troops broke ranks and disintegrated. No one liked it or looked forward to it, and it was fiendishly dangerous, as the casualties showed, but as an instant and visible contribution to the fighting it was unparalleled.

43 Squadron, under Alan Dore, one of the pioneers of trench strafing, was the last of the 1½-strutters to get Camels, and they continued with the old machine through most of September while they were converting, suffering further casualties. Yet their keenness to do the job was undiminished. 13 September, wrote Dore, was 'a sad day for us all'. To begin with, they were grounded by the weather. Then 'Rickards came to me and said he thought the weather was good enough for photos. He and Thompson went off.' Captain A.T. Rickards was one of Dore's flight commanders. They took their photos, but, as always with photographic work, their straight and level flying over-exposed them to Archie. 'Thompson was hit but got back; Rickards was seen to dive very steeply. Then his wings folded up and he fell for 8,000 feet ... Rickards fell out and was found 500 yards away from the machine.' His observer, too, was killed: 'Marshall-Lewis, one of my best observers, gone.' On the same day a second of Dore's senior pilots side-slipped while practising in a Camel and was very badly hurt. 'So I lose two flight commanders in one day.'

On 19 September, six machines were doing a line patrol when a raw Canadian, Second-Lieutenant M.G.M. Oxley, became separated, 'as is often the case with new pilots'. News that he and his observer were dead came from the pilot of a Hun scout shot down on the British side next day.

At last, on 25 September, they flew their final patrol in the Sopwith two-seater. 'Having accomplished much fine work,' wrote Dore, 'they are now the slowest thing on the line.' But the conversion to Camels did not eliminate casualties, included among them being some of the two-seater pilots who had been with the squadron six months. The death of Second-Lieutenant Charles H. Harriman, shot down on patrol, was described by Dore as 'one of the tragedies of the war'. That night Dore 'went up to trenches . . . to see if we could recover the body of Harriman'. The machine had come down in no man's land, not 50 yards from where they stood – 'a pitiful sight, upended in the moonlight'. If Dore entertained any hope that Harriman might be alive, it vanished now. 'It was impossible to get to him in that night of full moon.' Two stretcher-bearers later crawled to him and found him dead. Later, when Harriman's body had been recovered, Dore 'buried him at La Pugnoy, where so many of our lads lie'.[1]

A reminder that life was worse in the trenches came when Dore visited his old battalion, the 7th Worcesters, a few days later. 'At Ypres they lost 600 men and 28 officers. Hoare, one of the original 7th Battalion, was killed there. He died quite happy in the command of a company: all he desired in this war . . . The terrors of Ypres were told by the fireside. Running up to their armpits in mud. Messages so soaked that they tore apart and had to be pieced together. Men with the look in their eyes that borders on insanity.'

At least the 34-year-old Dore had an inkling of what all this meant. In his last days on 43 Squadron he had the satisfaction of shooting down a Hun, also the horror of cutting away the woodwork of a crashed Camel to release the mangled body of one of his pilots. 'How I loathe the war when these things happen.'[2]

* * *

1. Harriman had been feeling sick at heights for some time but had refused to give in. This probably cost him his life, as he was seen to come out of a cloud upside down and crash.
2. In 1930 Alan Sidney Whitehorn Dore raised and was the original commander of No. 604 (County of Middlesex) Squadron, Auxiliary Air Force. The squadron flew night-fighter Blenheims in the Battle of Britain.

The departure of Alan Dore coincided with the return to France of his former squadron commander, Sholto Douglas, recovered from his digression into horse-play and now in charge of a newly-formed SE5A squadron, No. 84. At this time the SE5A was probably superior to any other fighting machine at the front: indeed Douglas regarded it as the most successful of all the Allied single-seaters, inferior to the Camel numerically but otherwise superior. Douglas listed its qualities as:

Comfortable, with a good all-round view.
Retaining its performance and manoeuvrability at high level (unlike the Spad and the Camel).
Steady and quick to gather speed in the dive.
Capable of a very fine zoom.
Useful in both offence and defence.
Strong in design and construction.
Possessing a reliable engine, especially after the Wolseley Viper was fitted.

The squadron was granted a period of preliminary training before being committed to the battle. Meanwhile, in continuing bad weather, with the infantry floundering in the mud of Passchendaele, the RFC mounted bombing and machine-gun attacks from low level and all manner of patrols, often at near-prohibitive cost: fourteen pilots and observers were lost and five others wounded in one day alone. Even these losses were scarcely proportionate to those on the ground, and all hope of achieving the strategic aims of the campaign was abandoned. Yet Haig was still determined to secure the Passchendaele ridge. Although continuing the assault was against the advice of his subordinate commanders, success, he believed, would secure the British position for the winter months and make life uncomfortable for the Germans. And Haig did have other reasons. He wanted to divert attention from the French, who were planning an attack on the Aisne front, and from the surprise he himself was plotting for late in the year by attacking with a massed force of tanks near Cambrai. Thus the failure of the first attack on Passchendaele, begun on 12 October, did not deter him, and the attack was renewed a fortnight later. Only the soldier can tell of the horrors that followed, but Norman Macmillan was one of a great many airmen who 'looked down on the sodden mass of shell-pocked mud that was the swamp of Passchendaele'. And Garland wrote: 'I can never forget Passchendaele – a nightmare of mud and unmentionable visions.' At one point the advancing troops had to withdraw because their rifles were choked with mud.

When the weather improved on 27 October it was the turn of the British troops to be hounded by bombing and machine-gun attacks. Ten enemy machines were claimed as destroyed, but RFC casualties too were severe – one killed, nine wounded, and thirteen missing.

Four days earlier, McCudden had gone on leave, Rhys Davids taking over the flight in his absence. RD was one of only four of the squadron's original complement still alive and in France, and he too was due for home posting. He was the top scorer in his flight, with twenty-one victories. 'This officer', reported Blomfield, 'came out to France with 56 on April 7th 1917 and has abundantly proved his capabilities in the air and on the ground during the past six months. I strongly recommend him for transfer to Home Establishment as a flight commander.' But RD was looking forward to running the flight. 'I shall be really sorry when I have to come home,' he told his mother. 'With luck I may get another month or six weeks out here.' At this news Caroline, who had been looking forward anxiously to the end of the six-month period, was seriously alarmed; Arthur was surely tempting fate. On 14 October she heard from her son again. 'I shall be here now till the end of the month at least.' Four days later she received chilling news. 'I am now the only original flying officer left.'

Blomfield was doing his best to keep RD on the ground, but in McCudden's absence it was difficult. And McCudden's restraining influence had more than once been responsible for saving RD's life. For some days after McCudden's departure, the squadron was grounded by bad weather, but on 27 October, a day, as has been mentioned, of heavy losses, No. 56 resumed patrolling. When they returned, three pilots were missing. One of them was Maybery, another was RD. Soon it was known that Maybery had landed safely. But of RD there was no sign.

'It would take a damn good Hun', the pilots told themselves, 'to get RD,' and for a long time they refused to believe he was dead. So did his mother, who, starved of news, addressed letters to her son as a prisoner. It was two months before the Germans, evidently uncovering some scrap of identification, dropped a message to say he was dead.

Caroline Rhys Davids, her hopes shattered, wrote at once to the CO of 56 Squadron (Blomfield had been succeeded by New Zealander Rainsford Balcombe-Brown): 'We have received, since early November, *absolutely no news* save the CO's and the War Office's messages "missing October 27th" and the latter's letter of December 29th that German airmen had dropped apparently the baldest announcement of his death. No burial place, no relics.

'Not a soul of those who knew him and were on patrol with him that day have sent us a single word. I know that his best friends either preceded him on leave or have themselves become missing, but surely others must have seen something of him during that fatal flight?' She began to suspect that he must, in some way, 'after all his swiftly won fame, have disgraced the squadron in the end'.

Balcombe-Brown was able to set her mind at rest on that score. He could well have added that new pilots arriving on 56 Squadron were always reminded of the distinction conferred upon them. 'This is the squadron', they were told, 'of Ball, Maybery, Rhys Davids, and McCudden.'

Before the year was out, Maybery, too, had gone, killed on 19 December after recording his twenty-first victory, equalling RD.

The weather again restricted RFC cooperation in the last days of the Passchendaele battle, but on the ground the fighting was bitter, the ridge being gained but at terrible cost. On 8 November, according to the historian A.J.P. Taylor, Haig's chief of staff visited the fighting zone for the first time. 'Good God!' he exclaimed. 'Did we really send men to fight in that?' He was silenced by his companion's laconic reply. *It's worse further up.*

16

THE ALLIED OFFENSIVE FLOUNDERS:
COUNTER-ATTACKED AT CAMBRAI

AFTER three and a half months of bitter fighting, causing some 250,000 casualties on each side, Haig's Flanders offensive had finally floundered in a morass of liquid mud at Passchendaele, leaving his armies with inadequate reserves for further adventures that winter. Yet, by mid-November, the pilots of III Brigade RFC under J.F.A. 'Josh' Higgins, one of the original flight commanders from August 1914, had reason to suspect that something unpleasant was brewing. First the brigade was being hastily reinforced, with two Camel squadrons, Nos 3 and 46, two new DH5 Squadrons, Nos 64 and 68 (Australian), two flights of a newly-arrived day-bombing squadron (DH4's), and the acquisition of Sholto Douglas's 84 Squadron (SE5A's). A pilot still serving in 46 squadron, converted from Pups, was Arthur Gould Lee. He thoroughly approved of the Camel, which he found lighter even on the controls than a Pup, and the 130 hp Clerget engine gave a wonderful surge of power. But why, he asked himself, were Camels appearing in such numbers in such a hurry? Why was his squadron being ordered to practise low-level bombing and low-level cross-country flying so assiduously? Every village in the back areas teemed with British troops, the cavalry were massing, and hundreds of tanks were assembling. Clearly a big push was imminent.

III Brigade now comprised the bulk of fifteen squadrons totalling nearly 300 aeroplanes, giving it an advantage on the Third Army front opposite Cambrai, of some three and a half to one. It was on this front, because of the rolling terrain that characterised it, that the Tank Corps commander, now disposing of 381 tanks, envisaged a major raid. Haig, with the Third Army commander, General Julian Byng, planned to expand and develop this raid into something more ambitious. Although seen as a limited offensive, it might be exploited if successful. German strength on southern sectors of the front had been denuded to bolster their resistance at Ypres; it would be a salutary reminder that they were vulnerable elsewhere.

There were wider implications. Soon, with the imminent collapse of Russia as an ally, large enemy forces would become available for the western front and for Italy, where the Italians were already in retreat after the Battle of Caporetto. By mounting an immediate diversion in France, an opportunity might be seized which might not recur, bringing relief to the hard-pressed Italians and making a significant breach in the German defences.

In order to achieve surprise, the standard pre-battle artillery bombardment, precursor of a likely assault, was dispensed with, and, on the morning of 20 November, in massed formation, the tanks rolled forward. Surprise was achieved, and the formidable Hindenburg Line and its main support line were overrun on a six-mile front to a depth of four miles. Meanwhile, from first light, despite low clouds and mist, army pilots began the strafing, practised earlier, of forward areas and aerodromes and other targets behind the enemy lines.

Pilots going into action for the first time were facing a tempestuous baptism. 'Many casualties occurred through pilots flying into the ground,' wrote Lee, 'but the majority were from ground fire.' Returning to the advanced landing ground several times to reload, Lee flew so low that he had to leap over the tanks when he glimpsed them labouring through the haze, drawing little groups of infantry in their wake, 'trudging forward', as he noted, 'with cigarettes alight'. He was dismayed to see flames belching from some of the tanks, not so much disabled as destroyed. Such was the confusion that to check his bearings he landed in a field, to find himself far to the east of

Cambrai, with marching German troops on a nearby road precipitating a panic take-off.

The commander of 64 Squadron (DH5's), Major Bernard Smythies, linguist and intellectual, formerly of 9 Squadron, realised from an early stage that he was ignorant of what was happening on the ground and was likely to remain so. This was typical of the army squadrons. They had their specific objectives and were fully occupied with those. Only the corps squadrons could normally hope to follow the course of the battle. The pilots of the DH5's, in their first taste of action, scattered troops with bombs and machine-gun fire, routed horse-drawn gun teams, silenced batteries, pounded dug-outs, blasted fortified shell-holes, and fired into trenches and gun emplacements. Those who escaped more or less unscathed rearmed and went again. But their single Vickers machine-guns, although synchronised to fire forward, and although supplemented by a bomb rack carrying four 20 lb bombs, combined with other inadequacies to make the DH5 a somewhat disappointing successor to the DH2. The change to a tractor configuration still gave a good forward view, but the rear view, where hostile attacks mostly originated, was obstructed by the wings. A poor performance above 10,000 feet did not matter for low-level strafing, but bombs could only be aimed in a dive. This was a particularly severe strain on the newer pilots, and casualties were heavy. On that first day alone the squadron had one man killed, one wounded, and two missing, a sobering introduction. Yet the squadron had within its ranks men of high calibre, and their performance drew a message of sympathy and commendation from Trenchard. 'Deeply regret your casualties today. Congratulations to all pilots on their splendid work under very difficult conditions.'

No. 64 Squadron was also notable for having three of the first pilots to be trained in Canada, under a scheme first examined by RFC veteran C.J. Burke ('Pregnant Percy'), and established in January 1917 by two more veterans in C.G. Hoare and Dermott Allen. To the 19-year-old Walter Daniel, who was one of the pupils, the early casualties imposed an additional strain: this was his first experience of life – and the loss of it – among the British. Previously, his countrymen had had plenty of time to adapt to the British while training in England, but Daniel, lacking this advantage, dubbed his flight commander 'a remote Englishman,' and thought he might have given him and other new pilots more encouragement. He was happier when the flight was taken over by Captain Philip Burge, who chose Daniel as his No. 2: 'I was very much encouraged by his personality and leadership.' Burge, from Potters Bar, had earned an MM in the trenches before transfer, and he later became an ace, with eleven victories and an MC to add to his MM. He was shot down in flames in a dogfight in July 1918.

Others who helped to restore the squadron's confidence included Captains Jimmy Slater (thirty-four victories) and E.R. Tempest (seventeen), although these victories were mostly gained after the DH5 was replaced by the SE5A. Meanwhile, during the battle for Bourlon Wood, Lieutenant J.A.V. Boddy had the misfortune to encounter not only the Richthofen *Jadgstaffeln*, swiftly transferred to this sector, but the Red Baron himself, returning after convalescence. Boddy was on a strafing mission when Richthofen intervened. But it was not quite the same old Richthofen. 'I am in wretched spirits after every aerial battle. That no doubt is an after-effect of my head wound.' But he was good enough to account for Boddy and his DH5 in what was his sixty-second victory, his first shots wounding Boddy in the head. Boddy was no stranger to being shot down, and he managed to glide in and crash-land in a corner of the wood.

He was not alone: moments earlier a squadron colleague, while strafing German troops retreating from the wood, had been brought down nearby. This was Captain Albert Morford, who extricated himself from his own pile-up in time to see Boddy's. Wounded himself, he managed to help Boddy out of his cockpit, and together they stumbled through the British forward positions to a dressing station. But both men had completed their task, earning the squadron another commendation for their work, this time from pioneer photographic pilot George Pretyman, now commanding the 13th (Corps) Wing under Higgins. 'Your people were simply magnificent today and probably created a record in showing what can be done in helping infantry with aeroplanes.'

These were deserved tributes to a squadron that had landed in

France less than a fortnight earlier and was facing a degree of exposure, in an inferior machine, which even hardened pilots cordially disliked. Perhaps this is why the beginners did so well. 'Trench strafing', wrote Lee, 'was all chance no matter how skilled you were.' It was a lottery, and it bore no comparison to air fighting, where experience, skill, tactics, good flying and accurate shooting gave the advantage, and luck, although essential for survival, was not the only factor. Strafing behind the lines Lee found less objectionable. Answering fire was nothing like so intense and the pilot could usually see the results of his attack, which was seldom feasible when trench-strafing. 'So much fire was directed at you that you felt every moment must be your last.'

Nevertheless Lee found releasing bombs at 100 feet before shooting up columns of lorries and other mechanical transport, seeing them swerve into ditches, and looking back on a scene of confusion, had its satisfactions, anyway in retrospect. 'I probably killed more Huns than in all my air fighting . . . But I don't like it overmuch, in fact, I don't like it at all. Nor does anybody else on the squadron.'

How long could one's luck last? Sick at the prospect of diving yet again into those nests of machine-guns, he knew that he still had to do it. Superstitions, like touching wood before a flight, had long since been forgotten by Lee: all that was left was a numb indifference to his fate. This was preferable to the nightmares of some of his colleagues as they sweated and screamed in imaginary death-throes. He was sorry, too, for the horses.

The Germans were meanwhile bringing up reinforcements and resisting strongly. British reinforcements on a significant scale were simply not available, tank losses and tank failures mounted, and an important objective in the left-centre of the front remained untaken, partly through poor visibility hampering reconnaissance. Attempts to make the position on the Bourlon ridge secure were challenged, and on 27 November the Germans recaptured it. When the expected enemy counter-attack came on 30 November, the dependence of air operations on the weather was again underlined. Early morning mist clinging to the valleys obscured infantry movements from the prying eyes of the corps squadrons, surprise was achieved, and the British were compelled to withdraw.

It was now the turn of the British forces to be subjected to incessant attacks by low-flying aircraft, and for British commanders to complain of the casualties caused and their demoralising effect. The Germans had learned their lesson from the British, and they attached great importance to it. Hoist with their own petard, the British subsequently recorded: 'Our men did not seem to know what to do to minimise the moral effect of these low-flying machines.'

The RFC responded by strengthening formations and shifting their offensive patrols to the battle area, and a hotch-potch of some fifty machines from each side, writhing and cavorting above Bourlon Wood, was a familiar sight. But the low-flying aircraft got through. Forced to give ground at Bourlon, the British were in some peril as they extricated themselves but had successfully completed their withdrawal by 7 December. Neither side had been able to exploit its moments of gain.

If the Cambrai battle was a pointer to the end of trench warfare, it also revealed the mounting threat to infantry of low-flying aircraft. 'The object of the battle flights', said a German memorandum, 'is to shatter the enemy's nerve by repeated attacks in close formation and thus to obtain a decisive influence on the course of the fighting.' At Cambrai, as the British admitted, 'The moral effect of this was very great and no doubt tended to facilitate the enemy's success.'

Two factors militated against undue reliance on troop-strafing. One, as ever, was the weather. The other was the casualty rate. For each day at Cambrai on which this form of attack was employed by the British, losses averaged 30 per cent. If a similar loss rate could be inflicted on the Germans it would be equally prohibitive. It was a rate at which whole squadrons would need replacing every four days. Such losses, even more certainly than bad weather, would have brought the RFC's whole system of army support to a standstill.

By the end of the first week in December, many of the surviving pilots, too, had fought themselves to a standstill. Lee was one of them. Suffering himself now from nightmares, he was told he should have a rest before he cracked up, yet he continued to fly. One of the five MC's awarded that week to 46 Squadron went to him, an excuse for a party. 'There's nothing wrong with me,' insisted Lee, 'that a good binge won't cure.' When he led a patrol next morning he was still seeing double.

Fierce abdominal pain suggested that there was indeed something wrong; by the end of the year he was living on brandy and milk. The medicos, diagnosing appendicitis, took him off flying. He had been longer on the squadron than anyone, half his colleagues were strangers, he had done 222 hours actually over the lines, been reported missing four times, had fifty-six combats and shot down eleven Huns. Only the chance of his survival enabled his experiences to be recorded, and his name to become known.

17

FIGHTER TACTICS: THE PEAK OF McCUDDEN AND MANNOCK

T HE rush to reinforce the Cambrai front had contrasting effects on the men drafted from England. The DH5's of 64 and 68 Squadrons, for all their deficiencies as fighting machines, were well led and well handled: the same could not be said of the two flights of DH4 bombers of 49 Squadron which had been adjudged ready for France. Despite past experience, and the long-term efforts of Smith-Barry and others, pilots, and even squadrons, or in this case parts of squadrons, were still being sent to the front in answer to emergency calls before they were operationally ready.

Lieutenant John Herbert Morris, although only just 19, had served with the Royal Horse Artillery in the Loos sector, on the Somme, and during the German retreat to the Hindenburg Line, and he was accustomed not only to the severities but also to the comforting presence of military discipline. He found it impossible to imagine anything more chaotic than the flight of 49 Squadron to join the BEF. Taking off on 11 November to cross the Channel, they ran into bad weather, circled in confusion, and eventually turned back. 'I never received one definite order from anyone,' complained the methodical Morris. He had given up hope of continuing that day when suddenly, at about three o'clock, they were told to hurry up and get off. They were to join the first formation they came across and take up any position they liked. 'Can you imagine anything more indefinite?' Each formation, contended Morris, should have been properly detailed, with a leader and a deputy leader. Clearly the squadron was totally unready for action. Engine trouble on the way – they had been equipped with the Farnborough-built 200 hp 3a engine, not the standard Rolls-Royce 'Eagle' – resulted in several forced-landings, but somehow they all got through to their aerodrome at Bellevue – a tribute more to their resourcefulness than their skill.

They were given a fortnight's familiarisation, during which they had continual trouble with the new engines. Wondering whether the servicing was at fault, Morris began to take his own mechanic up with him on test, 'to make certain he takes an interest'. But the mechanics were equally frustrated, and the teething troubles persisted. Eventually, on 26 November, all twelve machines took off on their first bombing raid, with an escort of SE5A's to defend them against the known depredations of Richthofen's Circus. According to Morris, they failed to establish contact with their escort, and although a further attempt was made later in the day it was foiled by clouds.

Morris describes another raid soon afterwards when there should have been nine of them present. This was reduced to seven by mechanical troubles, and at the rendezvous over the lines only four turned up. Morris had meanwhile been appointed deputy flight commander to a 22-year-old Londoner named William Chambers, formerly of the Lincolnshire Regiment, whom he respected. Their target, a town, was eight miles beyond the lines, and although monitored by hostiles they had a height advantage and continued to the target. Morris actually dropped his first bomb while there were five Hun machines directly beneath him, vaguely hoping he might hit one on the way – a somewhat bizarre notion. But he was well supported by his observer, Second-Lieutenant W.H. Hasler. 'Hasler was carrying on a war of his own, against a gentleman who had climbed a little higher than the others and was shooting at us with tracer. Hasler gave him a good burst and down he went.' At least two of their bombs hit the town, after which they fought a rearguard action back to the lines, some of the Hun pilots betraying a lack of persistence. Morris found he could outmanoeuvre them easily at 15,000 feet and above, and this and the speed of the DH4's facilitated their escape. 'We all got back safely.'

Lack of persistence was not confined to the German side, and there were times when Morris did not mince his words. A disastrous bombing raid on 4 December when nearly everyone got lost and five machines were missing did not improve morale. Morris described the shelling as 'terrible': he was the rear man, and everything seemed to burst around him. 'Crump, crump, crump they went ... What could I do? Ducking was useless. Hundreds of little black dots filled the sky around me ... 14,000 feet to fall if one hit me.' He threw the machine about and somehow avoided most of the bursts. A hole near his seat, pointed out to him when he landed, made him shiver.

Next day there was news of some of their casualties. 'I hadn't been in an hour when someone came in and said they'd just come back from Whyte's and Coddington's funerals.[1] It is extraordinary. A fellow comes up on a stunt with you at nine o'clock one morning and at eleven o'clock next day he's dead and buried and another pilot has taken his place.'

For a time all shows were stopped. When they restarted, Morris's letters, addressed to his family in Blandford, Dorset, continued. 'On nearly all expeditions, eight or nine machines would be detailed but seldom more than three or four could get the height to get over, thanks to our rotten engines.' It may not always have been the engines. 'Some made a nuisance of themselves by continually turning back with a dud engine,' continued Morris, who strongly disapproved. 'I hated letting anyone else do a job which had been given to me.'

The harassed squadron commander, Major Basil Turner, a South African, was forced to rely on Morris more than was reasonable, and Morris complained that his CO was working him to death. 'The more you do for him the more he wants, whereas if you never do

---

1. Second-Lieutenants G.H. Whyte and C.E. Coddington, killed in action on 4 December 1917.

anything, like some of our people, who have never been over the line even once, he doesn't expect anything from them, and they never need to do anything.' Turner, like most squadron commanders, was under continual pressure to get results, and Morris, unlike some of his colleagues, generally got them. It was not a unique situation. There were shirkers on most squadrons, and the best men were generally entrusted with the vital tasks. Ewart Garland was a case in point. Even Charles Smart, on 5 Squadron, had acknowledged that there were exceptions to the general high standard. Advantage was inevitably taken of outstanding men.

Among the other newly-arrived squadrons, even No. 84 under Sholto Douglas started badly. Following its period of preliminary training, the squadron flew their first offensive patrols on the Passchendaele front. All through October they fought up and down the Menin-Roulers road, which ran north and south some six miles east of Ypres. Of the pilots, only the three flight commanders had experience in France, and at first there were many casualties, so much so that Douglas fell to analysing what was wrong. He came to believe that the policy of mounting OPs in single flights was mistaken. Three separate squadrons of SE5A's might each put up a single flight to patrol a single section of the front, but they would be operating independently, with no unified plan. 'Thus a single flight was often attacked and defeated before the other two were aware of it.' Douglas's preference would have been for all three flights of a single squadron to work together as a unit, but this did not get the blessing of his superiors until the spring of 1918.

Towards the end of October the squadron was transferred to the 13th Wing under George Pretyman, to strengthen the forces cooperating with the Fourth Army at Cambrai. Their task was to keep the sky clear not only for the corps squadrons but also for the low-flying strafers. But the fog, mists and drizzle that hindered reconnaissance forced Douglas to reduce rather than increase the size of his patrols and operate his machines in pairs and even singly. With the Germans also intent on giving protection to their low-flying and reconnaissance machines, the SE5A's succeeded in shooting down some half-a-dozen enemy scouts without loss. Douglas called this 'the fruits of our arduous apprenticeship on the Menin–Roulers road'.

The experience of 84 Squadron was that the most practicable fighting formation was not a flight of six machines, as often supposed, but a Vee-shaped formation of five, two machines stepped up behind the leader on either side. Another discovery was that losses occurred when a flight was attacking, rather than when it was being attacked. When under attack, the pilots stuck together for mutual protection; when attacking, they tended to break off in pursuit of individual targets, get separated from their colleagues, and be jumped on by superior numbers. The remedy, concluded Douglas, was for the flight leader to be regarded as paramount. When he dived to attack, the flight must dive with him. When he zoomed, they must zoom. This, during combat, was the only way to keep the flight together. Inevitably it meant that it was the flight leader who did most of the shooting. They learnt too, as McCudden had learnt, that they must always try to take the enemy at a disadvantage, and that it was often sensible, failing that, to refuse combat. In essence they were simply adopting the methods long favoured by Manfred von Richthofen.

Fortunate were the men posted to squadrons where strategy and tactics were so closely studied. Their chances of survival were dramatically improved. One of the luckiest was Ted Galley, whose vicissitudes as observer have been referred to. Joining up originally as a despatch rider, he had graduated from Sandhurst with a regular commission, and he had been serving on the Somme when he was attracted by the notice about transferring to the RFC as an observer, and he had soon found himself flying photo recces on FE2b's with 22 Squadron. Eventually his misfortunes with over-cautious drivers had got him home on a pilot's course. Told by his flight commander at CFS – it was Balcombe-Brown – that he'd never make a pilot, he had resolved to prove him wrong, promising that he would win the sweepstake for the quickest pupil on his course to go solo – and making good his boast. He was waiting at King's Cross for the train to Scotland to begin his combat training when an orderly accosted him. 'Report to Postings immediately.' There had been heavy casualties in France, there was a shortage of pilots, and he was to leave for France that night. It was a familiar story, though for Galley it was to have a fortunate outcome.

Balcombe-Brown, as already recorded, had meanwhile replaced Blomfield at 56 Squadron, and when he heard of Galley's arrival in France, soon after the loss of Rhys Davids, he sent for him. Galley then had the further good fortune to be assigned to McCudden's flight. Of McCudden and 56 he wrote: 'There were some dashing fellows there, but he and I saw eye to eye about things.' (If this seemed presumptuous in a newcomer, Galley, besides having had considerable experience as an observer, was, as we have seen, no shrinking violet.) 'He always got height before he attacked,' he wrote approvingly of McCudden. Strategy and tactics, as Galley soon saw, were McCudden's forte. 'He only lost one man [from his flight] the whole time I was with him.' It was the same with combat damage. 'I've only ever seen about three bullet holes through his machine.'

McCudden, indeed, was enjoying his finest period, building up to a remarkable sequence over Christmas 1917. Four enemy two-seaters fell to his guns on 23 December, and a hat trick five days later took his personal score to thirty-seven. A telegram from Trenchard ended with the words 'You are wonderful!' Despite Trenchard's dislike of publicity for so-called aces ('The British Army does not permit the names of its flying heroes to be published,' said an American news agency), anonymity could no longer be preserved. On 16 January 1918 the front page of the *Sunday Herald* was devoted to a picture gallery of the McCudden family – ex-Sergeant-Major W.H. McCudden, his wife Amelia McCudden, and their pilot sons, Willie (already killed, in 1915), Jimmy, and a third son, the impetuous Jack, who was making a name for himself on SE5A's with 84 Squadron (six victims in January–February). When Jimmy eventually went home on rest in March 1918 he had fulfilled the half-jocular toast that his initial victory with 56 Squadron should be the first of fifty: his score, the highest so far on the Allied side, was fifty-seven.

Mick Mannock, too, in the last weeks of 1917, was scoring victories almost daily. He was still with 40 Squadron under Leonard Tilney, but he was now flying SE5A's. His temperament, always volatile, had fluctuated wildly in previous months. Early in his career he had landed from a scrap with his knees shaking and his nervous system temporarily shattered; but there were others worse than him. 'Old Mackenzie goes on leave today,' he wrote. 'He is in need of it. If ever a lad was cracked up, Mac is. I wonder if I shall ever get like that?'

Mannock was befriended by a Scot named William MacLanachan, whom he dubbed McScotch, to distinguish him from another Mac on the squadron, Dubliner George McElroy, whom he called McIrish. It seemed to McScotch that the inner life that he was aware Mannock led was turning him into a loner. But he could do little about it. Emotional battles, he supposed, could only be fought alone. 'Feeling nervy and ill,' wrote Mannock. 'Afraid I am breaking up. Oh for a fortnight in the country at home.' Three days later the 22-year-old Tilney sent his 30-year-old flight commander home on leave. But there was no relaxation for Mannock in what was a broken home. His mother had become an alcoholic, and he sought sanctuary with friends. There he worked hard to crystallise his ideas about air fighting. Back in France the pace had hotted up and he was ready for it. 'Fights galore and thrilling escapes!' was all he had time to record.

After his award of the MC, and promotion to captain and flight commander, at first on probation, there was resentment at what some saw as his recklessness. In deliberate protest, Maclanachan left the patrol and continued alone. It was a salutary reminder to Mannock that his days as an individualist were over. As a flight commander he must think first of his flight. They did not know that Mannock, alone in his room, sometimes cried heartbrokenly when a colleague was lost.

From this point on he devoted his spare time to training his flight and to developing his talent for leadership. 'My nerves better lately,' he noted. And his violin-playing, which had stopped when a colleague who accompanied him at the piano was killed, was resumed. The tall, gaunt figure, standing in the shadows in a corner of the Mess, playing without accompaniment, displayed an emotional depth that proved spell-binding. Lest he reveal too much of himself, he would turn his face to the wall as he played.

He had been fighting continuously for eight months, and the strain was showing. His abiding horror of a flamer was becoming obsessive, and on 2 January 1918, with a bar to his MC, he was sent home again by Tilney; this time on rest.

18

'THEM AND US': THE GROUND CREWS

WHEN Arthur Gould Lee relinquished command of his flight in 46 Squadron, bound for Home Establishment, he put up three of his ground crew tradesmen for decorations for outstanding work – and was surprised and gratified when he heard they had been awarded. How many other squadron and flight commanders, he wondered, remembered the men who serviced their machines, the fitters and riggers and armourers on whose care and devotion their lives daily depended? 'We're cut off from them,' wrote Lee, 'we live in a separate world, simply because they don't fly and fight as we do.' (There was also the social gulf, widened rather than narrowed by the wearing of uniform.) Lee welcomed the chance, as he saw it, to cross the bridge between what he called 'them and us.'

Here the RFC was at a basic disadvantage compared with the front line troops, where officers and men were all in it together. Yet this dichotomy, felt Lee, should not obscure recognition of exceptional effort behind the lines.

It does seem that standards in the RFC were above average. Whereas, back in 1911, the first officer recruits to the original Air Battalion could be selected from any regular branch of the army, other ranks could be recruited only from the Corps of Royal Engineers, lending a sense of exclusivity from the start. Later, with the expansion that followed the creation of the RFC and the outbreak of war, the favourable terms offered for ground tradesmen made attracting the best men possible. Alan Dore, after transfer from the Worcestershire Regiment, expressed his amazement at the wealth of talent around him. He wrote that, in his squadron alone, 'we have the best mechanics in England, the best wireless operators, the best instrument makers, and the most highly-skilled armourers.' Many of these men took the opportunity to fly.

The negative reaction of one engine fitter ('No fear!') to the extra two shillings a day blood money paid to air gunners ('They get all the dirty long-distance bombing jobs'), emphasises the spirit of the men who took up the challenge. Of those who did, the number who lost their lives runs into hundreds, many were taken prisoner, and some were decorated. But it was of the ground tradesman dedicated to his job that Trenchard had declaimed: 'These men are the back-bone of all our efforts.'

An average squadron might include as many as 200 other ranks of various trades, but it was usually the men working directly with the machines and the pilots who volunteered for flying. Not all such volunteers could be accepted: the ranks of expert tradesmen would have been seriously denuded had this been so. One engine fitter, who later graduated to senior NCO and then engineer officer, applied for pilot training but was told: 'We can recruit fit young men and train them as pilots in three months: we can't do that for engine fitters.' Another mechanic, after volunteering, was ordered to cease pilot training and revert to his ground trade.

Squadron commanders were fully aware of their dependence on their ground tradesmen. 'Josh' Higgins once told a pilot whose careless flying with a mechanic as passenger had alarmed and enraged him: 'If you want to kill yourself you can, but don't kill one of my men.'

During the March 1918 retreat, Trenchard put a harsher complexion on the responsibilities of the ground crews. 'You men must guard these machines with your lives. Without these machines the army is blind ... And if it's between you and the machine, the machine comes first.' Few aerodromes were more than perfunctorily guarded.

The relationship between pilot and ground tradesman was on a level of trust, not always absolute. John Morris, of 49 Squadron, has been mentioned as one who encouraged responsibility by insisting that his mechanic accompany him on air test. Charles Smart wrote: 'Took the engine sergeant up to prove to him that the engine was dud.' It was in test flights like these that adventurous air mechanics got the bug for flying.

Machines that ran well on the ground sometimes under-performed in the air, but the pilot who continually blamed his engine when he failed to reach his target was soon rumbled, while the careless mechanic was disciplined. More often than not, though, an attachment grew.

Bert Harris, in speaking of this three-cornered team, listed his machine, his observer, and himself; but he then made special mention of 'your own favourite mechanic, who looked after your machine. You felt you were just a team together.' The mechanics, too, shared this team spirit, never more poignantly than when, gazing eastwards, they waited in vain for man and machine to return, knowing that something in their lives which they valued had gone.

The rapid arrival of replacement pilots, and the intensive work involved in keeping the aircraft flying, checked morbidity. Some of the most genuine mourners were batmen, who got to know the officers they looked after, their idiosyncrasies and their weaknesses, better than most. 'Lost two more nice gentlemen,' was one sad comment.

Hugh Walmsley – later Air Marshal Sir Hugh – had a fitter named Laidlaw and a rigger named Taylor who before the war had both worked at Avro's in Manchester. 'They looked after my aeroplane', said Walmsley, 'as though it were their own child.' There was no such thing as working hours. 'If there was anything to do they did it, they used to work like blazes night and day.' Only years later did Walmsley realise how close he had been to these men, the perception coming when he discovered that his mother had been sending them food parcels throughout.

Such contacts were based on mutual regard. Each knew the other's worth. 'We respected them,' wrote Walmsley, 'and they respected us because of the high casualty rate; they knew that compared with us they had a cushy job.' Air mechanic Callender put it more humorously – and humour was a vital ingredient. 'Our relationship with the officers was very good indeed. We kept our place and we kept them in theirs.' They were asked to do things, he says, but never ordered. As for discipline, on a front-line squadron, rough justice was inevitable, and the men accepted it.

Ewart Garland believed that ground crews understood the gulf that was bound to exist between flyer and non-flyer, quite apart from any question of rank. One incident he never forgot was when, after a particularly rough day in the air, pilots and observers, on taking their seats in a hangar for a concert, were applauded by the men.

Signing himself 'Your faithful mechanic', Leslie P. Tupling wrote from France in April 1917 of his pride in having had Garland's 'valuable life in my keeping' over a period of ten months. Respect, as in this case, was frequently tinged with affection. 'I am absolutely fed up now and have been ever since you left good old 10th Squadron.' He consoled himself with the thought of what Garland's fate would inevitably have been had he stayed any longer. 'Every time I saw you take wing my thoughts were far from happy until you returned.'

Men who had transferred to the RFC from the army appreciated the contrast and were eternally grateful. Walter Cobb, a photographer, wrote: 'What a relief from the infantry! We never had enough to eat in the line as there were too many pickings on the way up, but in the squadron [No. 59] we were never short.' Life was much more bearable in other ways. 'NCO's were not drill-and-yapping experts but men with some trade who knew what they were doing and worked with others more as a team. They got the best out of us by cooperation and help.' Sport and entertainment were other fields of contact.

It was not that ground tradesmen were immune from danger. When aerodromes were bombed, as they increasingly were, other ranks suffered in proportion to their numbers. Battery wireless operators were special targets of enemy action. 'Conspicuous Gallantry' was the verdict on an operator named H.V. Howlett, of 52 Squadron, who left his dug-out three times to re-rig a damaged aerial under heavy shell-fire. The citation for his Military Medal stressed how the accurate shooting of the artillery depended on operators maintaining contact with pilots and observers, thus saving the lives of thousands of troops.

In the course of the war, casualties among Battery wireless operators ran into hundreds. One who had a lucky escape was Stanley Gorringe, of 21 Squadron. Dissatisfied with the trade of Stoker offered him by the RNAS, he transferred to the RFC via the Wireless School at Aldershot, but must surely have regretted it when his dug-out was hit. His diary and log-book were pierced by shell-splinters and splashed with the blood of a comrade, but he himself escaped. 'I was on the scene in about half an hour,' wrote his CO to his parents, 'and found your son badly shaken but quite unwounded. He has a mild dose of shell-shock.'

Willie Read, as already mentioned, invited his batman to join him in the air, knowing that he was eager to do so. 'He would always come aboard with a packet of sandwiches and a Thermos . . . During a raid he would come aft and serve me with sandwiches, as if he were waiting at table.' This was in a Handley Page bomber. Read's reputation for looking after his men was very properly accompanied by a habit of looking after himself.

It was mostly the older men who kept diaries. Among pilots, Read by this time was 33, so was Smart, and Dore was 34. Among mechanics, diarist Alexander Paice, originally of No. 34 Squadron under John Chamier and Eric Routh, was 33 and married, with a small son. A cabinet-maker by trade, working for a family firm in Gloucestershire which designed and built folding furniture for the top London hotels and stores, he heard of the RFC's desperate need for tradesmen and was quickly signed on as an air mechanic (flight rigger). Despite a crisp shorthand style his diary confirms a greater-than-average maturity. At Christmas 1916, for instance, he was a sober witness of festivities that left 'nearly everyone in the billet drunk . . . What a Christmas'.

In 1917 he moved to 70 Squadron, where he teamed up with an engine fitter of equal conscientiousness named Tom Webb. The most dangerous job on the squadron appears to have been Pay Parade: three times Paice tells of officers who had paid them that morning and who were casualties virtually within the hour. One of his pilots was New Zealander Clive Collett, the test pilot and guinea-pig parachutist; he records with pride Collett's eighth Hun on 18 August.[1] But early in 1918 he and Webb got a new pilot, Lieutenant John Todd, formerly a student at Edinburgh University: Todd had been punished as an infantryman, wrote Paice, for 'shooting himself in the foot'. Whether this was true physically or metaphorically Paice did not elaborate; no doubt Todd kept it a secret. But it was to prove a rewarding partnership. In recording Todd's exploits, Paice basked in reflected glory, and his pride in 'his pilot' grew.

'*19th January – New pilot, Lieutenant Todd. 20th January – Lieutenant Todd gave me five francs.*' (Presumably Webb was treated the same. There were 25 francs to the pound.)

'*22nd January – Lieutenant Todd brought his first Hun down.*' It was an Albatros DV: within three days, Todd had achieved something that took most men weeks and even months.

'*24th January – Todd nearly brought a Nieuport down in a fight with an Albatros.*' The older but vastly junior man was becoming the father confessor: Todd, as before, appears to have kept his escapade to himself.

On 28 and 29 January Todd made claims, anyway to Paice, but only the first was confirmed. It was a Fokker Triplane. Then:-

'*9th February – Up early for special flying. Lieutenant Todd volunteered to go over the lines at daybreak to catch a Hun which comes over bombing every morning. But weather wet and rough.*' The attempt was repeated a few days later, when Todd brought down an Albatros DV.

1. Collett later returned to test flying with twelve victories, but was killed in December 1917 testing a captured Albatros scout over the Firth of Forth.

[411]

'*24th – My machine came back awfully damaged. Todd all right, only dazed. There were pieces of shrapnel sticking to his flying coat. The Major had it photographed.*'

On 5 March Paice is made acting corporal. On the 11th, with the great German March offensive imminent, Todd takes delivery of a new Camel, and next day he shoots down another Hun, his fourth. But the new machine, with a longeron perforated, has to go away to be rebuilt. Meanwhile Todd is promoted to captain, and Paice, for the first time, is appointed to take charge of the Guard.

A move by road to Marieux on 15 March, one of many in the ensuing weeks, brings out Paice's aesthetic appreciation. '*Best aerodrome I've been to, on the edge of a large wood. The daffodils, primroses, and cowslips are in lovely bloom.*' He also evinces an impartial appreciation of man-made things. '*A captured Albatros brought to Marieux, a splendidly-built machine.*'

There was appreciation, too, perhaps less aesthetic, from Todd. '*19th March – Captain Todd gave me fifty francs for looking after his machine.*' (£2, more than a week's wages; again one can perhaps assume that Tom Webb got the same.) On the 21st, Ludendorff launched the offensive that was to win the war before the Americans could intervene. '*Worked day and night,*' recorded Paice.

On the 22nd, as the Allies retreated: '*Busy erecting hangars, German POWs helping. Todd got two Huns, squadron got ten. Fritz was over again tonight.*' German night bombing was becoming severe.

On the night of 23 March, as recorded earlier, Paice worked right through until 5 a.m., and then for another eight hours until midnight on the 24th. '*Terrible fighting just in front of us. May have to leave any time.*' Todd's new machine was damaged but Paice repaired it, and 70 Squadron never let up, bombing and strafing all day. This was the day when Paice's flight broke all records by getting thirty-six hours' flying out of their machines. Next day they began digging trenches.

'*Terrible raid on our aerodrome. Many of our chaps wounded and five killed.*' Continually forced to retreat to fresh aerodromes, bombed and machine-gunned as they went, their conditions

Werner Voss with his Triplane.
'His flying was wonderful, his
courage magnificent.'

V.P. 'Versh' Cronyn. 'The relief
from tension was so great that I
nearly collapsed.'

A group of German Aces. From left to right: Sebastian Festner, Emil
Schaefer, Manfred von Richthofen, Lothar von Richthofen, Kurt Wolff.

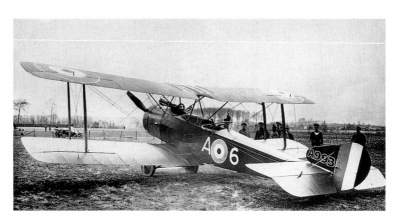

A Sopwith 1½-strutter of 43 Squadron, forced down beyond the lines with its crew during Bloody April.

Sopwith Pups of 46 Squadron about to return to the UK to repel the Gothas, July 1917. (Note, a Nieuport of 40 Squadron centre.)

An Armstrong–Whitworth FK8 of 82 Squadron. The sluggish 'Big Ack' required skilful handling.

Left: P.N.M. 'Puggy' Shone and his pilot caused untold havoc amongst off-duty German pilots with their pranks.

Below right: S.J. 'Squibs' Sibley. 'The trouble with this war is that it's so bloody dangerous.'

DH4 two-seaters of 217 Squadron lined up for action, some with 320 lb bombs ready for loading. By general consent 'the best day bomber of the war'.

A Sopwith Camel of 46 Squadron, showing flight commander's streamers and two Cooper (20 lb) bombs.

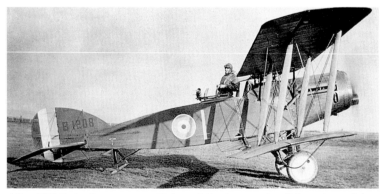

The F2B Bristol two-seater Fighter. Mistaken tactics did not long delay its effectiveness.

Jimmy Slater – a true professional (34 victories on DH5's and SE5A's).

C.M. 'Billy' Crowe (15 victories) followed Ball into cloud – but then lost him.

Arthur Gould Lee called Trenchard 'a leader after the hearts of Service pilots.'

Clive Collett, test and scout pilot, made the RFC's first parachute descent from an aeroplane, 13 January 1917.

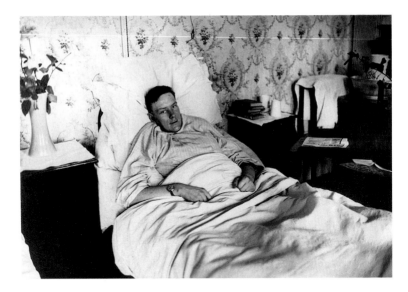

Above: 'Alan would take on anything.' A 6'2", big-boned 18-year-old from Winnipeg, Alan McLeod won the RFC's last VC, but succumbed soon after to Spanish flu.

Left: Arthur Hammond, a 23-year-old English observer with McLeod, lost a leg but later emigrated . . . to Winnipeg.

John Todd (18 victories)   Oscar Heron (13 victories)

'My machine came back awfully damaged,'
wrote Paice in his diary. 'Todd all right.'

Caught at the
workshop bench –
Alec Paice.

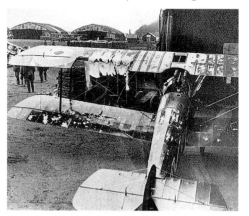

Left: Ewart Stock, the Camel pilot who kept an illustrated diary of the March 1918 Retreat. 'We had very few pilots left.'

Below: Another Ewart, also a notable diarist – the Australian Ewart Garland, second from left, with members of his flight on DH9A bombers of the Independent Force, 1918.

worsened. '*No bread, only biscuits. Fatal crashes almost daily, mid-air collisions frequent.*'

So it continued for Todd and for Paice, and for countless others, throughout the retreat and on into May, June and the first half of July, moving from one aerodrome to another, hounded out at first and subsequently advancing, but bombed continually, with many casualties. Pilots and machines went missing or were shot down in flames, or collided or broke up in mid-air, or crashed fatally on landing, to be faithfully diarised by Paice. But Paice himself survived, and so too did Todd. Promoted to flight commander in May, and awarded the new Royal Air Force decoration, the Distinguished Flying Cross, in July, John Todd went home next day after six months at the Front with eighteen confirmed victories – and with no more wounds in the foot. A modest enough ace by comparison, he was a hero of heroes to Paice, as Paice was to him.

For Paice the war went on. Soon he was involved with another hero, Oscar Heron: of Heron's thirteen victories before the armistice, all in a Camel serviced by Webb and Paice, ten were the formidable Fokker DVII. No doubt Heron was equally appreciative of his mechanics, but his generosity may not have matched John Todd's: anyway there is no mention in Paice's diary of francs changing hands.[1]

1. Alexander Paice returned to the family business in 1919. When the new Dorchester Hotel was being furnished in 1931, the firm were asked to build a simple but attractive folding trunk-stand in Swedish birch for each of its 283 rooms. When Queen Mary visited the hotel she was so taken with these trunk-stands that she said she would like some at Buckingham Palace. They were duly made, in solid walnut, leading to further orders. Paice died in 1946.

1918

19

FACING THE GERMAN OFFENSIVE: THE RFC IN DEFENCE

THE reputation of General Smuts as a visionary was confirmed and enhanced when he presented his report to the War Cabinet on 17 August 1917. He looked ahead to a time when air power, because of its potential for the 'devastation of enemy lands and the destruction of industrial and populous centres on a vast scale', might actually take precedence over those naval and military operations to which it was then subordinate and ancillary. In pursuit of his vision, he recommended the amalgamation of the two air services into a unified command, spelling an end to duplication and to the competing and often conflicting demands that had exacerbated the supply problem. With surprising alacrity the War Cabinet approved; Smuts was appointed to chair a committee to work out the details; and one of his principal advisers throughout remained David Henderson, the RFC's first commander in the field.

Trenchard, so often called the Father of the Air Force, ahead of Henderson, resisted rather than sought an amalgamation. The RFC, he felt, had only just settled down after the changes and uncertainties of previous years. Why disturb the present set-up? He feared that a separate air force, uncontrolled by the Navy or the Army, would be drawn towards the spectacular, at the expense of the job of work it was doing. How were the duties of the new force to be allocated? Competition between the Navy and Army for existing resources was fierce: wouldn't they simply be introducing a third competitor? He feared, too, that such a major reorganisation would have an adverse effect on production. Then there was the personnel side. Operational pilots soon wore themselves out. What would happen to them? At present, where appropriate, they could be absorbed back into their relevant service or regiment. Finally, Trenchard expressed a personal wish to remain in the job he was doing, where he felt he was being employed most fittingly, rather than be tied, as suggested, to an office and staff work, to which he felt he was unsuited. But the decision was made.

On 29 November the Air Force Bill duly received the Royal Assent, and an Air Ministry, on a par with the Admiralty and the War Office, was formed on 2 January 1918. Lord Rothermere, the newspaper baron, was appointed Air Minister, and Trenchard, who was knighted, was designated Chief of a newly established Air Staff. An Air Council, with executive powers, assumed the functions of the old non-executive Air Board, and Jack Salmond succeeded Trenchard in command of the RFC in France. The new service, to be named the Royal Air Force, was to come into being on 1 April 1918.

For the Royal Flying Corps, as for the Royal Naval Air Service, the year 1918 thus began with intimations of mortality. Jealousies and friction in Whitehall had sometimes been reflected at squadron level, and a distaste for the merger was general. The RNAS, having been part of the senior service, felt superior, 'and they acted it', according to Lieutenant H.R. Puncher, who flew alongside them on what had been a naval squadron. The RFC, in the front line of the ground fighting for so long, could not accept inferiority. Both services were proud of their origins and achievements and had developed loyalties almost as fierce as those of a regiment. They were lukewarm, if not hostile, to the change, which, as typically understated by Bryan Sharwood-Smith, was 'greeted with no great enthusiasm'. Tommy Traill wrote more frankly: 'We were proud of the RFC and of our-selves, and we wanted none of this new thing.' Yet the ugliness was often in the eye of the beholder. 'I can only say that as a squadron officer,' wrote Lieutenant-Commander R.M. Bailey, RN, of the alleged animosity, 'I never experienced it at all in France.'

The greatest achievement of the RNAS up to this point lay in its contribution to the anti-U-boat war, specifically in the Channel and the North Sea, an area of 4,000 square miles which they systematically combed in spider's-web fashion from coastal bases in Britain and France. In 1917 alone they made 175 U-boat sightings and 107 attacks, and although their claims of sinkings were modest they greatly assisted the surface forces besides acting as a deterrent. They had also undertaken most of the strategic bombing that had been attempted thus far. For the RFC, however, in what were to prove its climactic months of existence, its greatest challenge still lay ahead.

During the winter of 1917–18 the pendulum between attack and defence had swung drastically away from Haig and towards Ludendorff. The Bolsheviks, following the October revolution, were negotiating a separate peace, and an armistice between Russia and Germany was signed on 15 December, removing, for Ludendorff, the bane of war on two fronts. Furthermore, vast quantities of manpower and material were thereby released for transfer to the western front. Yet although these welcome accessions would eclipse any immediate infusion of American strength, they would be a diminishing and irreplaceable asset, which American strength was not. The Austrian breakthrough at Caporetto had been arrested (with the help of eleven divisions from the British and French) by a determined stand on the natural barrier of the river Piave, stabilising the front; but the Austrian army remained in a strong position, unlikely to need early reinforcement. And whereas the U-boat campaign, as a means of securing a negotiated peace, had disappointed, the Allied blockade was beginning to bite. Clearly, in Ludendorff's mind, the time to strike was now, before American manpower and industrial output tipped the scales.

On the Allied side, the French were still consolidating with an eye to the American build-up, while disillusion with Haig as a commander-in-chief, after the exhausting campaigns of 1917, had led to a reluctance by the British War Cabinet to back him wholeheartedly, for fear that resources might be squandered. Indeed there was a move afoot to replace him, to Trenchard's disgust, though it came to nothing. Meanwhile the armies in the field were smarting under the experience of Cambrai, which had begun so well and ended in stalemate after a thoroughly daunting reverse.

It was the daunting reverse that exercised the minds of the General Staff. British troops had taken part in a more open engagement than the trench warfare to which they had become accustomed, and the Germans had adapted the more readily. The German principle involved the use, as a spearhead, of specially trained *sturmtruppen* who by infiltrating their adversary's forward positions caused confusion and panic. As an antidote, the British adapted a German method of defence which relied on a thinly-held front line or Forward Zone, with a Battle Zone a mile or two behind it, supported by strong-points in depth, and a Rear Zone, four to eight miles behind the Battle Zone, on which the defence could fall back if necessary. But anything approaching mobile warfare was subject to the same imponderable as air support, namely, the weather.

While the tactics of elastic defence were being overhauled and practised by the army, in preparation for the imminent German offensive foreshadowed by Intelligence reports and by aerial reconnaissance, Trenchard, as his last contribution before leaving France, fell to considering how the RFC should best be employed in a ground campaign based on defence. Obviously the first and foremost duties would lie in reconnaissance, watching for signs of possible attack and helping army commanders to determine whence and in what strength such attacks might come. Secondly, once preparations for an attack were established, would come the routine work of (a) artillery cooperation, (b) bombing aimed at hindering the enemy's preparations and harassing his troops, and (c) an energetic offensive against the enemy's air force to facilitate (a) and (b).

Once an attack started, the primary duty would lie, as always, with the corps squadrons, 'to render our artillery fire effective.' If this object could be attained, thought Trenchard, 'it will be the most material help which can be rendered to the infantry although it may be invisible to them.' Trenchard had always insisted that the RFC should work as an integral part of the army, and he was anxious to reassure Haig, who feared, with the introduction of a separate air service, a conflict of interests. He had argued logically and lucidly against the practicality and moral advisability of Smuts's theories, without effect. He was fortunate in having, in Trenchard, a man devoted to the army, for whom nothing must detract from the RFC's primary duty.

Trenchard also saw a secondary duty: the violent low-level strafing of enemy reinforcements behind the lines, of his communications, and of his advance troops, in close cooperation with the infantry. He specifically stressed the moral effect. And it was in low-level strafing, when the battle started, that pilots and observers of the RFC were to take perhaps the greatest personal risks of any of the combatants in their endeavours to halt the German advance.

Trenchard's homily on 'The Employment of the Royal Flying Corps in Defence' did not end without a reminder of the basic philosophy on which he had always insisted, and always would. Success was only possible through gaining and maintaining an overall ascendancy. This could be achieved only by attacking and defeating the enemy's air forces. Even when the Army was forced temporarily on the defensive, as now, the action of the RFC must always remain essentially offensive. In this he had no more fervent a disciple than Jack Salmond.

The agitation in the UK, in the summer of 1917, for the formation of an Air Ministry, and the news that Winston Churchill, who had long since argued for an Air Ministry, had been appointed Minister of Munitions, seemed to the Germans to portend a substantial growth in British air strength, and in response they formulated and hastened a programme of expansion which gave priority to their air service. The result was that enemy aircraft production was more than doubled, from 8,100 in 1916 to 19,400 in 1917. The British, too, were expanding, and their assessments of where the blow might fall were based on hard-won evidence, but as defenders they were bound to spread their strength, which must inevitably give the attackers a numerical advantage wherever they struck. Haig had good reasons for keeping the Second and First Armies in the northern sector, fearing a drive for the Channel ports, but he also had to be prepared for an attack somewhere in the centre, in the area Arras–Cambrai–St Quentin–La Fére, aimed at separating the British armies from each other, and perhaps from the French farther south. Thirdly was the fear of a drive southwards for Paris. To increase the problems of prediction, Ludendorff seems to have planned tactically rather than strategically, the intention being to strike hard at what he considered the weakest points in the line and be ready to exploit any success achieved.

German efforts to keep the Allies guessing as to the precise direction of their attack were less successful than their masking of its scale. In the centre, where the indications remained strongest that the main assault would come, the British Third and Fifth Armies, of fourteen and twelve divisions respectively, faced three German armies totalling twice that number, a disparity that was soon to become distressingly evident.

In this period of nervous apprehension, waiting for the attack that everyone knew must come, the work of surveillance was paramount. But the corps squadrons, under the protection of offensive patrolling, and with minimum interference, did not neglect the artillery, while bombing, by day and by night, mostly of aerodromes and communications – to which the Corps squadrons contributed – attracted few casualties. An example was a major raid on 9 March, when fifty-three machines of various types, with strong fighter protection, took off to bomb a clutch of German aerodromes from low level. Eighty-eight bombs were dropped, direct hits were recorded on hangars and buildings, and all machines returned safely. But only a fortnight earlier, the General Staff had declared that 'spasmodic bombing is wasteful', and the principle of concentration in time and space had yet to be learned. The profusion of targets listed by the General Staff was in direct contradiction to their declaration, and the raid of 9 March might have been more effective had all the bombs been aimed at a single target. Another recommendation, that a succession of attacks on the same target multiplied the effect, did not register immediately.

Inevitably the winter weather brought a lull in air activity, although the RFC, true to Trenchard's dictum, were much more active than their adversaries, continually probing for signs of unusual movement and, where appropriate, bombing what they found. The accent in the German Air Force was on consolidation, and it was difficult to bring them to battle, even Richthofen going for several weeks without a victory. But the Circus, like many of the RFC's fighter squadrons, was based in the central sector, and by early February there were some spectacular clashes. One of these involved a 19-year-old Camel pilot named A.D.G. 'Grey' Alderson of No. 3 Squadron, whose CO's policy was to allow his pilots forty-eight hours' grace before they went on leave and another forty-eight hours' on their return 'to get over it', subject always to the 'exigencies'. And it was the exigencies that forced Alderson into a patrol late in January, on the morning he was due to go on leave.

He soon appreciated the CO's point: he had never known so much Archie, the sky was full of it, and he fancied it was all directed at him. He admitted to having 'the breeze vertical', and he feared he would never live to go on leave.

As compensation the CO arranged for him to fly a Spad back to England, instead of going by sea, and he was lucky, too, after a fortnight in his native Yorkshire, to find a reinforcement DH4 to fly back. Next day he took his Camel up on test, but again the promised interval was denied him: that afternoon he and three others were sitting by the fire in the Mess when they were called to the squadron office. The Circus was out, it was a chance not to be missed, wing headquarters were calling for an offensive patrol, and they were the only pilots immediately available. They ran to the hangars, pulled on their flying kits, and were airborne within minutes.

Before they reached the lines, one of the four turned back with engine trouble, a serious loss in view of what faced them. Soon they sighted six Albatros single-seaters at 13,500 feet and noted their vivid colours and squadron markings: the Circus, for sure. When the firing started the flight commander sheered off at once with a damaged tailplane, which left only two to cope with six.

How long the fight lasted Alderson never knew, but an Archie gunner who witnessed it wrote: 'One Hun was sent down in flames by the remaining two Camels, shortly followed by a second. Then one of our two went down, shot out of control, and the remaining machine went down in flames. It was a fight against impossible odds.'

There was no chance for the chap in the flamer, but Alderson was in the Camel going down out of control. No chance, it seemed, for him either. An explosive bullet had hit the rudder bar, shattering his right leg, and as he saw the second Albatros burst into flames he passed out. From two and a half miles up his Camel dived, zoomed, somersaulted and spun under its own volition, engine full on, with Alderson still in it, unconscious.

He had often wondered what a man felt like in those last despairing moments, and he had convinced himself that a pilot would be so engrossed in the task of trying to lessen the force of the crash that he would have no time to think of anything else. But once, in a formation that was diving steeply on a Hun battery, he had seen the wings of one of the Camels suddenly fold back, the machine plunging like a meteor and bursting into flames on impact. He had conceded that when a machine broke up in the air like that, the pilot's anguish might be prolonged. But as it was, he was aware of none of these things. A week elapsed before he recovered even a proportion of his senses, and then, suffering from a fractured skull and delirium, he imagined he was in a London hospital, surrounded by exotic blossoms and no less exotic nurses. In reality he lay in a small, bare, dimly-lit room, and a German sentry stood guard at the foot of his bed. It was then that he wrote the postcard which, as related earlier, so outraged the German general.

The day-bomber squadron on the Third Army front, opposite Cambrai, was No. 49, and throughout February it was engaged on high-level reconnaissance. A 260 hp Fiat engine was being tested in some of the DH4's, replacing the disappointing Farnborough 3a, and John Morris, the man who had been so overworked the previous year, wrote that 'it went rippingly'. But he was deafened by the noise it made. With the engine 'bang in front of my head', and with 'practically no exhaust pipe to quieten it', it was 'like a motor-bike without a silencer'. He was becoming aware, too, of the problems of high altitude. One pilot, on a height test, reached 18,000 feet in thirty-three minutes, but anoxia at these heights was causing drowsiness for some and physical debility for others. Some suffered from headaches, others found themselves fighting for breath. A pilot named G. Fox-Rule, 'really only a boy,' said Morris, 'he looks like a kid of about fifteen', was taking photographs over the line when he felt faint. He managed to get back to the aerodrome and land before collapsing, but it was several minutes before he could be revived – with the oxygen that should surely have been fitted in his machine. He seems to have suffered no ill-effects, as he was later credited with seven victories, a high score for a bomber pilot, and the best on 49 Squadron.

Medical studies into what was known as 'mountain sickness' were begun. The Germans were already one step ahead, as with parachutes: they had already begun to fit oxygen into some of their high-flying machines.

Morris was certainly no malcontent, but the tenacity of some of his colleagues could still not be relied upon, and he was sickened by the continuing tendency of some of them to abort. Of ten crews detailed on one bombing show, only eight started – and even that, felt Morris, rightly as it turned out, was too good to be true. 'Sure enough one by one they departed with engine trouble.' The smallest formation of DH4's allowed to cross the lines was four, and Morris had climbed to 13,500 feet with three others when another crew dropped out and back they all had to go. On a similar occasion, again on a bombing show, Morris couldn't bear to take his bombs back, and seeing no Huns about he went on and bombed the target alone.

Although Morris took great care of his engine, he too had problems. Descending from the heights at which they operated was a long process and needed patience and care, lest the engine, throttled back, went cold. Wise pilots throttled down only just enough to lose height. Morris was far over the lines late one afternoon when his engine started playing up. It was getting dark, and captivity beckoned, but he just managed to get clear of the lines before being forced down, breaking his propeller. The nervous tension had been such that 'I sat there for a few minutes without attempting to get out'.

No. 49 Squadron continued for some time to operate with only two flights, and the CO, recognising Morris as a future flight commander, borrowed him on one occasion from A Flight to go as deputy leader with B Flight. Morris was 'a bit put out about this, as both flights are equally denuded', but he recognised it as a compliment. They were on a photographic job, but again Morris found something to criticise: the flight leader failed to keep them together. Morris had now done more shows than anyone in either flight except Chambers, his flight commander and the man he most admired.

The discerning Morris always gave credit where it was due. 'We always teach the observer something about flying, so that if the pilot is knocked out, they can save themselves and perhaps the pilot, if he is only wounded.' He spent a whole day flying around with a new observer named Cuttle, familiarising him with the machine and the countryside, then took him up again for an hour and a half in the evening, showing him the lines. 'Cuttle put up a good show when he once got started, and after a few more shots he should be able to get down at any rate without killing himself.'[1] But with another youth he was less patient: he was 'too slow and thick-witted', and he was returned to his unit.

These and similar contretemps and imperfections did not feature in RFC communiqués, but they were the stuff of squadron life, revealing yet again how, in the average squadron, fortitude depended on the few. These were the men the RFC relied on to eliminate faults and foibles before the offensive broke, and to lead the way when it did.

In early March No. 49 Squadron was switched from long-range photo reconnaissance to the bombing of villages where enemy troops were billeted, and of ammunition dumps. It was on one of these raids, on 6 March 1918, that the squadron suffered a loss it could

1. Lieutenant G.R. Cuttle, from Victoria, Australia. He had won the MC on the Somme, but was killed in air combat as an observer in No. 49 Squadron on 9 May 1918.

ill afford. The estimable John Morris, whose letters from the front to his family in Blandford, Dorset had numbered two a week over a four-month period, and whose name, like so many, does not appear in any list of awards, was killed in action. He was still only 19. Flight-commander Chambers did not long survive him.

Among the fighters cooperating with the Fifth Army under General Gough were the SE5A's of Sholto Douglas's 84 Squadron, and they used the hiatus between January and March to work out their most efficient fighting formations and to plot how best to tempt or trap their adversaries into action, in pursuit of the ascendancy Trenchard had demanded. Lieutenant-Colonel F.V. Holt, DSO, commanding the Wing, was an advocate of strong offensive patrols, even at the expense of leaving parts of the line thinly protected, and Douglas, by trial and error, arrived at what he regarded as the ideal squadron formation. Of his three flights, the lowest led the squadron, normally at about 15,000 feet. Five hundred feet above it, and a mile distant, behind and to the flank, flew the second flight, whose absolute duty was to conform to the movements of the leading flight. The third flight formed a covering force, 3,000 feet above the leading flight, some two to three miles behind it and on the other flank. This flight only came to the assistance of the other flights in extreme emergency: its very presence often acted as a deterrent. When working as a complete squadron, this was the formation arrived at.

There were attempts, in this period, to operate three squadrons together, in one large formation at different heights, Camels at 15,000 feet, SE5A's at 16–17,000, Brisfits at 18–19,000 – but this only frightened the enemy off. More subtlety was needed, and the alternative tried was for three squadrons, flying independently, to meet at a prearranged point – say over an enemy aerodrome – then return westwards together, enfolding any enemy patrols between them and the lines into their net. For whatever reason, on the three occasions when this manoeuvre was tried, the enemy responded with vigour, and tremendous dogfights developed. Unfortunately these did not always end with advantage to the RFC, victories being gained at sobering cost. 'As the fighting took place fifteen or twenty miles east of the lines,' wrote Douglas, 'our casualties were fairly severe.' Pilots tended to lose formation in the mêlée and often had to return independently, with perhaps a damaged machine or a failing engine, all too liable to be picked off. Nevertheless Douglas was convinced that this was the best method of carrying out multi-squadron offensive patrols, assuming the need for them, giving the best chance of surprising a small number of enemy machines with a large concentration of fighters.

Not everyone was happy with these attempts at enticing the enemy into combat, and Gwilym Lewis, of 40 Squadron, also flying SE5A's, thought the Huns, by using the winter months to rest and re-equip their scouts, as they were obviously doing, were 'showing twice as much common sense as we were'. His squadron existed, or so he believed, to protect the corps machines, indirectly more than directly, but most of their work that winter lay in seeking out the enemy's reconnaissance two-seaters at various levels, up to 20,000 feet, and escorting bombers in daylight. He confessed to having moments over the lines when he was so paralysed with fright that he longed to turn back, and sometimes did, but he already had five hostiles to his credit, had been promoted to flight commander, and had a reputation as a disciplinarian. Yet he did not compare himself with the top scout pilots, men like George McElroy, Mannock's 'McIrish', who 'has been going absolutely full out. He is quite mad and seldom returns without having brought something down'.

The man Lewis admired most of all was Mannock himself. 'He strafes about on his own – he is an excellent fellow.' Yet, paradoxically, while Lewis, who looked up to Trenchard and admired his ascetic way of life, could see no merit in the policy of maintaining the offensive at all costs, and wrote of the work of escorting DH4's in raids on German aerodromes that winter as 'stupid daylight bombing stunts', the socialist Mannock, who associated Trenchard with the top-brass, upper-class mentality and wrote that he 'talked bilge, don't like him', exerted himself in support of that policy to an exceptional degree. 'Our expert', wrote Lewis of Mannock in January 1918, 'has recently been sent home, very much against his will. He has been out here about eight or ten months, and has 18 Huns to his credit . . . He even went up on the morning he was due to leave.'

Lewis's opinion of Trenchard had improved on acquaintance. Having disliked him at first on principle, he now believed him to be an exceptional man. He had built up the RFC in France with immense pertinacity, yet there was nothing of the regular soldier about him. 'He doesn't smoke, I have never seen him drink anything but water, and one stares at a general who lives like that. Very strong minded and independent. Our present position out here is largely the result of his efforts.' He added: 'He thinks nothing of Sykes.' This was Major-General Frederick H. Sykes, who had gone to France in August 1914 as chief staff officer and deputy to David Henderson, a big blow at the time to Trenchard, who had had to be content with being left in charge at Farnborough. But when Henderson returned to the War Office in August 1915, he was succeeded not by Sykes but by Trenchard.

Trenchard's straightforward manner contrasted and frequently clashed with that of the more politically astute Sykes, of whom it was said that he was hampered by a personality which 'strongly engendered mistrust'. But he remained a powerful rival.

Trenchard went home on 18 January to take over as the new Chief of the Air staff, only to find, in the next few weeks, the machinations of Rothermere intolerable. Eventually he resigned, making way for none other than Sykes. This brought a second resignation, that of Henderson, who was no happier than Trenchard with Sykes.

The day after Trenchard's return to the UK, the RFC lost its youngest and best-loved brigadier-general, Gordon Shephard, one of the early flight leaders and by then commanding No. I Brigade at Bruay. In addition to taking every opportunity to fly reconnaissance sorties himself, Shephard visited the squadrons under his command almost daily in his Nieuport scout, making a point of getting to know all his pilots and observers personally, and taking a special interest in newcomers. He was about to land at Auchel aerodrome when he spun in and was killed. Trenchard rated him with pioneers Don Lewis and Bron James as one of the begetters of aerial reconnaissance. He was 32.

Flying of all kinds still held its hazards, even for so experienced a veteran as Gordon Shephard. His reputation as an operational pilot had been 'bold, but safe', yet he made what seems to have been a simple error, stalling in the turn and spinning in. Others to lose their lives in non-operational flying that winter included two of McCudden's original flight in 56 Squadron, Keith Muspratt and Leonard Barlow: both were killed while test-flying at Martlesham Heath. Of McCudden's famous flight on No. 56, only Rhys Davids actually died in combat. Coote and Cronyn survived the war.

German reticence in the air, as Ludendorff completed his preparations for the offensive, became less pronounced, and it was not long before Richthofen himself was leading his Circus again. The rest had done him good. But much of the old conceit had evaporated. His book, *The Red Air Fighter*, had meanwhile been published, and he blushed when he read it, it was so brash and immature. 'I no longer possess such an insolent spirit.' He was now leading thirty machines and more into battle, and on 12 March his Fokker triplanes and Albatris shot down four out of a formation of nine Bristol Fighters for the loss of half that number, Richthofen scoring his sixty-fourth victory. He seems at last to have been back to his best, and the Brisfit pilot he shot down, who like his observer was captured, later paid a warm tribute to Richthofen's skill and marksmanship. Richthofen, for his part, did not forget the courtesies between opposing airmen that still informed the air war. 'During my second day in hospital,' wrote the observer, 'a German officer came in and said he had come from Baron von Richthofen, who wished me to accept half a dozen cigars with his compliments. I did, with thanks.'

Next day Richthofen shot down a Camel, but in an ensuing dogfight his brother Lothar was wounded, needing several weeks in hospital to recover. From this point on, Manfred seems to have acquired or inherited some of his brother's panache, revising his earlier tactics of caution and stealth. He had taken part that winter in discussions on military strategy, and was aware that the war situation was 'very grim'. Of his destruction of another Camel soon afterwards, one of his pilots demurred. 'We all saw you fly so close to him that a collision seemed inevitable.'

The RFC was still bidding for the ascendancy, and a favourite ploy remained trying to trap the enemy at a disadvantage. The Circus was caught out on 17 March when five DH4's mounted a bombing attack with the sole purpose of luring them into an ambush, and in the resultant dogfight three single-seaters were destroyed by SE5A's without loss. But an attempt to repeat the ruse next day was answered by some fifty of the latest German fighters in a ferocious mêlée in which the British came off decidedly the worse, losing five Camels, two SE5A's and a DH4, against a bag of four Germans. The morale of the German Air Force, powerfully reinforced as it had been, remained high.

The RFC, too, was approaching a peak, equipped with the machines with which it would be obliged – and tolerably happy – to fight the rest of the war. On the western front the basic corps machine, finally replacing the BE2c, was the RE8, of which there were sixteen squadrons, complemented by five squadrons of Armstrong Whitworth FK8 two-seaters – 'Big Acks'. Another machine that had disappeared, its passing unmourned, was the Martinsyde Elephant – largely peculiar to 27 Squadron – which had been succeeded by the DH4. This machine was now equipping six bomber squadrons and was confirmed as the best day bomber of the war. Ten Sopwith Camel, ten SE5A, five Bristol Fighter and two Sopwith Dolphin squadrons – the last-named widely used on escort duties – formed the bulk of the so-called fighting or army machines. The four FE2b squadrons that remained in service were mostly employed on night bombing.

In the Third and Fifth Army areas the RFC had mustered a total of 579 serviceable aircraft, of which 261 were single-seater fighters. Ranged against them the Germans could bring to bear a total of 730 machines, of which 326 were single-seater fighters. So although the Germans could no longer claim any technical advantage, numerical superiority, which the RFC had hitherto enjoyed, had passed to them.

The readiness of the Circus to mix it with the RFC on 17 and 18 March was only one of many indications that the great German spring offensive was about to begin.

20

THE MARCH RETREAT: LOW-LEVEL STRAFING AIMS TO STEM THE TIDE

'... into our minds had crept for the first time the secret, incredible fear that we might lose the war.'

VERA BRITTAIN, *Testament of Youth*.

S OON after 4.30 on the morning of 21 March, the pilots of the three army squadrons based at the aerodrome at Flez, nine miles west of German-held St Quentin, were awakened by a tumultuous roar. The German spring offensive, as confidently predicted by aerial observation, the interrogation of prisoners, and other forms of Intelligence, had begun.

Sleep became impossible, the whistling of shells overhead provided a strident descant, and the pilots, pulling warm clothes over their pyjamas, stood in half-dazed groups outside their huts, gas masks at the ready. This was it: soon they would be called into action. But for all the chill apprehensions of early morning, their minds, saturated by the barrage, still registered fellow-feeling for the less fortunate. *'Thank God we're not in the trenches.'*

The tasks allotted to the RFC to assist in repelling the coming onslaught were well rehearsed and well known. Of the two brigades immediately involved, both commanded by men who had led elements of the original Channel crossing three and a half years earlier, No. III, under Josh Higgins, was attached to the Third Army. It comprised four RE8 squadrons for gun-spotting and photography, three Camel squadrons to protect the corps machines, three SE5 squadrons for engaging enemy fighters, a Brisfit squadron for low-level strafing, and two bomber squadrons, one day and one night. No. V Brigade, under Lionel Charlton, had five corps squadrons (three Armstrong-Whitworth and two RE8), and, in fighters, one Camel, two SE5, one Brisfit and one Spad squadron, and again two bomber squadrons, one day and one night. Although outnumbered by the enemy – because of his ability to concentrate his forces – they were at least his equal in quality, well able to make him pay a heavy price for his aggression. Every pilot knew his specific duties and the targets and tasks to which he was assigned. But as they groped around in the candlelight that morning, at Flez and at a dozen other bases, to prepare for the dawn patrols that were ordered, the din of bombardment, accompanied by the whining of terrified pets, continued to assail their ears despite a curious muffling of sound. Not until dawn came at 06.30 was the blanket of mist that clung like an adhesive to the earth belatedly revealed. Sound, however attenuated, might penetrate it, but not aeroplanes. The multiple tasks allotted to the RFC could not be discharged because they could not even get airborne.

Massed along more than fifty miles of front were fifty-six German divisions, with twelve more in reserve. In all they had assembled close-on a million men. When, an hour or so later, they began to move forward, staggering their times between sectors, the British, although forewarned, knew nothing until enemy troops suddenly swarmed out of the fog, penetrating and infiltrating their positions before they were properly aware of it. Plans for enfilading fire that would devastate advancing *sturmtruppen* were aborted, and for vital hours no one knew what was happening. Many of the forward troops, already overwhelmed by the bombardment, were annihilated, and by noon the enemy assault troops had reached the battle zone. Although the timing of the assault had been predicted to the minute, the scale of it, and the unparalleled concentration of firepower, with a gas attack for good measure, came as a cataclysm.

For the RFC it was a case of *déjà vu*, of seeing the picture round again. This was where they came in. In the retreat from Mons they had contributed decisively by spotting first the threatened isolation of the BEF, then the great wheeling movement which left von Kluck's army vulnerable to counter-attack. Now British armies were in headlong retreat again, disastrously, or so it seemed. Could they contribute decisively now?

The Germans were advancing along the entire Somme front, facing Arras and the Third Army in the north, down to St Quentin and La Fére, where the Fifth Army joined the French, in the south. The initial thrust seemed to threaten the junction between the Third and Fifth Armies, but no one could be sure where the major blow might fall.

The only successful attempts at reconnaissance that morning were made in the north, where visibility was clearer. The RE8 crews of 59 Squadron did best, reporting with precision on a bulge in the line along seven miles of front south of Arras. Some of the early wireless calls to batteries were dealt with expeditiously, one call for fire on groups of advancing German infantry being answered – so it was recorded – 'with devastating effect': but all too often the batteries themselves were enacting or contemplating retreat and had not erected their aerials, so that countless such calls went unheeded. The first low-flying attacks were also mounted on this front, six Camel pilots of 46 Squadron bombing and machine-gunning active German batteries north of Bourlon Wood.

When visibility in the south improved, the three army squadrons at Flez, Nos 48 (Bristols), 54 (Camels), and 84 (SE5A's) lined up their machines in front of the hangars in readiness. Meanwhile the bombardment continued with undiminished fury, and four miles to the north, at Mons-en-Chaussées, the DH4's of No. 5 (Naval) Squadron were driven out by the shelling, moving south-west to Champien, fifteen miles south of Flez, near the town of Roye, and burning their buildings and hangars before they left.

The first reports from the corps squadrons in this sector brought alarming news: south of St Quentin, in an area thought to be impregnable, the enemy had broken through. Among the first of the army pilots to take off from Flez were Lieutenants Stock and Drysdale. Their CO, George Maxwell, was on leave and had been temporarily replaced by Captain Francis Kitto, commanding C Flight. This left 19-year-old Ewart Stock, Kitto's deputy, to take over the flight. A few months earlier he had been opening the batting – and had been adjudged the best fielder – at Caterham School. Now he was opening for C Flight, 54 Squadron. He had given up a place at Hertford College, Oxford to join up.

Stock and Drysdale left at 11.30 on a low-level reconnaissance of a section of the St Quentin canal. They found the mist still clinging to the contours, giving them some protection. As they neared the lines the glutinous fog was penetrated by bursts of flame as gun after gun exploded; they could also see groups of British infantry returning the enemy fire. Flying at 500 feet towards the canal, they passed column after column of grey uniforms on the roads beneath them, heading west.

Stock estimated that there were many thousands on these roads, with not a single shell bursting amongst them. They passed over the canal, and still the roads were crammed with troops and transport, splendid targets if their role had been troop-strafing. But their job was to glean as much information as they could on the strength of the enemy in this area. They continued east until they were beyond the enemy's observation balloons, then headed back for Flez, engines full out until they were clear of the battle zone. As they approached Flez they could see British artillery in hurried retreat, with every cross-roads behind the lines so jam-packed as to be impassable. Stock was surprised on landing when his mechanic pointed to a rash of bullet-holes in his machine.

In the afternoon and early evening, contact patrols, in improving weather, clarified the situation – generally for the worse – on the Fifth Army front. Efforts by the DH4 squadrons to fulfil the bombing programme were neutralised not only by the weather but also by an outdated order, not yet rescinded, that they must not bomb from lower than 15,000 feet. Against the kind of opportunity targets that presented themselves, this condemned them to failure. As an instance, two hundred 25 lb bombs were dropped on bridges over the St Quentin canal but they all survived more or less intact.

Despite protective patrols at low level along the Fifth Army front, the corps squadrons all suffered casualties. More successful were the SE5A's of 56 and 64 squadrons farther north, who clashed with a formation of twenty-six hostiles over Bourlon Wood, shooting down four. But the German Air Force, intent on supporting the advance, mostly avoided combat.

The one major success scored by the RFC on that first day was the low-level strafing of enemy infantry. Some pilots were familiar with this form of attack, others were not, but all responded in spirited fashion. 'After lunch,' noted Stock, 'I was ordered to head a formation along the St Quentin/Estrees-en-Chaussée road and bomb and fire at enemy infantry and transport. We had never undertaken this sort of job before.' Leading his flight of six Camels, he covered the four miles north to the road and then followed it eastwards, diving to 500 feet and peering ahead for a target. Each machine was carrying two 20 lb bombs and 800 rounds of ammunition. 'Enemy infantry everywhere,' noted Stock, 'advancing in the open and in large columns on the road.' The first necessity was to get rid of the handicap of the bombs, and he gave the sign to drop when he recognised grey uniforms directly ahead, accoutred with large helmets and long bayonets. His bombs 'must have hit the road squarely in the centre. I could hear the explosions.'

The others followed, scattering the enemy columns. Stock then led them west and dived on the troops in the open. 'At one time I must have been at the level of their heads: they lay down on the ground when they saw us coming.' The Camels repeated this until their ammunition was exhausted, when Stock led them home. They lost one machine but heard later that the pilot had escaped to the Fifth Army lines.

Returning for afternoon tea at 16.30, Stock went out again in what was now a glorious evening, paired, as in the morning, with Drysdale. They spotted an RE8 being chased by a hostile and dived to its aid, forcing the German pilot to head east, his observer slumped over his gun.

On the ground the enemy was still advancing, with shells bursting incessantly in the British lines, and they returned to report what they'd seen. 'We retired that night at an early hour as another day's work, equally strenuous, lay before us.' The Third and Fifth Armies were in universal retreat, and the enemy had made formidable inroads along the whole length of the line.

As pilots and crews adapted to the changed pattern of air operations, all played their part in the bombing and machine-gunning. Most of the RFC casualties were caused by small arms fire from the ground. Sensing that their most treasured possessions were exposed to the greatest danger, pilots sat on flattened steel helmets for protection.

The biggest disappointment continued to be the breakdown of communications between pilots and battery commanders, and in an effort to correct this failure the commander of No. 8 Squadron (Armstrong-Whitworths, Major Trafford Leigh-Mallory), supporting the Fifth Army, sent his wireless officer to locate the batteries with which he was trying to cooperate, only to find that most of them had discarded their wireless equipment. 'As soon as the retreat started,' complained Leigh-Mallory, 'all idea of cooperating with aeroplanes seems to have been abandoned.'

The overall situation was critical, if not desperate, the immediate danger being that a gap would be driven between the Third and Fifth Armies. Plans for repelling the assault had been totally distorted by the fog, both on the ground and in the air. For many vital hours the RFC had been grounded, and they had been deprived, in the panic and confusion of the retreat, of their long-practised liaison with the artillery. This was the function on which Trenchard had set the greatest store. Yet in their frustration and impotence they had turned to the alternative of low-level strafing and bombing of enemy troops and transport with outstanding success.

Again and again the battered German regiments reported with understandable vexation – but with ungrudging admiration – on how, when visibility improved, the British airmen flew 'in the most daring manner very low over the ground and threw bombs causing us considerable losses'. Concentrations were spotted and bombs were rained upon them. In a raid south of St Quentin, 'the signal officer, the excellent Weisz, was killed instantly. The regimental staff was decimated.' At Honnecourt, behind the German lines south of

Cambrai, an artillery unit had 'sixty horses killed by a British airman who caught them on the march'. Another regiment which had halted temporarily in a hollow was so heavily bombarded from the air that they were ordered to fall back. Also on the Third Army front: 'About a dozen English low-flying battle aeroplanes whizzed up, and from an incredibly low height bombed our advancing troops. This caused great confusion.' These were the Camels of 46 Squadron. And again, 'The English got valuable support from their aircraft, which attacked regardless of the consequences . . . Our own airmen were absent.'

The greatest damage was still done on the rare occasions when aeroplane and artillery were able to cooperate; but when this was denied them, the RFC found a way of helping directly to slow the German advance. It was a form of attack that the enemy, despite their much-vaunted battle flights, seemed unable to mount in comparable violence; it was a form which their troops were to dislike even more intensely than the pilots who mounted it.

21

CAMEL PILOTS EWART STOCK AND
ROY CROWDEN

'We are again at a crisis of the War'
DOUGLAS HAIG

FOR the British, the first day of Ludendorff's offensive had been one of the most disastrous of the war, with casualties estimated, in round figures, at 7,500 killed, 10,000 wounded, and 21,000 taken prisoner – losses exceeded only by the slaughter on the first day on the Somme. The number of guns lost was unprecedented – 382 by the Fifth Army, 150 by the Third, about one-fifth of the whole. Retreat was universal over the entire 50-mile front, to a depth, at its farthest point, of nearly ten miles. Yet although British losses mounted daily, and the retreat continued, the Germans suffered even more severely as the two defending armies, far from collapsing, continued to inflict heavy losses on their pursuers. The moment of crisis, though, was yet to come.

On the second morning, 22 March, the fog was thicker than ever, but when it cleared, at about eleven o'clock, corps and army machines went into action again. In the south, the enemy were now clear of Holman Wood and well on their way to Mons-Estree, on the St Quentin–Amiens road. Pilots from Flez, on strafing missions both morning and afternoon, reported masses of the enemy still advancing, pushing the defenders back by their sheer weight. But the thin line of infantry that confronted them was still making them pay for their gains. Ewart Stock had dramatic evidence of this in the afternoon when firing on troops in the open. 'I saw what seemed to be a long wall of sandbags. I could not understand for a moment why I had not seen it before, until diving at the enemy behind it I noticed that it was a wall of dead bodies heaped one upon the other. The enemy were on the east side of it, so I was able to sweep this wall with machine-gun fire until there must have been a hundred or so German soldiers to add to their human wall.'

By this time Stock's former companion Drysdale, replacing a casualty, was leading A Flight; but that afternoon he too was wounded, and he left the squadron that evening. Casualties were getting unacceptably high, and Stock revealed in his diary a dissatisfaction with the squadron's tactics so far. Formations of six machines, he judged, were too cumbersome for ground-strafing; they got in each other's way, risking collision. The decision taken for the future was to work in pairs, a method that other squadrons either copied or were already practising.

No. 84 Squadron's activity was equally unceasing, and they too were working in pairs. But their actual style of attack, according to Hugh Saunders, a South African, differed from the converging method of the Camels of No. 54: each pilot dived separately, firing from 500 feet down to 50 before zooming away in a climbing turn. Whether this was as effective as the converging attack is impossible to gauge, but it eliminated the risk of collision, and Sholto Douglas was also able to claim that it was safer, not one of his pilots being lost to ground fire in the March retreat. Saunders added that it was a method made possible by the robustness of the SE5A, the dive and steep pull-out being made without fear of structural failure.

In paying tribute to Douglas as their inspiration, 'Dingbat' Saunders, as he was known, described him as 'a very stern CO'. Although he himself was a future air chief marshal, Saunders admitted to being 'quite frightened of him'.

Such was the weight of the German attack that they were still pouring through the gap opposite St Quentin, and low-flying attacks by squadron after squadron could not dislodge them, despite losses of some thirty machines on both sides. Yet German accounts testify to the awe in which the RFC pilots were held and the confusion and casualties they caused. All told, 730 25-pounders were dropped by a variety of squadrons, causing extreme pessimism in one regiment: 'Under the heavy artillery and machine-gun fire and frequent attacks by air squadrons the attack cannot go on.'

Air fighting that day was again of a desultory nature, the German air force, for all its concentration in numbers, seeming to operate to no coherent plan. Against this, the RFC pounded away at the same railway junctions they had bombed the previous day, while that night the FE2b's, on roving commissions, aimed their bombs wherever they saw evidence of activity. More than that, they spotted fresh masses of troops moving in darkness towards the fragile Fifth Army line, in time for General Gough to reverse his earlier resolve to offer battle east of the Somme. Instead, a gradual withdrawal west of the river was ordered, almost certainly saving the Fifth Army from a defeat that would have opened the approaches to Amiens. This was where the RFC had first landed on French soil three and a half years earlier, and it was a communications pivot that had to be held if a retreat to the coast was to be averted.

Relentless German pressure continued along the entire battlefront on 23 March, and the RFC were called upon to redouble their low-level strikes. Every machine not otherwise gainfully employed was switched to harassing the enemy troops. The withdrawal of the Fifth Army obliged the Third Army to adjust to the same line, and for a time the two armies actually lost touch. All this was reported in lucid detail by contact patrol observers who, although frequently attacked, were granted a panoramic view by improved visibility. With batteries in retreat still unable to erect wireless aerials for reception, or lay out ground strips, the corps crews themselves, flying below 1,000 feet, bombed any targets they saw.

Crews were flying several patrols daily, assessing whether or not bridges had been destroyed, bombing and firing at advancing infantry, and sending urgent signals for specific masses of troops to be blasted by all available batteries. One such report, by Lieutenants W.E. Joseph and G.W. Owen of 35 Squadron, concluded: 'Attacked by seven enemy aircraft (Scouts) at 300 feet and followed as far as Foucaucourt.' Yet the enemy pilots, strangely irresolute, pursued them no farther. Within half an hour of landing, Joseph and Owen were airborne again on another patrol.

The enemy were now so close to Flez aerodrome that the rattle of machine-gun fire, three miles to the north, disturbed the pilots at breakfast. Targets that morning again lay along the St Quentin–Amiens road, and 'after a hasty lunch', with the aerodrome about to be overrun, they took off for the Ham area, a town eleven miles south-west of St Quentin. There they attacked transport on the Ham–La Fére road before joining No. 5 (Naval) Squadron at Champien. What upset them most was that the Hun was now in possession of their old aerodrome, 'where we had lived in peace for several months', though ground crews had burnt the Mess and the hangars before leaving. Again there were parallels with the Mons retreat as they dined in a hotel in Noyon and slept the night in a chateau. Other squadrons, too, were forced to move, one of the FE2b night bombing squadrons suffering a temporary pause in operations for that reason.

The fourth day of the retreat, Sunday 24 March, was no day to return from leave, let alone find oneself in command of a squadron for the first time, but this was the fate of Gwilym Lewis of 40 Squadron at Bruay, nominally attached to the First Army farther north but now working with the Third. Leonard Tilney had been killed leading the squadron on 9 March, and with the imminent merger of the two air services, the new commander was to be the RNAS Australian ace Roderick Dallas – but not until 1 April. It seemed to Lewis that from this point on he lived in the air. Five squadrons were crammed into Bruay, instead of the usual two, and they were all feverishly bombarding the German infantry.

The SE5A pilots carried four 20 lb bombs, and Lewis found a macabre humour in 'laying nice little eggs' on what he described as 'rows of fat Huns' (Lewis's sense of humour – and of propriety – demanded that every Hun should be 'fat'). The eggs were the curtain-raiser, preliminary to the main entertainment of shooting them up and 'seeing them run in all directions'. But it was not so

[443]

funny when one was being Archied and hosed point-blank with small-arms fire. It was good for a laugh afterwards, perhaps, but 'everything is spoiled at the time by being so frightened'. Life became so hectic that more than once he nearly fell asleep in the cockpit.

On high-level patrol, Lewis got numbed and frozen at 17–19,000 feet. Coming down to refuel, he had barely thawed out when he was off again. But, as with low-level strafing, he could recall little of what happened, one patrol running like damp colours into another. 'Sometimes we get Huns and sometimes we don't.' But thirty-nine German machines were claimed as destroyed on this day, for only five British losses, although twenty-eight more, as squadrons were chased out of one aerodrome into another, were wrecked. Enemy casualties included Ludendorff's son, buried unnamed by the British. Later Ludendorff was to have the task of identifying him.

For the British the news on that Sunday morning was grave. The German thrust in the centre, as confirmed by air observation, was continuing, and a critical situation was developing between Peronne and the Bapaume–Cambrai road, where the wedge between the two British armies had been widened to nearly three miles. 'We are again at a crisis of the war,' warned Haig in a special order of the day. He reminded his forces that the enemy was aiming at nothing less than the destruction of the British Army, which they must do their utmost to prevent. Clery, near Peronne, had fallen, and the retreat was continuing under extreme difficulty. Yet the RFC reacted so ferociously throughout the day that several German regiments were forced to pause, one admitting that 'very active fighting and bombing squadrons of the enemy in the clear air imposed a very cautious advance on us'. Another regiment, aiming to cross the Bapaume–Peronne road, was delayed by 'hostile airmen, flying low', their weapons machine-guns and bombs.

South of Peronne, too, where German troops were assembling after crossing the Somme, low-level strafing was ordered. One German account told of the sudden appearance of twenty or more British aeroplanes diving until they were virtually scraping the earth. 'My company commander, Lieutenant Nocke, had to fling himself flat on the ground, but for all that he was struck on the back by the wheels of one machine, thus being literally run over.' Typically of the dive-bombed, the writer imagined himself under personal attack. 'At the last moment I was able to spring clear as the machine whizzed past me.' This madcap, trigger-happy low flying and bombing created havoc wherever it occurred, but not without cost. The German account went on to describe how one attacking machine was brought down, with four others destroyed in the same area.

Farther south, facing the thrust from St Quentin, Camel pilots Ewart Stock and Roy Crowden, who were rooming together, were called at 6 a.m.; they walked to their heavily-patched machines and headed for Ham with the usual load – two bombs and 800 rounds of ammunition. Approaching the Somme they noted that their compatriots were digging trenches on the west bank, where they were preparing to make a stand. Flying low on the east side of the river, they spotted Hun cavalry advancing through Matigny, four miles north-west of Ham. Here was an ideal target.

After climbing to 2,000 feet and scanning the sky to make sure there were no Huns about, they flew flat out towards Matigny. The bulk of the cavalry were on a straight road running east of the village, and, with Crowden following, Stock released his bombs. Simultaneously his Camel was hit, severing a landing wire, a piece of which just missed his goggles, but he was able to turn in time to see the results of his strike. 'I had never seen such confusion amongst horses as I saw then. They were darting all over the field, knocking men down who were trying to catch them.'

Seeing another squad of about twenty horses galloping across a field, he tried to line them up, but his wheels struck the ground with such force that his Camel leapt into the air before he could shoot. He dived a second time and got in a lengthy burst, then, as he was pulling out, he saw a group of four mounted officers on the road, with a fifth squatting nearby. 'I distinctly saw one firing with a revolver at Crowden.' This was enough, and he dived on them and fired about a hundred rounds. 'Two of them fell off their horses and one galloped off along the road. He was a tall man and was wearing the spiked Hun helmet.' Stock hit either him or his horse and they crashed together into a hedge. Then a machine-gun opened up at him and he could not shake it off. He had lost touch with Crowden and did not see him again till after he landed. Stock's wings were riddled, two flying wires were severed and there was a bullet through his rev counter, but he was off again that evening in a different machine, this time leading a formation of five to bomb enemy transport at Athies, close to their old aerodrome at Flez. With Champien also becoming untenable, they were to retreat afterwards as far as Bertangles, four miles north of Amiens.

With gaggles of retreating artillery, transport and French peasant carts hurrying west below them, they followed the Somme until they were in sight of Flez. Looking round to check that the formation was with him, Stock saw a clutch of six Huns flying 2,000 feet higher and about a mile on the far side of the river. He immediately turned and climbed towards the sun. As they were all carrying bombs the climb was sluggish, but 'before we got far the Huns went east, thus showing their usual spirit of avoiding a scrap unless the advantage is with them'. The German Air Force, in turn, was paying the price for too-rapid expansion.

At Athies they descended to 500 feet and bombed a large convoy parked on the east side of a wood. Then they made for Bertangles. No transport had arrived for them, but they borrowed a car from another squadron, dined in Amiens – 'I never wanted a hot bath and a big meal and bed as I did then' – and found another chateau to sleep in. Good news was that the CO was back and that Captain Kitto had shot down two Albatros DV's, the fifth and sixth victories of his career. As always there was bad news too. 'We had very few pilots left of the old squadron by this time, about six were missing and at least five had been wounded. This meant more work for those that were left, so we were up early again next morning for another day's work.'

At Marieux, seventeen miles west of Bapaume, mechanics worked all night on the Camels of 70 Squadron, finishing at five o'clock, starting again at tea-time, and working until midnight. On 22 March the squadron had shot down ten hostiles, but they had suffered for it. 'Own aircraft badly shot about,' noted John Todd's mechanic Alexander Paice, 'rather stirring times. Fritz dropped six bombs not far away.' This was when he commented: 'Terrible fighting just in front of us. May have to leave any time.' And on the 24th his flight broke all records for flying hours in one day.

The most spectacular achievement of 24 March, however, belonged to a flight commander on 43 Squadron (Camels) named John Trollope. Like Kitto he was a veteran of 1½-strutters. Already credited with seven victories, he actually scored six more in the course of two patrols that day, morning and afternoon, five two-seaters and an Albatros DV. He was still scrapping on the afternoon patrol when he ran out of ammunition. Forty-two German aircraft were shot down during the day, but the British losses exceeded these – eleven missing, eight burnt or abandoned, forty-six wrecked.

A new crisis emerged on 25 March when an RE8 crew of 59 Squadron reported a powerful enemy thrust against the Third Army in the north. On the Cambrai front the enemy had been reinforced by nine fresh divisions, Bapaume had fallen, and masses of infantry were concentrating east of the town. Meanwhile, in the south, a great bulge towards Roye, where the Fifth Army was contiguous with the French, produced a second wedge which aimed at capturing Montdidier and cutting the lateral railway link that served the whole front. The Fifth Army, outflanked on both sides, with the French on their right tempted to fall back on Paris, and the Third Army on their left protecting the Channel ports, was threatened with extinction. Soon after eleven o'clock, with the line crumbling, Salmond ordered every available machine on to a designated line west of Bapaume. *'These squadrons will bomb and shoot up everything they can see on the enemy side of this line. Very low flying is essential. All risks to be taken. Urgent.'*

22

FOCH TAKES OVER: 'MANY GALLANT DEEDS WERE DONE'

ARLY on the morning of 25 March, some hours before Salmond issued his order, squadrons at Bertangles and elsewhere were alerted to the crisis. Among the first to be called, at five o'clock, were Stock and Crowden, who were ordered to harass the enemy as much as possible on the Bapaume–Albert road. All pilots were aware that the fateful hour had come. 'The situation is apparently very serious,' noted Stock. The Hun was now in Peronne and Bapaume and was likely to be in Albert at any moment.

'It was a glorious morning when we set out for the lines,' wrote Stock. 'As far as I could see we were the only machines in the air around Albert when we reached it.' Albert was in ruins, but the church, crowned by its statue of the Virgin, still stood. 'The area over which we flew was the old Somme battleground of 1916, one mass of trenches and shellholes and a stump of a tree here and there.' A thin haze covered the ground and there was cloud at 2,000 feet, perfect conditions for ground strafing. They worked the entire day on this front, going out twice before breakfast and five times in all, 'dropping twenty Cooper bombs and firing 4,000 rounds of ammunition each before dark appeared and we went to bed.' Compared with some squadrons, 54 were lucky in that no one was missing from the day's strikes. Even the pilots who were wounded managed to get back to Bertangles, to be whisked away by Red Cross car to hospital, 'envied by those who remained whole'.

With the maximum possible effort diverted to low-flying attacks in the north, following Salmond's order, the influence of the RFC on the day's fighting was indisputable, as German accounts confirm. In the hutted camps east of Bapaume, life was 'not very pleasant because airmen bombed us causing heavy losses', while west of Bapaume the advancing troops were given no respite. 'After only twenty minutes' marching the first hostile airmen flying low appear and seek to delay the advance with machine-gun fire. There were about twenty-five airmen over the regiment. There is very little cover.' And again: 'This afternoon the hostile airmen are present in crowds. We count more than thirty above us at the same time.'

Expanding his emergency order, Salmond called that evening for every available machine to be concentrated in the same area next morning, and, of a total of sixty squadrons on the western front, no fewer than thirty-seven directly intervened on the right of the Third Army. At Pozières, little more than three miles north-east of Albert, Camels of 54 Squadron and SE5A's of 84 flew up and down the road continuously from early morning attacking troops, while DH4 bombers caused extensive damage at Bapaume, Peronne, and also at Pozières, where they set fire to trains containing ammunition and supplies, and where 'continual heavy explosions could be heard which destroyed one wagon after another'. On the Bapaume area alone, 117 heavy bombs and 1300 25-pounders were dropped, and more than a quarter of a million rounds were discharged at advancing troops. With this crucial assistance, the situation north of Albert was eventually stabilised by Commonwealth forces.

No sooner had the crisis on the Third Army front been relieved, if only temporarily, than an escalation of the enemy's threat to separate the British from the French in the south seemed imminent. Ludendorff was keeping his options open. Massive German forces, as seen and reported from the air, were concentrating in an arc around Roye, where a gap had been forced. Fifth Army squadrons that had been cooperating in the Bapaume area were quickly redeployed, testing the resilience of pilots almost to destruction. Called early for breakfast, pilots could face nothing more than a cup of tea and a slice of bread. Food had lost its attraction; the strain of low-level strafing quelled appetite. The only thing Stock, for one, looked forward to now was a cigarette at the end of a flight.

Early on the morning of 26 March, 'with a Gold Flake between our lips', as Stock recorded, he and Crowden strapped their helmets on, wound scarves round their necks against the cold, adjusted their goggles, and walked to the hangars, where the faithful flight sergeant awaited them. All he ever said was 'Good morning, sir,' as they arrived, and 'Good luck, sir,' as they prepared to take off. Once airborne, Crowden followed Stock in his usual position, slightly behind and to the right. 'We had flown together so many times now that we were able to keep together in the thick of machine-gun fire from the ground.'

Heading south-east for Roye along the road from Amiens, they had the familiar experience of seeing clusters of British troops, hampered by peasant carts, hurrying in the opposite direction. A pall of smoke lay over Roye, and with the French evidently still fighting in the town they concentrated their fire on enemy infantry battalions debussing from the north-east. As the day advanced a thick mist reduced air activity, and indeed little was seen of the Hun air force all day. 'There are many British but no German flying men up,' complained one enemy account.

Most of the pilots at Bertangles went into Amiens that night for dinner at the Savoy. 'One would have thought that we had had enough excitement during the last few days,' wrote Stock, but not so. Energies miraculously restored, they homed on Charlie's Bar 'like needles to a magnet', holding animated discussions on the latest snippets of news. They returned before midnight to be greeted with congratulations on their work during the past week from a visiting general, who emphasised, with the aid of a pocket flashlight and a map, that Amiens itself was still in grave danger and that they were to do all they could next morning to harass the enemy on the Bray–Corbie road, another approach road to Amiens.

Strategically, the best news on 26 March was the appointment of General Ferdinand Foch to coordinate the Allied armies on the western front – a measure, long overdue, now forced on the hitherto reluctant generals by events. Haig's plan to assemble the First and Second Armies near Arras for a counter-attack had met with a cautious response from Pétain, who seemed more concerned with covering Paris, threatening a catastrophic split. At a conference at Doullens attended by the French Prime Minister Georges Clemenceau (an ardent disciple of total Allied victory), Lord Milner, Secretary of State for War and a campaigner for closer Anglo-French military accord, and Generals Haig, Foch, Weygand, Pétain and Wilson, Chief of the Imperial General Staff, Foch was appointed to coordinate all Allied Armies on the western front. He became, in effect, Supreme Allied Commander; his first task would be to save Amiens.

Bombing on the night of 26 March reached a new intensity, stimulated by an RFC Headquarters message that 'It is hoped that a record number of bombs will be dropped'. Beginning with an assault on Ham, the FE2b's were soon switched to the north, where air reconnaissance reported abnormal train movements southwards from Lille and the arrival of reinforcements at Cambrai. 'It is of the utmost importance', continued the message, 'to delay enemy reinforcements coming up at this crisis . . .' The target for J.C.F. Hopkins, a pilot on 83 Squadron at Auchel, was the Bapaume–Albert road, which showed up incredibly white in the frosty moonlight. From 1,500 feet he picked out individual vehicles, then a long black blob of marching troops, perfect targets for his anti-personnel bombs. He did two shows that night, as did many others. Two Handley Page squadrons (Naval), carrying 250- and 112-pounders, joined in the bombardment.

From dawn on the 27th onwards, low-level strikes were resumed in unremitting sequence. At last the DH4's were freed from height limitations, and, in bombing and strafing generally, the RFC reached a peak on this day. 'Our efforts were of course entirely directed to the assistance of our hard-pressed infantry,' wrote Sholto Douglas. 'All machines and pilots were concentrated on low-flying attacks against the advancing enemy.' He felt afterwards that the value of much of this work was obscured by the rush of events. 'Many very gallant deeds were done by our low-flying aircraft of which only the scantiest records were kept: we had little time for writing up our achievements.' Lack of documentary evidence later militated against a full appreciation of what was done.

Douglas also dilated on the difficulties of having to move almost daily from one aerodrome to another. 'It was impossible to carry out any but the smallest repairs to machines and engines; our machines stood out in the rain for days at a time. But both pilots and mechanics, inspired by the importance of the occasion, worked themselves to a standstill ... One felt that one was directly helping to stop the enemy's victorious advance.'

Losses varied widely from squadron to squadron, illustrating how opposition differed between sectors; but the discrepancy in skill and experience between pilot and pilot was also a factor. Whereas 84 Squadron escaped lightly, casualties in 70 Squadron, where Jock Andrews was a flight commander, were high. New pilots were arriving with as much as forty hours' solo experience, but there was no time to give them squadron training, and almost at once they were sent to the line. They were exposed, too, to some atrocious weather, which contributed to many crashes, due to the inability of newcomers to cope.

Andrews' own flight disappeared completely, as eventually did Stock's, but in neither case could the fault be pinned on the leadership. Andrews realised he was fortunate in knowing every inch of the country; whereas he could hug the ground at 50 feet, pilots without his knowledge had to climb occasionally to locate themselves, thus exposing themselves to sharpshooters. Yet even Andrews found the strain too much, and after seven days of the retreat he was given a break.

Australia's toughest and highest-scoring air ace, 24-year-old Arthur Cobby, of No. 4 Squadron Australian Flying Corps, who was to become renowned, despite many indisciplined escapades, as a good shot and a brilliant tactician, got his first two confirmed victims during the retreat, both Albatros DVs. But he confessed that once he got involved in troop-strafing he could no longer eat, because of overstrain, nervousness, and a mixture of fear and hypertension. He lived on champagne and brandy and the occasional biscuit. Yet air combat (in which he eventually achieved a score of twenty-nine), never worried him.

Another squadron fully committed was 64, much happier since their DH5's had been swapped for the SE5A. Like most squadrons they had their stars. Flight commander Jimmy Slater, already mentioned, got two Albatros DVs and a half-share of a Fokker triplane on the day the retreat started. A true professional, still only 22, Slater had graduated through regimental service as a private, five months as a commissioned observer, nine months on Nieuport Scouts, and a spell as an instructor. A more junior member of the squadron, Walter Daniel, the Canadian who had begun by finding the English aloof, wrote: 'We were really in the thick of it, flying and sleeping and flying again . . . The turbulence from passing shells and bursts on the ground and in the air made me more airsick than I have ever been before.' He was passing over an ammunition dump when it blew up. 'I went up over a thousand feet with the blast and debris before I righted the plane and found it to be all in one piece.'

Many squadrons received attention from German bombers in this period, and 64 was no exception. Daniel was blasted from his hut one night to find a huge crater outside, with a visiting chaplain lying face down peering into it, evidently looking for victims to rescue. Whether or not this influenced Daniel, he served with the RCAF as a chaplain in World War II.

Meanwhile the corps squadrons, too, were playing their part in the bombing and strafing, all too often unsung. There was rarely a story to tell when a crew were shot down. But there were exceptions. An exuberant young Canadian from Winnipeg named Alan McLeod, 6' 2", raw, big-boned, and chubby-cheeked, still only 18, was briefed to fly with five other Armstrong-Whitworth FK8's of No. 2 Squadron, their mission to strike at German infantry and artillery massing at Bray-sur-Somme, near Albert. With McLeod as observer was a 23-year-old Englishman named Arthur Hammond. McLeod liked Hammond for his directness, but most of all because he could shoot. Experience had taught 'Babe' McLeod, as he came to be known, that, in the sluggish Big Ack, skilful handling needed to be allied to deadly shooting.

After two bombing trips the previous night, McLeod and Hammond were in bed when they were called for the attack on Bray-sur-Somme. They had scarcely got airborne when down came the fog. After two hours of trying to find a pinpoint, McLeod turned west to look for an Allied airfield to refuel. He found one, but in landing on a strange airfield with a full load of bombs he touched down heavily and cracked his tail skid. While a replacement was being sent for, he and Hammond had lunch with 43 Squadron (Camels), on whose aerodrome they had landed.

At one o'clock the Camel pilots took off, but within minutes they were back, reporting that conditions were hopeless. Yet McLeod and Hammond, remembering the importance attached to their mission, decided, when their repair was completed, to make an effort. The Germans had now taken Albert, and a hot reception at Bray-sur-Somme seemed certain, especially as their approach coincided with a lifting of the cloud base.

Casualties for the strafers had mostly come from ground fire, but the German scout squadrons, forced back on the defensive, still had to be reckoned with. Richthofen alone claimed three victims on this day. Hammond, although preoccupied with the bombing run, spotted the approach of a Fokker triplane just in time, tapped McLeod on the shoulder, and pointed down. McLeod immediately executed a tight turn to port, increasing height marginally, and held the turn, describing a perpetual circle. It made the Fokker pilot's twin Spandaus difficult to bring to bear, while allowing Hammond, swinging his Lewis on its swivel mounting, to fire almost at will.

Many German scout pilots would sheer away from a well-handled two-seater: but not this one. He was a member of Richthofen's Circus. Hammond's aim, though, was deadly, and the Fokker fell into a spin from which it never recovered. Waving excitedly to each other, McLeod and Hammond resumed their bombing run. But as they did so, the clouds above them parted to reveal bright sunshine, out of which another triplane was diving at them. Six more were tagging along behind.

Running away from a fight was against McLeod's instincts, but he was no hothead. If he couldn't plant his bombs where they were wanted right now, he would live to drop them later. But he judged that flight would be even more certain to bring destruction than fight. He would stay to do battle.

'Alan would take on anything,' a previous crew-mate had averred. 'He would turn round to me and laugh out loud.' But seven Fokkers were no laughing matter. One pilot, losing patience, dived to close range, McLeod pulled abruptly to port, and Hammond fired, so destructively that the triplane broke in half, ejecting the pilot. But the Germans, aware now that they were up against a worthy adversary, and led by 21-year-old Leutnant Hans Kirchstein of *Jasta 10*, reformed for the kill. Both McLeod and Hammond were wounded, yet a second triplane exploded and broke up when Hammond's bullets punctured its fuel tank.

It was Kirchstein who, in an attack from astern and below, ruptured the Big Ack's fuel tank in turn. The petrol immediately ignited, the flames blowing back under the cockpit seats. Fanned by the slipstream, they burned through the wooden floor, scorching McLeod's flying boots and setting fire to his wicker chair. His response was to throttle back, set the rudder pedals to neutral, ease the stick forward, and climb out of the burning chair, stepping on to the lower port wing and manoeuvring the joystick from there, in a crabbing side-slip that kept him clear of the flames.

Satisfied that plane and crew were doomed, Kirchstein and others went off to look for alternative prey. But one pilot determined to finish them off. Hammond had perched himself on the cockpit coaming, and as he struggled to manipulate his gun the floor of his cockpit gave way, carrying with it the revolving stool on which he had planted his feet. Grabbing the half-circular gun-ring aft of his cockpit and straddling the fuselage, facing aft, he was wounded again as the Fokker closed. Grappling with the Lewis, he fired a burst that drove the triplane off. .

Still manoeuvring so as to direct the flames away from himself and Hammond, McLeod was preparing to land. As soon as he flattened off he was choked by smoke and flames and the fabric around him caught fire. Hammond, forced to abandon the cockpit area, dragged himself up until he was standing on the cockpit coaming, steadying himself by clutching the trailing edge of the upper wing. One last effort from McLeod and the machine ploughed into the earth and slithered to the edge of a mud-filled crater. They had landed in the morass of no man's land and were under ground fire.

There were eight bombs still strapped to the FK8, and about a thousand rounds of ammunition in Hammond's cockpit. McLeod had been thrown clear, but Hammond was lying close to the burning mainplane, half-buried in the surrounding quagmire, unconscious.

Wounded in five places, his burnt flying clothing hanging in shreds, with bullets already exploding like firecrackers, and with the bombs about to go off, McLeod returned to the burning wreck and dragged Hammond clear.

For weeks McLeod's life hung by a thread; but Hammond, after having a leg amputated, made good progress. McLeod was recommended for a DSO, Hammond for a Bar to the MC he already had. Hammond got his Bar, but McLeod's DSO was upgraded to a VC.

Alan McLeod recovered sufficiently to return to Canada to a rapturous welcome, only to succumb in his weakened state to a plague of Spanish influenza. Arthur Hammond, after emigrating to Canada, chose to settle in Winnipeg, where he lived another forty-one years. McLeod's was the RFC's last VC.

Although the enemy advance north of the Somme had been halted, withdrawal from Bray-sur-Somme had exposed the left flank of the Fifth Army, and at 08:30 that morning, 27 March, Ludendorff began an attack south of the Somme on the Fifth Army, and farther south still on the French.

Determined to protect Amiens, the Fifth Army fought hard to hold on, greatly assisted by the transfer of low-level air attack to the Somme. Despite an inevitable weariness, little ground was given, but the weight of the attack on the French was such that they were forced to cede Montdidier.

Some of the squadrons at Bertangles were cheered that morning to find themselves warned for an old-style offensive patrol at altitude, ground strafing being postponed till the afternoon. The enemy were so fully occupied in trying to check the peppering of their own troops that they had largely deserted the upper air, but their scouts were known to be out in strength that morning.

With the return of George Maxwell, commanding 54 Squadron, Francis Kitto had resumed the task of running C flight. They took off at 10.30 in a formation of six, with Stock as deputy leader, and after following the twistings and turnings of the Somme they spotted a formation of eight enemy scouts over Peronne. Kitto had the advantage of height and he went straight into a dive, the rest following. Then Stock, whose job it was to protect the rear, was surprised to see a second Hun formation, some way above them, beginning to nosedive in turn. With Kitto intent on attack, Stock fired a burst over his top plane to attract his attention, then turned to face their attackers.

The nearest Hun was now about to fire and Stock met him head on. He could sense the German pilot's hesitation, and he zoomed up over him and turned sharply round to get on his tail, at the same time trying to keep Kitto in sight; but the German turned too. 'Thus we turned round and round, each trying to make a sharper turn than his adversary . . . But the Hun did the wrong thing . . . He changed or attempted to change from a left-hand to a right-hand circuit, thus giving me my opportunity, and I let him have it . . . he went down in a steep nosedive and burst into flames . . . A glorious sight at the time, since one does not realise that a human being like oneself is within, for after all as far as war is concerned it is merely a mechanical bird.'

In Stock's experience, the scene after landing from an offensive patrol was always the same. First, from the flight commander:

'What luck, old man?'
'One. And you?'
'Two, one near Athies and the other near St Quentin.'
'You've been to hell and gone over, then?'
'Yes, didn't realise where I was until the scrap was over. Got a gasper?'
Up walks the major. 'What luck, Kitto?'

'Three so far, sir. The rest are not back yet.'
Maxwell: 'Good old C Flight. Go and make the report, Kitto. Oh, by the way, Russell's wounded.'
Stock: 'Is he sir? Where?'
'In the leg.'
Kitto (under his breath): 'Lucky devil.'

After lunch on 27 March it was pairs again, a low reconnaissance in the Noyon area, during which Stock and Crowden for once got separated, and Stock, having penetrated much farther than he had intended, noted large enemy groups moving westward and a variety of transport. He memorised the different roads and the direction the troops were taking, ready to report back at Bertangles. His was one of the scores of reports that afternoon that enabled army dispositions to be adjusted.

After dark, bombing was again aimed at stifling the enemy's reinforcement routes, and 840 lbs of bombs were dropped and over 18,000 rounds of ammunition fired by the four FE2b squadrons. Unconfirmed though the results were, the crews reported many hits on columns of transport and on encampments and dumps. More convincing perhaps were the widespread reports of confusion and delay culled later from enemy documents.

23

THE CLIMACTIC DAY

NEXT morning, 28 March, after a brief but intense bombardment, Ludendorff launched another series of attacks, beginning north of the Somme towards Arras. Here the British resistance was at its strongest and the attack was repulsed, with Camels, SE5A's and DH4's causing panic and stampedes. By the end of the day the main battle north of the Somme was virtually at an end, but south of the Somme, where the exhausted and outnumbered Fifth Army remained under pressure, German troops had infiltrated across the river during the night, reaching the Amiens–St Quentin road. The battle for Amiens was boiling up, and a further assault on the Fifth Army front and on the French was simmering. At this point Ludendorff, confident of success, did not perhaps realise the extent of his own troops' exhaustion and demoralisation.

In front of Amiens the Fifth Army were withdrawing to a defensive line on a north–south axis, from the Somme in the north through Hamel and Ignaucourt to Mezières, at the junction with the French in the south. The withdrawal was conducted in good order, as confirmed by contact patrols. The Fifth Army, supported by its air component, was still defending grimly despite all its handicaps, and indeed General Gough, although aware of the crisis, felt that the challenge was being repulsed. It was at this moment, following political intervention, that Gough and his staff were relieved of their duties, being replaced in command of the British troops south of the Somme by General Rawlinson and the staff of the Fourth Army, which had hitherto been held in reserve.

Whatever the justification for this, for the RFC it changed nothing: maximum effort was still demanded. Records kept remained scant, and even some that were kept were subsequently lost; but Stock was still keeping notes from which, when time allowed, he made up his diary. His first reaction, on waking up on the morning of the 28th, was one of intense relief: rain at last! Crowden was still asleep. At 07.30 their batman Neville appeared with two large cups of tea. 'Dud, sir,' he whispered.

Stock could not resist passing the good news on. 'Crowden!' 'Go to hell.' 'Look at it!'

Crowden was sceptical; he had had his leg pulled by Stock before, and he threatened to throw his cup at him. 'Neville,' called Stock. 'Open the door.' The aperture revealed low cloud clinging to distant hills and sheets of rain falling on hutment roofs. 'Does that satisfy you?'

Crowden brightened. 'Neville,' he said, 'go over to the Mess and order me breakfast for eleven o'clock.' Both men dropped off to sleep again instantly, but within minutes the door opened again and another voice, recognised at once as that of authority, penetrated their slumber. 'Get into flying kit at once.' They sat up and stared in amazement: it was Major Maxwell. 'Can't help it,' they heard him say, 'Wing orders.' As Maxwell left, Stock swore that he heard him mutter: 'Damned shame.'

'Hell!' said Crowden. 'Things must be getting critical.' Stock agreed. To send them up in driving rain was unheard of.

The mechanics were waiting for them at the hangars, and despite the rain they were already starting engines. All remaining fit pilots had been called. With the clouds at 200 feet they were compelled to fly underneath them, and when Stock glanced over the side to try to pick up a landmark the rain blinded him and slashed his face. He lost sight of Crowden, and the first warning he got that he was near the lines was a staccato thud underneath him which bumped his machine crazily. He was down to 100 feet, and there was a battery of 60-pounders directly below him, firing frenziedly towards the river.

He could see that the Hun was attacking across the river at two points, at Maricourt and Cerisy-Gailly, apparently trying to outflank the British troops defending the Amiens road four miles to the south. 'Everywhere was a mass of smoke and flame, of 60-pounders and heavies of all kinds, all firing at Mericourt and Cerisy.' On reaching these riverside villages he was greeted by a bombardment such as he had never experienced before. His outer struts were immediately splintered, and he throttled down and twisted and turned as much as he could – 'to fly straight would be fatal' – then saw what all the noise was about. The large stone bridge over the river at Cerisy was covered by a mass of Hun troops edging across, under fire from the British artillery south of the river.

The Germans had lined the river-bank with field guns and were also bringing up machine-guns. A determined effort was being made to cross the river and outflank Villiers-Bretonneux, the last village before Amiens. Stock resolved on an equally determined attempt to stop them.

He was unlikely to destroy the bridge itself with a couple of 25-pounders. Flying through a blizzard of fire towards the bridge, he decided to drop his bombs on the mass of troops who were approaching the bridge, then to machine-gun from low level the men who were actually endeavouring to cross. How well he succeeded may best be judged from the citation for his subsequent award of a Military Cross, the incident having been watched by hundreds of British artillerymen. First, he 'caused great confusion' with his bombs among the men approaching the bridge. Then,

diving on several parties of the enemy who remained on the bridge in a state of indecision, he almost completely annihilated them. His action undoubtedly hampered the enemy by making the bridge impassable for half an hour ... On numerous other occasions he disorganised and hindered the enemy's advance by his attacks on troops and transport. He has destroyed three hostile machines, and has always set an excellent example of courage and enterprise.

Owing to the dense smoke caused by his bombs and by bursting shrapnel, Stock himself was unable to evaluate his attack, nor could he locate the precise position of the British artillery or assess the strength of the enemy forces. Crowden had meanwhile bombed the bridge (he too got an MC later), and they joined up and headed back to Bertangles.

Many other fighting squadrons, together with the DH4 day-bombers, were diverted that day south of the Somme, ground targets southwards of Cerisy-Gailly attracting special attention. The corps squadrons, too, when patrol work allowed, made a maximum low-strafing effort. 'It was on this day,' said one report, 'that an extraordinary number of enemy troops were reported and our machines had a field day attacking columns in fours. Heavy casualties were inflicted . . .'. The bridge at Cerisy-Gailly was attacked again, this time with 112-pounders, and a party attempting to repair it was slaughtered. At Hamel, west of Cerisy, much of the German artillery was brought forward successfully, but, according to a German account, 'the replenishment of ammunition broke down owing to bombardment by the enemy's aeroplanes', and the attack was beaten off.

There was little fighting in the upper air that day, the enemy doing their best to avoid combat, although seven of their machines were shot down. More surprising was the failure of the German battle squadrons to persist with the low-level assault they had planned on the retreating army and its communications. Heavy losses in the first few days, and preoccupation with defence against the aggression of the RFC, contributed to this. For the RFC, too, casualties were high, nearly all from ground fire. 'March 28th,' wrote Stock 'was perhaps worse as far as we were concerned than all the others during the push. We lost more on our squadron than on any other single day. I feel certain that if it had not been for the splendid example shown by our CO we could never have carried on . . . We came back from the firing line several times utterly done, and caring naught for anything or anyone, to find the CO awaiting us or perhaps about to take off on his own and trench-strafe.'

By nightfall their machines were in an appalling state, cobbled together like patchwork but still showing bullet-holes everywhere. 'Some poor fellows', wrote Stock, 'came back with half an arm or leg, and others not at all.' Stock had a special word for Roy Crowden. 'He looked upon these gruesome sights with perfect calm. In fact it was partly through his cheerfulness that we managed to carry on together when nearly everyone was either wounded or missing.' Experience was similar in squadron after squadron, RFC losses that day amounting to seventeen machines missing with twenty-five crew, thirty-five machines wrecked, and six more burnt out or abandoned, not to mention the wounded. But on the ground, the day had gone well.

In retrospect, 28 March can be seen as climactic, and when German pressure continued on the morning of the 29th, the British line south of the Somme was dominated by the relieving Fourth Army. The French were driven from Mezières, at the junction with the British, and were forced back towards Moreuil, twelve miles southeast of Amiens, but they recaptured Montdidier. Night bombing of distant targets was attempted when the weather allowed, and vigorous offensive action on ground targets was continued on the 30th.

Already the dense enemy columns approaching Moreuil had suffered from the V Brigade squadrons and those that had reinforced them, and further low-flying attacks on the 30th drew bitter complaint. 'The French and British flying men circle over Moreuil Wood and join in the battle, attacking with bombs and machine-gun fire . . .' Disappointment was voiced when a pair of British aviators, after almost destroying themselves by hitting the ground, just avoided the tree-tops. 'They have dropped their bombs and used their machine-guns, and now, flying at the speed of arrows, attack our batteries . . . one bomb dropped from a negligible height places the whole staff of the 1st Battalion *hors de combat*. Moreuil Wood is hell.' It would be hard to find more convincing evidence of the influence of the air on the battle.

The one disappointment remained the loss of reliable contact with the artillery, belying Trenchard's contention that it would be through rendering artillery fire effective that the RFC would make its greatest contribution. The blame for this, if blame there was, could certainly not be attached to the RFC. But by this time the enemy battle flights, baffled by lack of liaison with their army commands, and deprived by the stricken landscape of suitable aerodromes near the front, were again showing signs of returning to the upper air, and for a time the RFC fighting squadrons were switched from ground targets to high-level patrolling. This order was reversed when Foch, in an effort to co-ordinate the British and French air services in the battle area, ordered, for the bombers, the concentration of every resource on a few vital railway junctions, rather than dissipation over a wide area, and, for fighting aircraft, the primary duty of assisting the troops on the ground by incessant low-level attacks.

Meanwhile, on 1 April, the Royal Flying Corps was absorbed, with the Royal Naval Air Service, into the Royal Air Force. On the same day, Ewart Stock was wounded in yet another low-level attack and invalided home. Soon he was back at Hertford College, Oxford, where, in 1920, he matriculated. Lucky devil, he must surely have said.

Under Trenchard's leadership the RFC had espoused the doctrine of the offensive, the forcing of the enemy air service on the defensive and the establishing of a degree of superiority in the air, whatever the cost. From this all blessings would flow. That this was repeated during the March retreat, in spite of the enemy's numerical concentrations, is unarguable, in view of the torments of the German ground forces in comparison with the British. A German document on the employment of their battle flights dated 20 February 1918 makes it clear that the General Staff fully understood what was required. 'The object of the *battle flights* is to shatter the enemy's nerve by repeated attacks in close formation and thus to obtain a decisive influence on the course of the fighting.' But it was the RFC that exerted this influence. That the enemy did not achieve it was because they were not allowed to, through the offensive posture adopted by the RFC, not just during the retreat but over the years. It was a posture foreign to the German pilots, who in any case were thrown on the defensive almost from the start. This was in accordance with Trenchard's predication that the only effective way to counter a more aggressive stance by the enemy, if it were ever adopted, was to pursue a still more aggressive policy oneself.

There was plenty of room in the RFC, as has been shown, for qualities of doggedness, perseverance, and staying power, but it was the 'sporting audacity' – as General von Hoeppner had described it – of the scout pilot which won air superiority, and incidentally won fame, perhaps at the expense of a full understanding of the more direct but humdrum, routine, cumulative contribution, with only the occasional highspot, of the corps squadrons, still underestimated by history.

If it is true that the British tend to glorify retreats, according them an almost mythical quality, then the part played by the RFC in the March 1918 retreat has been monstrously neglected by the myth-makers. No less a military historian than B.H. Liddell Hart paid tribute to the low-flying form of attack perfected by the RFC in this battle, calling it 'an important factor in stemming the German onrush, and one that has been inadequately recognised by historians'. It is paradoxical, for a force that prided itself above all on its ethos of attack and aggression, that the RFC should have first earned respect in one retreat, and reached the zenith of its achievement in another.

Perhaps some nations really are at their best in retreats. Both sides were fighting in conditions bordering on the chaotic. The most serious problem for the British was to keep the squadrons flying, to find them new aerodromes when they were chased or shelled out of the old ones, to keep them supplied with essentials, and to replace losses in aircraft, arms, and personnel. Due to the foresight of Jack Salmond, a substantial increase in transport had been agreed and provided just in time. The Deputy Assistant Quartermaster-General at RFC Headquarters, Brigadier H.R.M. Brooke-Popham, had done the job once before, admittedly on an infinitely smaller scale, in the retreat from Mons, and he initiated emergency schemes for rushing convoys from the supply depots and parks to the squadrons, which kept them up to strength as the enemy's re-supply problems mounted.

Thanks to the expansion schemes that bore fruit that winter, the supply of new aeroplanes to make good the losses was never a problem, and the pilots required to replace casualties, now better trained, flew them where they were wanted. All this was achieved while the supply depots were themselves on the move, and when fall-back arrangements included such precautions as the planning of new routes for reinforcements from England in case the Channel ports were lost.

Against this, the comparative ineffectiveness of the German air service in this period stands out. Their opportunities for the intensive bombing and strafing of British columns in retreat, along roads often blocked by refugees, must have been unequalled. 'Congestion behind our Third Army was extraordinary,' wrote one airman who witnessed it, with peasants fleeing westward, blocking the roads with their carts and barrows, while relief battalions struggled against the tide to reinforce the front-line. The British troops were certainly not unmolested from the air, but the enemy pilots, after the losses of the first few days, were never able to approach the carnage wrought by the RFC. General von Hoeppner himself admitted that the operations of his forces had not been coordinated with the march of events on the ground. 'It therefore happened that the infantry were deprived, at the decisive times and places, of the help of the fighting pilots.' The supply problems of the advance, for the German air force, were not foreseen: they had no Brooke-Popham. The supply problems of the retreat, for the RFC, were brilliantly resolved.

It may be, too, that when the initial impetus of the attack had abated, and success seemed assured, there was not the inspired resolve on the German side that stems from forces at bay. The enemy pilots had no such rallying call to respond to as Salmond's *'Very low flying is essential. All risks to be taken. Urgent.'*

The RFC's concentration on low-flying attacks in moments of crisis, as against spotting for the artillery, which Trenchard had seen as the best way of helping the infantry, aroused controversy, but it argued a new flexibility, and it was justified by the impossibility of keeping track of battery positions in the fluidity of mobile warfare. Captured enemy documents fully confirmed the RFC's impact on the land battle. The German air service was not technically inferior, and they were ahead in such matters as providing parachutes and oxygen for their pilots, but the quality of these pilots was not maintained. The *Jastas* still fought magnificently, but their overall tactics were haphazard, while the Royal Flying Corps had become a fully-fledged Air Force, in fact as well as in name.

24

GROWTH OF THE RAF: MEMORABILIA, RFC

I N the seven and a half months that were to elapse before final victory, the Royal Air Force grew to a size and potency unimagined six years earlier when the RFC was formed. From a force of 146 RFC officers in August 1914, the RAF worldwide in November 1918 had more than 27,000 officers. Other ranks swelled the total to over 290,000. A force of less than 100 machines in a handful of squadrons in 1914 had grown to an estimated 22,677 by November 1918, spread over 188 squadrons. Over half of these were in France.

The number of air actions in support of the army in those final months was vastly greater than anything that had gone before, and many new reputations were deservedly made; but they are not a part of this story. It remains to follow, in brief, the fortunes of some of the RFC men who had survived this far, men who had helped to set the example, to lay the foundations on which the independent air force was built.

Even before the end of the March Retreat, Ludendorff's Somme offensive was beginning to falter. Despite having made advances of up to forty miles in places, by far the deepest penetrations in any campaign since 1914, no decisive results were achieved. Resistance, whether on the ground or from the air, was undiminished. The vital communications centre of Amiens lay only ten miles distant, but it remained tantalisingly inviolate, and a final attempt to break through on 4 April failed. 'Our strength is exhausted,' admitted Hindenburg, and Ludendorff wrote: 'The enemy's resistance was beyond our powers.' Next day, 5 April, he abandoned the offensive against Amiens, at least for the moment, electing to try elsewhere.

His second attempt was not long delayed. Switching to the north, he attacked on 9 April in Flanders, at a point where the River Lys separated the British First and Second Armies. The immediate objective was the communications centre of Hazebrouck, the ultimate a new threat to the Channel ports. The Army general staff, refusing to believe that the offensive in the south, which had come so close to success, would be abandoned, were sceptical of air reports which offered clear evidence of Ludendorff's intentions, and his preparations went ahead unhampered. Then, when Ludendorff struck, bad weather restricted flying and contributed to a situation of extreme gravity until, on 12 April, Haig issued his famous 'backs to the wall' order, enjoining that 'each one of us must fight to the end.'

The RAF's answer, as visibility cleared, was to fly more hours, drop more bombs, and take more photographs than on any other day in the war so far. 'Throughout the whole of this vital day of the battle,' says the Official History, 'the advancing German divisions were subjected to relentless attacks by the British air squadrons . . . every squadron was used unsparingly from dawn to dusk.' Observers in kite balloons enjoyed panoramic views in the crystalline atmosphere, while incessant contact patrols made the progress of the battle 'clear as had never been made clear before'.

There was no break either in the air fighting. Anxious to redeem themselves for their failure to protect their troops in the Amiens débâcle, German low-flying machines, supported at altitude, disputed the RAF's ascendancy – and were sharply rebuffed. On 12 April, forty-nine hostiles were brought down and another twenty-five driven down out of control. One squadron alone recorded thirteen victories: this was No. 43 (Camels), where the extrovert H.W. 'Willie' Woollett, already credited with thirteen victories and two balloons from RFC days, and acknowledged by colleagues as having an uncanny flair for air fighting, destroyed six machines, three in the morning and three in the afternoon, thus equalling the record set by John Trollope, also of 43 Squadron, three weeks earlier. Trollope had meanwhile been shot down and taken prisoner, with wounds that resulted in the amputation of a hand – and much later, of the arm itself. Woollett eventually raised his score to thirty-five.

Another man with a reputation from RFC days who scored that day – two single-seaters – was Mick Mannock. Sent home on rest by Tilney on 1 January, he had talked his way back as a flight commander on 74 Squadron. These were his seventeenth and eighteenth victories, and they began a remarkable sequence of success, both for him and his new squadron commander, 'Grid' Cald-well, who also scored that day.

By 18 April, with the help of French reinforcements, the German advance had been halted. The main weight of the RAF effort, although restricted by the weather, was again directed at stemming the advance, and by 29 April Ludendorff's second great offensive had been held. German casualties since 21 March amounted to some 350,000, while Allied casualties, most of them British, exceeded 300,000. The wastage in aircraft was proportionately high: over the same period, of 1,232 machines on the strength of the RFC in France on 21 March, all but 200 had been lost or wrecked beyond repair. But again, the aircraft supply and repair depots, and the rail and road organisation, had coped.

The same could not be said on the German side, where early superiority was again rapidly checked and reversed. Whereas the Allies could fall back on undamaged aerodromes, fresh landing grounds remained impossible for the Germans to find in the devastated battle areas, leaving their bases out of touch. There were complaints from the troops, as before, that they were inadequately protected from strafing.

These and other battles that summer were different in one major respect from those to which the RFC had become accustomed: mobile warfare had superseded static. But it was a change to which the RFC had already adjusted, and the new service adapted similarly. Speed became a vital factor, the fighting coming in bursts, two or three days of rapid movement being followed by a lull of perhaps a week, during which artillery moved forward or back, new positions were registered by air reconnaissance, and photographs to a depth of four miles behind the lines were taken and circulated. The work was done under intense pressure, with the German Air Force active although sometimes non-aggressive.

As new stars appeared in the firmament, some of the old ones shone less brilliantly, or were extinguished. An old opponent, so much a part of the RFC story, was Manfred von Richthofen, and he did not long survive the amalgamation. Can it be said that the RAF achieved what the RFC could not? That remains a matter of debate to this day.

The pilot credited with shooting down the Red Baron, on 21 April 1918, in the middle of the Lys offensive, was not even ex-RFC. His name was Captain Roy Brown, a Canadian, and before amalgamation he had been in the RNAS. But there were other claimants, namely a group of machine-gunners from the Australian Field Artillery, who fired at Richthofen's Fokker Dreidecker 1 more or less simultaneously with Brown's attack. The impact of the crash was not lethal, and the gunners ran excitedly towards the damaged machine, intent on capturing the pilot. But the man in the cockpit, head pitched forward, was dead.

They lifted the body from the cockpit and riffled through what papers they could find, casually at first, then with mounting incredulity. '*My God! We've got the bloody Baron!*'

Studies of the probable trajectory of the single bullet that killed Richthofen were contradictory. But whatever the truth, Richthofen was dead.

Hundreds of soldiers and airmen filed past his body next morning as it lay in state, like that of a deceased monarch, on a dais in a hangar at Bertangles. That afternoon, eleven days short of his 26th birthday, he was buried with full military honours, mourned, perversely enough, by friend and foe alike. His score of eighty victories, involving 123 pilots or crewmen killed or captured, was compiled almost exclusively against British and Commonwealth airmen. It remained unequalled.

A special floral tribute came from survivors who had flown against him, with the inscription: 'To Captain von Richthofen, our valiant and worthy foe.' But lest too much emphasis be placed on sentiments not perhaps universally shared, Mannock's reaction, when asked to drink a toast to the dead Baron, may be quoted. *'I won't drink to that bastard.'*

Ludendorff's policy now became to weaken Allied reserves with a succession of minor attacks at selected points, meanwhile preparing for an offensive on a grand scale. The responsibility for guarding against surprise when the major attack came rested squarely on the reconnaissance crews. And although, on the Aisne river (27 May– 2 June), and further south against the French between Montdidier and Noyon (9–13 June), Ludendorff kept up the pressure, his early successes were again neutralised.

Ludendorff's last great gamble was to be in Flanders, but first, on 15 July, as a diversion, he attacked in strength on the Marne. Driven back by the French, he then had to face an Allied counter-attack which caused the postponement, and finally, after 8 August (Ludendorff's 'black day for the German Army'), the abandonment, of any further major German offensive action. There were still three months of desperate fighting ahead, but from this point on the German army was battling for its very existence, the RAF, despite enormous losses, was achieving something approaching mastery of the air, and Germany had nothing to hope for but what might be rescued from an armistice.

When Jimmy McCudden left 56 Squadron for Home Establishment on 5 March he resumed his role of fighting instructor, this time at Ayr. But first he enjoyed a brief spell of leave with his younger brother Jack, now flying with 84 Squadron and boasting eight victories and an MC. Whatever Jimmy may have said to try to curb Jack's impetuosity was of no avail, as Jack got into a scrap with the Richthofen Circus on the day he got back and was killed. This left Jimmy and a sister the only survivors of the McCudden brood. Eleven days later Jimmy's career may be said to have peaked when he was awarded the VC, the citation stressing his responsible leadership as well as his personal triumphs. Meanwhile he was completing the manuscript of a book, as Richthofen had done.

McCudden stood out, with Albert Ball, as the most highly decorated and most charismatic of British scout pilots, his theories on air fighting being widely respected and copied. By combining superb leadership of his flight with a flair for the lone stalking of potential victims he had established himself as a unique all-rounder, at the pinnacle of his profession. Yet there were others threatening to challenge his supremacy.

Billy Bishop, after recording forty-seven victories with 60 Squadron, had returned to Canada briefly to help with a recruiting drive, and to marry. He too wrote a book at this stage. Then, over a brief period from 27 May to 19 June, while commanding 85 Squadron (SE5A's), and before being recalled again to Canada, he scored another twenty-five victories in twenty-four days, passing McCudden's record of fifty-seven in the process and ending with a total claimed of seventy-two. Since so many of his victories were scored on lone patrols, unsubstantiated by colleagues, and have often been queried, it is noteworthy that his total claims were approved at this point by Wing Headquarters.

Whereas Bishop, as an individualist, was not unduly concerned with welding his squadron into a team, Mannock, who replaced him as commander of 85 Squadron, 'planned every manoeuvre like a chess player', according to one of his pilots. In three months as a flight commander on 74 Squadron (also SE5A's), from mid-April to mid-June, he added another thirty-six victims to his sixteen with 40 Squadron, taking his score to fifty-two. He had become an outstanding tactician and leader, nursing newcomers, shedding those he deemed not up to standard, and inspiring a respect and affection in his pilots approaching idolatry. But many others were increasing their scores dramatically in this period, among them Mannock's old friend from 40 Squadron days, the Irishman George McElroy.

In the following month McCudden, after pleading for a quicker return to action than the authorities were planning, was posted back to France to command another famous fighting squadron, No. 60. The threat to his supremacy, it seemed, was not to go unchallenged.

He was on his way back in an SE5A on 9 July when he landed by mistake at an aerodrome close to his destination. Checking his bearings, he took off, circled the field, and, according to an eye-witness, carried out the conventional dive-and-zoom salutation that courtesy demanded. At the top of the zoom his motor cut out and he had no chance to recover. A wrongly-fitted carburettor has been blamed.

Accounts which record McCudden as making the novice's mistake of attempting to turn back towards the airfield when his engine failed on take-off seem less plausible – or perhaps too painful to contemplate. All three McCudden brothers were gone.

Neither Mannock nor McElroy was to survive McCudden for long. At a farewell party on 18 July for Gwilym Lewis, going home, so he said, 'a physical wreck', the two aces upbraided each other for taking unnecessary risks in pursuit of the enemy at low level. Eight days later, machine-gun fire from the ground was to prove Mannock's undoing. He had meanwhile raised his score to sixty-one. Another five days and McElroy (forty-six victories), fell in similar fashion.

The Germans dropped a note about McElroy; such courtesies were still being observed. As for Mannock, the area where he had crashed in flames, as he had always predicted he would, was blasted soon afterwards by artillery. The Germans just had time to take possession of documents, which were later returned to the family, and to bury the body. Attempts to locate the grave still persist.

To his colleagues Mick Mannock was incomparable, the ace of aces, and it was only through their sense of dismay and injustice, expressed by no one better than Captain Ira 'Taffy' Jones, one of Mannock's flight commanders and himself an ace with thirty-seven victories, that his achievement was properly recognised. Mannock, his colleagues knew, had allowed many of his victories to be credited to others, and an investigation, at the Air Ministry itself, amended his official tally to seventy-three. That this reassessment made him top-scorer on the Allied side, one more than Billy Bishop, inevitably raised eyebrows, and it is probable that both totals should be scaled down. However, to quote the Official History on Mannock, 'there are grounds for the claim . . . that he was the greatest fighting pilot of the war'. Eventually, nearly a year after his death, and with the backing of the then Air Minister, Winston Churchill, he was awarded a posthumous VC.

There was no shortage of newcomers to fill the empty chairs still tragically vacated, an inevitable diminution in the quality of candidates from Great Britain being redeemed by the influx from the schools established in Canada. 'All the Canadians', Garland had written, when he was instructing at Andover, 'are very quick and seem adapted to the air.'

In support of Ludendorff's offensives, a night bombing campaign against selected military targets behind the Western Front was waged by the Gothas, reaching a culmination in May, when huge losses were inflicted on congested ordnance depots and dumps. But the Gotha units lacked the capacity to keep up a simultaneous campaign against southern England, where their losses had anyway been prohibitive, and this enabled a squadron to be formed from Home Defence units for service in France. Major C.J. Quintin-Brand, a South African, many years later to command No. 10 Group in the Battle of Britain, was promoted from flight commander of a home-based squadron to command a new squadron of Camels specially adapted for night fighting, No. 151. Quintin-Brand's previous record included seven victories in Nieuports while a member of No. 1 Squadron in France, and the rare distinction of shooting down a Gotha bomber over Kent: most of the sixty-one lost in raiding England fell to anti-aircraft guns and to accidents.

Among the pilots transferred with Quintin-Brand was Captain A.B. Yuille, and it was Yuille who claimed the first Gotha victim for No. 151, on 23 July. Searchlights and guns assembled at strategic points assisted the night flyers, and Yuille was successful again when he destroyed a five-engined Giant on 10 August, shot down in flames with its nine-man crew.

Most successful of the night-fighters was Quintin-Brand himself, with four, but the squadron accounted for twenty-six Gothas of various types, often in spectacular fashion when unreleased bombs exploded in mid-air, or when bombers broke up while illuminated by searchlights. Eventually the pilots took to intercepting the Gothas over their own aerodromes as they attempted to land. So great was the effect on morale that by the time the ground forces had reached the Hindenburg Line in early September, having recovered all the ground lost in the March Retreat, night bombing by the Gothas had virtually ceased.

Another major development, in the final months of the war, was the expansion of the 41st (Bomber) Wing into the so-called Independent Force. Inheriting the bombing policy stimulated by the Gotha raids on London ('to carry the war into Germany by attacking her industry, commerce and population'), and originally intended to function as an Inter-Allied force, it was restricted, at its inception on 6 June 1918, to five RAF squadrons, three day and two night. Later four more squadrons were added. Commanding the force, after refusing several other possible appointments following his resignation as CAS, was Trenchard himself.

At least two of the pioneers who had crossed the Channel four years previously, on 13 August 1914, were still flying operationally in the final months: one of these was the pertinacious Willie Read, now 33. His stubborn refusal to take no for an answer had eventually overcome an equally stubborn Trenchard. 'If I *did* take you back,' warned Boom, 'it would be as a lieutenant, and you'd go to England as an instructor.'

Read accepted this, convinced that if he committed some minor breach of discipline he'd be posted back overseas, as was the fashion. But he would have to make sure it came to the notice of the authorities. He chose a fine day, saddled a Sopwith Pup from his training school, headed for London, and flew provocatively under Tower Bridge, then back under it again as an encore. He was lucky to escape unscathed – he had forgotten about the pigeons. Nothing happened for a fortnight – and then came a posting to command No. 216 Handley Page bomber squadron of the Independent Force under

Trenchard. Had Boom heard about the Tower Bridge incident? Anyway he must have relented.

No. 216 Squadron had formerly been 16 (Naval), and Read found a residue of animosity between old RFC and RNAS men which needed prompt action. To complicate matters, he was the first non-Naval man to command the unit. There was one consolation. 'There was no silly order about squadron commanders not being allowed to fly over the lines.' This gave him an idea. When he landed back from his first night raid on industrial Germany he reloaded and went again, an innovation that he hoped might encourage *esprit de corps*. In the morning there was a congratulatory signal from Boom; and the squadron responded. 'Read soon became a popular CO,' wrote one member, 'and made many operational flights as pilot during the latter weeks of the war.' With his batman, of course, manning the front gun and providing the comforts.

Despite heavy casualties, Read seems to have been perfectly content to be running a squadron again under Trenchard. Earlier that summer he had submitted a plan to the Air Ministry for the bombing of Germany by the new four-engined Handley Page V/1500's, staging at Prague, and he was hoping 216 would be chosen. (A Wing to undertake this project was indeed formed but was overtaken by the armistice.) Of Boom himself, Read wrote: 'Trenchard was always practical. We didn't think he had a great brain, but he had a great personality and strength of character and ability for getting things done.'

Among other pioneers still active operationally was Louis Strange. Ever the innovator, as a lieutenant-colonel commanding an all-purpose wing – fighters, bombers and reconnaissance machines, under brigade commander Ludlow-Hewitt – he conceived and developed the low-level tactical strike, involving massed assaults on German airfields and communications. Many of these strikes, designated 'Voluntary Offensive Patrols,' were virtually impromptu, involving aerial combat, attacks on airfields, and the disruption of enemy supply columns far behind the lines, often with devastating effect. Strange flew on these strikes himself, tucked in behind the Australian Arthur Cobby, whom he appointed leader; but it was

Strange's 'high influence and unexampled leadership' which characterised these operations. They excited Ludlow-Hewitt, who planned
them, and provided many tactical lessons.

Air superiority had become essential for success in all operations
over the battlefield, coordination reaching a stage at which aircraft
were cooperating directly with tanks. It was in this period, according to Vincent Orange, biographer of Arthur Coningham (better
known as Maori or 'Mary'), that Coningham, then commanding
an SE5A squadron under Strange, learnt the tactical lessons 'which
he would apply with excellent effect in the Western Desert' in a
later war.

The Germans defended desperately, and inevitably there were
losses, but Strange survived and was awarded the DSO. To the end
there was no let-up in the scale of the air fighting: as late as 30
October the enemy lost sixty-seven machines on the British front
alone and the British forty-one, their casualties including three killed,
eight wounded and twenty-six missing.

The crews of the Independent Force, beset by mechanical troubles,
confronted by strengthened defences, and hampered by foul weather,
rated their chances of survival even lower. One young observer,
Lieutenant Roy Shillinglaw, on arrival at Nancy, was taken aback
at the sums of money that changed hands amongst the card players
in the Mess. Cheques for £50, £100, even for £250, a huge sum for
the time, were, as he put it, 'flying around'. 'What does it matter?'
he was asked. 'We shall all be dead in a week – we're being swatted
like flies.'

Trenchard's attitude to casualties was the same as it had always
been: if their efforts could shorten the war by a single day, and thus
relieve the men fighting the ground battle, losses must be accepted.
This was soon obvious to another former RFC man whose
impatience for action had been blunted by a belated appreciation of
social life and female company while stationed in England on rest.
Depression and foreboding, normally quite foreign to him, were activated by a posting as senior flight commander to 104 Squadron

(DH9's), about whose crippling losses he had just been reading in the newspapers. This was the Australian Ewart Garland.

Garland had served with the squadron's CO, John Quinnell, twice before, on 10 Squadron in France, and again, after he had been ordered home in September 1917, on a reserve squadron at Andover. The months at Andover had been traumatic, the leadership (not Quinnell's) brutal. 'Crashes are so usual now I don't think of mentioning them,' he noted in his diary. 'Things are worse than ever as regards the Col. He asks the most impossible things and then strafes the heart out of you for not doing what is humanly impossible.' The 'Col.', promoted after running 40 Squadron efficiently – but by all accounts ruthlessly – before Leonard Tilney took over, was Bobbie Loraine, DSO, MC. 'He was a holy terror as a CO,' wrote Garland, 'but I found him good company off duty.'

Others at Andover more senior than Garland, led by John Quinnell, combined to get rid of Loraine. By what Garland called 'a dirty trick', they got him court-martialled for being drunk on duty. Garland was in hospital at the time after an appendectomy and was glad to be out of it. Loraine was acquitted but was demoted to major after pleading, in his indignation, to be sent back to France. There for the next two months he was attached to a night bomber squadron, until a gunshot wound in the left knee-joint ended his operational career. He had gone to France as an observer almost at the beginning, and had still been flying in France almost at the end. Garland acknowledged him, for all his faults, as 'a brave flying man'. The 'Actor-Airman', as the Press called him, returned to the theatre.

It was soon after this that Garland arrived at No. 104. 'This is the very squadron which the newspapers reported as losing seven machines out of nine on one raid . . . The casualties are enormous . . . The squadron consists almost all of new pilots and observers, as so many were wiped out recently.' The squadron had already been closed down twice for rehabilitation, casualties amounting to 250 per cent overall.

At first Garland's nerve almost failed him. 'Damn me for a frightened fool! But not a coward – it's one thing to be in a funk and yet do your job and another to shirk because you are frightened.' In

September he was ordered, in a hushed, sepulchral tone, to lead a raid on Mannheim: it was on Mannheim a few weeks earlier, on 22 August, that forty enemy fighters had attacked the DH9's and shot down seven. '*Mannheim! It's like being under sentence of death.*' But perhaps his luck would hold. 'I will trust in God and all that, but at the same time I'll take with me spare socks, a cheque book, and my vest-pocket Shakespeare.'

Next day his mood was almost euphoric. 'Hurrah! We have bombed Mannheim and only lost three machines.' Two of them were from his flight – but they were seen to go down under control. This was followed by many other raids, often led by Garland, generally with losses, reducing the squadron to impotence. But the news on the western front was of the breaking and then the capture of the Hindenburg Line. Right through October Garland pronounced the news good almost everywhere. 'Bulgaria surrenders, Cambrai fallen,' and so on.

Then at last: '*Germany has agreed to peace terms!*' Yet the war staggered on. Quinnell went on leave, others, wounded, languished in hospital, still more were dead or had been sent home. 'No sign of a rest for me.' Thus it happened that he was in sole charge when the news of the armistice was confirmed.

'*November 11th. So! It's over! I can scarce realise the stupendous event. Cease hostilities! Good Lord is it really true!*'

He wrote this diary entry at noon, having paraded the squadron. 'Everyone has taken it very quietly, just as a Britisher would!' There were about a hundred officers and men present. 'I think I must have felt the "history" of the occasion, standing out there addressing all these men, the majority much older than I, and quietly asking them to behave "properly" when celebrating. I was 21 years old.'

Nearer the fighting, and more distant from it, in Paris, in London and almost everywhere, the scenes were irresponsible and even hysterical. 'Heard the news at nine o'clock,' wrote First-class Air Mechanic Alexander Paice. 'Shall never forget the sight from all the aerodromes around, and ours too, of Very lights being fired. We marched round Menin with a Scotch regiment. They had a bagpipe band.'

Within a few weeks the RAF had shed huge numbers of personnel, and room in a greatly truncated peacetime service could be found for very few. Most of those selected were glad to stay, and many eventually reached high rank, but one who refused a permanent commission was Garland. He never piloted an aeroplane again. 'Strangely enough I lost interest completely the moment the war was over.' For some, like Gordon Taylor, flying had become a vocation; but civil aviation as yet had barely been born. Some became barnstormers, touring the country giving flying displays, others entered the precarious world of long-distance first-timing and record-breaking. Most of the 'intrepid flyers' of the twenties and thirties had begun their careers in the flying services. But the vast majority, like Garland, resumed or reactivated their peacetime careers.

Figures of aircraft deliveries confirm the massive expansion of the Royal Air Force in 1918. The total for 1916 was 6,633; this more than doubled in 1917 to 14,832; and in 1918 it more than doubled again, to 30,782. The figures were reflected in the swarms of machines which fought the aerial battles that year, also in the wartime aggregate of casualties, more than a third being sustained in the last seven and a half months of the war.

Was Trenchard's policy of the offensive, with all its tragic losses, justified by results? Was his basic aim of easing the burden of the men on the ground achieved?

Much depends on whether the work of the corps two-seaters really made a decisive contribution to the ground battles; and if they did, whether the information they gleaned, and the fire-power they enhanced, could have been accomplished without the elbow room provided by the scout squadrons. Could it all have been achieved by some other means? Was there an alternative?

The tasks allotted to the RFC were dictated by the ground situation and by military strategy. Apart from the work of the 41st Wing and the Independent Force, a tiny proportion of the whole, and then only in the last year of the war, the RFC, and then the RAF, functioned as an integral part of the army. Only the armies involved, British and German especially, can make a true assessment.

Whether the squadrons could or should have been better equipped, better trained and better handled remains open to study; but the leaders of the armies on both sides agreed, time and time again, and certainly from 1916 on, that air support had become indispensable to all ground operations. More than that, in periods of crisis, air superiority had become decisive.

PUBLISHED SOURCES

A. G. D. ALDERSON, *The First War in the Air* (Published privately 1990)

HAROLD BALFOUR, *An Airman Marches* (Hutchinson 1973)

MAURICE BARING, *Flying Corps Headquarters – 1914–1918* (G. Bell and Sons 1920)

RICHARD TOWNSHEND BICKERS, *The First Great Air War* (Hodder 1988)

W. A. BISHOP, *Winged Warfare* (Blackwood 1968)

EZRA BOWEN, *Knights of the Air* (Time-Life 1980)

CHAZ BOWYER, *The Air VCs* (Kimber 1978 and Grub Street 1993)

— *History of the RAF* (Hamlyn 1977)

— *The Flying Elephants* (Macdonald 1972)

ANDREW BOYLE, *Trenchard, Man of Vision* (Collins 1962)

ANTHONY BRUCE, *An Illustrated Companion to the First World War* (M. Joseph 1989)

JOHN BUCHAN, *A History of the First World War* (Lochar 1991)

J. A. CHAMBER, *The Birth of the Royal Air Force* (Pitman 1943)

LIONEL CHARLTON, *Charlton, an autobiography* (Faber 1931)

ALAN CLARK, *Aces High* (Fontana/Collins 1973)

CHRISTOPHER COLE, *McCudden VC* (Kimber 1967)

— *RFC Communiqués 1915–1916* (Kimber 1969)

— *RFC Communiqués, 1918* (Kimber 1988)

BASIL COLLIER, *Leader of the Few* (Jarrolds)

BRYAN COOPER, *The Story of the Bombers 1914–1915* (Octopus 1974)

A. CORBETT-SMITH, *The Retreat from Mons* (Cassell 1916)

V. P. CRONYN, *Other Days* (Published privately 1976)

LORD DOUGLAS OF KIRTLESIDE, *Years of Combat* (Collins 1963)

MARTIN GILBERT, *First World War Atlas* (Weidenfeld and Nicolson 1970)

DUNCAN GRINNELL-MILNE, *Wind in the Wires* (Aviation Book Club 1933)

JOHN HAMMERTON (EDITOR), *War in the Air, Aerial Wonders of Our Time* (Amalgated Press, c. 1936)

HAROLD E. HARTNEY, *Up and At 'Em* (Bailey and Swinfen 1974)

W. J. F. HARVEY, *Pie in the Sky* (Colin Huston 1971)

TYRREL M. HAWKER, *Hawker VC* (Mitre Press 1965)

PETER HEARN, *The Sky People – A History of Parachuting* (Airlife 1990)

— *Flying ebel, A Biography of Louis Strange* (HMSO 1994)

DAVID HENDERSON, *The Art of Reconnaissance* (Murray 1914)

PRUDENCE HILL, *To Know the Sky* (Kimber 1962)

GODERIC HODGES, *Memoirs of an Old Balloonatic* (Kimber 1972

ROBERT JACKSON, *Fighter Pilots of World War I* (Barker 1977)

J. E. JOHNSON, *Full Circle* (Chatto 1964)

IRA JONES, *King of the Air Fighters* (Ivor Nicholson and Watson 1938)

ARTHUR GOULD LEE, *No Parachute* (Kimber 1968)

— *Open Cockpit* (Jarrolds 1969)

PHILIP JOURBERT, *The Third Service* (Thames and Hudson 1955)

CECIL LEWIS, *Sagittarius Rising* (Peter Davies 1936 and Greenhill 1993)

GWILYM H. LEWIS, *Wings Over the Somme* (Kimber 1976 and – a new edition – Bridge Books 1994)

PETER LIDDLE, *The Airman's War* (Blanford Press 1989)

WINIFRED LORAINE, *Robert Loraine* (Collins 1938)

JAMES MCCUDDEN, *Five Years in the RFC* (Aeroplane and General 1918)

ALEXANDER MCKEE, *The Friendless Sky* (Souvenir Press 1962)

WILLIAM MACLANACHAN, *McScotch* (Routledge 1936)

NORMAN MACMILLAN, *Into the Blue* (Jarrolds 1929)

T. B. MARSON, *Scarlet and Khaki* (Jonathan Cape 1930)

L. MILLER, *The Chronicles of 55 Squadron RAF and RFC* (Unwin Bros 1919)

R. R. MONEY, *Flying and Soldiering* (Nicolson and Watson 1936)

ALAN MORRIS, *Bloody April* (Jarrolds 1967)

— *The Balloonatics* (Jarrolds 1970)

JOHN H. MORROW JR, *The Great War in the Air* (Airlife 1993)

JACQUES MORTANE, *Special Missions* (Aeroplane and General 1919)

GEOFFREY NORRIS, *The Royal Flying Corps, A History* (Muller 1965)

VINCENT ORANGE, *Coningham* (Methuen 1990)

WALTER RALEIGH AND H. A. JONES, *The War in the Air, Vols I to III* (The Clarendon Press Oxford 1923–1931)

— *The War in the Air, Vols I to VI, with Maps and Appendices* (Clarendon Press Oxford 1923–1937)

ALEX REVELL, *British Fighter Units on the Western Front, 1914–1916* (Osprey 1978)

LINDA RHODES-MOORHOUSE, *Kaleidoscope* (Barker 1960)

MANFRED VON RICHTHOFEN, *The Red Air Fighter* (Aeroplane and General 1918)

R. L. RIMELL, *The Airship VC* (Aston Publications 1989)

D. H. ROBINSON, *The Dangerous Sky: A History of Aviation Medicine* (Foulis 1973)

ROBERT SAUNDBY, *Air Bombardment: The Story of Its Development* (Chatto 1961)

HILARY ST G. SAUNDERS, *Per Ardua* (OUP 1944)

A. J. L. SCOTT, *Sixty Squadron* (Heinemann 1920)

MICHAEL SHAW, *Twice Vertical, the History of No. 1 Squadron* (Macdonald 1971 and Ian Allen 1986)

GORDON S. SHEPHARD, *Memoirs* (Published privately 1924)

CHRISTOPHER SHORES, NORMAN FRANKS, AND RUSSELL GUEST, *Above The Trenches* (Grub Street 1990)

GUY SLATER (EDITOR), *My Warrior Sons: the Borton Family Diaries* (Peter Davies 1973)

JOHN SLESSOR, *The Central Blue* (Cassell 1968)

HORACE SMITH-DORRIEN, *Memoirs of 48 Years Service* (Murray 1925)

OLIVER STEWART, *Words and Music for a Mechanical Man* (Faber 1967)

LOUIS STRANGE, *Recollections of an Airman* (John Hamilton 1933

A. J. P. TAYLOR, *The First World War* (Hamish Hamilton 1963))

J. W. R. TAYLOR, *CFS – Birthplace of Air Power* (Putnam 1953)

ROBERT THOMPSON, *The Royal Flying Corps* (Hamish Hamilton 1968)

FRANK D. TREDREY, *Pioneer Pilot – The Great Smith-Barry* (Peter Davies 1976)

S. F. VINCENT, *Flying Fever* (Jarrolds 1972)

HERBERT S. WARD, *An Erratic Odyssey* (Odyssey Books 1988)

W. ALISTER WILLIAMS, *Against the Odds: The Life of Group Captain Lionel Rees* (Bridge Books 1989)

H. J. WILLIAMSON, *The Roll of Honour RFC and RAF for the Great War 1914–1918* (Naval and Military Press 1972)

DENIS WINTER, *The First of the Few* (Allen Lane 1982)

FRED WINTERBOTHAM, *The Ultra Spy* (Macmillan 1989)

Encyclopaedias: *Encyclopaedia of Air Warfare* (Spring Books 1975)

Magazines: Aeronautics, Aeroplane, Aerospace, Aviation News, Flight, Cross and Cockade (GB) Society Journal, Journal of the RAF Historical Society, Air Mail (Journal of the RAF Association).

INDEX

Note: Ranks where given are those current at the time